In Memory of our beloved

RUNU

(Sarita Bhowmick)

PREFACE

It was in hot summer in the month of June 1982, I was in Bidisa, a remote village under Narayangarh Police Station in the district of Midnapur, West Bengal about 19 Kms. from Kharagpur Railway Station. I was there to participate in a seminar on Tribal Problems and Development organised by the Institute of Social Research and Applied Anthropology in its premises at Bidisa. A large number of eminent scholars belonging to anthropology and other allied disciplines were also present there for the same purpose. The seminar was scheduled to be inaugurated at 11.00 a.m., but was delayed as till then Dr. J. K. Bose, President of the Institute (ISRAA) could not reach Bidisa. He was scheduled to come by a car with our beloved Runu (Sarita Bhowmick) and also Doordarshan cameraman As they could not reach even at 3.00 p.m., the seminar was inaugurated in absence of the President of ISRAA. It was at about 4.00 p.m. that the news came as a bolt from the blue. Palash Chandra Coomar, my associate in editing this book, brought the news which made everybody torpid as nobody could believe it. Runu died of car accident near Pashkura in the district of Midnapur. The car which was carrying Dr. J. K. Bose, Runu, Palash Chandra Coomar, Sujit Pradhan and two T.V. men, met an accident and this accident tolled two lives, that of J. K. Bose and Runu.

It was a great shock, we all were stunned, we all were stupefied with grief. It was so painful to all of us as Runu was so dear to us (news of death of Dr. J. K. Bose came much later). It was unbelievable yet it was the reality. Thus a budding but bright anthropologist demised so untimely. The God Almighty snatched her from us at the dawn of her career. It was so early, so sudden !

Preface

Runu i.e. Sarita Bhowmick, daughter of Professor P.K. Bhowmick of the Department of Anthropology, Calcutta University and Honorary Secretary, Institute of Social Research and Applied Anthropology, was born on September 24, 1956. She had a brilliant academic career. She graduated from the University of Calcutta in 1976 as the best graduate student securing first class first position and obtaining highest marks among all successful candidates in Science and Arts faculties. It was a rare distinction. She became first class first in M.Sc. and got a number of prizes, awards and scholarships. She took immense interest in the activities of the Institute of Social Research and Applied Anthropology as she had much interest in applied anthropological research.

Sometimes after that seminar on *Tribal Problems and Development* when Professor Bhowmick, of the Institute of Social Research and Applied Anthropology, requested me to edit a book on the theme of this seminar, I thought of dedicating the same in the loving memory of Runu. I wrote to a number of scholars, who were experts in this field. Many of them readily responded. But I had to select a few more articles on the theme I thought for this book, from the Journal 'Man and Life', organ of the Institute of Social Research and Applied Anthropology to give this book a complete shape. So finally I earmarked twenty-eight articles unpublished and published, for the two separate volumes of this book, in order to cover different aspects of the problem, development and prospect of our tribal brethren.

The present book in two separate volumes, is no doubt an addition to a number of books on this theme so far published. But this book has the distinction of having articles on the general issues relating to the policies of the tribal welfare, the problems and development of our tribal brethren, area specific or state level issues, issues relating to the impact of the problems like industrialization, agricultural development, etc. and also on certain other specific issues. As a result our readers, the administrators, planners, social scientists, social workers, politicians and even the village level workers, will gather first-hand knowledge about the nature of problems and the extent of development taking place among the Scheduled Tribes of our country. The book will also help the tribal leaders to know what is happening in regard to their problems, and development. Further, this book, I believe, will be of immense help to the students and scholars of Applied Anthropology.

Considering the number of the articles selected for this book, I had to distribute them in two separate volumes. The present volume i.e. Volume One has given the vivid account on the policies regarding tribal development in general for India as a whole and for some States and Union Territories in particular.

M.K. RAHA

ACKNOWLEDGEMENT

Man is the most versatile, complex, intelligent and interesting creature of Nature. He is not only surviving for much over a hundred thousand years, but thriving with high rate of multiplication braving the various odds and adversities of the nature. The ethnic, culture, psychological and intellectual diversities have made him the most interesting and superior creation. The anthropologists who study man both in the remotest and most inaccessible areas as well as in the most advanced metropolis, have given man the knowledge about man and brought him closer and nearer to one another and thereby helping him to think of his welfare.

Being an anthropologist, my discipline, Anthropology and my profession have helped generating keen interest in me to know the problems of the people, my countrymen, particularly of our tribal brethren and looking at the welfare of the tribal people. This interest and urge was further strengthened when I served in the Cultural Research Institute, Scheduled Castes and Tribes Welfare Department, Government of West Bengal, at the beginning of my service career. Since then my profession took me to different parts of our country to know our tribal brethren and identify and understand their problems. I also got some opportunity to evaluate some of the development projects meant for them and also to see whether those actually benefit them and if so how much. At this juncture Professor P.K. Bhowmick of the Department of Anthropology, University of Calcutta and Honorary Secretary, Institute of Social Research and Applied Anthropology, requested me to edit such a book. It is undoubtedly a great encouragement for expressing my feelings and experience about the tribal world in black and white. I offer my deep sense of gratitude to Professor Bhowmick. I am also grateful to the authorities of the Institute of Social Research and Applied Anthropology for their kind encouragement to edit and publish this book. Thanks are due to the authorities of the Journal *Man and Life* and also *Bulletin of the Cultural Research Institute* for permitting me to incorporate some of the articles in this book which are already published in different issues of the journals.

My sincere thanks are due to all the contributors who are scholars in their respective fields. Without their active co-operation this project of mine could not have been successful. To Shri D.Banerjee, Mrs. Vimla, Miss Geeta, Shri E. Pitambaru, Shri Anand Minz and Miss Mala Mukherjee, my sincere thanks as they took much pains in typing the manuscripts whenever required. I am also thankful to all my colleagues of the Anthropological Survey of India and also others for their kind cooperation and active assistance in one way or other.

Finally, I express my extreme gratitude to my publishers, Gian Publishing House, New Delhi. Their sincere and active co-operation, experience and skill have made the publication of this book possible at a very short time.

CONTRIBUTORS

Dr. Bhupinder Singh	Special Commissioner for Scheduled Tribes, New Delhi.
Dr. Ajit K. Danda	Director, Anthropological Survey of India, Government of India, Calcutta.
Dr. Samarendra Saraf	Professor, Department of Anthropology, Dr. Hari Singh Gour Vishwavidyalaya, Sagar, Madhya Pradesh.
Dr. R. S. Mann	Joint Director, Anthropological Survey of India, Dehra Dun, Uttar Pradesh.
Dr. D. L. Prasada Rao	Professor, Department of Anthropology, Andhra University, Waltair, Andhra Pradesh.
Shri. P. Venkata Rao	Department of Anthropology, Andhra University, Waltair, Andhra Pradesh.
Dr. Rajat Kanti Das	Reader, Department of Anthropology, Vidyasagar University, Midnapur, West Bengal.
Dr. Soumen Sen	Department of Political Science, Shillong College, Shillong, Meghalaya.
Dr. B. N. Bordoloi	Director, Tribal Research Institute, Govt. of Assam, Guwahati, Assam.
Dr. Tanka Bahadur Subba	Lecturer, Centre for Himalayan Studies, University of North Bengal, Darjeeling, West Bengal.

Dr. Amal Kumar Das	Director, Cultural Research Institute, Govt. of West Bengal, Calcutta, West Bengal.
Dr. K. Mohan Rao	Director, Tribal Cultural Research and Training Institute, Govt. of Andhra Pradesh, Hyderabad, Andhra Pradesh.
Shri P. C. Coomar	Senior Technical Assistant, Anthropological Survey of India, Port Blair, Andaman.
Dr. M. K. Raha	Deputy Director, Anthropological Survey of India, Nagpur.

CONTENTS

INTRODUCTION

Introduction

M. K. Raha

The vast territory of India with diverse ecological, cultural and linguistic zones, have given shelter to 685,184,692 souls who also include 51,628,638 tribal people with 26,038,535 males and 25,590,103 females (Padmanabha, 1983). These people who constitute 7.53 per cent of the total population in India, come under the fold of four hundred and odd tribal groups. They are found to inhabit almost throughout the length and breadth of India barring a few States and Union Territories. While the majority of the tribal people are found to reside in the very remote areas, particularly in the forest and hilly tracts, a good number of them also live in the urban centres, industrial belts, mines and collieries, tea gardens and such other places.

According to 1981 Census (Padmanabha, 1983) 51,628,638 tribal people in India, are found to inhabit in all States and Union Territories except States of Punjab, Haryana, Jammu and Kashmir and Union Territories of Delhi, Chandigarh and Pondicherry. Madhya Pradesh is the State where highest number of these people (23.22 per cent) live. Next in order come Orissa (11.46 per cent), Bihar (11.26 per cent) and Maharashtra (11.18) per cent). While Gujarat has 9.39 per cent, Rajasthan bears 8.12 per cent. All the other States have the strength of the tribal populace each below 4.00 per cent of the total tribal people of India. Again five of these States, namely, Himachal Pradesh, Kerala, Manipur,

Sikkim and Uttar Pradesh cover below 1.00 per cent of the total tribal population of India. In case of the Union Territories, it may be said that according to 1981 Census each of the six Union Territories having tribal population, bears less than 1.00 per cent of the total tribal population of India. It is interesting to point out here that the four States namely Madhya Pradesh, Orissa, Bihar and Maharashtra, who have more than 10.00 per cent of the tribal population of India each, together cover 57.12 per cent, and each of the eight States namely Madhya Pradesh, Orissa, Bihar, Maharashtra, Gujarat, Rajasthan, Andhra Pradesh and West Bengal which has over 5.00 per cent of the total tribal population in India, together bear the overwhelming majority(86.71 per cent) of the total tribal population of India. All the nine Union Territories together share only 2.03 per cent of the total tribal population of India. That means the States of India together cover 97.97 per cent of these people.

When we examine the frequency of the tribal population in each State and Union territory out of the total population there according to 1981 Census, we see that among the States, Nagaland has the highest tribal population covering 83.00 per cent of the total population of the State. Next to Nagaland come Meghalaya where the share of the tribal population out of the total population is 80.58 per cent. There are five States each of which covers between 20.00 and 30.00 per cent of tribal population out of the total population of that State. These States are Tripura(28.44 per cent), Manipur(27.30 per cent), Sikkim(23.27 per cent), Madhya Pradesh(22.97 per cent) and Orissa(23.43 per cent). The States of Gujarat(14.22 per cent) and Rajasthan(12.21 per cent) have tribal population between 10.00 and 20.00 per cent of the total population. Each of the remaining States has tribal population below 10.00 per cent out of total population.

In case of the Union Territories, Lakshadweep has the highest tribal population. Except a few non-tribals, almost the whole population of Lakshadweep (93.82 per cent) are tribals. Lakshadweep is followed closely by Mizoram where 93.55 per cent of the total population are tribals. In Dadra and Nagar Haveli 78.82 per cent of the total population are tribals. Similarly in Arunachal Pradesh 69.82 per cent of the total population belong to tribal groups. But in Andaman and Nicobar Islands only 11.85 per cent and in Goa, Daman and Diu only 0.99 per cent of the total population have the tribal status.

The history of India reveals that the tribal people co-existed with the general mass and also with the ruling administration since the dawn of Indian civilization. But there is little knowledge about the interactions of the rulers of that bygone era with the tribals and the action of the administrators taken for the development and welfare of these tribal folk. The kings and rulers of ancient India of course, knew some of the problems of the tribal people of their time and tried to solve those. From King Ashoka's inscription we come to know that the great king was aware of the problems of the tribals inhabiting the forests and he thought it to be his duty and responsibility to do welfare of these people.

> "Upon the forest tribes in his dominions His Majesty has compassion... For His Majesty desires for all animate beings security, control over passion, peace of mind and joyousness."

But it may be assumed that very little the tribal could taste the fruits of the development works in the remote past. They could get very little of facilities granted by the royalty during the pre-British era. This might be due to their confinement in the remotest and very inaccessible areas like forests and forest-clad hilly terrains. Very little or almost no communication was there to reach them, and rarely they could come out to open from their far-away domains. The result was obvious. While they remained with their own world of joy and misery, sorrows and happiness, they bothered little about the realities of the outside world. The world outside their domain was almost unknown to them. Similarly due to the lack of communication the kings and the rulers of the past knew very little of them, cared very little for them and therefore, did very little for them. They allowed them to stay in their own world undisturbed except during war, conflict and natural calamities. Only a very few kings and rulers thought of their well-being.

Long after the British rulers established their colonial rule in India and settled permanently, they thought of the tribal people. In most of the cases they allowed the tribal people to remain as they were. The British Government never liked to disturb the isolated condition of the tribal habitat. In most of the cases the policy they adopted for the tribal people, was the policy of isolation. As a result the tribal people of this country received very little of the modern facilities and western thought the British brought to this country and granted to the Indian people. The approach of the British Government towards the tribal world of our country, was to keep them isolated in order to prevent any contact with the Indian general mass. The British Government deliberately adopted this policy of keeping the tribals in isolation and to create a barrier between them and the general mass, mainly to prevent the possible contact of the tribal people with the general mass so that the idea of freedom movement did not infiltrate among them. Their another interest was not to face any trouble created by the tribals. Some cases of movements and insurrections by the tribals taught them this lesson. Their basic motive was to fulfil their colonial interest.

> "The British Government(was) inclined, on the whole, to leave the tribesmen alone partly because the task of administration especially in the wild border areas, was difficult and unrewarding, partly from a desire to quarantine the tribes from possible political infection and partly because a number of officers sincerely held the view that the people were better and happier as they were ...." (Elwin, 1960).

So the colonial administration adopted the policy 'to leave them alone'. But was that true ? The history tells us something different. The British Government never hesitated to intervene and to suppress any move adopted by these tribals against the oppression which the former felt might go against their colonial interest. We get innumerable number of such examples where the British Government used brutal force to wipe out such agitation without caring to think that the latter resolve to such movement for their survival only. Sometimes again they employed the method of appeasement of tribal chiefs and other influential elite groups to get rid of the crisis(Raha & Das, 1982).The reason for such actions of the British Government was to secure their own stability and not necessarily to help the people to advance on the road to progress (Ghurye, 1963).

This British policy of keeping the tribals segregated from the main-stream also helped the administration in another way. They encouraged the Christian missionaries to move into the tribal areas with two definite purposes - firstly to do the welfare works and secondly, which possibly was more important for the British Government, was to convert the tribal people to Christianity. This they rightly thought, would help them in two ways. Firstly the influence and assistance of the Christian missionaries and the conversion of the tribal people into Christianity would prevent the tribals from going against the colonial administration; even these would make them loyal and faithful subjects, and secondly these would also shield the tribals from the impact of the freedom movement which was rapidly gaining ground day by day. The missionary activities were sought to isolate the tribal people mentally and emotionally from the people of India who were eagerly waiting for the freedom of India and active in achieving it. No doubt the Christian missionaries devoted themselves for the service of these downtroddens and helped them constantly to remove their poverty and backwardness by bringing socio-economic transformation but it is at the sametime, equally true that this baptization in some cases helped the British Government to implement their colonial policies and to fulfil their interest. This is also interesting that the British Government allowed none but the Christian missions to undertake voluntary welfare works in the tribal belt.

> "A careful analysis of the missionary activities thus leads to the conclusion that under the garb of humanitarianism, the obnoxious political motives of the colonial rules were rampant. It was a sort of intellectual and moral aggression on Indian life strongly patronized by the British Government which aimed, gradually, to alienate a chunk of population from the main national stream by generating a kind of 'sentimental and emotional detachment' with the rest of the people -- a process which could be effectively carried out under the auspices of the policy of Isolation" (Raha & Das, 1982).

The isolated and the segregated condition in which the tribals lived, did not allow the tribals to live in all peace and happiness as the same also allured many vested interests. This condition invited the greedy interests of the money-lenders, contractors, feudal lords, middlemen and others to exploit the tribals and to suck the nectar of life from these poor helpless illiterate people.

But this policy of the British Government took abrupt turn when India won freedom. The Union Government of the Independent India adopted a totally different policy towards our tribal brethren.

> "...the approaches of the two administrative machineries show a striking difference in terms of deep motivational principles. While the approach of the British Government was fundamentally political, being purely guided by the colonial interests, the present Government's attitude promoted by a desire of welfare and an uncompromising concern for the socio-economic upliftment of our tribal folk''. (Raha & Das, 1982).

The tribal people of our country are suffering from innumerable problems. Poverty and economic crisis are rampant among them. Most of them are below poverty line. They have problems concerning the very basic needs which the humanity requires - the problems of food, clothing and shelter--are acute among them. Added to these are education and health. The other aspects are equally worse. The illiteracy, economic crisis and superstitions have put them at a very backward state - at a level much below the standard maintained by the average Indian people. The very economic crisis are taking them to the clutches of the money-lenders, forcing them to act as bonded labours and to alienate their most precious thing, the small holding of land they possess. The condition continued from bad to worse without any ray of hope until independence when in order to lessen their plights a number of welfare schemes have been undertaken. Various development programmes have been taken in hand by the Government for the overall improvement of the conditions of the tribal people. These development schemes cover agriculture, irrigation, animal husbandry, house and house site, agricultural land, roads and communication, co-operatives, education, health and many others including job opportunities, reservation of their representation in the Parliament and State Legislative Assemblies, etc.

The concept of the tribal development is based on twin approaches, firstly the protection of interest of the tribal people through legal-administrative support and secondly to implement development programmes to promote their standard and level of living. Presently the main instrument of such development is tribal sub-Plan launched in 1974-75 the sub-Plans implemented in different States and Union Territories have benefited a large number of tribals. These sub-Plans are implemented through the State Plan, special Central Assistance, Centrally sponsored programmes and institutional finance. Under the revised 20 Point Programme, a high priority has been given to the development of the Scheduled Castes and Scheduled Tribes.

After the promulgation of the Constitution of India, which provides a number of safeguards for the welfare and development of the backward people, particularly the Scheduled Castes and Scheduled Tribes, the Government of India and also the State Governments and Union Territory administrations started looking after the interests of the tribal people. A large number of schemes for the overall development of the Scheduled Castes and Scheduled Tribes of India have been launched and a good amount of money has been spent for the successful implementation of these schemes. Not only their representations in the both Houses of Parliament and State Legislative Assemblies are guaranteed by the Constitutional provisions, but they also enjoy the facility of the reservation of the services in the government and semi-government organisations. The Tribal advisory Council in State is meant for rendering advice on such matters pertaining to welfare and uplift of these people. The Commissioner for the Scheduled Tribes and Scheduled Castes is to look after their interest.

Thus we see that the Indian Government after reversing the policy adopted by the colonial administration, have come out with a number of measures to promote economic condition and educational standard of the tribal people and to bring over all development of these people. But no doubt the rate of development is not uniform everywhere nor it is 'remarkable'. It is much below the rate it should have achieved. The reasons of the 'unsatisfactory' growth rate are manifold. Administrative procedural problems, lack of knowledge about the selection of proper area and time of implementation of the schemes, lack of coordination among implementing agencies, difficulty in implementing welfare schemes in remote, difficult and inaccessible tribal areas, lack of missionary zeal and helping attitudes in many cases among the implementing agencies, peculiar psychology of the tribal people, their reactions etc. are the main reasons for the slow growth and failure. But one of the most important reasons of unsatisfactory development works and partial failure is the lack of proper knowledge of the implementing agencies about the culture and psychology of the tribal people among whom the development programmes are to be implemented. It is never true that what the planners and the implementing agencies think best for the tribal people and what they think will render best benefits to the tribals, will be best and most profitable to the tribals who they think, will readily accept these whatever the cost of implementation may be. Often it is found that many welfare schemes meant for the uplift of these people have resulted in utter failure. The tribal people did not accept these and money spent on these schemes has gone in total waste. This problem could be solved if the authority could take into consideration the views of the experts who have long and intimate contact with the tribal people among whom they undertake research work to study their miseries and problems. These experts are the persons who know best about the likings and dislikings of the tribal people. But their views are often given little attention and importance. The net result is that the rate of development of the tribals is quite low and so the tribal people get little benefit of these though these are meant for their uplift.

However, it is a good sign that in recent years the planners and authorities meant for implementing the welfare schemes, have realised the gravity of the situation. They have started consulting experts who are anthropologists and other social scientists, and giving due importance to their views. It may thus be hoped that if there is proper knowledge, will and zeal to do the welfare works, proper benefits will go to those for whom the welfare works are meant.

My decades' long research experience and intimate contact with the tribal people inhabiting in different parts of India in different ecological settings and having different economic pursuits and social organization, inspired me to make public the basic problems of the tribal people, types of development work done among them and the nature and extent of benefits received by them with the idea that it may draw the attention the people of India about the miseries and troubles, economic bankruptcy and pains of indebtedness, tortures and oppression faced by a section of our countrymen. This, I hope, will enable us to realise the gravity of the problems, the real needs of our tribal brethren which may help in the formulation and implementation of *proper* welfare and development schemes from which these poor souls may harvest the *real* and maximum benefits and thereby the *purpose* for which these schêmes have been implemented, will achieve a real success. Thus these backward people who for countries, are remaining below the poverty line and are submerged in the sea of crisis, may see the ray of hope for a brighter and better prospect, if not for them, at least for their future progeny.

In order to reveal clearly the problems of tribal people, the nature and extent of development works for the uplift of these people and finally to assess the brightness of their prospect that these measures will bring to them, I have included twenty-nine articles and distributed them into two separate volumes of this book.

In Volume I of this book I have included a total of thirteen articles related to some problems or other of the tribals. I have grouped these articles into two parts. Part One includes six articles dealing with problems which the tribal people of India are in general, facing. These also highlight the policies of tribal welfare, the nature and extent of development undertaken among these people for the overall improvement of their socio-economic conditions particularly for the development of their economy, health and educational status so as to bring them closer if not at par with the mainstream.

The first article of Part One is of Dr. Bhupendra Singh; Dr. Singh has stated the objectives of the welfare of the tribals, asserted the need for the welfare of this weaker section of the society and also discussed about various welfare schemes for the benefit of these people.

Dr. Ajit K. Danda, through his article, has highlighted the policies framed at different period for the welfare of the tribal people of India. He has also narrated the history of early contact with tribals and also reviewed the various policies meant for the uplift of these people.

Professor Samarendra Saraf has through his article, discussed about different policies framed for the welfare of the tribal people in different period of time, the problems the tribals are facing and the role of the tribals in these matters.

Dr. R.S. Mann in his article, discusses about the various measures taken for the uplift of the condition of the tribals, the weakness of these schemes and suggested dimensions for strengthening the existing model of tribal welfare to impart maximum benefit to these people.

The article of Dr. Amal K.Das has pinpointed some very important issues relating to the promotion of the socio-economic condition of the tribal people. He has also shown the measures taken for the development of the tribal people.

Professor D.L. Prasad Rao and Dr. P. Venkata Rao have dealt in their article, the problem of the tribals, the priorities in the development measures for the tribals infrastructure required for the implementation of such scheme, proper utilisation of these benefits and other aspects.

In Part Two I have included seven articles each of which deals with the problems of the tribals of a particular State or Union Territory and also the process of development implemented for the overall improvement of their condition.

The first article of this part of the book is of Dr. Rajat Kanti Das who has dealt with the problems of the tribals of Manipur. Giving some details of the tribal people of Manipur and their culture, he has highlighted the various problems which the tribal people in Manipur are experiencing in different period of time. The reasons of these problems and the measures for their solution have also been detailed by him.

In his paper Dr. Soumen Sen has highlighted the problems of the tribals of Meghalaya, namely the Khasi-Jayantia and the Garo, are facing. The problem of under-development was and still is the major issue of the tribals of Meghalaya, the author asserts. The tribals of Meghalaya have always faced some particular problems besides general problems of economic and educational under nourishment.

Dr.B.N. Bordoloi has in details, shown the strategies taken during both pre and post-independence period for the upliftment of the tribals of Assam, the measures taken for solving those problems in recent years and the benefits the tribals of Assam have got out of these welfare schemes.

Dr. Tanka Bahadur Subha has attempted to focus the socio-economic condition of the tribals of Sikkim like the Bhotia and the Lapcha vis-a-vis the various caste groups of the dominant Nepalese. He has also shown the various development schemes and reflections of these on the tribals.

Dr. Amal K.Das has given a detailed account on the measures taken to promote the socio-economic conditions and educational standard of the tribal people of West Bengal since the First Five Year Plan.

In his article Dr. K. Mohan Rao has described his experience about the problems faced by the tribal people of Andhra Pradesh and steps taken to remove these problems. He has also stated the need for devising the development schemes for these people in the light of the socio-cultural factors and economic needs of the tribals.

The problems of the Negrito tribes of Andaman islands is very peculiar and totally different from those of the tribal people of the mainland of India. The most important problem is the question of their survival. These tribal people are rapidly declining in their numerical strength. The authors have highlighted this acute and crucial problem of the decline of the population of these tribals which the authors think as the most important and vital one, and have also discussed the reasons behind this.

This is undoubtedly a very critical problem of the Andaman Negrito tribes, particularly the great Andamanese and the Onge, though no doubt other problems, particularly the problems of their economy and education, are equally crucial.

Volume II of this book, a separate publication, has included sixteen articles, which have been distributed in two parts. Some articles are specifically on the economic issues of the tribals, the peculiar economic crisis they are facing in different situations, and the measures to solve these economic problems. Besides, many other problems and issues related to the different aspects of the life and culture of these people, have also been included in this volume.

Part One of the Volume II of this book has accommodated five articles dealing with impact of industrialization on the tribals, problems of the tribal labourers in the coal mines and tea estates, impact of conservation of forest on the tribals, rope industry among the tribals and agriculture among the non-agriculturist tribals.

Part-Two of Volume II includes, eleven articles. These deal with varied subjects concerning the tribal life such as the problems of the denotified tribes, tribal manpower, tribal leadership, development of curriculum for the tribal students, tribal education, problems of the displacement of tribals, co-operatives among the tribals, activities of the missionaries, tribal drinks, anthropology and tribal welfare etc.

In the two volumes of this book I have included twenty-nine articles of varied interest as stated earlier. While some deal with the policies relating to the development of the tribal people of different States and Union Territories of India, some are related to their economic development. Some articles are on various other aspects of tribal life. At the planning stage of this book, I thought of including articles on the problems of the tribals and the development programmes among them of all the States and Union Territories of India wherever they are found. But unfortunately due to some difficulties, constraints and limitations, I failed to fulfil the aim. Even then I have included the problems and development among the tribals of some States and Union Territories. These will, I believe, give a comprehensive idea about the problems and development of the tribals in India, in general, and those of States and Union Territories in particular. The problems of these people in different other spheres and the ways of their solution, will give enough idea about the prospect of these miserable people of our country.

This book, I believe, will not only be helpful to the planners, administrators, social workers and others who are directly involved in the welfare programmes of the Scheduled Tribes and other backward classes of our country, but also to the academicians, particularly to the members of the discipline of anthropology. They diagnose the problems of the tribal people and prescribe the solution of these problems in order to help these people in promoting their socio-economic condition and educational standard and also in bringing themselves above the poverty line if not at par with the general mass of India.

References

Elwin, Verrier (1960) *A Philosophy for NEFA*, Shillong NEFA,

Ghurye, G.S. (1977) *The Scheduled Tribe*, Bombay, Popular Prakashan.

Padmanabha, P. (1983) *Primary Census Abstract, Scheduled Tribes, Series --India, Part II B (III), Census of India 1981*, New Delhi, Controller of Publication.

Raha, M.K. & J.C. Das (1982) Constitutional Safeguards for the Scheduled Tribes : Their Relevance and Implication in *Tribal Dpvelopment in India*. Ed. Dr. B. Choudhury, New Delhi, Inter India Publishers.

Part One : General Issues

CHAPTER 1

Tribal Development In Retrospect And Prospect*

Bhupinder Singh

The broad historical currents of development in this country since Independence are quite well known. The community development movement was launched in early fities with a view to achieve the objective of socio-economic development of the people. The Panchayati Raj institution was intermeshed with the official development machinery so that the broad direction of development should be infused with a sense of realism and felt needs of the people. But even in the fities, it became apparent that the fruits of development were sidetracking the weaker sections of the society, since control over resources passed on to the more powerful sections of the society. It began to be realised that a mechanism through which the lower strata of society could become recipient of such fruits should be evolved.

Article 46 of the Constitution explicitly recognises the scheduled castes and the scheduled tribes as the weaker sections of the society and

---

* Reproduced by the permission of the authority of 'Man and Life' and Institute of Social Research and Applied Anthropology, Calcutta from 'Man and Life', 9(1 + 2) : 11 -16, 1983.

calls for promotion of their educational and economic interest as well as their protection from exploitation. In the spirit of this directive policy of the Constitution, trials were fielded with a view to ensure that benefits of development reached the scheduled tribe people. The special multipurpose tribal projects which were a variant of the community development projects and, subsequently, the tribal development blocks, a variant of the community development blocks, were the experiments in this line. The idea was that through additional financial allocations, the special needs of the scheduled tribe population could be taken care of. But such a hope was believed as reviews by committees and teams appointed for the purpose showed.

The Tribal sub-Plan was launched as a new strategy in the beginning of the Fifth Plan period with the avowed purpose of earmarking definite quantum of funds from the State and Central Plans for Tribal Areas which were demarcated on the basis of blocks or talukas having a majority of the scheduled tribe population. To accelerate the pace of development, the Government of India sanctioned an additive in the form of special Central assistance. The Tribal sub-Plan was initially conceived as an area development plan with focus on tribals as the tribal areas had particularly been starved of infrastructural facilities from the pre-Independence times. Communications were poor, educational and health facilities were sparse and irrigation and power sources minimal. It was clear that unless these basic infrastructural requirements were met, there could be little advancement on both the economic and social fronts. Sixteen States and two Union Territories having a sizeable tribal concentration prepared their tribal sub-Plan each for the Fifth Plan period 1974-79 and a total investment of about a thousand crore of rupees was made. The net result was that there was improvement in infrastructural facilities in the tribal sub-Plan areas. Incidentally, the tribal sub-Plan areas have become, in almost all the States, co-terminus with the Scheduled Areas referred to in the Fifth Schedule of the Constitution.

The Tribal sub-Plan strategy has been continued in the Sixth Plan period. But the need has been increasingly felt of programmes which can make a dent into the income status of a tribal family. Assessment by the Tribal Research Institutes in the country through bench-mark surveys which have been conducted by them shows that in some States 80 per cent of scheduled tribe families live below the poverty-line while in some other States their percentage exceeds even 90. Thus, the bulk of the scheduled tribe families live on the verge of starvation; the prime objective of a Tribal sub-Plan has, therefore, to be to pull the families back from the brink of starvation. Thus, while development of infrastructure in the form of creation of irrigation, communication, co-operation, transport, health, education and such facilities continues to be important during the Sixth Plan period, an important planning dimension recently added is the thrust towards raising the scheduled tribe families above the poverty-line. In fact, it becomes even more important after the announcement by the Prime Minister advocating 20-Point Programme on 14 January, 1982. The four important objectives of Tribal sub-Plan during the Sixth Plan period have been formulated as:

(a) Raising the productivity levels in the fields of agriculture, horticulture animal husbandry, forestry, cottage-village and small industry, etc. so as to create economic impact of an order which will enable a targeted number of families(say 50%) in the tribal sub-Plan area to cross the poverty line. With the house-hold as the basic unit of planning, in poverty reduction the poorest and then the poor should be taken up on a progressive scale.

(b) Apart from the effort in the core economic sectors indicated in (a) above, education should become the key sector in the Sixth Plan period.

(c) The attainment of the objectives in (a) and (b) above would vitally depend on an adequate infrastructure for the creation of which there should be commensurate financial and physical effort.

(d) Concomitant with the aforesaid three-fold aims and, perhaps, the most important, assiduous exertions are necessary to eliminate exploitation of tribals in the fields of alienation of land, money-lending, debt bondage, trade, excise, forest etc.

The introduction of integrated rural development programmes and the national rural employment programme has added a further impetus to family-oriented programmes. Along-side the infrastructure and family-oriented economic programmes, the anxiety is also to ensure development of human resources and improvement of the quality of life in tribal areas, the latter aims being sought to be achieved through dissemination of general and technical education, catering to the health needs, ensuring drinking water supply, special nutritional programmes etc. Thus, the Tribal sub-Plan should ideally represent a harmonious blend of infra-structure supporting schemes, family-oriented economic schemes and social service programmes. The investment estimated in the Sixth Plan period in tribal development is between four thousand and five thousand crores of rupees and this order of investment should make a significant impact.

If the objective is to be realised, more than 50 per cent of scheduled tribe families should be able to cross the poverty-line in the Sixth Plan period 1980-85. But experienced planners and administrators will aver the course of development does not run smooth. A number of other requisites come into the picture. In the first instance, the plans drawn up should be apt, answering to the needs, aspirations of the tribal people and attuned to the local environment. The reference is to not only States' Tribal sub-Plans but more to the plan and programmes nearer the ground. In the tribal sub-Plan area of the country, 180 Integrated Tribal Development Projects(ITDPs) have been established, each ITDP being either coterminous with one development block or, more often an aggregate of two or more blocks. The block plans have to be sensitive to the people's needs and should get integrated a project report for an ITDP. In turn, such realistic project reports should get into worthwhile the State Tribal sub-Plan. It is obvious that a mere official effort at preparation of block plans, ITDP project reports and tribal sub-Plans, howsoever sincere it may be, may not produce the desired results. For one thing, most of the members of the administrative machinery belong to the non-tribal section of the society. Secondly, even if large number of tribal members were apart of the administrative machinery, still they would not be able to reflect the felt needs. There has to be a ceaseless and lively dialogue between the development participants and the development agents. Such an exchange has to take place right from the village level upwards through panchayat, block, ITDP, district, state and national levels. To some extent, this has been attempted in as much as at the ITDP-level committees to advise on project formulation and review of implementation have been constituted comprised of officials as well as people's representatives like MPs, MLAs and local tribal leaders. Some consultation mechanism has been built at the state and national levels through Tribes Advisory Councils, Legislative Assembly bodies, Parliamentary bodies etc. But, it has been felt that the interaction process should be multi-level extending both below and upward and should be more intense. It should commence from the village level.

Notwithstanding the special administrative structure created in the tribal sub-Plan and the involvement of the people's representatives in the development process, it has been expressed that the process has been going awry. Recently, the Home Minister happened to express the view that the benefits of development were, by and large, not reaching the tribals. This needs to be examined thoroughly with a view to evolving remedial measures. One reason seems to be apparent. The level of awareness and articulation of tribals being limited, they are not able to make the administration accountable. Perhaps, we shall have to live with this state of affairs for quite some time to come. But, in the meantime, ways and means of meeting the handicaps and ensuring flow of benefits to tribals have to be ensured. For the long run, there should be a much bigger drive towards general enlightenment of tribals by way of more intensive efforts at primary and adult education. Their general level of consciousness is likely to rise this way and the time will not be far off when they can make decisions relating to their development and watch implementation of the various development measures. Secondly, without waiting for the emergence of an educated tribal stratum, there ought to be an attempt to build up leadership among them through their active participation in panchayati raj bodies, co-operatives like LAMPS, informal forums and traditional social and political institutes. Thirdly, voluntary organisations can play a big role in trying a interpret sympathetically their felt needs and aspirations to the administration, thus acting as a bridgehead between the tribal mass and the development agents. Voluntary organization can mobilise the efforts in various sectors like credit, cooperation, social forestry. In fact, there is hardly any field in which dedicated and selfless workers and voluntary organisations cannot play the role of effective extension agents.

Not infrequently, we hear and read about the incidents of tribal unrest and law and order situations arising therefrom. It is a symptom of a disease that is deeper. The unrest is an expression of resentment and anger against their exploitation, deprivation and their low socio-economic status. Surely, as equal members of the society and as citizens of this country, they deserve a better deal. But, even on merely pragmatic grounds, it is necessary to intensify the efforts for their socio-economic development, as that is the only way of removal of their imaginary and substantive grievances. We shall thereby help to build a tension-free social milieu. This is the minimum price we have to pay for evolving a progressive society. For progress demands peace, order and stability. Let us, therefore, proceed with a certain amount of foresight and wisdom. Therein lies the hope for our children and grand-children.

CHAPTER 2

Policies of Tribal Welfare in India*

Ajit K. Danda

I

There is hardly any nation in the contemporary world that does not represent a state of ethnic heterogeneity. The differences between the culturally defined groups of those composite wholes vary from situation to situation and over time. Since prehistoric times, India had been the home of multiple ethno-cultural stocks (Basham, 1954:13). By the early historical period, cultural diversities between the various ethnic groups of her population became enormous. This implies not only coexistence of non-identical ethnocultural groups in the Indian sub-continent, but also a situation where there could be contacts in harmony as well as conflict. Such natural settings ordinarily provide scopes for assimilation

*** This is a slightly revised and somewhat updated version of the lecture entitled 'A Brief Account of the Principles and Policies of Tribal Welfare in India' delivered at the Raosaheb Thaware Memorial Social Welfare Lecture Series of 1969.**

and consequent merger of smaller groups of discrete cultures into the body of the larger ones. According to Ghurye (1943) such a process was already in motion in India until the British rule appeared on the scene and intervened. In his own words, "Considering the original differences, the results achieved up to the middle of the third quarter of the 18th Century were very hopeful. Owing to a variety of reasons, not the least among them being the nature of the method employed, there were still large sections of the Hindu populace which, in comparison with the upper-most sections, appeared to belong to a different culture altogether, when the British appeared on the scene as the rulers of the land. The old process of assimilation was upset. New problems arose". (1959 : XI). The groups of people who remained unassimilated drew attention of the then rulers who out of their subjective sympathy and humanism decided to treat them as distinct from the rest of the people. This discretely treated groups constitute the tribals of India. The main theme of discussion of this paper is built around the measures of welfare of these people.

In the course of my discussion, at the outset, I shall try to give you a general outline of the history of early contact of the tribals of India with the alien people. Then I propose to review the policies of tribal welfare in general terms.

If we trace the history of our knowledge about the tribal communities, we find that at the initial stage two different kinds of interests led our pioneers to establish contact with these peoples. For the purpose of this essay, these may broadly be called (i) academic interest and (ii) administrative interest. The academic interest can in turn be sub-divided into three successive phases each of which bearing marked evidence of temper of the times and thus reflecting the trends of their respective contemporary world.

Since the publication of Darwin's *On the Origin of Species* in 1859, for sometime there grew a general tendency among scholars to examine whether the biological evolutionary sequences could have any parallel in the spheres of cultural evolution and whether similar evolutionary sequences in the case of cultures can possibly be established. This led to the development of interest in studying archaic cultures that consequently culminated into the study of the so-called primitive societies. During the first phase of studies of various tribes due to influence of the West, the main purpose was to know one's own position in the biological and cultural evolutionary sequences. The major emphasis of the study of tribes during this period has been rather on the static aspects of their culture, that is, the study of customs and material culture, particularly to highlight their exotic nature. The second phase of the academic interest did not emerge until scholars discovered the existence of similar cultural traits in spatially and geographically distant and distinct regions. They were somewhat flabbergasted in their concern to explain the cause of such occurrences. After having observed the cultural similarities between the people of separate geographical regions, scholars of tribal society became interested in the study of dynamic aspects of culture. As a result, interests in the studies of diffusion, acculturation, transculturation, and so on arose. It is from the studies of these dynamic aspects of culture, that there developed a major concern for the welfare of the tribals. This marks the beginning of the third phase (Wilkinson, 1962 : 19). There is, however, a marked difference between the former two phases on the one hand, that are characterized by apparent lack of concern for fellow beings and the last phase on the other, that expresses an overtone of fellow feelings.

As far as the administrative interest is concerned, the history of the civilized man's relationship with the tribal people falls into two distinct phases. The first phase represents an initial period of conquest and spoilation driving the tribals in general to a precarious existence. This is followed by the second phase that characterizes attempts to redeem, to some extent, the wrongs done to them and recognition of their right of existence and own mode of living (Guha, 1951 :35).

One important observation of the above review is that both the academic and administrative interests arrived at more or less the same conclusion, that is some welfare was urgently needed to be done among the tribal peoples of India. The term, 'welfare' presupposes a condition of disparity, economic, social, cultural and such others. Before we get involved into the discussion of parity and disparity in order to obtain the required background information, it would be worthwhile to examine the situation of the tribals in India from the early period and the nature of their early contact. For our appreciation of the overall situation however, I shall primarily depend on the observations of Guha (1951:36-38).

Ancient Sanskrit literatures bear ample evidences of clashes and contact between the Aryan invaders and the autochthonus aborigines of India. Ancient Tamil books also write of similar encounter between the two groups in the early Christian era (Kanakasabhai, 1904 : 65). This, however, did not lead to extermination of either of the feuding groups. One section of the vanquished group was, as a result, driven out of the immediate neighbourhood and another was absorbed to a limited extent to form a low layer of the Hindu social hierarchy (Ghurye, 1959:XI). The wider section of non-Aryan tribes was though partly influenced by the Hindu thoughts, ideas, and customs, their tribal identity remained undisturbed.

II

With the British occupation of the country and the rapid opening up of communication channels, the tribal people came to the notice of the rulers, particularly when punitive measures had to be undertaken against their raids on the loyal subjects occupying the plains. Beginning with the Mal Paharias under Warren Hastings in 1772, who were brought under control by Augustus Cleveland between 1778-84, the primitive tribes were pacified, if not subjugated, one by one until the majority of the tribal populations of Chota Nagpur, Central India, and South India, and those of the North-eastern hill tracts and Assam were brought under the British subjugation.

Annexation of the tribal territories with the British administration posed many serious problems of administration as the tribal lands began wholly passing into the hands of the non-tribal landlords and the money-lenders of the plains. This led to dissatisfaction and consequent tribal uprisings that challenged the integrity of the State and endangered the law and order situation of the country. The Mal Paharia raids of 1772 showed for the first time the necessity of the system of indirect rule and as a result of the mutinies of the Hos of Singbhum in 1831, the Khond uprisings in 1846, and the Santal rebellions in 1855, it was felt necessary to bring these regions under the specially constituted non-regulation tracts to be administered by simpler codes, directly by the Deputy Commissioners in a manner suitable to the aborigines. Consequently such a system was introduced by the Act XXIV of 1839 in Madras Presidency whereby civil and criminal jurisdiction of Ganjam, Visakhapatnam, and Godavari Hill tract was vested in an Agent and his staff. In Bombay, the tribal area of the Mewasi estates of West Khandesh was excluded by Act XI of 1846 and special rules were framed for the administration of these estates. Similarly the first contact with the hill tribes of Assam began with an expedition sent against the Jaintia estates in 1774. But not until the murder of a survey party by the people of Nongkhlaw in 1829, did the British Government seriously attempt the subjugation of the Khasi Hills, which was completed in 1833 after the Confederacy of the Khasi Chiefs was successfully defeated. In 1854 North Cachar was annexed. Several expeditions had to be sent to the Chin-Lushai Hills between 1850 and 1890 when the Lushai Hills was brought under the British administration. The Naga Hills came under the British control in 1878, with Kohima as the capital, and finally the Abor (Adi) expedition of 1912 established the British influence over the entire territory of this section.

In order to organize a special administration particularly to check alienation of lands for the primitive tribes that would be more or less the same throughout the tribal territories, the Scheduled Districts Act was passed in 1874 by the Indian Legislature. This specified the tribal areas all over the country into Scheduled Tracts. In spite of these legislative safeguards, alienation of the tribal lands could not be altogether checked. Even after these enactments the aboriginal populations suffered enormous disabilities from the enforcement of the rather ill-conceived forest and game laws and interference with tribal festivals on moral grounds. The result was, as pointed out by Elwin (1957), an extraordinary increase in incidences of drunkenness which augmented excise revenues and profit of the contractors and wine dealers at the expense of the bewildered aboriginals.

The second phase in the administration of the tribals began with the passing of the Government of India Act of 1919 when the tribal areas were reconstituted under section 52-A of that Act into backward tracts after removing them either fully or partially from the jurisdiction of the administrative ministries. There were altogether 19 areas thus classified, of which four were entirely beyond the pale of the legislatures. With respect to the others, the legislatures were empowered to pass laws but in that case, too, the operation was dependent on the decision of the Governor General.

In the Government of India Act of 1935, more stringent provision for special treatment of tribal areas was made by converting the backward tracts into Areas of Total Exclusion or Partial Exclusion. In the Sixth

Schedule of the said Act, four areas under the first head and 11 areas under the second were at first proposed. It may be noted here that the Wazirs of Lahul and Spiti were exceptions in this respect as though declared as excluded areas, they were not considered as such as backward tracts. Their inclusion was, however, due solely to the political and administrative reasons.

These enactments were primarily aimed at protecting the aboriginal people from exploitation and for allowing them freedom to pursue their traditional method of living. Some tribes in India who needed the protection most, because of the area approach of tribal problems and the blanket policy of tribal welfare, were not considered important to be included in this scheme. Mention may be made about the Andamanese, Kadars, Pulayans of Annamalai Hills and the forest tribes of the Wynad in this respect. Nor the Todas of Nilgiri Hills, who were among those tribals of India that are steadily declining in population were entitled to the benefits of this Act. However, the total area covered by the Act for special treatment was 126,576 sq. miles of which 28,134 sq. miles consisted of entirely excluded area and 98,442 sq. miles for the partially excluded area.

A review of the special constitutional measures taken for the protection of the tribal population shows that the purpose behind these has neither been fulfilled, nor economic exploitation could be checked to ensure social justice. Any tangible evidence of increase in the adaptability of the tribes changing situation is not visible either. The steady addition and inclusion to the number of special reserved areas with each succeeding constitutional change, if anything, rather proves it the other way.

III

The tribal policies in India were subjected to two major controversies. The first among them belongs to the pre-independence period that arose around the thirties and forties of the present century. The early students of Indian aborigines and their subjective ideas and observations were, to some extent, responsible for this controversy. Those who are familiar with the empirical anthropological records of the Indian subcontinent, I believe, would acknowledge the contributions of S. C. Roy, Von Finer Haimendorf ,Verrier Elwin, K. P. Chattopadhyay, T. C. Das,

D. N. Majumdar, and other distinguished scholars to our repertory of knowledge with reverence. But the observations of most of these scholars had one thing in common, that is, whenever they analysed the changing tribal life, probably because of their attachment to and sympathy for the people, they mostly highlighted the misery and distress of the tribal communities that have come about because of contact of the tribal communities with the alien people. Even the early British ethnographers were not exceptions in this respect. Probably there was a common *leit motif* that guided the authors that is, to draw attention of the administrators, politicians, and social workers to the precarious existence of these downtrodden neglected communities. In a way, they were apparently successful in their efforts, but as a consequence, the question that immediately came up was what could be done to wipe out the misery of the tribals. In his attempt to reply to this question, Ghurye (1943) came forward with his thesis of assimilation. As already referred to, according to him the various tribal communities in India were at different levels of the process of Hinduisation. This was the case with pre-British India as well as in the later date except with an intermittent period of confusion due to British contact and influence. So in order to ensure benefit to the tribals and also for the sake of national solidarity, the absorption of the tribal communities to the Hindu fold was recommended to be the only remedy. Bose (1941) though did not advocate it as a solution to the problem of tribal welfare, even before Ghurye came forward with his thesis of assimilation, demonstrated the on-going process of the Hindu method of tribal absorption.

In an earlier publication, Elwin had already pleaded an altogether different strategy. In his concluding Chapter of The Baigas (1939), he discussed at length the extent of evils that have come about to the life of the tribals through their contact with the neighbouring alien populations. He substantiated his view by citations from the celebrated authors like S. C. Roy, J.H. Hutton, J.P. Mills and demonstrated with evidence the misery and distress that have come about to the tribal community because of their contact with the non-tribals. It may be mentioned here that the anthropologists of the thirties and forties of this century seldom found any positive effect, that the tribal folks have experienced due to their contact with the alien people. Among the contributors of tribal studies, those who were silent about the negative aspects of contact, were not very vocal about the positive contributions either. As a result of this, a strong feeling grew among the anthropologists to reduce the extent of contact of the tribals and Elwin was taken to be the spokesman of this view. According to him, due to contact between the tribals and non-tribals it is the former group who always suffered from a number of setbacks. In his own words, "Some of their simple and innocent dances, under Hindu influence, have been given up. The souls of the people are soiled and grimy with the dust of passing motor-buses. In the village, you are in the midst not of a living community, but of a collection of isolated units. Tribal life and tradition appears slightly ludicrous, even to the tribesmen themselves. And once that point is reached, there is no hope for the tribe" (1939:514). Therefore, in order to protect interest of these people he advocated a policy of controlled isolationism which he himself called the establishment of a sort of national park. According to this policy, in order to protect interest of the tribal people, it is necessary to keep the alien people away from the tribals. As per his recommendation, areas of maximum tribal concentration should be declared as special areas. "This special area" according to him, "should be under the direct control of a Tribes Commissioner"(1939:515).

As indicated earlier in pre-independence India, this view received a mixed appreciation. When the social workers and some anthropologists were extremely bitter about this policy of what they interpreted as isolationism, it gained the status of being more or less the accepted official view of the government of British India. The anthropologists and the social scientists, however, as a result of this controversy, became divided into two camps. When a section found some meaning in this policy, others considered it a utopia especially designed to weaken India and the national solidarity movement. There was, however, a third group of anthropologists who were cautious in their very approach and refused to support or advocate either of the policies of assimilation or controlled isolation without having sufficient background knowledge about the way of life of the tribal people themselves.

IV

After the independence of India, discussions on the problems of the tribals and other backward communities again came to the limelight. As a result of this, the old controversy became revised in a new form. In the post independence controversy also the principal theme was either assimilation or isolation. But it no longer remained an academician's dilemma.

With the independence of India the national government was looking for constructive policies to tackle the tribal situation and in this endeavour the social workers and the anthropologists became the rival partners. In fact, a major portion of their respective arguments was a dialogue at cross purposes and neither of the groups were ready to look at the problem from the opponents' frame of reference. As a result, Elwin's policy of national park, which was bitterly criticized by a number of anthropologists and social scientists and when Elwin himself made many amendments to his former position, was taken to be by the social workers, as if the unanimous view of the anthropologists. Even the social workers of eminence sometimes attacked the anthropologists on this issue and branded them as 'isolationists', 'revivalists', and 'no changers'.

There is, of course, another factor that contributed to the development of misunderstandings between the anthropologists and social workers. As indicated earlier, the two groups took two different kinds of attitude towards this national issue. When the social workers were in a hurry to advocate their policy, as they desired to assimilate these people without any loss of time, the anthropologists were rather 'cautious' to say anything outright. It is the initial hesitation of the anthropologists that earned the name 'no changer' for them. Further, they did not support the policy of assimilation either, that was so strongly advocated by the social workers. However, because of various reasons, the social workers initially could occupy an established position in framing national policy and this made the anthropologists, too, somewhat aggressive and vocal. Soon they were also able to form public opinion in their favour and press their demand for the recognition to applied or action anthropology. But, this, instead of help developing understanding between the two groups, invited further slur and bitterness.

Apart from the above differences there was another area where the anthropologists and the social workers did not see eye to eye, or rather, were poles apart. This difference was fundamental as the two groups looked at the tribal problems from two different frames of reference and suggested diverse solutions. The social workers viewed the tribes as neglected backward communities who deserved sympathy, at least on humanitarian ground. The anthropologists, on the other hand, pleaded for their right of being uplifted. So it was not a question of a charity but a demand. But what made the already tense situation worse is that for safeguarding their own recognized position, the social workers found a challenge from anthropologists as their rivals and the former sometimes attacked the latter on personal grounds. Probably it went a bit too far as the criticism of the social workers no longer remained against the policy of anthropologists as such. A social worker of the eminence of Thakkar Bapa also once challenged the integrity of the discipline of anthropology. In his Kale Memorial lecture in 1941, he accused the anthropologists for keeping the tribals confined to and isolated in their inaccessible hills and jungles and to him it was something like keeping them in glass cases of a museum for the curiosity of purely academic persons.

Some of the anthropologists, in return, accused the social workers as interventionists. The main attack of the anthropologists, however,was not on intervention as such, as the social workers sometimes assumed it. Their main objection was against social workers' attitude of parentalism which presupposes an order of cultural superiority and inferiority that the anthropologists resent.

Though anthropologists, for the first instance, are accused of advocating isolationism, there is a great deal of misunderstanding here as none of them really pleaded so as a permanent measure. Even the advocate of the so-called national park theory did not want to leave the tribes alone, he rather opposed it. What Elwin really pleaded for was to put a check on uncontrolled exploitation. As he observed, "I see no reason why the tribal areas should be 'excluded' or 'partially excluded' as they are under the present Government of India Act, but it is obvious that some expert should stand between them and the Legislature" (1939 : 515). He further revised his opinion in his *A Philosophy for NEFA* and said, "It is true that I myself, writing many years ago when India was under British rule, advocated a policy of temporary isolation for certain small tribes but this was not to keep them as they were, but because at that time the only contacts they had with the outside world were debarring contacts, leading to economic exploitation and cultural destruction.... But a policy advocated to meet a set of special circumstances does not hold when those circumstances have changed, and neither I nor any other anthropologist would dream of suggesting such a policy since the independence" (1957:46). In order to avoid misunderstanding he again, reassured, "Isolation in the modern world is impossible; it would not be desirable even if it was possible. The old controversy about zoo and museums has long been dead...To try to preserve and develop the best elements of tribal art, religion and culture is something very different from wishing to keep the people in a zoo'' (1957:59).

V

I have already mentioned that a section of the anthropologists labelled the social workers as interventionists. This was, for obvious reasons, never liked by the latter, rather, the social workers took objection to the use of word interventionist. In the second half of his lecture referred to earlier, Thakkar Bapa raised the issue and pleaded that the policy advocated by the Indian social workers and nationalist politicians was one of assimilation and not of just haphazard intervention. There he also tried to give an outline of the areas of problems of the tribals and classified them under six major headings. These are poverty, illiteracy, lack of communication, ill health, defects in administration, and lack of appropriate leadership. He strongly urged a quick elimination of all these problems from tribal areas. Emphasizing the importance of need for contacts, he explained that unless the aboriginal people through their contact with the advanced group realise their own backwardness in the economic, social, and political fields, they would hardly make any progress.

Whatever the justification of either of the feuding groups might be, the controversy did not help framing a clear cut national policy of the tribals, and from time to time the government policies were found to sway between the opinions of either of the groups. As a result, both the planners and administrators confronted a great deal of confusion in the whole situation.

There were, no doubt, suggestions for close coordination between the anthropologists and social workers. I may refer to Bose (1957), an anthropologist and an associate of Gandhi in this respect. ''Anthropologists have often not been social workers, and social workers have not usually been anthropologists. Specialization has its obvious merits in any scientific discipline, but, when, as in social science, thought and action run hand in hand, it may be more fruitful to bring about a controlled coordination between the two'' (1957 : 178).

What may be suggested heré is that neither the anthropologists nor the social workers were entirely correct nor either of them was altogether wrong in their approach to the problems of tribal welfare. What seems unfortunate is that none of them was ready to look into the problems from the other's point of view. Expertise and specialized experience both are needed at the initial stage, particularly when a new nation launches upon an important programme like that of tribal welfare. Instead of becoming possessive if we have tried to be accommodative, many such misunderstandings could have been averted.

VI

So far, I broadly dealt with the history of contact of the tribal people in India and the two major controversies on the policy of tribal welfare that arose out of some misunderstandings between the professionals and practitioners, one during the pre-independence period and the other after India won freedom. Here at the outset I propose to describe the official position of the Government of India regarding tribal welfare. After a brief evaluation of the various approaches to tribal welfare I would highlight the recent changes in the official policy and their implications.

The Directive Principles of the State Policy on tribal welfare is laid down in Article 46 of the Constitution of India. It says, "The State shall promote with special care the educational and economic interests of the weaker sections of the people, and, in particular, of the Scheduled Castes and the Scheduled Tribes, and shall protect them from social injustice and all forms of exploitation." The above provides an outline of the State Policy regarding the Scheduled Tribes and other weaker sections of the population though, does not spell out the method for attaining this goal. The Report of the Study Team, nevertheless, outlines the policy in the following words:

> "There are two very clear implications of the policy adopted by the Government of India towards the Backward classes. On the one hand there is recognition of the fact that certain sections of the population are socially, educationally and economically not even with the rest of the community. Alongside there is an equally important stipulation that the wide disparities

in the socio-economic levels of various sections of the community should be narrowed down and finally eliminated. It has been fully realised that special arrangements would have to be made for them in order to bring them to a position of equality with other citizens. In essence, therefore, this is a policy of social justice (1959:123)."

The above quotation, though outlines the policy in fairly clear terms, it remains rather silent about the very approach. In fact, as already indicated, the controversy of the anthropologists and the social workers created a situation which was quite disturbing from the administrative point of view. This is partly reflected in the Report of the Study Team when it comments :

"The problem of Scheduled Tribes is somewhat different because of several anthropological reasons. Each tribe has a distinct cultural pattern of its own. It was, therefore, necessary to prepare any programme for the development and welfare of Scheduled Tribes with a clearcut national policy. Anthropologists, planners, welfare administrators and social workers have all been interested alike in defining this policy in the light of their own understanding of the problem. Opinions expressed by various groups on this subject constitute divergent schools of thought which have evoked considerable controversy. Because of the forces released by the plans for the overall national development, the process of acculturation of tribes has been further accelerated. With the linking up of the tribal areas with the outside world, the question whether we should adopt a policy of assimilation or otherwise is no more than of mere academic interest (1959:124)."

A close examination of the above citation clearly demonstrates that regarding controversy of anthropologists and social workers the report of the Study Team tries to remain non-committal though, one gets the feel that it more or less endorsed the view that was once advocated by the eminent social worker Thakkar Bapa.

So far as the pre-independence tribal policies are concerned, the then British Government of India adopted the policy of 'exclusion' and 'partial exclusion' of tribal areas. So some sort of segregation was envisaged which was argued to be for the benefit of the tribal themselves. This policy was strongly criticized by the bulk of anthropologists as well as other social scientists and social workers. Irawati Karve in this connection observed:

> "It is necessary to accomplish a rapid and complete assimilation of these people to the culture and language of the State in which they find themselves. This would enable them to participate fully in the political and social life of the State and become full citizens of India (1959:143)."

The above quotation from an eminent social scientist of India though generally supports the views of the social workers, as far as the question of assimilation is concerned, the anthropologists and social scientists in general were equally blamed for creating the confusion.

The policy on tribals of post-independence India has been most explicitly outlined by Jawaharlal Nehru himself, who in his Foreword to the second edition of *A Philosophy for NEFA* by Verrier Elwin stated:

> "We cannot allow matters to drift in the tribal areas or just not take interest in them. In the world of today that is not possible or desirable. At the same time we should avoid over-administering these areas and, in particular, sending too many outsiders into tribal territory."

It is between these two extreme positions that we have to function. Development in various ways there has to be, such as communications, medical facilities, education and better agriculture. These avenues of development should, however, be pursued within the broad framework or the following five fundamental principles:

(i) People should develop along the lines of their own genius, we should avoid imposing anything on them. We should try to encourage in every way their own traditional arts and culture.

(ii) Tribal rights in land and forests should be respected.

(iii) We should try to train and build up a team of their own people to do the work of administration and development. Some technical personnel from outside will, no doubt, be needed, especially in the beginning. But we should avoid introducing too many outsiders into tribal territory.

(iv) We should not over-administer these areas or over-whelm them with the multiplicity of schemes. We should rather work through and not in rivalry to, their own social and cultural institutions.

(v) We should judge results, not by statistics or the amount of money spent, but by quality of human character that was evolved.

If we accept the above views of Nehru as the Government of India's views regarding the tribal policy then there is no doubt that the anthropologists' position got some recognition in the government policy matter. But this probably remained more or less a matter of principle than planning and implementation of programmes. Because, in practical administration initially it is the group of social workers who handled the whole thing and planned programmes for them. And as expected, this was by and large, not liked by the anthropologists. Though this has been expressed somewhat bluntly by L.P. Vidyarthi, the following quotation of him is fairly revealing:

> "The social workers...found the political and administrative climate very favourable for the expansion of their activities. They found their own colleagues and partymen at the helm of the government affairs. They were already biased against the anthropological approach to the tribal problems. They sought all cooperation from the social workers in framing tribal policies and delegated their powers to them in the execution of welfare scheme among the tribal population. In this way, as a matter of fact, the social workers assumed the roles of both semi-officials and scientists. They began to make recommendations to the Government on tribal matters, they began to get substantial grants from the Government fund for

> helping the tribals, and later began to hold administrative posts for tribal welfare schemes on small honoraria. They began to organize tribal welfare conferences on an all India level (1959:62)''

Whatever the amount of truth might be in it, such accusation or counteraccusation does not lead to the development of any mutual understanding; it rather breeds ill-feeling among the persons involved. T.C. Das was rather extra-cautious in his views on policy matters when he suggested that before framing any tribal policy it is important that the tribal people are classified first for their proper identification and it is as per need of these tribal people the policies might be framed. In the Fourth Tribal Welfare Conference held at Koraput in April-May 1957, T. C. Das proposed a fivefold classification of the tribals of India. These are (i) the nomadic food gatherers and pastorals, (ii) the shifting cultivators of the hill-slopes, (iii) the plough cultivators of the plateau and foot-hills, (iv) the tribals partially assimilated into the Hindu social system, and (v) the fully assimilated tribal groups occupying a fairly high social status among the Hindus (1957:61-66). N. K. Bose did not put forward any classification though, outlined a device for such a classification. In his own words, ''In a memorandum submitted to the Backward Classes Commission, the writer once suggested that only those should be considered backward who are so by three joint tests. One is that economically the particular group should be poorer in terms of the average income among all classes in the neighbourhood. Secondly, the percentage of education or literacy among them should be lower than the average in the neighburhood. And, thirdly the people are reckoned as among those from whom water is not acceptable to Brahmins, or who are not served by Brahmin priests such as also serve other castes'' (1958:20).

As pointed out by Bose, neither economy, nor social differences, nor the educational backwardness individually is responsible for the disparities or discrepancies between the tribals and the rest of the Indian population. It is the combination of these three factors together that determines the degree of backwardness of individuals or groups. His joint tests suggest an integrated formula that takes care of literacy, economy and social distances together and forms a new indicator that might be used successfully for locating the individuals or groups who deserve special attention. Bose further suggests, ''While promoting new industries, while educating young people from among the Adivasis, our purpose must be not reformist, but revolutionary. We must not aim at raising the status of the tribal people and find place for them in caste's social scale, but should do away with all class-wise scales attaching to birth or to occupation altogether'' (1958:22). Bose probably could realise the intricacy of the problem in its appropriate depth and suggested an effective method to handle it. But unfortunately this approach to tribal welfare was not given due attention. In the later policies of the government, however, integrated approach got official recognition.

VII

There were some further changes in the official position of tribal welfare. But before we get into the discussion of later changes in the policy matters, I would like to say a few words about the various approaches to the tribal problems and would endeavour to make an assessment of relative merits of each of those approaches.

In pre-independence India the major directed changes that came about to the life of the tribals were through the activities of the missionaries. Even prior to that, because of their contact with alien people some changes were taking place. However, there was no well organized agency to provide support to such change. Probably the administrative agencies of the government were the next to come in close contact with the tribal life. There was, nevertheless, a major difference between the approaches of the two agencies to the tribal problems as they were working to achieve rather two non-identical goals. When the missionaries were primarily interested in converting the tribal people into Christianity, the government agency was primarily concerned about their economic betterment. The missionaries also, in order to earn confidence of the tribal people introduced certain educational, health, and other welfare programmes. But as the motive force behind their developmental activities was conversion, there were certain built-in constraints in their approach to tribal welfare.

During the last few decades of India's foreign rule, some voluntary agencies also initiated developmental activities in the tribal areas. At the outset their attempts were meagre and extremely localised. But since India achieved independence, the role of voluntary agencies became very important. Accordingly, they became viable agencies for introducing changed programmes to the tribal areas.

Anthropologists are probably the last to appear in the scene. As stated earlier, because of their involvement in two major controversies about tribal policies, initially their assistance appeared somewhat unwelcome in tribal affairs. Their commitment to academic exercise and apathy toward shouldering the responsibility of developmental activities were to some extent responsible for that.

Lacking adequate well-established model for tribal welfare in the world arena and also adequate personal experience, the Indian anthropologists appeared not sure to the extent they should get involved in the reconstruction work of new India. When the programmes were about to set in, they were rather caught unprepared to bear the burden. As a result, at the initial stage there was a period of apparent apathy. In spite of their sufficient responses in intellectual exercises, the Indian anthropologists' preparedness to undertake any developmental programme was rare. Even today, in comparison with the other agencies, anthropologists' share of involvement in the implementation of welfare programme is extremely insignificant.

An important factor separates the anthropologists from the other agencies of development. Missionaries, administrators, and social workers were all convinced that the tribals are backward. They are unfed, or half-fed, half-naked, illiterate and they should be provided all these. Thus to the agencies mentioned above the end was predetermined and so was the means. "Imposition and parentalism are their working tools" (Vidyarthi, 1960:24). On the contrary the anthropologists refused to start with any preconceived notion. Naturally, the goals as well as the means were yet to be worked out. As Sachchidananda observed in this connection: "The development of these people is very much more than mere implementation of the works programme. It involves social processes to be set in motion, through a correct grasp of their culture, traditions and current problems of life" (1960:50). There was another point on which the anthropologists and the non-anthropologists differed in their approach. When the non-anthropologists generally bracketed all the tribes together ignoring the inter-tribal and intra-tribal distinctions, the anthropologists not only refused to accept the blanket policy but pleaded for preliminary studies emphasizing differences prior to implementation of any programme (Das, 1959:127).

VIII

There are altogether four major approaches to tribal welfare. The approaches of the missionaries, which may be called the religious approach, is the oldest among them. As far as their welfare activities are concerned, no doubt they are doing a commendable job. But a question remains to be answered is whether the tribals'conversion to a new faith adds to their social solidarity and integrates them to the mainstream of national life, which is the ultimate objective of all welfare measures. As S. C. Dube points out, ''If the conversion of tribes to a new faith adds to their social solidarity, without alienating them from the majority of the neighbouring communities, and equips them better for participation in modern life, if cannot reasonably be opposed. But if it detribalizes and disintegrates these communities without offering them any alternative satisfactions, the approach can hardly be said to be offering any serious solution to the tribal problem'' (1960:14).

The administrative approach to tribal welfare was subject to some amount of changes in the context of the British rule in India and of the post independence period. As mentioned earlier, for the purpose of administrative advantage, the then British Government of India demarcated the tribal territories as excluded and partially excluded areas and separate political representation to the tribes was awarded. This again became an issue of bitter criticism from the nationalist Indians and these were viewed ''....as part of a diabolic conspiracy to create a new separatist minority....'' (Dube, 1960:13). The government of independent India modified the exclusion policy altogether. But the policy of awarding separate representation to the tribes has practically remained unchanged. This poses a very serious question which is somewhat related to the earlier mentioned blanket policy. How far did the various tribal groups inhabiting a common territory themselves recognise the collectivity that got separate representation? The major handicap of this policy is that it did not take the inter-tribal and intra-tribal differences into account at all, neither did it pay any attention to the exploitation of one or a number of tribes by other tribal group or groups.

As far as the approach of the social workers is concerned, one has to admit that various voluntary agencies have done a considerable amount of humanitarian social service in tribal areas. But the problem there, as already mentioned, is that their over-involvement in the situation often costs them their valued objectivity. Further, there idealism and spirit of service have often not been matched by their understanding of tribal organization, their values and problems. Though L. P. Vidyarthi appears to over-stretch it a bit, there is some amount of truth in it when he points out "...they do not care for the 'value', volition, and the right of self-determination of the tribal folk". (1960:24).

The solutions to the tribal problems as envisaged by the anthropologists may be called the anthropological approach. As indicated earlier, the anthropologists' primary concern was to know the problem and about the tribes before suggesting any solution. Naturally, instead of depending on an omnibus solution of tribal problems, they have been contemplating a number of possible solutions. Further the anthropologists, particularly the action anthropologists, have given due consideration to the question of value position also "For them 'end', and 'means' are inter-dependent and are determined in course of enquiry" (Vidyarthi, 1960-24):

Anthropologists have been much discredited as welfare workers because of Elwin's recommendation of temporary isolation of the tribal groups in extreme cases. In spite of that, personally he remained not only a respected member of the NEFA (now Arunachal Pradesh) Administration, his policies were implemented there almost in full. However, from an analysis of the suggestions put forward by anthropologists, ultimate integration of the tribes into the mainstream of Indian life emerges to be the natural and desirable goal which is to be attained with utmost care, restraint, and cautious planning.

Of late, elements of anthropological thinking on the problems of tribal welfare have been incorporated in the national policies. The anthropologists' suggestions, in short, are (i) understanding of tribal organization and values through sustained scientific studies, (ii) identifying the problems of tribes at different levels of technological, economic and cultural development, (iii) identifying the integrative forces in tribal life, (iv) identifying the areas of minimum and maximum resistance to innovation in their culture, (v) recognising vital linkages in their cultural fabric, (vi) orienting the administrators to tribal life and culture in all aspects considered and giving them special training for the tasks they have to undertake among the tribes, (vii) cautious formulation of welfare plans with a view to accommodating tribal needs with regional and national interests and (viii) careful watch on the trends set in motion by these measures, with a view to eliminating elements that destroy the social solidarity of the tribes and kill their zest for life (Dube, 1960:14).

Anthropologists' concern for integration of the tribal people has found repeated expression. T. C. Das, in this connection remarked,

> "The Christian and Muslim approaches to assimilation are through religion. They are dynamic in character. But Hindu approach is neither dynamic nor through religion. Hinduism sought solution of the problem through socio-economic means, allowing the tribals to exercise their free will to move into the Hindu fold. The scientific approach which we advocate for tribal assimilation is similar to Hindu method excepting its dynamic character. We cannot wait indefinitely for the psychological change suitable for modernization though its value is not denied. But circumstances in the outer world do not warrant delay in modernizing the tribals. India cannot afford to keep 20 millions of her tribal children in a static condition for an indefinite period. It would be ruinous to her national development (1960:9)"

N.K. Bose also follows the same line of thinking when he says:

> "It thus became abundantly clear that when constitutional reforms are proposed for a community which has not earned its way to reforms by added internal strength, it eventually leads to separatism rather than clear integration. The moral is also obvious. It is at the grassroots that democracy must begin. The lives of the citizens of India are being changed considerably in many ways. If those who are in the same economic position combine in spite of linguistic or cultural differences in a joint endeavour to build up a new life and convert those who oppose it by means of peaceful persuasion, then only will integration of right type take place. We can obviate the dangers of a latent

> two-nation theory only by trying to encourage unities of economic and social interests as they arise in course of the nations changing life (1964:104)''

B. K. Roy Burman moves somewhat further in this direction when he identifies various types of integration and analyses them at different levels (1961:13). Thus national integration as such, has been envisaged as a combination of various types of integration at different levels. The important among them are (i) emotional integration, (ii) technological integration, (iii) civil integration and (iv) cultural integration. The types of integration that should be fostered in the case of a particular tribe can be determined only through a thorough analysis of the way of life of that particular tribe.

According to him, so far as the emotional integration is concerned, it developed through a sense of belongingness to the nation. Nation is actually the ultimate aggregate of meaningful symbols of emotional integration. In the Indian context, there are evidences of positive steps towards the promotion of emotional integration of the tribals through special constitutional provisions. ''It is thus expected that the political privileges provided for in the constitution, supplemented by the huge experiment in democracy through national extension service programme, will go a long way in emotional integration of the tribals in the national society'' (Roy Burman, 1961:14).

The ultimate aim to technological integration as Roy Burman observes, is to bring about a change in the standard of living of the tribals and to equalize them with the other sectors of the nation. Article 275 of the Constitution of India provides for grant of capital and recurring sums from the Consolidated Fund of India for promoting welfare of the Scheduled Tribes and it is expected that through implementation of various schemes for economic development the desired changes could be achieved.

The civil integration of the tribals according to him, involves a long drawn process. The Preamble of the Constitution of India has ruled out the possibility of any discrimination and assured social justice. The modern concepts of social justice are in shaping inter personal relationship and intra familial relationship, more or less in the same way all over the world. Naturally, it can be expected that with the attainment of social maturity, tribal societies in India also will more or less conform to the general pattern. But as it has to develop from within as the situation stands now, the emergence of such elite promoting civi' ıegration may take somewhat a long time.

As far as the cultural integration is concerned, it may be made clear here that cultural integration does not mean cultural fusion. "Seen in this light cultural integration means cross-cultural co-existence of the different cultures in mutual respect and understanding so that one may promote healthy development of another. Cultural integration is thus a double way process involving both tribal and non-tribal cultures. Integration of tribal culture and non-tribal culture can take place in a democracy only by democratizing both tribal culture and non-tribal culture" (Roy Burman, 1961:15). While framing the Constitution of India this basic tenet of democracy was given special attention and Article 29 of the Constitution of India laid down that "any section of the citizens residing in the territory of India or any part thereof having a distinct language, script or culture of its own shall have the right to conserve the same". In other words, cultural integration in a democracy means freedom of choice for individuals in adopting formalities of different cultures, while maintaining the basic humanism of every culture.

IX

The changes that have come about in the policies of tribal welfare, due to change in the administrative machinery have already been discussed. We have noticed that even after the independence of India the policies have undergone several major changes. It has already been stated that at the initial stage the problems of tribal welfare were looked upon as a salvation work of the downtrodden communities. The approach was visualized purely as humanitarian exercise. Naturally the spirit of the task of national reconstruction was absent there. With the commencement of the Constitution of India, a major shift of the approach to tribal welfare did take place. It was realized that only the humanitarian approach or tribal welfare will neither satisfy the members of the tribal communities, nor will it serve the need for reconstruction of the country. As a result the work that was so long considered a charity became substituted by the spirit of development. Even then, the programmes were not fully satisfactory as the development activities were primarily oriented to serve the needs of only the vocal individuals of the tribal communities. It was as late as during the Second Five Year Plan period that the need for an well-integrated approach to tribal welfare was recognized and positive efforts were made for their implementation through the programme of Special Multipurpose Tribal Blocks. But unfortunately the activities of these Special Multipurpose Tribal Blocks were, somewhat unjudiciously mixed up with the activities of the over-published Community Development Blocks. As an outcome of that, during later years when the Community Development Projects came under severe criticism of both officials and non-officials, the programme of Special Multipurpose Tribal Blocks was also made to share the blame and in several states in India a major portion of the programme was shelved. That brought about another change in the tribal welfare programme as the well-integrated tribal welfare schemes were replaced by a broad-based area programme. This change seems to be quite fundamental as it suggests the replacement of the ethnic basis of tribal development by the territorial basis (Roy Burman, 1967). The rationale behind this change was: (i) that the ethnic basis of tribal development would keep the members of the tribal communities separate from the rest of the nation. While giving full protection to the distinctive traits of the tribal communities, attempts should be made to build up an integrated community life of the tribals and their non-tribal neighbours, (ii) that while the tribal people should be provided with special assistance to come at par with the rest of the nation, such an assistance should not be looked upon as a perpetual right for the tribals. It will not only become a liability, at the same time it will hinder the tribals to become self-reliant and self-confident.

On the face of it, as Roy Burman observes (1967), the above perspective of area approach for the development of the tribal population seems to be quite sound. There are also additional advantages of broad-based area approach as it links together the operational aspects of the various schemes and thus maximizes the benefits for the population as a whole. But there are some limitations of area approach as well. An analysis of early records shows that the improvement of economic conditions of a region does not necessarily mean that all the inhabitants of the region concerned share a portion of the benefit more or less equally. On the contrary past experiences prove the reverse. Unless the people are prepared psychologically and technologically to internalize advantage of the changes thus brought about they may, in fact, suffer impoverishment of their conditions. It is, therefore, necessary that before the area development programme for the benefit of the tribes of a region is introduced, suitable social actions are required to be initiated and legislations are enacted to reduce the holds of those segments of the population who would stand in the way of absorption of the maximum benefits of the developments by the tribal communities concerned. Attempts should also be made through strategic encouragement and support, to bring about desirable orientation in the attitudes of the tribal communities concerned, so that they can derive maximum benefits, out of the growth potentials of the region. Further, area approach for improving the social and economic conditions of the tribal communities should visualize phasing of the programme in such a manner that as far as possible the development of the physical resources remains in harmony with the development of human resources.

X

During the years that followed, the programme of implementation of tribal welfare measures in India experienced a great deal of change. The initial anxiety of extending benefits of such programmes to the majority of the tribal populations at the minimum possible time manifested itself through periodic shift of emphasis between ethnic approach and area approach. What is important to note down here is that the programmes of the early plan schemes were as such never very compartmentalized. Special benefits in general were extended to the tribal people identified on ethnic basis from the areas of their major concentrations. Tribal Development Blocks, Special Multipurpose Tribal Development Blocks, Tribal Development Projects, Integrated Tribal Development Projects, all had the same objective and more or less similar approach.

Although areas of tribal concentration are still considered very important for implementation of the tribal welfare programmes, at the same time there grew an impression that the weakest elements of the tribal societies, due to their peripheral location are usually left out of the scope of any such welfare measures. In fact, since they were either found in the non-tribal milieu or at the fringe, they by and large skipped attention. Of late, through introduction of the concept of tribal sub-plan a serious attempt has been made to extend tribal welfare benefits particularly to those tribals who are left at the fringe. Since they could not be fully covered either through ethnic approach or through area approach, the programme executors had to narrow down the focus from area or community to family.

This, nevertheless, speaks of a revision of the strategy for implementation of programmes initiated on the basis of the policies already defined. Obviously, at the policy level, there has been hardly any major shift since.

The down-trodden having no control over resources, would not be in a position to absorb optimum benefits out of such programmes, in spite of the adjustments in strategies, unless they are specifically groomed for the purpose. And even after implementation of the programmes, unless the area as a whole receives the benefits of developmental measures, the isolated tribal families would hardly be in a position to retain such benefits. Therefore, when there cannot be any two opinions about the desirability of extending special programme for the tribals, they may perhaps be in a relatively better position to absorb such benefits, if such programmes take up the locals as a whole for extension of developmental measures.

References

Basham, A. L. (1954) *The Wonder that was India*. London : Sidgwick and Jackson.

Bose, Nirmal Kumar (1941) "The Hindu Method of Tribal Absorption", *Science and Culture*. Vol. VII, No. 4,

Bose, Nirmal Kumar (1957) "Anthropology and Tribal Welfare", *Man in India*. Vol. 37, No. 3, 169 -181.

Bose, Nirmal Kumar (1958) "Anthropology and Tribal Welfare", *Report of the Fourth Conference for Tribes & Tribal (Scheduled) Areas*. New Delhi : Bharatiya Adimjati Sevak Sangh, 17-25.

Bose Nirmal Kumar (1984) "Integration of Tribes in Andhra Pradesh", *Man in India*. Vol. 44, No. 2, 97-104

Drawin, Charles (1859) *On the Origin of Species*. London : John Murray.

Das, T. C. (1957) "Classification of Tribals of India", *Report of the Fourth Conference for Tribes and Tribal (Scheduled)Areas*. New Delhi : Bharatiya Adimjati Sevak Sangh. 61-66.

Das, T. C. (1959) "A Plan for Assimilation of the Tribals of India", *Report of the Fifth Conference for Tribes & Tribal (Scheduled)Areas*. Delhi : Bharatiya Adimjati Sevak Sangh, 127-137.

Das, T. C. (1960) "Assimilation : Integration : Acculturation", *Indian Anthropology in Action*. L. P. Vidyarthi (ed,). Ranchi : Council of Social and Cultural Research, 6-10.

Dube, S. C. (1960) "Approaches to the Tribal Problems in *Indian Anthropology in Action*. L. P. Vidyarthi (ed). Ranchi : Council of Social and Cultural Research, 11-15.

Elwin, Verrier (1939) *The Baigas* London : John Murray.

Elwin, Verrier (1964) *A Philosophy for NEFA*. Shillong : Adviser to the Governor of Assam, (First published in 1957).

Ghurye, G. S. (1943) *The Aborigines So-called and their Future*. Bombay : Popular Prakashan.

Ghurye, G. S. (1959) *The Scheduled Tribes*. Bombay : Popular Book Depot.

Guha, B. S. (1951) "The Indian Aborigines and their Administration", *Journal of the Asiatic Society*. Science. Vol. XVII, No. 1, 19-44

Kanakasabhai, V. (1904) *The Tamils Eighteen Hundred Years Ago*. Madras : Higginbotham & Co.,

Karve, I. (1958) "A Few Observations about the Work among Primitive Tribes", *Report of the Fourth Conference for Tribes and Tribal(Scheduled) Areas*. New Delhi : Bharatiya Adimjati Sevak Sangh, 143-144.

Nehru, Jawaharlal. (1964) "Foreword to the Second Edition", *A Philosophy for NEFA*. by Verrier Elwin. Shillong : Adviser to the Governor of Assam (First Published in 1957).

Study Team on Social Welfare (1959) *Report of the Study Team on Social Welfare* and Welfare of Backward Classes. Vol. I, New Delhi : The Manager of Publications.

Roy Burman, B. K. (1961) "Perspective of Tribal Welfare", *Bulletin of the Tribal Research Institute*. Vol. I, No.1, 12-16.

Roy Burman, B. K. (1967) "Area Approach to the Socio-Economic Development of Tribal Communities", (Mimeographed).

Sachchidananda (1960) "Community Development in Tribal Areas", *Indian Anthropology in Action*. L P Vidyarthi (ed.). Ranchi : Council of Social and Cultural Research, 49-56.

Vidyarthi, L. P. (1959) "Anthropology and Administration in India", *Anthropology and Tribal Welfare in India*. L. P. Vidyarthi (ed.). Ranchi : Council of Social and Cultural Research, 59-71.

Vidyarthi, L. P. (1960) "Anthropology and Tribal Policy : A Case Study among the Mal Paharia : Some Preliminary Thought", *Indian Anthropology in Action*. L. P. Vidyarthi (ed.) Ranchi :

Council of Social and Cultural Research, 25-34.

Wilkinson, T. S. (1962) "Isolation, Assimilation and Integration in their Historical Perspective", *Bulletin of the Tribal Research Institute*. Vol. 2, No. 1, 19-28.

CHAPTER 3

Tribal Development and The Role of Tribals

Samarendra Saraf

India's Independence followed close on the heels of the conclusion of World War II-- a period when the emerging intellectual ethos of scientific humanism had nearly started making its impact felt. Several new nation states were fast emerging, opting for the democratic system of government *of* the people, *by* the people and *for* the people; and the new nation states got founded on the firm bedrock of the ideology wedded to the welfare of its people. As sheer coincidence would have it, the post-War phase got marked with the emergence of several new and independent nations on the globe, and the international consensus relating to the ideals of a welfare state reverberated in the political ethos of the nations that emerged anew.

The scourge of the two World Wars over a short span of two-and-a-half decades had made the world realize that the only way to materialize a global community of nations was to bury full fathom five all political rivalries and shed away all colonial ambitions. Peace, progress and prosperity on the globe could be ensured only when the milieu of international understanding and cooperation came to prevail.

From the matrix of such consensus was born the United Nations and with the birth of the United Nations, a new era of mutual help and trust got ushered in with the signing of the historic document by many a nation of the world, that is, the 'Charter' of the United Nations. The signatories to the document resolved:

> "(not only) to save succeeding generations from the scourge of the war which twice in our lifetime has brought untold sorrow to mankind (but also) *to reaffirm faith in fundamental human rights, in the dignity and worth of the human person, in the equal rights of men and women and of nations large and small* (in order) *to promote social progress and better standards of life in larger freedom* (by employing) international machinery for the promotion of the economic and social advancement of all peoples" (emphasis supplied).

The slogans of the French Revolution --Equality, Liberty and Fraternity--had started echoing with all zeal and fervour only because nations of the world had witnessed utter devastation and the scientists had started warning men and nations about the dire consequences of nuclear warfare. Moreover, the political situation around the globe had necessitated it too:

> "Fast-disappearing colonies and fast-appearing independent nation states rapidly changed the political map of the world... Trade and commerce brought about great economic interdependence. Networks of modern means of transport and communication shortened distances and promoted closer contacts and interaction between different nations, thereby leading them not only towards a world community but also a *global village*, as Marshal McLuhan would have it, 'where contending nations can grind ponderously for peace and wars, and where they could also ' muster the moral and material forces of mankind' for human betterment. Such enlightened hope was charged with determination and optimism to help the people of the undeveloped world get more and better food to eat, better houses to live in, besides freeing them from the

> shackles of epidemics, ignorance and poverty; and the prospects to start hoping for a better future through the instrumentality of national and international agencies became ever brighter'' (Saraf,1983:2).

The world, thus, got a foot and heading determinedly towards a phase of sanity after the spell of insanity of the world wars, charged with all optimism and enthusiasm with a view to materializing a 'Brave New World' or, what the UN's Assistant Secretary General Dr. Robert Muller has called, 'The New Genesis'. As the master architect of the entire cosmos, God is believed to have inaugurated the mythical genesis : as the master of science and technology, man is preparing himself for ushering in a new, historical genesis, as it were.

In his recent publication Dr. Muller has encapsulated his a-doctrinaire views in a poetic vein so characteristic of "The UN's Prophet of Hope'' (that is how the free-lance journalist from Massachusetts, Pam Robbins, goes to characterize Dr. Muller), while dedicating his work as follows:

> "...to the innumerable good people of this planet who want to live in peace, friendship, freedom and justice, and to enjoy the miracle of life under the generous rays of our sun and the good guidance of the God of the universe....
>
> "[to those who are committed] to start a new history and prepare the advent of a new age, a new world, a new philosophy and new human relationships...
>
> "[to the people who] coalesce with all strength, mind, heart and soul around a New Genesis, a true global, God-abiding political, moral and spiritual renaissance to make this planet at long last what it was always meant to be: the planet God'' (Muller,1982:vii).

The wasting woes of war and the pressing problems of peace upon the conclusion of the World War II inaugurated the era of massive and concerted efforts for development in the international context; many young democracies, committed to the ideals of welfare state and operating in the world community of nations, also felt the urgent need to gear into action their programmes of national development:

> "Growing interest in scientific humanism, the emergence of and subscription to the ideals of welfare state against the eighteenth century political philosophy of *laissez faire*, the new political ideologies promising to meet the challenge of the changing times, the desire for fuller participation in the world community through the technological advancement and the recognition of the dignity of human person have all had their respective share in crystallizing the philosophy of planned change which has come to find more coherent and articulate expression as a philosophy of life and society in the present century when many undeveloped and underdeveloped countries of the world have chosen to commit themselves to nation-building by initiating well laid-out programmes of change under the guidance of qualified personnel. Development-mindedness has thus become almost an obsession with virtually every nation... the newly emerging free nations showing greater concern, reposing greater confidence, and relegating greater responsibility to such plans in their efforts at nation-building" (Saraf,1971:50).

Soon after India won independence, the national leadership drafted the charter of her social, cultural, economic and political destiny in the form of the *Constitution of India*, and the secular nation comprising several castes and creeds, colours and communities, languages and sub-cultures came to have the most sacrosanct scripture of its political unity and identity. The 'Preamble' spells out the objectives of the *sovereign democratic republic*, thus:

> "We, the people of India, having solemnly resolved to constitute India into a SOVEREIGN DEMOCRATIC REPUBLIC and to secure to all its citizens:
>
> JUSTICE, social, economic and political;
>
> LIBERTY of thought, expression, belief, faith and worship; EQUALITY of status and of opportunity; and to promote among them all.

> FRATERNITY assuring the dignity of the individual and the unity of the Nation;
>
> in our Constituent Assembly this twenty-sixth day of November, 1949, do hereby adopt, enact and give to ourselves this Constitution''.

In consonance with the spirit of the 'Preamble', the *Constitution* was committed to the ideals and tasks of a welfare state, making several provisions to safeguard and promote the interests of the weaker sections of the people, especially the Scheduled Castes and Scheduled Tribes that form a sizeable section of the country's population. Such provisions were made with a view to protecting the weaker sections from 'social injustice and all forms of exploitation''. For several low castes and tribes had long suffered from social inequalities and/or exploitation.

Right from the Vedic times down to the present day, several tribes have lived throughout the vast expanse of the sub continent and passed through different phases and styles of interaction with the non-tribal world around, witnessing all sorts of vicissitudes that ranged from sympathy to antipathy:

> ''Our present-day tribal people whose remote ancestors of the Vedic or even pre-Vedic antiquity had peopled the Indian sub-continent, have a long historicity as the autochthons. Their informal history, as only partially reconstructed on the basis of the Hindu scriptures, sheds scanty but definitive light on the fact that the Aryans and the autochthonous people had bled and bred together in the past. With the passage of time, their hostilities either partly sublimated into mutual understanding and peaceful coexistence or they resulted in voluntary or involuntary withdrawal of the uncompromising ones into the inhospitable and sleepy quarters amid hills and forests.
>
> ''Through all this vast expanse of time since the Vedic era, our ancient classical literature has shown its general acquaintance with such autochthonous groups as the Nisada, the Kirata and the Sabara, to name a few.

> The ancient literature has presented before us rather ambivalent images of our ancient tribal folk. Such images, however, suffer in their depiction either from too much of glorification or too liberal humanism, on the one hand, or from too much of sophistication of cultural bias of the civilized high-brow, on the other'' (Saraf,1969:118).

Our present-day tribal canvas presents a rich assortment of colours and contours. These tribal groups represent the rich cultural heritage of the land, contributing to its ethnic and socio-cultural diversity:

> ''Spread almost throughout the country, the tribal world represents a wide variety of linguistic and ethnic elements. For, here we encounter their rich diversity. From primitive hunters and food-gatherers to settled agriculturists, from the unacculturated, tribals down to their educated, westernized counterparts, and from the animistic/animatistic folk down to the church/temple-going devotees--all are to be met here'' (ibid:119).

While making specific provisions for the weaker sections, the *Constitution* has envisaged our contemporary tribal folk who have lived for centuries in the relatively calm, quiet and in-accessible hinterland, preserving their native nerve, maintaining their tribal identity and fostering their distinctive socio-cultural traditions despite braving all sorts of odds. Until recently, their fortunes had been all-too-limited but their problems became all-too-numerous. The pace of their acculturisation, especially during the British rule, had resulted in the transformation of the tribal world, although the pace of change has varied in the different tribal zones of the country. There is no gainsaying the fact that the social, political, economic and religious factors and forces of the non-tribal world had long started invading the calm and quiet tribal precincts, releasing definite stirs of change and giving rise to several problems of varying magnitude:

> ''Ever since the socio-religio-politico-economic processes of the non-tribal society invaded the tribal world, thereby inaugurating a kind of cultural transfor-

> mation hitherto unknown in the history of tribal India, the boundaries that marked the tribal and the non-tribal worlds, have been dissolving and a new milieu has been emerging--a milieu of exploitation of the indigenous folk by the well-to-do Hindu caste people and the feudal institutions, the massive proselytization, the resultant political awakening and the active participation of the people in the political processes... the episodes of mistrust and misunderstanding, of hostilities and tensions, of our failures and their frustrations, of our poor performance and their high expectations... of our diplomatic oscillations and their political pressures, especially in certain sensitive areas'' (Ibid).

The British rule bequeathed more liabilities than assets, more problems than solutions, in regard to the tribal areas and their people. It followed the policy of isolation or 'Leave Them Alone', for obvious reasons:

> ''The British Government inclined, on the whole, to leave the tribesmen alone, partly because the task of administration, especially in the wild border areas, was difficult and unrewarding, partly from a desire to quarantine the tribes from possible political infection, and partly because a number of officers sincerely held the view that the people were better and happier as they were'' (Elwin 1960:45).

Adoption of the isolationist approach resulted in the widening of the gulf between the tribal and the non-tribal worlds and in the preservation of distinctive identity of the tribals, thereby minimizing their interaction and inhibiting their integration into the mainstream of the national life: their distinctive identity and their relative isolation only fostered separatism. While the British administration was endorsing the isolationist approach, it gave the Christian missionaries an unbriddled liberty to go ahead with their proselytization campaign. The missionaries adopted various means to bring the tribals to bear the burden of the Cross without caring for the fact whether or not the burden would be carried without breaking the back of the bearer! For, mere conversion of faith was no solution of the various urgent and pressing problems of the acculturated tribals. In George Bernard Shaw's words, "The conversion of a savage to Christianity was nothing but the conversion of Christianity to savagery"!

The policy of assimilation worked as a double-edged weapon: it effected the loss of identity while it also fostered emotional and cultural alienation. Strongly reacting to the assimilationist approach, Jairamdas Daulatram, the then Governor of Assam, had epitomized his reactions in a figurative and rhetorical vein:

> "Each section of our large population contributes to the making of the nation in the same manner as each flower helps to make a garden. Every flower has the right to grow according to its own laws of growth; has the right to enrich and develop its own colour and form and to spread its own fragrance to make up the cumulative beauty and splendour of the garden. I would not like to change my roses into lilies nor my lilies into roses. Nor do I want to sacrifice my lovely orchids and rhododendrons of the hills" (Ibid:57).

That neither isolation nor assimilation can solve the tribal problems, was long ago stressed by Prime Minister Jawaharlal Nehru in his 'Forewrod' to Verrier Elwin's book, *A Philosophy for NEFA*:

> "I came across the tribal people first, rather distantly, in various parts of India other than the North-East Frontier....
>
> "Later, I came in touch with the tribal people of the North-East Frontier of India... My liking for them grew and with it came respect. I had no sensation of superiority over them. My ideas were not clear at all, but I felt that we should avoid two extreme courses: one was to treat them as anthropological specimens for study and the other was to allow them to be engulfed by the masses of Indian humanity...
>
> Above all, I hope there will be no attempt made to impose other ways of life on them in a hurry. *Let the*

changes come gradually and be worked out by the tribals themselves'' (Ibid: 'Foreword to the First Edition'--emphasis supplied).

''*We cannot allow matters to drift in the tribal areas or just not take interest in them. In the world of today that is not possible or desirable.* At the same time we should avoid over-administering these areas and, in particular, sending too many outsiders into tribal territory.

It is between these two extrême positions that we have to function. Development in various ways there has to be, such as communications, medical facilities, education and better agriculture'' (Ibid : 'Foreword to the Second Edition'-- emphasis supplied).

As a messiah of peace and a prophet of progress, the Prime Minister outlined the broad framework of the fivefold fundamental principle, an abridgement of which is as follows:

- ''People should develop along the lines of their own genius and we should avoid imposing anything on them. We should try to encourage in every way their own traditional arts and culture.

- Tribal rights in land and forests should be respected.

- *We should try to train and build up a team of their own people to do the work of administration and development. Some technical personnel from outside will, no doubt, be needed, especially in the beginning...*

- *We should not over-administer these areas or overwhelm them with a multiplicity of schemes. We should rather work through, and not in rivalry to, their own social and cultural institutions.*

> *We should judge results, not by statistics or the amount of money spent, but by the quality of human character that is evolved*'' (Ibid--emphasis supplied).

It is interesting to note that, motivated by a genuine interest in and humanitarian concern towards the development of the tribal world, the late Prime Minister had articulated his views as a culture relativist and a scientific humanist. In his advocacy of steering the middle course, neither toeing the line with the isolationists nor with the assimilationists, he had struck the note of prudence of a moderatist--something that had led Gautama the Buddha to opt for the middle course (*madhyama pratipada*) in the midst of the extremist positions of indulgence and abstinence. While spelling out the nature and content of his fivefold fundamental principles, Prime Minister Nehru had specifically emphasized the urgency of training of the tribals and of building up a core of such trained personnel from amongst the tribals with a view to relegating to them the task of tribal administration and development----that is the import of the third principle above.

The Prime Minister was not only a leader and a diplomat, a humanist and a scientist, a renowned author and a scholar, a radical and a visionary but he was also a social and cultural historian of definite stature and renown. His *Discovery of India* stands a testimony to it. The social/cultural anthropologist in him had visualized that the task of development in a welfare state needs must begin at the grass-roots level in order to help the young democracy emerge in due course of time as a viable force and an enviable institution--the object of social cynosure for the young democracies of the world. To him, merely going to the polls and exercising adult franchise once or twice (in the event of a mid-term poll) every five years was not the *summum bonum* of political awareness or political participation. His conception of the participant political culture can be encapsulated as follows: political awareness envisages the cognizance of social, economic, political and the like issues in their regional, national and/or international contexts: likewise, political participation implies an active role-playing in the decision-making processes that relate to the people's own issues, oftentimes urgent and pressing. That is why he had added the following saving clause to the third fundamental principle: ''Some technical personnel from outside will, no doubt,be needed, especially in the beginning''. In other words, he had visualized, and very rightly indeed, an initial phase of spoon-feeding by the foster-mother till such time when the baby comes to feed itself, to meet its needs as and when they are left by it. From an initial phase of government-reliance to a subsequent phase or self-reliance--that was the objective of development, whether tribal or non-tribal, as an on-going process, as Prime Minister Nehru had envisioned it.

There is no denying the fact that the late Prime Minister had an abiding interest in social and cultural history, that he had a measure of sympathy for the tribals, and that he had an artist's love for the rich diversity of the tribal population and a social philosopher's zeal and enthusiasm for the preservation of the bases of identity and unity. But he had also sounded the emphatic note of an integrationist while giving tongue to his critique of assimilationism:

> "There is no point in trying to make a second rate copy of ourselves...
>
> "What we ought to do is to develop a sense of oneness with these people, a sense of unity and understanding ...the greatest problem in India today is not so much political as psychological integration and consolidation"(Saraf,1976:202)"

Prime Minister Nehru's philosophy of tribal development has been best epitomized in the following passage:

> *"The Government of India is determined to help the tribal people to grow according to their own genius and tradition*; it is not the intention to impose anything on them...
>
> *"Development must be according to their own genius and not something that they cannot absorb or imbibe and which merely uproots them. I would much rather go slow in our plans for development than risk the danger of this uprooting... let this development and change be natural and be in the nature of self-development with all the help one can give in the process"* (Elwin, 1960:56 - emphasis supplied).

The very idea of formation of a nucleus of trained and qualified bureaucrats and technocrats from amongst the tribals goes cheek by jowl with the spirit of the *Constitution*, as it is also in consonance with the philosophy of the democratic principle of people's participation in shaping the political destiny of the nation. It has found its epigrammatic expression in Prime Minister Nehru's following axiom: *"Let the changes come gradually and be worked out by the tribals themselves"* ('Foreword to the First Edition'- emphasis supplied).

History tells us that, under the inspiration of John Collier, the Commissioner of the Bureau of Indian Affairs, a similar approach was advocated and implemented in regard to the Indian Reservations in the United States. The central thrust of their Indianist Policy, as contemplated by the *Indian Reorganization Act of 1934* (also known as the *Wheeler-Howard Act*), made room for several challenging and ambitious provisions, keeping in view the long-term planning to safeguard and promote the Indian interests:

> "Tribal constitutions were drafted. Adult franchise was introduced and the Indians voted very enthusiastically in order to elect their office-bearers for the reservations. For, they were sought to be introduced to the participant political culture through democratic institutions. Moreover, *a special Indian Civil Service was organized with a view to raising from amongst the Indians a core of administrative personnel by opening the doors to qualify the Indians 'to take a dignified and responsible part in the guidance of their own people*" (Saraf,1983:16-emphasis supplied).

John Collier had outlined the spirit of the Indianist Policy in the following words:

> "The present policy [as enunicated in the *Indian Reorganization Act*] is: that Indian property must not pass to Whites, that Indian organization must be encouraged and assisted that Indian family life must be respected and reinforced, that Indian culture must be appreciated, used, and brought into the stream of American culture as a whole, and that the Indian as a race must not die, but must grow and live" (Goldenweiser,1946:438-39.

When the problem of tribal development and the role of the tribals is examined and evaluated, it becomes all-too-clear that a very rational and pragmatic blueprint was offered by Prime Minister Nehru: but the country has not been able to translate his fivefold fundamental principles into concrete action, giving them "a local habitation and a name", as it were. Have we been able to build up the nucleus of the tribal elite for an effective role-playing in the participant political culture of the country? Have we been able to bring about national and emotional integration with them? While assessing the progress of tribal development, do we not judge results by "statistics [and]the amount of money spent" rather than judging it "by the quality of human character that is evolved" through such developmental programmes? For, there is no gainsaying the fact that, despite all well-intentioned and well worded invocations and exhortation appeals of the national leaders ever since the mid-fifties and despite the mass-mediated bombardment of such appeals, day in and day out, through the net-works, of all sophisticated audio-visual gadgets, very little (perhaps, negligible) response of understanding participation of the tribals has been recorded, either in the direction of national and emotional under-standing or political awareness and participation in terms of larger national interests; likewise, no size able "team of their own people" has been trained and built up "to do the work of administration and development."

Had the country followed the blueprint that was offered by Prime Minister Nehru, it may be argued, the pace of change would have been faster, the direction of change rational, the content of change healthy and the dividends of the developmental plans much more spectacular in terms of "the quality of human character". It is, therefore, high time to reoerient the tribal development plan and policy where -withal a team of trained bureaucrats and technocrats gets nurtured from amongst the tribals themselves, the plans get reached to the tribals in their own idiom through such personnel, and the emphasis and priorities get identified and implemented by the trained tribal man power in consultation with the tribal people, on the one hand, and the central and state governments, on the other.

References

Elwin, Verrier. (1960) — *A Philosophy for NEFA,* Shillong : Advisor to the Governor of Assam.

Goldenweiser, A. (1946) — *Anthropology : An Introduction to Primitive* Culture, F.S. Crofts & Co., New York.

Muller, Robert. (1984) — *New Genesis : Shaping a Global Spirituality.* Doubleday & Co., New York.

Saraf, Samarendra. (1969) — Tribal Unrest : An Urgent Research Problem, *Vanyajati* Vol. XVIII.

---------------------- (1971) — Socio-Cultrual Barriers in Adult Education Programme in Rural India, *Society and Culture* Vol. II, No. 1.

--------------------- (1976) — Verrier Elwin : A Profile, *Vivekananda Kendra Patrika* Vol.V. No.1

--------------------- (1982) — Research Idiom for Contemporary Tribal Context, *Tribal Development in India : Problems and Prospects* (Ed) Buddhadib Chaudhury, Inter-India Publications, Delhi.

--------------------- (1983) — Economic Development and the Mass Media of Development (originally presented in 1968 at the Seminar on Economic Development, held at the University of Saugar, Saugar). *Interaction* Vol. I, No.1. (revised version published).

--------------------- (1983a) — The Indianist policy, *Studies in Applied Anthropology.* (in Press).

CHAPTER 4

Tribal Development : An Alternative Strategy*

R. S. Mann

It is slightly short of three decades that the issue of tribal development came into focus. When the idea of socio-economic transformation of village India was taking shape, with the introduction of Community Development Programme, the tribal pockets, and the inhabitants thereof, too started coming to light. This being a still weaker section than the non-tribal population of the country, it became added responsibility of the union government to develop them, socially and economically, so that they could come at par with the broader streams of national social and economic framework. Outcome of such ideology and commitment was the Tribal Development Programme. In spite of various experiments, made use of for the development of tribals, the picture does not seem to be satisfactory one. Problems do persist even when protective legislations and the practical programmes of planned change have come into effect. Of worry, at the moment, is the question

---

* Reproduced by the permission of the authority of 'Man and Life' and Institute of Social Research and Applied Anthropology, Calcutta from 'Man and Life', 9(1 + 2) : 53-63, 1983.

whether we can gain substantially through existing network of tribal development, or shall we go in for some alternative, keeping in view related current trends. It is in this context that a modest attempt has been made to divise additional elements as part of a new strategy. As a new approach, the strategy can initially be tried in some selected tribal pockets. And when the results prove comparatively more effective, its application may be extended to the remaining tribal habitations.

Even before the onset of deep concern for tribal development, that emerged in the fifties of this century, the British administrators and rulers did bother for this section of humanity. But it had a different background and perspective. Being scared of administrative difficulties and problems in far flung tribal belts, and considering that Indian Independence movement could spread infection among tribes too, the people in power announced that the tribals were happy under the then existing conditions. With this, they added that the tribals should not be disturbed by the outside administration, policies, programmes and elements. Such a thinking led to the rise of 'excluded' and 'partially excluded' tribal areas, treating them as 'reserves' against alien intervention. Thus originated the policy of isolation in respect of tribal population. Almost parallel to this emerged those who expressed concern about the problems and miseries inherent in tribal population. Among this lot were the missionaries, both Christians and Hindus, whose ideology asked for radical reforms and changes in tribal society. So much so that they expressed their feelings and ideas of making the tribals as second rate copies of Christians and Hindus. This was made abundantly clear when they tried to assimilate tribals into the broader tenets of Christianity and Hinduism. The trend promoted the policy of 'assimilation'. The later did not remain in tune with the then British government policy of isolation. It was almost immediately after India got freedom that the policy and approaches to the tribals were reviewed, jointly by the government representatives, non-officials, including social workers, social scientists, politicians etc. With unanimity and consensus the shift from the earlier policies was desired. It was agreed upon that the tribals were to be socially and economically develop and that they were to be protected from all forms of injustice and exploitation. This necessitated the adoption of policy of 'integration' of the tribals.

To stand by the above commitment, the government, to startwith, established 43 Special Multipurpose Tribal Blocks, in concentrated tribal belts. A mojor share of these went to Madhya Pradesh, Bihar and Orissa who contain larger tribal population. Others with less concentration of tribals, got meagre share. Verrier Elwin Committee, which examined the working and effect of Special Multipurpose Tribal Blocks, gave further suggestion for improvement, as also suggested for the expansion of programme in a slightly different form. The latter was also supplemented by the suggestions of Dhebar Commission on Sheduled Castes and Scheduled Tribes. With mild change in pattern, espeically in terms of percentage of tribal population and area coverage, a massive programme of tribal development came in. And in every successive Five Year Plans, more and more of Tribal Development Blocks were opened. The trend resulted into increased coverage of tribal poplulation. Correspondingly, the funds for tribal development also increased. From mid fifties to mid seventies of this century, the Tribal Development Blocks contiued to serve the cause of tribal development. Sometime in late seventies the idea of Integrated Tribal Development grew. The States, having more tribal population, went for making of Tribal Sub-Plans. In other words the government laid more stress on, and expressed increased concern for the welfare and betterment of tribal population. Under the Tribal Sub-Plans, provision could be made for sufficient funds for tribal development. It also guaranteed for additional coverage, especially of scanty and outlying tribal pockets. In other words there has been constant expansion of programmes for tribal development. However, how much we have practically achieved, in terms of our targets, is a debatable question. The position does not seem to be encouraging. Statistics might, at times speak high but the quality of character which was to be built is yet to grow satisfactorily. The latter also holds true in the context of healthy leadership which was to be generated among the tribals.

A review of the patterns of tribal development, adopted by the non-official and official agencies, from the second quarter of the current century to the late seventies, is convincing of the fact that some weaknesses, in one form or the other, were indentified at various levels. As such, time and again, adoption of new patterns was thought necessary. And most of the time necessity of change was agreed upon by programme planners, implementors and even social scientists. Faults in the ideology of various agencies were also pointed out many a times. Some procedures, adopted by the voluntary organisations, totally in isolation of government procedures, were not appreciated. This was at times, claimed true vice versa. But somehow no serious remedy could, in most of the situations, be suggested to evolve a common plan where thing would have been best delivered to the tribals. Lately, especially after the formation of sub-plans for tribal development, a huge amount of money has been sanctioned for improving the socio-economic condition of the tribals. In the name of integrated development, a massive expansion, through tribal corporations and other offices, in terms of machinery and schemes has taken place. But will it be sufficient for the cause of tribal development? Some reservations, in this respect, can always be considered. The existing model needs strengthening, and the same is possible through the incorporation of added dimensions suggested below.

1. The position of social workers and voluntary organizations, in the context of tribal development and its existing pattern, is to be understood and used in the right spirit. Their existing working pattern is to be assessed. It may not be proper and practical to assign, exclusively, the massive task of tribal development to the social workers and voluntary agencies, even if some of them are doing a good job. This has its own implications which need not be dealt with here. But there is certainly no harm if the "purposeful technology",used by some of them, is adopted. The formal procedures of official agencies may cater less to tribal requirements if kept in isolation of the know-how of purposeful technology possessed by some of the valuntary agencies. Another form of liaison (between voluntary and government agencies) which sounds indispensable in the interest of tribal development is the fixation of certain amount of added responsibility on the social workers and voluntary organizations. They should be authorized and encouraged to get into the ongoing tribal development efforts made by the official machinery. Further, it needs to be made clear that their findings would carry sufficient weight in government quarters. Even the official functionaries are to be made conversant with such a stand, with the expectation that they would cooperate with non-officials attached with voluntary organisations. Necessary steps for improvement are, then, to be jointly suggested. The best way may be to leave some room for voluntary organisations right at the level of planning. In order that the designing of procedures and patterns becomes more effective, it may partly be done on official line and partly on the lines in practice with the efficient voluntary organisations. Some of the voluntary organisations are undoubtedly rendering a good service to the tribal people. It would be advantageous if their methodology is taken help of. For this purpose,

certain constraints, posed by the official rules and regulations, may have to be relaxed. An area-wise division of voluntary organisations, working in tribal areas, is to be done. Then the liaison and coordination of each, with the specific official agency for tribal development in the area, are to be brought about.

2. Parallel to the healthy intrusion of voluntary organisations is another essential requirement which should be not with in the interest of successful implementation of tribal development programmes. The agents of change and the personnel associated with equally strong tribal front are also needed to go hand in hand with the above two agencies. The intervention at tribal level is even otherwise of significance. Their absence at planning and implementation levels keeps one devoid of certain very valid view-points, which the tribals alone understand better. The tribals, being insiders, better know what is the problem, and in what style can solutions be more practical and feasible. Thus, the insiders opinion has its own value in tribal development. And its absence is certainly undesirable. Now the question is as to which tribals are to be more actively involved along with the efforts of official change agents and the workers of voluntary organisations? Those representing Panchayati Raj bodies have not lived upto expectations. In a large number of cases their involvement has been sufficiently inactive. It has not adequately helped gear up tribal development programmes. Moreover, it has also been somewhat faulty to give excessive recognition only to the formally elected tribals who represented Panchayati Raj institutions at various levels. Their position is to be certainly respected but they should not be treated as the sole agents of tribal destiny. Traditional leadership which, by and large, continues to strongly survive, is also to be taken help of in the matter. Though the persons, representing traditional leadership have been catering more to the traditional and customary requirements, their induction in non-traditional programmes would be of no less value. The respect and authority they command over the tribals is, in most of the cases, far more than what the formally elected representatives do. The former more competent to feel the pulse of their own people. Therefore, when the question of involving insiders is taken up, those representing traditional leadership hierarchy are not to be neglected. They may play a very vital role in the progress, of their own people. For this purpose, they are to be properly handled and oriented. Such an orientation is bound to give them chance to favourably consider what is beyond pro-tradition. An effective and proportionate

representation, along with reorientation, of traditional leadership hierarchy will have its own impact. This does not, however, mean that non-traditional and formally elected leaders are to be dropped altogether. Useful ones, out of them, will share the responsibility, under a healthy understanding with traditional leaders. For a macrocoverage of such an involvement of insiders, one has to take stock of leadership at area, village segment, and tribe levels. A close co-ordination between them and the voluntary agencies is another prerequisite for efficient implementation of socio-economic programmes carried by the official agents of change.

3. Once the official agencies,voluntary agencies and the insiders infrastructure come closer for a common cause of tribal development, elements of a new front need be searched for. Such a front involves "institutional network" as a base, necessary for effective overall development of the tribals. To conceive of such institutional network all the agencies will pool their ideas and thinking. The model, emerged with common consensus, is then to be given a practical shape. While evolving the model of institutional network, an adequate representation of all the agencies is essential. It is not that the official views alone would prevail. The more scientific and broad-based the model is, the more useful will it prove in bettering the living standard of the tribal community. What will constitute such an institutional network would again be partly determined by the cultural and environmental systems of the tribal concerned. An element of institutional network, designed for tribe X may not be suitable for tribe Y. On the other hand, quite a few of the elements may even be of uniform nature, though meant for different tribes. What additional institution is to be created where will thus be decided after taking note of various considerations. However, a scientific layout of institutions, meant to introduce change, is an essential step. One cannot deny that it is not already being done, though haphazardly in most of the situations. It needs to be made more systematic and scientific on the lines suggested-above. What is to be further taken care of is the abrupt and excessive establishment of institutions. In other words, an evolutionary order is to be created, and what kind of institution is to be established when would go as per the order. Such an order, too, is to be jointly decided by various agencies. The creation of any infrastructure, as part of institutional network, requires material resources, which rest chiefly with the government. Therefore the investment, of whatever order, is to basically come from the government and the latter should

be held solely responsible for investment in the creation of institutions. But what is to be created when, and whether the institutions get created or not are to be persuaded by insider's leadership as well as by the voluntary organisations concerned. When one part of the institutional network gets through, the next one is to be established without undue delay. With such a systematic growth at practical level, of institutional network the community participation in connected ventures should also grow proportionately. For the latter purpose, the three agencies will have to be equally active again. It is expected that the establishment of complete institutional netwrok will represent massive participation of tribals in various programmes of directed social and economic change. Any imbalance in the creation of institutions is bound to reflect adversely on people's participation.

This has already been observed at number of places. In this respect, an added responsibility of all the agencies is to see that the institutions, born of their common thinking and ideals, do function efficiently. Then the institutions should be so designated and managed that they can cater to most of the requirements of tribals, chiefly in kind. Provision of loans and other assistance, in cash, needs to be thoroughly discouraged. Instead, the institutional network should be so strengthened that it can provide all kinds of articles, implements, commodities, facilities, etc. with their own arrangement. And in case the disbursing of cash is unavoidable, the money should straight away be deposited in bank, which should have a branch in tribal area itself, in the individual's name. The person concerned, may only be given the pass-book. He should be allowed to draw the money only when the three agencies are convinced that he is ready for the deal, for which the loan was sanctioned, or when he has completed the first phase of work and needs another instalment for the next.

4. For a large scale involvement in the institutional network, and hence in the process and programmes of tribal development, special steps are needed. From a review of what has already happened in this respect, one gathers an impression that a selected few could only be contacted. The bulk remained dispossessed of the benefits of tribal development. They could hardly be approached and their ignorance persisted. Those contacted and/or involved in various programmes were, in general, either the formally elected leaders or some others who can be treated as elites within the limits of tirbal living. Quite a few of them

took advantage of their position and contact in exploiting their own tribal brethren who continued to sink in ignorance and poverty. They hardly objected to such a treatment, and rather submitted to the lately emerged elites. The fact that many people failed to participate in the programmes of socio-economic development is not due to their reluctance alone. Rather, they could not be informed of the efforts of development. This happened because of lack of communication and contact with them. The functionaries or agents of change did not come in touch with such tribals. Their contact remained limited to a few whom they frequently met and helped. The rapport with others could not be established at all. This drawback may be taken care of when voluntary organisations and traditional leadership get their due place. Much difference can, however, be made only when "man-to-man" approach is planned. Though there are numerous hazards in tribal areas to take up man-to-man approach, it is unavoidable if masses are to be mobilised for their involvement in the processes and programmes of tribal development. The tribals of the last row need to be contacted more as they are the ones who continue to be out of touch with new, ideas, proposals and schemes. At the same time they form the most ignorant lot. Contact at individual level has its own advantages,and this may be made more feasible after holding group discussions at section or village level. If the exercise of man-to-man contact is not done, or half done, the results of efforts for tribal development will not be encouraging. Even the fruits of development will not reach the bulk of population. Situations of comparartively more physical isolation, like tribal regions, are bound to give further fillip to such unhealthy trends. To have man-to-man contact, the voluntary agencies and the selected insiders can be of much use. At the same time the official agencies, too, need to be reactivated and strenghened for the purpose.

5. After taking note of all the above four elements, as new dimensions of the strategy of tribal development, three issues are clear. First, the machinery on which lies the major responsibility of diffusion of innovations in tribal communities. This is composed of official and non-official agencies, including the tribals themselves. Second, the assumed claim of its efficiency to gear up directed progress in tribal villages. Third, the procedure suggested for each agency in terms of its roles in the total complex of tribal development. Further other important factors are the actual existence and co-ordination of various agencies, their practical pattern of playing roles meant for them, the utility of set

procedures, and the impact of all of them on tribal life and culture. Therefore, an additional requirement is of a research cell, not necessarily of the government alone, which can regularly evaluate the agency structure, their co-ordination, procedures adopted and the nature of impact all of these make on the way of life of tribal people. The research findings would tell the way programmes are moving, and will also reveal why they went in a particular direction. In other words, all kinds of positive and negative involvements would be analysed and results presented for improvement and further course of action. The operational researches are really meaningful in on-going programmes, as one of the tribal development. While organising such a research cell, due care is to be taken of its independent identity. Otherwise, any bias from any corner is bound to prove misleading.

To start with, some elements of the above startegy might look difficult to handle. They may not meet some of the official procedural demands. And this can make the officials indifferent as far as their initial reaction is concerned. Many of them will not like to share their things with the non-officials working in the voluntary organisations. At the same time they would outrightly condemn the idea of their being evaluated by the non-officials as well as the tribals. Even the functionaries at lower level of hierarchical formation are likely to be upset when they find additional men and machniery surrounding their field of operation. Psychologically this holds true for majority of human beings. From the side of functionaries the resistance can assume more momentum, especially when they have already operated in the atmosphere of freedom. So far, the only fear prevailing upon them emanates from the official hierarchy. At higher echelons too, the induction, with defined and ascribed privileges, of non-officials and tribals is unlikely to be welcomed. Many shall take it imposing and unwanted while feeling that their say is interrupted. Under the hazy clouds marking the existing tribal development formation, the change-over to new strategy does not seem to be easy, but if the development of the tribals is to be shown priority, and is to be taken up in right ernest, and with zeal and dedication the initial hurdles are to be side-tracked making convenient arrangement here and there. With latter, the switch over need not come heavy on anyone, or at any phase. Proper and smooth adaptation with new procedures and conditions will save functionaries from being discouraged and disheartened. As made clear with five major points of strategy, there is more urgency of inter-play and co-ordination of concerned agencies, rather than any kind of intervention. Since the official machinery is heavy, both in terms of manpower and resources their co-operation and positive attitude to various requirements will make others, mentioned in the strategy, at ease. Tension free and co-operative attitude will largely provide impetus to the commonly intended aim of tribal development.

Another major advantage of this strategy is that it would give, to all concerned, almost equal opportunity to prove their worth and importance. Neither the members of target population that is the tribals themselves, nor the agents of change, both official would have complaint that they have not been consulted or involved. Under the ongoing system if anything goes wrong, or if the objective are not achieved, there is lot of mud slinging on one another. Official functionaries usually express that the tribals are not cooperative, and that they put up resistance at various levels. But the tribals feel that the functionaries are not discharging their role honestly and as per the requirements. Likewise, some members of voluntary agencies charge the offcial functionaries for neglect of their duties, and for their attitude of indifference to the tribals. Some functionaries highlight the undesirable activities of certain non officials, and the agencies to which they belong to. Such a mutual criticism, in isolation, does not allow one to fix responsibility anywhere. And so long as such a compartmentalization is maintained, the complexity and uncertainty are likely to prevail, barring the existence of congenial atmosphere needed for tribal development. To create a congenial atmosphere, to curb the tendency of escaping responsibility, to fix areas of responsibility and to provide fillip to tribal development the alternative strategy, mentioned herein, needs to be tried at. Let us not leave any section disgruntled and grumbling for the simple reason that they are not consulted, respected, or not given their due. However, at the forefront should remain the common aim of soico-economic advancement of the tribals. All need to seriously subscribe to it, without giving further way to mistakes already commited.

Note: The views expressed in this paper are of the author and not of Anthropological Survey of India.

References

Bhowmick, P. K. (1980) *Some Aspects of Indian Anthropology,* Subarnarekha, Calcutta.

Foster, G. M. (1962) *Traditional Societies and Technological change,* Allied Publishers Private Limited, Bombay.

Sharma, B.D. (1978) *Tribal Development : The Concept and the Frame,* Pradip Prakashan, New Delhi.

Vidyarthi, L. P. & Sahay, B. N. (1980) *Applied Anthropology and Development in India,* National; New Delhi.

Occasional Papers on Tribal Development : Government of India, Ministry of Home Affairs, New Delhi.

CHAPTER 5

Some Leading Issues in Tribal Development*

Amal Kumar Das

India holds a unique position in the tribal map of the world. Except perhaps Africa nowhere such a vast majority of tribal population is concentrated. There are about 400 Tribal Communities spread over throughout the length and breadth of the country. Due to various types of exposures at various phases of historical development these tribal groups are at present found at different points of socio-economic and cultural ladder. The present day tribal situation varies from region to region and tribe to tribe. In many areas their way of life and thinking have greatly been affected due to various forces of changes, though the tribal life in some areas still remain in quite calm due to their isolated nature of habitat and mental makeup. Due to the impact of modern education and other forces of changes a section of tribals has become very much conscious about their rights and organising movements 'in search of their identity'! The new socio-economic forces have suddenly made

---

* Reproduced by the permission of the authority of the Cultural Research Institute from the Bulletin of the Cultural Research Institute, Vol. XV No. 1 & 2.

tremendous effect on the tribal society which had hitherto been kept aloof and isolated from the rest of the country due to the policy of alien rulers. The State is committed to a policy of allowing the tribals, this vital limb of the Indian Community, to develop according to their own genius. Now the time has come, after a period of three and a half decades, to evaluate how far we have succeeded in achieving our goal relating to the tribal brethren. On the other hand the tribals also may like to pause for a while to examine and to take decision about the course of their development.

Since the beginning of our Five Year Plans, schemes were drawn up for an overall development of the social, economic and cultural life of the tribal communities. At the end of the Fourth Five Year Plan the whole situation was reviewed. It was found that some of the communities made substantial progress in relation to economic and educational achievements whereas a vast majority of them lagged far behind. This happened also in the case of individual communities amongst whom some persons were found quite well off in comparison with others of the said community. This gave rise to conflict and tension in the inter as well as intra community level. In addition to the above there persisted a wide gap in between different areas in the level of development as happened in the ethnic level. A number of factors was responsible for giving rise to such situation. For bridging up the gap of imbalance that existed at regional level, programmes under TD Blocks were prepared but the ambit of the same in operational terms was very limited. These TD Blocks were mainly concerned themselves largely with the usual developmental schemes and social services. These schemes were generally formulated for the comparatively advanced areas and extended to the tribal areas in the same form. There was emphasis in principle towards protective aspects but they were not organically linked with other facets of administration and development. Therefore, a new strategy for tribal development was adopted since the beginning of the Fifth Five Year Plan. The areas having 50% or more tribal population were identified and special plans (Tribal sub-Plan) were prepared. This new strategy could cover only two-thirds of the total tribal population of the country whereas the rest one-third remained outside the orbit of the development plan. No special attention was given to their problems.

The approach needed for tribal development would be clear from the following words of the Prime Minister:

"We have evolved the strategy of sub-plans and have systematically identified the areas of tribal concentration sometimes these strategies and plans become bottlenecks. We should see that whatever is decided is implemented straight away.

"The most important element is the personnel. We should find out dedicated persons who have the competence and the correct attitude,the correct emotional involvement with this work...people should be urged to do something because it is in the national interest and it is something worth doing and it is a rewarding thing even for the individual.

"A simple situation requires a simple organisation so that the unsophisticated people with whom one has to deal can understand and not get confused by complicated procedures".

These strategy adopted during the Fifth Plan was "area development with focus on the develpment of tribal communities, for areas where tribals are a predominent community". The above concept was formulated on the basis of the following prevailing situation in the tribal areas.

(a) Amongst the Scheduled Tribe Communities there remains variations in the social, political, economic and cultural levels.

(b) The demographic situation reveals that in certian States the tribals have concentrated pockets whereas in other parts they are scattered and live interspersed with general population.

(c) There are a number of primitive tribal communities who are at pre-agricultural and pre-literate stage and live in secluded regions in isolation. In a nut shell it may be stated that Tribal Development was related to their level of development and pattern of distribution. In concentrated tribal regions, areas approach with focus on development of tribal Communities was favoured while for primitive groups, community oriented programmes were preferred. The main purpose was to eliminate exploitation in all forms and to build up inner strength of the people and to improve their organisational capability.

The working group on Tribal Development (1980-85) observed that though the approach and strategy were clearly worked out but the success in relation to planning and implementation of programmes were very limited. The elimination of exploitation which was one of the basic objectives during the Fifth Plan has had only very limited success. The Administrative unpreparedness appeared to be main constraint in implementation of programmes and protective policies. A review of different documents dealing with tribal development reveals that the benefits meant for tribals have not yet reached to is a substantial section of the population concerned. This has resulted in widening the gap between the tribals and non-tribals of a particular area and also accelerated the processes of exploitation in a more effective and organised way. The fear of exploitation has also resulted in some cases in the rejection of larger programmes by tribal bodies (Ratha, 1981).

The post Fifth Plan strategy tries to attack the tribal problem from three angles classifying the tribals into three categories:

(a) Tribals in the area of tribal concentration,

(b) Dispersed tribals in other areas; and

(c) Primitive tribal communities.

Thus the developmental measures are designed to be area oriented, community oriented and individual family oriented for the respective categories of population.

The urgent task, according to the report of the working group on Tribal Development during the Sixth Plan, is to create in the economic field impact of an order which will enable a targeted number of families belonging to a scheduled tribe community cross the poverty line.

In other words this indicates adoption of well calculated step for increasing income level of the tribal folk. Thus the economic development becomes the primary concern. It is a common experience that the exploitative process gradually becomes strengthened side by side with the developmental programmes. Therefore, for achieving the target the step needed at the very beginning is to adopt adequate measures for saving the tribals in general from economic and other social, political deprivation. The forest policy, excise policy, land alienation, marketing especially of forest produce are to be closely examined in relation to the tribal way of life and culture, and in the context of prevailing tribal situation in differnt regions of the State (Ratha:1981).

The economic betterment may be a part of the overall development process but that should not be treated as sole criterion for the overall human development. Belshaw (1972) states that development should be looked upon as an organised activity with the aim of satisfying certain basic needs and to orient the tribals mentally to adopt new skills, attitudes and life styles. This is necessary for building up the inner strength with appropriate social and cultural infrastructure to stand the pressure of the new programmes and maintain higher levels. In other words development is a process of multi-dimensional nature for an overall well integrated improvement of the social, cultural, economic and human conditions of the people necessary for a balanced growth of a society. According to Schneider (1975) due emphasis is required for establishing a meaningful link between the local and national levels of development and of the World at large. The Government agencies have given emphasis on the organisational structure and formulated action and end oriented programmes in education, health services, agriculture, marketing, forestry, nutrition, communication, etc. sectors.

The pre-requisite for formulation and implementation of any development project is a thorough knowledge about the socio-cultural situation and historical process of development of a particular ethnic group or a section of a community or a group of individual along with a clear cut idea about the eco-system of their locality. These will help in selecting programmes on priority basis for each area, community, section thereof or individuals concerned. Side by side, the clear conception about the methodology of approach is required. All these are necessary as because no single cause can be made responsible for economic underdevelopment and or cultural stagnation. A number of factors and forces (economic, social, political, religious, historical, cultural) singularly or jointly give rise to a particular situation of underdevelopment and cultural stagnation.

Present day outburst here and there in tribal areas and other experiences reveal that the development programmes have in a direct or an indirect way widened the psychological gap between the tribals and non-tribals and implementing agencies. The atmosphere of distrust and lack of confidence are not congenial for development activities. Elwin

(1963) further observed that the tribal folk are open, frank and willing to change when faith and reason convince them that the change is necessary.

Keeping the above facts in view, some of the leading emergent issues concerning tribal development are mentioned below in a nutshell.

1. The tribal population in general still suffer from mental isolation due to lack of confidence in them. The outsiders are in general considered 'exploiters' due to historical tradition.

2. It is to be examined how far the basic principle of tribal development, that is, "the tribals should develop in accordance with their own genius" still holds effective and meaningful under the existing tribal situation.

3. Major portion of tribal population still remains outside the operation of tribal sub-Plan. Therefore, suitable step is to be devised for bringing the remaining portion in the development fold. Otherwise the situation may lead to widening of the gap between tribals living in sub-Plan area and those remaining outside.

4. A major portion of the administrative machinery involved with the sub-Plan activities is neither conscious about the seriousness of the prevailing tribal situation nor fully aware of the concept and mechanism of operation of sub-Plan.

5. Side by side ,the functionaries lack in sufficient knowledge about tribal life and activities, their culture, mode of thinking, their level of aspiration etc. which are pre-requisite for any development activity.

6. Serious attempt is therefore, called for keeping abreast all the functionaries of tribal development administration with the latest situation prevailing in each area through intensive and peripatetic training otherwise there remains scope for non-appreciation of the proper approach needed for the purpose.

7. Suitable means are to be found out to see how far the local indigenous institutions can be best utilised for development

purpose for ensuring meaningful participation of the concerned population. This will help in creating confidence.

8. It is accepted that the Village Panchayat should oversee all developmental programmes in the tribal areas. In this connection, it is to be examined whether the traditional tribal Panch (community council) can also be associated with the development process so as to ensure a bigger participation from the tribal side.

9. An emergent consciousness for self-identification possess a great challenge. This is to be taken note of while drawing up plans and programmes. Maximum effort is to be made so that a batch of efficient workers from amongst the tribals themselves are trained and involved in the process of development.

10. The present administrative machinery is to be properly equipped and the monitoring system should be geared up and made quite effective.

11. At present there is no systematic mechanism for flow of information at various levels. This should be formalised so that there remains no scope for communication gap in between different functionaries.

12. The spirit of 'co-operation' is the fundamental principle of tribal society. The expected roles of the LAMPS are yet to be fulfilled.

13. Lack of knowledge regarding tribal folk quite often lead to selection of beneficiaries etc. outside the tribal fold by the Panchayat machinery.

References

1. Belshaw, C. S., (1972) "Development : The contribution of Anthropology", *International Social Science Journal*, 24 : 83-94.

2. Schneider, Harold K. (1975) "Economic Development and Anthropology ". *In the Annual Review of Anthropology*, B. J. Siegel *et al* (ed.) : 271-292.

3. Ratha, S. N. (1981) "Tribal Development Programme an Appraisal". In the Tribal Development and Its Administration. L.P. Vidyarthi (ed.) : 1981, 83-91.

4. Report of the Working Group on Tribal Development During Sixth Plan (1980-85), Government of India, Ministry of Home Affaris. New Delhi, October,1980.
5. Tribal Development--Retrospect and Prospect, Government of India, Ministry of Home Affairs, New Delhi.

CHAPTER 6

Tribal Development : An Appraisal*

D. L. Prasada Rao
P. Venkata Rao

Since the beginning of First Five Year Plan several developmental programmes are being implemented in the tribal areas of the country in addition to the special privileges and constitutional safeguards accorded to the tribals. With the introduction of special and multipurpose projects in the year 1956 during Second Plan Period, with a small beginning of about five per cent, is later on developed to cover about 39 per cent of the total population by the end of Fourth Plan. Along with the introduction of special and multipurpose projects various schemes were formulated for the benefit of tribal populations. These programmes are found to be formulated for individual sectors at different levels in an un-coordinated manner without taking into account the potential and priorities of the areas and the capabilities of the existing institutions[1]. This fragmentary approach has effected the process of development by

---

* Reproduced by the permission of the authority of 'Man and Life' and Institute of Social Research and Applied Anthropology, Calcutta from 'Man and Life', 6(3 + 4) : 130 - 142, 1980.

preferring exogenous priorities. These drawbacks led to the development of a new strategy for the Fifth Plan. This new strategy recognizes that there is no uniform solution for the multiferous problems of tribals which are at different levels of development. Hence it was argued that the solutions prescribed shall have to take into account the needs of the area covered by the plan. It implies that in the new strategy the socio-economic activities are to be located over a physical space for the balanced development of the area and ultimately culminating in the spatial integration through development programmes.

In line with the recommendations of the task forces appointed by Planning Commission, following the above mentioned spatial approach which is otherwise called as area planning or regional planning, sub-Plans are prepared for areas in 16 States and two Union Territories, for areas having more than 50% of concentration of tribals and Scheduled areas. The sub-Plans for each State were drawn in such a way as to become viable project areas based on the administrative boundaries, topography, level of socio-economic development, ethnic composition, natural resources and potential for development. By 1976 about 40 out of 145 integrated tribal development projects came into existence and, an amount of 65 crores was allotted for the first three years i.e.,'74-77'. For the remaining projects which are supposed to come into existence in the latter half of Fifth Plan[2] an amount of Rs.125 crores was earmarked.

The present paper attempts to examine the possible effects of some of the discripencies in the tribal development planning and administration in ameliorating the conditions of the tribal populations. This exercise will help us to understand some of the important factors which hinder the achievement of the objectives of integrated tribal development planning. During the Multipurpose Project Period the authorities were criticised for neglecting the felt needs and the unenthusiastic role played by them in implementation of schemes. It was observed that "the extension agency sometimes assumes the mantle of an expert prescribing programmes without pondering over a moment as to how the tribal receives it. The other extreme is that the extenstion agency plays the role of a consultant expecting the tribals to approach it.... On the other hand the tribal is skeptical about the capability of the extension agency and the efficiency of the programme intended for his uplift".[3] In the light of the above observation, it is necessary to examine the plans and experiences in the implementation of Welfare Programmes.

Priorities in Tribal Development

While appreciating the introduction of planned change in tribal areas, the following question looms large in our mind: To what extent agricultural development and allied sectors that are receiving major share in the plan outlays, are really useful to ameliorate the conditions of the tribal mass? Indeed, doubts have been expressed by some on this policy of giving priority to agriculture as it does not inprove the economy of the masses. One strong agrument is that "the geophysical and ecological conditions to tribal areas imposes limits on the degree to which tribal agriculture can be modernised. Further traditionally many farmers supplement their livelihood from forest wealth and the forest department should assume greater responsibilities in developing the tribal economy and adapt its policies accordingly"[4]. Further it has been observed that even in tribal societies the few who are locally dominant, influential and have the economic resources drive the benefits of this development more than the masses. This happens because they have access to sources of information and this enables them to take full advantage of the government help in the form of grants, subsidies and services. In a multi-tribal setting the situation is still worse, where the dominant tribal community and elite get lion's share of the benefits. In contrast to these groups the subsistence or below subsistence level farmers and landless families constitute the disadvantaged and downtrodden groups who lose on every front. Indeed in many cases they "have nothing to begin with, nothing which can be improved, no means of an economic start and so they remain economically as well as socially disadvantaged. The gap between them and the villagers widens rather than diminishing on account of development projects"[5]. It was further observed that different factors such as small sized land--holdings, lack of assured water supply, low and unstable family income, exploitation by merchant, inaccessability of tribal areas, cultural values and norms, act as barriers in the process of agricultural development[6]. Besides, other deterrent factors are : prevalence of share- croppers and contract-croppers where realization of benefits is effected only by those who invest on land and not the actual cultivator. In this background of tribal agriculture, the emphasis on agriculture will benefit only big land owners and those who invest on land, and this leads to cumulative increase in the economic differential between the rich and poor.

Integrated tribal development projects, the latest mechanism developed for tribal uplift although has a sophisticated outlook, is being built on earlier foundations of community development and agricultural extension. For example, in the sub-Plan outlay of Andhra Pradesh 1/4th is earmarked for irrigation and animal husbandry. The net cultivated area works out to 13.41% out of the total geographical area and more than 15% of the land is under forests, barren lands, pastures etc.[7] In 1971 Census of Andhra Pradesh only 43.41% of the tribals in the State are recorded as cultivators; and others are either agricultural labourers or other types of workers. This shows that agricultural development will be actually helpful to a limited number of people as the categroy of cultivators may also include smaller farmers, contract-croppers and share-croppers, who may not gain much through agricultural development. Moreover profits on the produce go over to middlemen due to a number of factors like the inadequacy of marketing facilities, selling produce to creditors and money-lenders at rates stipulated to the advantage of the later, lack of transport, ignorance about business transaction etc. Another peculiar feature about agricultural programmes is that, most of the schemes of agricultural sector are either thrust upon tribals or are introduced on incentive basis-wherein in good number of cases one can find misuses.

An alternative to avoid the above mentioned situation is to emphasize on income augmenting opportunities through wage earning occupations. Many a time it has been suggested that providing income earning opportunities to poorer sections must be given importance while planning for tribal development[8]. Also, it was suggested that employment should be provided through forest based industries and, the share of the tribals must be recognised and part of the income derived on forests should be spent for their betterment[9]. The Integrated Tribal Development Programmes seem to have limited schemes for landless poor and have not much to say about providing employment.

Exploitation from within

Another important observation made on tribal development programmes is that certain institutions which are considered powerful mechanisms for the operation of the programmes, have actually become channels of exploitation. Institutions like Panchayat Raj, Co-operatives etc, have legitimized the position of traditional leaders of the tribals like chiefs, Muttadars; Pettandars, Headmen etc., who are known for their prominent role in the exploitation of tribals. These local leaders have their origin in the historical past, in the policy of indirect rule by the British which sought the help of the then existing institutions to strengthen and perpetuate their authority. These traditional leaders with their past experience and privileges enjoyed during the British period found a place in the modern political institutions and are playing a double role worth mentioning between the tribals and development authorities and also continue as leaders in the traditional system set up[10]. This unique position indeed helps them to grab most of the benefits for themselves. It is not uncommon for these persons to use the modern and traditional institutions for personal gains and also sometimes to oppress their opponents.

The above argument can be examplified by an observation of the role of formal leadership in the programmes of the Integrated Tribal Development Project located in Visakhapatnam District, Andhra Pradesh. Out of the 25 tribal groups inhabiting the region the Bagatha tribe is the dominant and most populous. Traditionally these people are Muttadars and are owners of fertile lands. With the introduction of Panchayat Raj they entered the regional politics and succeeded in getting elected to various offices. Out of the 55 Panchayats located in Paderu Block where the headquarter of the Intregrated Tribal Development Agency is located, 28 Panchayats have Bagathas as Sarpanchs (before 1975). Up to this day it is the Bagatha leaders who represented the area successively in the Legislative Assembly. These Bagatha leaders still exert control over the area and are influential. Another group which is mentionable here is Valmiki, a tribal community with entrepreneuring ability. These are agriculturists, local traders, litigants and constitute a sizeable part in the tribal literates. Elwin committee observes that they are some of the most determined exploiters of the tribal people excelling even the traditional merchant castes and money-lenders of the plains. Owing to their superior cunning nature and intelligence many of them have become well-to-do though of course there are many poor Valmikis. They buy land, take contracts, advance loans, and generally earn the rewards that come easily to those who deal with the simple tribal people[11]. Because of their being listed in the list of Scheduled Tribes, these people were able to do all acts of exploitation of tribals for which legally any non-tribal is liable for punishment.

In Visakhapatnam District the dominant Bagatha[12] and the entrepreneuring Valmikis seem to the have taken full advantage of developmental efforts than other tribal groups, while the principle behind the integrated tribal development approach is to integrate the backward tribal regions with other areas by eliminating the disparities between them. This implies that under the prevailing conditions, discussed above, development of the region need not mean improvement of all the tribal groups inhabiting the territory. It is not an exaggeration to say that the expenditure incurred by Integrated Tribal Development Programme under various schemes may even result in widening the gap between the Bagatha and Valmiki on one end and the other economically backward tribal communities on the other.

This situation calls forth for special consideration to really backward groups by Integrated Tribal Development Agency (ITDA) authorities. Probably after recognizing this aspect the Commissioner for Scheduled Castes and Sheduled Tribes stated that ''Selection of proper beneficieries is of vital importance for the very success of the schemes of democratic decentralization and therefore it is necessary that suitable rules should be framed on this subject''[13]. It was also pointed out that assistance in the form of grants and loans should be given to the weaker sections in order of priority based on their socio-economic conditions, that is to say among the weaker sections those who have low income should be given priority.

In a situation of planned change people who have direct access to change agents, and institutions; get the impact first than others, and play a crucial role in the directional process responsible for change. People who are interested in personal gains dominate the local scene and they manipulate the situation to their best advantage. In this connection it is worth remembering the observation made in the Report of Commissioner for Scheduled Castes and Scheduled Tribes, that Samithis dominated by vested interests who are not enthusiastic about programmes for weaker sections may not deliver the goods[14].Commenting on the role of educated tribal youth Roy Burman writes: ''It is heard from various sources that the tribal educated elite represent the classes but not masses''[15]. If this is true then the only remedy is to give preference to weaker sections among tribals in the planning for development of tribals. It may not be an exaggeration to say that injustice done to the communities at lower levels and inaccessible areas is perepetuated by developmental programming.

Unless Integrated Tribal Develoment Programmes make it their policy to give preference to lower section in the distribution of benefits, facilities and other forms of assistance, integrated development will become only a paper manifesto for the development of tribals.

Developmental Personnel

Personnel connected with the implementation of development programmes play a crucial role in the success of various programmes.

One of the important features of personnel system in tribal areas is, that employees at lower levels like village development officer are almost fixed in their respective jurisdictions, which enables them to work hand-in-hand with the local leaders, while the higher level employees are always from the other departments of the government. One of the drawbacks of tribal welfare administration is the employment of officials on deputation. In many States, no doubt, there is a provision for promoting extention staff as B.D.O.'s, but this quota is very limited. The absence of a permanent cadre of B.D.O.'s, and the present method of deputing employees from one cadre to the other is most detrimental to the success of welfare programmes, more so for tribal welfare.

Under the present practice of deputation an officer belongs to his parent department and work in the deputed post on a temporary basis. This arrangement makes the officers not to feel much responsibility due to the temporary nature of the posting. Their hearts always set on posts in their parent department and their loyalty to the job for which they are deputed is limited. And further this practice provides little incentive to extension officers who are the real agents of change. In a report on a tribal welfare organization, the Girijan Cooperative Corporation, Andhra Pradesh the impact of deputations is observed as follows: "Temporary and too frequent changes of deputations is resulting in less of experienced hands. The report between deputationists and regular employees is low and the latter have a common grievance against deputationists as their promotion opportunities are hampered. The deputationists are under the control of their parent departments which do not allow the receiving department to take action against them. The deputationists spend large amounts of funds without having the responsibility to account for them"[16]. From the experience we can assume that this practice of deputation will have the same effect on the

Integrated Tribal Development Programmes. Even to this day, it has become a policy to appoint persons with little or no experience in tribal areas as Project Officers and they are supposed to coordinate not only the activities of various departmental officials at project level, but also to know the values and culture of tribals. The Integrated Tribal Developemental Projects depend upon the Tribal Development Blocks for executing their plans which already became mere distributing channels.

Moreover this personnel policy of the Government does not have any compatability with the organization and functioning of welfare institutions where committment for development and a compassionate outlook is essential.

The problems faced by Block staff that the staff is bogged down under heavy paper work, attending meetings, sending reports, statistics, receiving visitors, inspections and audits with less time to look after extension work[17] are never considered with seriousness and no alternatives have been explored.

According to Dr. B.D.Sharma, the most important aspect of tribal development scene in the country at this stage is the compatibility of the local socio-economic system with the personnel system. The personnel system in backward areas has a more unique role to play. It is supposed to act as catalytic agent for change. This task has to be performed through carefully guided mutual interaction at various socio-economic levels. Commenting on the validity of the personnel system in tribal areas, Dr. Sharma questions ''Is it possible that the same system can function equally well indifferent regions? Since these tasks in these areas are different can the same system assume with equal ease the passive role in one situtation and an active catalytic role in another?''[18] The special training prescribed for employees deployed in tribal areas lost its initial importance as neither the government nor the officers regarded their positions as of having any permanency.

The infrastructure for tribal development is supposed to function as distributing and servicing channel for the developmental process. The present practice of deputing officials from Revenue Department to Welfare Departments is a point to be considered in this context. Its working is expected to be entirely different from the Revenue Department where time is not an important factor as procedural delays have become part of the administration. With excessive centralization of authority and strict regulatory mechanisms in which the personnel of Revenue Department are oriented it is doubtful of them to transform suddenly when they step into Development and Welfare agencies to adopt to the orientation of these departments.

Despite the drastic differences in approaches the unhealthy practice of sending deputationists from Revenue Department to Developmental Department is still continuing. The practice of deputing employees at Block Development Officer level is quite unwelcome as little coordination can be expected between the Revenue Department deputatioinist B.D.O. and the Technically trained Extension Officers; who may be nursing considerable grudge on the deputation system which blockades their promotion opportunities. This situation gets more complicated with the Village Development Officers joining hands with local elite and factional groups, the whole development mechanism is being subverted from achieving the objectives.

The above discussion ultimately takes us to the question, to what extent the newly constituted Integrated Tribal Development Programmes with deputationists from various departments can function effectively?

Utilization of Benefits

Special privileges and concessions are extended to tribal areas and special emphasis is laid on tribal development due to poor productive and infrastructural base along with continued exploitation in tribal areas. Various protective legislations were enacted and developmental projects launched to ameliorate the conditions of the tribals. The expenditure on tribal welfare at all India level was 19.03 crores during First Plan, which was raised to 305.00 crores for the Fifth Plan.[19] All these efforts are intended to improve the economic conditions of the tribal societies which have not been able to keep pace with other communities towards self-reliance. Although a higher allocation is made in Fifth Plan the objective of making the tribal communities better is constrained due to various handicaps. At the level of implementation, various development programmes became exercises in execution of targets. Developmental staff utilized people for achieving the targets only and, the participation of people in developmental effort has remained only a slogan. To give an example from the author's own field experience in a village of Srikakulam District, in Andhra Pradesh. Loans were given to tribals for the purchase of ploughs, bullocks, seeds, fertilizers and other agricultural implements on crops which were non-existent. Actually land was allotted to the tribals and Pattas were handed over ceremoniously. But the plots were not demarcated even after two years. To fulfil the targets the authorities in the area distributed various incentives and inputs on the basis of the pattas, which were grossly misused. Practices like this, besides leading to wastage of funds creates unhealthy attitude towards government help. Though another instance in the same district let us understand the attitude of tribal towards a particular programme. While talking to the beneficieries in a government built housing colony, a question was put forth, why the damaged houses in the colony were not repaired? The villagers complained that the B.D.O. was not attending to the job. They feel that it is the duty of the B.D.O. who got them constructed,to look after them. Here we can see the transformation in the tribal attitude who used to construct houses through collective labour becoming dependent upon government even for small repairs. Similarly in Visakhapatnam District it was observed that Governemnt supplied cattle and poultry are dispensed away with the exhaustion of government feed supplied for them freely. Instances like the above reveal the easy attitude of the tribals towards government help, defeating the objectives behind government welfare programmes. Indeed it is also due to the lenient attitude of the personnel responsible for the implementation of schemes with the sole aim of fulfilling targets. Sensing this attitude of government the tribal elite are getting habituated to seek assistance whenever a government or semi-government official visits their area.

Another tendency prevalent in tribal areas is their indifference towards repayment of government loans. Usually it is the local elite who encourages the tribals to develop the attitude by saying "government won't take any action against tribals".

The net result of this situation is stoppage of issuing loans when the recoveries are not satisfactory and, thus hindering further credit facilities. This non-repayment handicaps the functioning of institutions like G.C.C. as they operate with a revolving fund.

Primary co-operatives which were enthusiastically started in different areas were closed down for the same reason as mentioned above. In some cases, fresh loans were issued and were adjusted to the previous debts. To bring out a typical example in Rajavommangi Tribal Development Block of Andhra Pradesh, housing colonies were constructed for the tribals by Block authorities with financial assistance from L.I.C. The tribals who are supposed to repay the cost of the house in instalments did not pay even a single instalment and the Block authorities are under pressure by L.I.C. Enquiries revealed that local politicians advised the tribals that nothing is going to happen even if they do not repay a single rupee.

Under these conditions it is doubtful to what extent the different schemes will continue if incentives are withdrawn. In this context what is urgently needed is to examine the tribal perception towards government help and how best they can be prepared to take over the situation by themselves. Steps must be taken to encourage the participation of tribals without incentives. In this context it is appropriate to recall the definition of community development given by Cochrane that "it meant development of human potential through self-education concerned with helping people to define or appreciate their wants and letting them evolve the means of their satisfaction"[20].

From the discussion carried out so far it is doubtful whether the newly constituted Integrated Tribal Development Agencies serve the purpose for which they are setup; unless suitable steps were taken on the issues mentioned here. Further it has been argued by many that whether the area development approach which is successful in Western Countries is applicable to tribal areas where the problems are of different order.

The tribal areas are not homogeneous for allowing the percolation of benefits through growth centres. The administrative machinery of the Integrated Tribal Developement Programmes is still possessed by the age old drawbacks. Further despite the democratic set-up, the exploitative feudalistic, soico-political structure of the tribal areas has not changed much. Hence it is desirable to take up the following steps to revitalize the tribal development programmes. Provision should be made for fully trained executive cadre oriented towards welfare activities. Instead of stress on agricultural development, emphasis must be shifted to creation of income earning opportunities. This measure based on forest resources besides providing them economic betterment, also releases them from the authority of local elite. Preference must be given to less dominant and vulnerable groups while implementing ameliorative schemes. Steps should be taken to see that the beneficieries utilize the money for the purpose to which it is actually sanctioned. It is better to stop assistance where misuses have become rampant. In this connection it is necessary to understand the tribal perception towards Government help.This will help to foster healthy ideas in tribal mind towards governmental help and prepare them to participate in various activities in future for their betterment even without incentives and persuasion.

References

1. *Approach to the Fifth Plan*,1974-79, Government of India, 1977, p. 56.
2. *Fifth Five Year Plan,* 1974-79. Government of India, Planning Commission, pp. 84-85.
3. Kamala Manohara Rao, P. Report of the working of T. D. Blocks in Andhra Pradesh, (Mimeographed) T. C. R. & T. I. Hyderabad. p. 187.
4. Institutional framework for agriculture development in tribal areas by D.V. Raghavarao, in Guy Hunter and Anthony F. Bottral (Ed.) Serving the small Policy choices in Indian Agriculture, N.I.R.D., 1974.
5. Social Organization and planned culture change in India, by Mandelbaum, David G., 1960, in M. N. Srinivas(Ed.), *India's villages.*
6. Barriers to diffusion of farm innovations among tribal people by N.K. Jaiswal and N. V. Kolte : 1974; in *Perspectives on Tribal Development and Administration,* N. I. R. D., Hyderabad.
7. *Statistical compendium on agricultural sector of sub-plan area in Andhra Pradesh,* (Mimeograped) T. C. R, & T. I., Hyderabad-78. p. 30.
8. For example, see the recommendations of a seminar on Planning for tribal development. Regarding the approach to be followed for integrated tribal planning. Ranjit Gupta (1977), Planning for Tribal Development. p. 17.
9. Elwin Committee Report opines that the tribals had a moral right on forest if not legal. It is suggested to introduce forest based occupations and tribals should be given a share in the profit of the forest. Report of the Committee on special and Multi-purpose Tribal Blocks, 1960. pp. 57-67.
10. Regarding the election of traditional leaders and their role see F.G. Bailey- Decisions by Consensus in Councils and Committees in Michael Banton (Ed.), 1965. "Political systems and distribution of Power".A.S.A.Monograph, Tavistock Publishers.
11. Report of the Committee on speical and multipurpose tribal blocks (Above cited) p. 321.
12. Bagathas in this area claim superior status on the pretext that they are warriors who served in the courts of nearby rulers. Many of the tribes in this area when asked about the name of their tribe replied that they are Porojas. As far back as 1931 it was reported that (Census of India) the term Poroja in its agency origin connotes the idea 'subject' or subjected as opposed to the rulers epitomizes the history of Vizagpatnam people. This may be an indication of emergence of class distinction.
13. Report of the Commissioner for Scheduled Castes and Scheduled Tribes, by N. K. Bose, 1969-70.
14. Report of the Commissioner for Scheduled Castes and Scheduled Tribes as cited above.

15. Roy Burman, B. K., 1976; "Perspectives for administration and development" in *Perspectives on Tribal Development and Administration*. N. I. R. D. Hyderabad.
16. Committee of House to enquire into matters relating to deficits and misappropriations etc., in The Girijan Co-Operative Corporation, Report, A.P. Legislative Assembly.1976.
17. Report on the working of T. D. Blocks in A. P. T., C. R. and T. I. Hyderabad.
18. B. D. Sharma, 1976 : Environmental context and the Personnel System and its Implications for Tribal Areas. Ministry of Home Affairs.
19. *Tribal Development : The New Strategy* by Om Mehta, Ministry of Home Affairs.
20. Cochrane : *Development Anthropology*, 1971. p. 47.

Part Two : Area Specific Issues

CHAPTER 7

Tribal Development in Manipur with Reference to their Organizational Features

Rajat Kanti Das

Any development effort should be shared by the members of a community. This is particularly so when it concerns a tribe because of the integrative mechanism of the tribal group, so often advocated by the anthropologists. The organizational features of the Manipur tribes are, however, not that simple to follow a uniform integrated approach to development, which may be applied to all the tribes of Manipur. In order to stress upon this point examples of organizational features of a selected group of tribes are presented in this paper.

II

To understand the pattern of distribution of the tribal groups of Manipur one needs to identify the underlying process of cultural dynamics. The spread of social and cultural forms seems to have been effected through movement of different tribes, who were initially involved in a process of displacing each other. It may not be very difficult to identify the processes that activated the nature of displacements. Presumably, there were phases in the history of migration whereby smaller groups were displaced time and again by population from more prolific centres. These smaller groups have ultimately been transformed into peripheral groups and cultures. When it comes to the question of a single tribe inhabiting a more or less well-defined territory, one may notice a clear age-area stratification from a centre to the periphery with regard to settlement pattern of villages. This may be correlated with the segmentary nature of tribal social organization. It may also be possible to find a pattern of diffusion and assimilation whereby cultural elements were borrowed and ethnic identities changed in response to the greater defensive efficiency in the face of frequent raids. Smaller tribes did not have a fixed well-defined territory of their own. They were constantly on the move. In their endeavour to avoid contact with bigger tribes, they set up villages along the fringes of the valley thereby coming under direct protective cover of the Meitei King and the people. There are unmistakable signs of the Meitei influence on them. That they could maintain their separate identity in the midst of the dominant group only speaks of the enduring power and strength of their culture. Moreover, the policy of the Meitei king was also against complete absorption in the interest of kingship, which believed in extension of control over tribes. Even in case of bigger tribes there was at best, the regional integration activated through a process of nucleation of some villages. Lineage and clan sentiments used to be at the root of such a limited integration. For integrating their constituent scattered settlements the tribal communities in general had to depend more heavily on lineality and intermarriage. A wider regional network of kinship and opportunities for inter-visiting could be created only through intervillage marriages. Since by and large the exchange relationships were unequal or non-symmetrical, organization at the tribal level is bound to be minimal. The Kabui, the Thadou and the Chiru represent the three tribes with three different aspects of organizational pattern.

III

The Kabui, a tribe of the Naga group, can be said to belong to two different groups, namely, the Hill Kabuis and the Plains Kabuis. Of these, the Plains Kabuis have come under the direct influence of the Meities. Historically and ethnically, however, there is no justification for considering them apart from the Hill Kabuis. But because of their exposure, the Plains Kabuis reveal some influence of the towns in their material culture. Distillation of liquor and rearing of pigs are vigorously pursued by the Kabuis living in and around Imphal town not because these are two important traditional occupations, but because of their capacity to earn a reasonably good amount of money. Not only that, there has been a significant rise of service-holders in these villages. At Chingmeirong, a Kabui village at a distance of 3 km. from the centre of Imphal, there were 28 government employees out of a total population of 286--2 of whom were females. Only 19 had cultivation as a primary occupation. Even in social life the villagers made some adjustments. For instance, there were two household deities--the *Sanamahi,* who is the Meitei household deity, and the *Kaikhun,* the Kabui male creator. The *Sanamahi* was not regularly worshipped, but the *Kaikhun* was worshipped at regular intervals. There was a clan Daimei, which was supposed to have been originated from an area called Gomphuning near Lanka bordering Manipur and Nagaland, but very few of the clan members were aware of it. As a matter of fact, none could tell the mythological story regarding the origin of this clan. Age grade associations or *thiens* were unknown in this village. The villagers did not consider these to be important. The youth dormitories were replaced by modern clubs. Although the original settlers came from Tamenglong area, the people of this village were quite accustomed to urban habits and life style. As far as Chingmeirong was concerned, there was no marital connection with the Hill Kabuis. The simple fact is that the Plains Kabuis and the Hill Kabuis now function as more or less separate groups. Only at the political level they may be spoken of as a unified tribe. Admittedly, the geo-ethnic situation of the two groups is different, which has profound effects on their different modes of organization. It, however, needs to be stressed that the Plains Kabuis as a group, have very little credibility. They are a loose collection of villages, each of which grows unilaterally.

IV

The Thadou form the largest tribe of Manipur. They are, however, distributed over a wide area covering some parts of Nagaland, Manipur and also Cachar district of Assam. They are also found to inhabit the difficult mountainous tracts close to the borders of Nagaland and

Manipur on the west and Upper Chindwin district of Burma on the east. Their largest concentration is in Manipur. It is clear that they are dispersed over a wide tract without occupying a contiguous areas. Territorial integrity could be maintained only at the clan level and also at the sub-clan level. This is also reflected in the social organization. The Thadou genealogical tree shows a long list of descendants. The original ones appeared as families, which had grown into clans in course of time. Today many of the descending groups could not be traced out at all. It appears that at certain stages they had lost their identities and merged with the powerful clans. In the Thadou society those clans which could produce chiefs, are considered powerful clans. Not all clans could produce chiefs and as such became insignificant after sometime. The segmentary process is deep-rooted in the Thadou social system. Originally, the tribe is believed to have four families, all named after their progenitors. The four families are, Doungel, Sit-lhou, Kipgen and Haokip. These are stated to be further sub-divided into many eponymous branches. It may be mentioned here that in the Thadou society elder brother *upa* has the right to enjoy certain privileges over younger brother or *naopa*. Chieftainship is supposed to go to the members of the senior clans. Incidentally, besides *inpipu*, who is the hereditary chief, there is also a non-hereditary chief *hausapu*. The second type of chieftainship could be acquired by displaying fighting capabilities, valour or any special skill. There is reason to believe that the non-hereditary type of chieftainship was a sort of adjustment which had to be done to accommodate minor clans. *Hausapu* is nothing more than a local chief, who has control over a newly formed village. A study conducted at Khengjang, a Thadou village situated about 21 km north of Imphal, revealed that *chongloi* was the most dominant clan in the village and the chief Thankosi belonged to this clan. His parents first set their feet on this village in 1948. The patrilineal kinship ties which bind the clans together, are strongest within the local group or village mainly formed around a core of agnatically related males, their wives and children. Moreover, though affinal links with neighbouring groups are derived from the practice of local lineage exogamy, relations with them can also be regulated. Over and above, frequent migration does not allow the patrilineage to function properly. Usually, one clan dominates over other clans in a group of villages located close by. But the isolated Thadou pockets comprising villages dominated by a single clan can at best, bring about local or regional integration. The policy of the British Government was also to some extent responsible for the Thadou to function as a disjointed tribe. The Thadous acted as a sort of 'buffer group', placed as they were in between two warring Naga groups. The pattern of dispersal of the Thadous fits rather well with their segmental nature.

V

The Chiru represent one of the small Kuki tribes of Manipur. They are distributed along the fringes of the valley. Although their villages are dispersed, they are far from isolated. They live under the shadow of an economically and politically dominant society, i.e., the Meiteis, but unlike the Plains Kabuis their villages are away from the urban milieu. The limited number of the Chiru villages are all located along the lower slopes of Kangchup and the Phunal ranges of hills. At least on two more points they differ markedly with the Plains Kabuis. Firstly, although they live under the shadow of the Meiteis, their social surroundings are dominated by the tribes as well. Important among the neighbouring tribes are the Thadou and the Kom. Secondly, since they are a little away from the urban centres the Chirus are less adept to utilise the vagaries of urban life to their advantage. One should not, however, lay too much emphasis on the situational advantage of the Plains Kabui village. The influence of Christianity cannot be lost sight of. Christianity is deep-rooted in all the Chiru villages. The example of Kangchup Chiru, a Chiru village on the slopes of the Kangchup hill, may be cited with the purpose of finding out the distinctive organizational features of the Chiru. Kangchup Chiru is situated on the west of Imphal at the distance of about 17 km. The residential cluster is on the eastern slope of the Kangchup hill. The slope gradually descends into the bed of the Maklang river. The village is bounded on the east by Loi village of Phayang, on the north by Hmar village of Zoute, on the south by Thadou village of Ladak. On the west is the Maklang river. The villagers are Christians and are affiliated to the American Baptist Mission. In the year the survey was conducted, the village had a population of 188, of whom 91 were males and 97 females. Land close to the Maklang river was in the possession of a few households only. No wonder, these households were better off than the rest. They had more of the domestic animals like buffalo, cow, bullock, pig and fowl. Interestingly enough, they belonged to clans which might be considered dominant. These were Samper, Danla and Raj. Samper and Danla split further Samper into Mackek. Samper and Danla into Tuithai Danla, Laina Danla, and Thanga Danla. There were eleven more clans, which were actually lineage names and which put together accounted for only 15% of the total population. Four of these clans, namely, Tingpui, Jachidingthei, Ningthoi and Tingthei belonged to villages other than Kangchup Chiru. The members of these clans were females, all of whom were married to this village. But on the whole, cases of inter-village marital ties were a few thereby confirming the view that inter-village marital ties could be systematically maintained as long as clanship ties did not lose their effectiveness. The main festivals in the village were Christmas, New Year's Day, Good Friday, *sathar-shekna* and *muchi-choina* or *tukna*. The list shows an amalgamation of the old and new beliefs and practices. *Sathar-shekna* and *muchi-choina* were the remnants of the traditional faith. These were associated with agricultural activities. Only because of that probably, they could not altogether be dispensed with. The role of the pastor in social life deserves mention. He now takes the leading part in organizing a festival. With his emergence as an important person in the village social life, the medicine man(*thimpu*) has almost been reduced to insignificance. In the olden days, the *thimpu* was the leading figure in all religious activities. It is clear that the element or elements that served as the focus for the activities of the villagers had not much of traditionalism in them. But they did not show much of material progress either. In the ultimate analysis, everything depends on the capacity to utilise economic resources at one's disposal and it is no wonder that a small tribe like Chiru would lack in that.

VI

Three tribes represent three different situations. The Kabui and Thadou, two bigger tribes, show very little in common. The Kabuis are clearly differentiated into two geographical groups, while the Thadous distributed all over in the form of some isolated pockets. The natural economic resources of the Chiru, who represent a small tribe, have shrunk considerably. It may appear that the ecological constraints they are subjected to, are of the immediate environment of the settlement, but actually these have far-reaching implications. A wider region inhabited by a number of communities, both tribes and non-tribes, come into the picture. The Chiru cannot be disentangled from others. They are a part of a wider regional unit and share with other constituent groups geographically localised economic interests. One would wonder whether the same developmental strategy would be followed in all the three cases. But one thing is clear. That a tribe cannot be treated in isolation. In the existing tribal situation in Manipur a unilateral development of a tribe may not be the answer. The situation calls for a multilateral development programme involving a number of tribes in a way that would help generating in them a sense of cooperation without disturbing their basic identity. But the matter is not that simple. The successful implementation of a multiethnic development programme depends on a correct assessment of the development needs of the groups concerned. It may be argued that in the case of tribes like the Tangkhul and the Maring such an approach may not be necessary since they have an almost continuous distribution. But even in these tribes one may find the existence of localised groups. The southern Tangkhuls may be clearly differentiated from the northern Tangkhuls and it needs no special training in contact ethnography to know that they have more of contact with the Thadou or the Maring than they have with latter. Similarly, the western group of the Maring are economically linked with the Meiteis at the foothills. They have no such link with the eastern group of the Marings. It is not a question of exercise of choice, as if to determine who matters most. The fact remains that every tribe has certain variants--urban or semi-urban, rural, local etc.--and it is not unusual for a particular variant of a tribe to be tagged with another such variant of another tribe belonging to the same area. The sense of solidarity may still be centered in the local group, but it may be qualified in some regions by a sense of participation in the multivariant regional group. The main task here will be to determine the exact nature and character of the regional group.

References

Das, R.K. (1979) Some Aspects of Changing Social Relations : A Study of a Thadou Village, *Journal of Social Research* Ranchi, Vol. XXII, No. 1.

CHAPTER 8

Development in a Tribal Setting: A Case of Meghalaya

Soumen Sen

Meghalaya, the twenty-first State of the Indian Union, came into existence first as a sub-State in 1970 and then as a full-fledged state in 1972 following the re-organisation of Assam after a decade-long movement for autonomy led by the All Party Hill Leaders' Conference. It is predominantly a tribal state. According to 1981 Census, the total population of Meghalaya is 13,35,819 of which tribal population is 10,76,345 i.e. 80.58%. The major tribes that inhabit the State are the Khasi-Jaintias of the Khasi and Jaintia Hills and the Garos of the Garo Hills. Both the tribes are matrilineal.

Development Scene

One of the major issues raised by the tribal leaders during the movement for a hill State was the issue of underdevelopment. As the demands for self-determination of small nation is always linked with the problem of growth which is articulated in political movements, the allegation was more or less legitimate, particularly in the light of regional imbalances of Indian economy and the chronic problem of backwardness within backwardness.

But even after the establishment of the State, the problem of under-development persists. Since planning for development is a socio-economic responsibility and in India this responsibility has been assumed by the government in the 'mixed economy' set-up, development strategy remains primarily the concern of the government. This concern becomes all the more important in a backward region, and more so in a tribal state. But as yet a clearcut economic policy reflecting a planned direction of socio-economic growth has not been formulated. No reform and modernization has been envisaged to vitalize the agrarian sector, nor there is any industrial policy to bring about a structural transformation of the economy. The absolute dependence on agriculture and that also of shifting cultivation stage with very low level of productivity speaks of a collossal failure in creating employment opportunities.The net result is a huge labour force depending on a static primary sector. The very simple goal of development planning, meeting the socio-economic objective of generating income and assets and social distribution of both, creating employment opportunities, remained unfulfilled.

Agrarian Sector

The urban-rural break-up of the total population of Meghalaya is 2,41,333 and 10,94,486 respectively. Bulk of the non-tribal population being settlers in urban centres-the percentage of non-tribal population of the State is 19.01 and in the rural category only 13.60% (SHB 1982.20), the Meghalayan rural population is distinctively tribal (86.13%). The maximum burden of tribal labour force is thus on the primary sector--about 79% of the total working population. The most disturbing trend of the economy is that more than 50% of the rural population of the State are non-workers. In the absence of any alternative avenues of employment, more than 50% of the rural population remain half starved. The following table (Table1) showing the number of main workers, marginal workers and non-workers indicates a very sad state of affairs in the agrarian sector. The situation is not bright either in the urban centres. Even taking that a sizeable portion of these population is female, the situation does not alter much because by tradition females constitute a major portion of the tribal working force in Meghalaya, both in the

Table 1

RURAL AND URBAN WORKING POPULATION IN MEGHALAYA-1981

Total Rural Urban	*Main workers*	*Marginal workers*	*Non-workers*	*Total*
T	5,87,158	19.912	7,21,273	1,328,343
R	5,10,654	17,933	5,61,255	10,88,842
U	76,504	1,979	1,61,018	2,39,501

Source : *Statistical Hand Book, Meghalaya*,1982, Directorate of Economics, Statistics and Evaluation, Meghalaya, p. 141.

town and in the villages.

The land utilisation figures (Table 2) show that of the total geographical area, forest occupies 36.12%, the area not available for cultivation is 13.89%, fallow land is 13.87% the land that remained uncultivated constitutes 27.55% and the net area sown is only 8.57%. The available net cropped area is now mostly mono-cropped(1,47,000 hectares approximately) and only approximately 35,000 hectares or 16% of the net cropped area is under double cropping (Sarma 1981). This is also reflected in the production of rice, the staple crop, which remained almost static for last few year (Table 3).

Shifting cultivation (*jhum*) still continues to be a popular and natural mode of production in Meghalaya. Approximately, 41% of the net sown area is under *jhum*. This is a system of production which is a typical case of a stationary economy where production is predominantly for self-consumption only and the system of exchange is almost non-existent. The yield rate is about half of al! India average. The Directorate of Agriculture of the State has also very candidly admitted that the State will continue as deficit for several more years to come at the present pace of food grain production (Sarma,1981). The rate of growth of food production is much slower than the rate of population. Percentage variation of Meghalaya Population between 1971-81 is 32.04 (SHB,1982:5). The present density of population, that varies between 33 per sq.km. in West Khari Hills to 98 in East Khasi Hills (Table 4) also suggests an increasing pressure on land. On the other hand, it has been calculated that lands under shifting cultivation can hardly support a population of more than 20 per sq mile (Borthakur *et al*, 1976:85). It is, therefore, not surprising that 74% of the rural population and 57% of the urban population in the State were found to be below poverty line at the beginning of the Sixth Plan. It has also been estimated that the States production alone is unable to meet even 60% of the total foodgrains requirement and that 4.6 lakh people of the state are victims of under-nutrition and remain hungry at their food intake level (Chaudhury 1985:54).

From the angle of productivity there cannot be two opinion about the urgency of a changeover from shifting cultivation to settled cultivation. Agricultural Scientists also speak of an urgent necessity to develop suitable technologies and land use system in order to increase productivity in the areas now under *jhum* cultivation (Borthakur,1979:4). Administrators and planners are equally aware of the problem (Sinha,1976; Khongwir,1979;Sarma,1981).

Table 2

LAND UTILISATION IN MEGHALAYA 1975-76 TO 1978-79

(In hectares)

Heading 1	*1975-76* 2	*1976-77* 3	*1977-78* 4	*1978-79* 5
I. Geographical area	22,48,900	22,48,900	22,48,900	22,48,900
II. Reporting area for Land Utilization Statistics	22,48,900	22,48,900	22,48,900	22,48,900
1. Forest	8,22,998	8,22,934	8,13,330	8,12,420
2. Not available for cultivation	3,09,182	3,09,161	3,13,050	3,12,525
3. Other uncultivated land excluding fallow land	6,13,572	6,13,400	6,22,000	6,19,662
4. Fallow land	3,29,324	3,29,282	3,22,290	3,11,968
5. Net area sown	1,73,824	1,74,123	1,78,250	1,92,773
6. Area sown more than once	29,193	29,484	30,580	30,597
7. Total cropped area	2,03,017	2,03,607	2,08,830	2,23,370
III. 1. Net Irrigated area	43,230	44,851	46,836	47,943
2. Gross irrigated area	45,748	49,327	48,187	49,917

Source : Statistical HandBook, Meghalaya, 1982 Directorate of Economics, Statistics and Evaluation, Meghalaya, Shillong. pp.36-37.

Table 3

AREA AND PRODUCTION OF RICE IN MEGHALAYA

Area-Hectares

Production-'000 Tonnes

	1979-80		*1980-81*		*1981-82*	
	Area	*Production*	*Area*	*Production*	*Area*	*Production*
	1	*2*	*3*	*4*	*5*	*6*
Rice						
(a) Autumn	30,487	28	30,755	32	34,387	36
(b) Winter	66,542	91	67,035	98	71,047	86
(c) Spring	1,655	3	1,250	2	1,795	3
Total	98,684	122	99,040	132	1,07,229	125

Source : *Statistical Hand Book, Meghalaya,* 1982. Directorate of Economics, Statistics and Evaluation,Meghalaya, Shillong, pp. 38-39.

Table 4

DENSITY OF POPULATION PER SQ. KM. IN THE DISTRICTS OF MEGHALAYA 1981

Jaintia Hills	-	41
East Khasi Hills	-	98
West Khasi Hills	-	33
East Garo Hills	-	52
West Garo Hills	-	66

Source : *Statistical Hand Book, Meghalaya, 1982*. Directorate of Economics, Statistics and Evaluation, Meghalaya, Shillong, pp.12-13.

But except some half-hazard scheme and piecemeal measures the Government has not done anything important to vitalize the agrarian sector by adopting a scientific land use system and introducing progressive land reforms.

One of the constraints, it appears, is the existing land system. Land here is not merely an economic category; it is bound up with the social, political and cultural institutions. But planned development requires drastic changes in tribal land system and any attempt to such change may face shifting cultivation to settled cultivation could not be made effective. But a question is involved here: Whether the opposition is real at the popular level or manipulated. The question arises because the land system in the State has long since deviated from the tribal egalitarian mould. If the communal ownership of land was real, it might not be altogether difficult for the government to plan for a communal holding in an enlarged form under a new setting, what is rather difficult in other regions with exclusive private rights on land. We have shown elsewhere (Sen,1985:54-64) that new agrarian relations have developed in Khasi-Jaintia Hills of Meghalaya. A good portion of land is now under private ownership, the extent of which is impossible to measure in the absence of cadastral survey and records of rights. A number of case studies in recent years has also shown concentration of landholdings under the ownership of a few families in a village with consequent rise in landlessness and share cropping in Khasi-Jaintia Hills of Meghalaya (Vincent, 1976;Lahiri, 1979; Blah,1981). A typical case is the village Hat Mawdon in Mawsynram Block where out of fifteen families, eleven were found to be landless and were share croppers in the lands owned by the other four families (Dutta,1981). This is a situation which negates the hitherto believed notion that land in the Khasi and Jaintia Hills are under communal ownership. The situation in Garo Hills is not different either. (Kar, 1981). That the government was aware of this situation is manifest in the appointment of a Land Reforms Commission for Khasi Hills as early as 1973. This was felt necessary to remove the confusion and misunderstanding with regard to the real land tenure in the hills (MLA Proceedings, March 1973). But though a number of memoranda submitted to the Commission indicated a large scale alienation of land and a phenomenal growth of landless labour and the Commission also admitted that the customary laws on land management allowed absolute private ownership under a category known as *Ri-Kynti* distinguishable from another category known as *ri raid* under communal management, it merely documented the existing pattern and did not recommend any reform of the existing land tenure. The government also did not take any further step in this regard. The obvious reasons were political opposition. We have shown elsewhere (Sen, 1984) that no political party in Meghalaya, neither national nor regional, except the CPI, has any comment to make on the prevailing land tenure or to suggest any reform for agricultural growth towards a desired direction. Some of these parties are distinctly in favour of retaining the existing land management. They project the traditional system. In Garo Hills it was also observed that through various development schemes the State government virtually sponsored such fissions of communal ownership. For example, all terrace-plots initially prepared and financed by the government were subsequently allotted permanently to different householders (Kar,1981).

This policy might be the outcome of certain formulations of the development planning canvassed by some on the plea that when a tribal society is involved in the process of modern economic development it has gradually to tear itself away from such a system and to consider land only as an economic category (Dutta,1985). Land viewed simply as an economic category shall also has to be taken as economically productive source for profit. That in Meghalaya it has already been viewed as a source of profit is evident from the clandestine usurption of communal right into private rights. A fifty year old report states that in Khasi-Jaintia Hills much of the communal land (*ri raid*) was converted into private possession (*ri kynti*) and in the areas nearer Shillong where land fetched high prices certain village headmen claimed that the raid durbar had a right to sell raid lands and give these lands to people as *rikynti* (David Roy,1934:121).It is to be remembered that the *ri kynti* owners, known as bakhraws are considered as aristocrats controlled the village and State councils (Sen,1985: 132-53). These aristocratic clans always owned better and more fertile lands in the villages and mostly waste and less fertile lands were distributed among other clans known as *khian kur* or commoners' clans (Pakem,1984). A research conducted in the Umroi Village in East Khasi Hills indicates that many structural changes have occured in the land system due to the influence of economic lust of wealth acquisition of a few outstanding clans (Blah 1981). The land Reforms Commission for Khasi Hills (1974) also admits such processes of conversion. The Chairman of the land Reforms Commission laments that land tenure remained feudal even after so many years of independence and land is owned mostly as private property and partly as community property (Rymbai,1976: 231-40). According to the Khasi custom and the very logic of communal ownership of land suggests that a family can hold land only in the village where they reside. But there has been transfer of land between persons who are residents of different areas giving rise to absentee landlordism and share cropping. A field investigation report of 1948 states that in the village Mawphlang in the East Khasi Hills a family owned says that in Mynsain village out of 30 families, 6 families have land of their own for cultivation and the major portion of paddy gowing land is owned by a person who is not a resident of that village (Lahiri,1979:87). In Garo Hills also the traditionally ownership pattern has been replaced by private ownership. Traditionally land belonged to the community that granted usufructuary rights to individual families. The settlements are divided into a number of well-defined areas (*akhing*) each under the common ownership and usufruct rights to the members of a particular clan (*mahan*). Plots of lands were distributed among the families and the clan chief (*nokma*) was the distributing authority. This arrangement itself has given rise to a class of landed interests. The British Government had also encouraged a fission in the egalitarian set up and created Zamidars and Mahari-Lakeraj particularly along the foothills. Some recent case studies in certain areas such as Rongram and Asanang in West Garo Hills indicate transfer to cultivable lands from communal ownership to the possessions of individual families.

Thus when development requirement demands the treatment of land as an economic category, a question arises immediately whether the erstwhile egalitarian system of communal ownership be replaced by private ownership with fragmentation of land into plots under legal sanction or the traditional system be strengthened by removing the obstacles to communal management. The first alternative tacitly allows the fast growing trends of alienation of land by a class that holds economic power and probably regulates the political power centres whereas the second alternative suggests putting a stop to all the obvious methods by which the communally owned land are gradually being converted into private land. The choice is both economic and political. But yet no political party in the State has spelt out its choice. The only suggestion that the manifestoes of the parties operating in the State, except the CPI, made is that the traditional system of land management should continue (Sen,1983). If it is so done ignoring the deviations that affected the very core of the tribal life, then probably the first causalty will be 'development'. We have shown elsewhere (Sen1985 b) that the customary tenure itself has allowed the growth of private holding of land and a class of landed gentry who wields political power. The choice for the government in a tribal State line Meghalaya should have been obvious: streamlining the customary tenure to evolve communal/co-operative farming under communal or state management. The traditional egalitarian mould also provided a congenial setting. But the government has not yet shown any preference for such a choice.

Industrial Scene and Employment Situation

From the industrial point of view Meghalaya is one of the most backward States in the country with only 55 registered factories with 3,075 employees in 1981 (SHB, 1982:64). In 1980 the registered small scale industries were only 177 with an average daily employment of 1,440 person (SHB,1982:66). The situation has not improved since. It is also significant that according to government statistics the number of employees in the 55 registered industrial units has come down to 2638 in 1982. (Maghalaya at a Glance, 1983:5). This indicates a very sad state of affairs in the industrial sector. It seems, for reason other than economic, there is lack of much interest towards industrialisation of the State. Neither the political parties have ever demanded industrialisation (Sen, 1984).

In the absence of industrialisation the maximum of labour force is on the primary sector which bears 79.02% of the State's total working force. We have already observed the state of economy in the primary sector with very low productivity, and a phenomenal growth of share cropping and landless labour. In the absence of alternative channel of employment which could be ensured by industrialisation, unemployment in the primary sector, both real and disguised, is bound to be on the increase.

There is another disturbing trend in the employment scene. With the increasing burden of unemployment in the primary sector there will be a push towards urban centres. But with a negligible industrial employment potential, the service sector remains the only employment source in the urban centres. Table 5 will show the increasing pressure on this sector and the maximum burden is on the State Government. Between 1978 to 1982 the number of employees in the State Government services has increased from 17,317 to 24,199 i.e. a phenomenal increase of 39.74%. If this trend continues, the service sector employment opportunities will also reach a saturation point in the near future. This also signifies an unequal distribution of employment opportunities between the different urban centres in the State and between different districts because most of the offices are located in Shillong, the capital. It has been estimated that the East Khasi Hills district where Shillong is situated has largest share of 60.64% of the total employment. Followed by 20.22% of the West Garo Hills district, 10.84% of the Jaintia Hills district, 4.39% of the East Garo Hills district and 3.91% of the West Khasi Hills district (Dutta, 1982).

A potential danger is seen in the growth of education in the general stream. The literacy rate as per 1981 Census is 33.35% in the State, of which the scheduled tribe literacy rate counts 31.55% (SHB 1982: 186-88). With the increasing preference for higher education in the general stream there will be further burden in years to come on the service sector which is the second largest source of employment. Man-power development in the proper sense of the term is in a very low key in the state.

Table 5

SECTORAL EMPLOYMENT IN MEGHALAYA AS ON 31ST MARCH

Sector	*1978*	*1979*	*1980*	*1981*	*1982*
Public					
i. General Government	9007	8811	8786	9900	10012
ii State Government	17317	18707	19491	22528	24199
iii. State Quasi Government	4780	4948	5075	5353	5424
iv. Central Quasi-Government	1060	1778	2278	2945	3482
v. Local Bodies	4956	5005	5028	3041	3077
Private					
Larger Establishments	2663	2695	2986	3218	3951
Smaller Establishments	1087	1151	1367	1311	1194
TOTAL	40870	43095	45011	48296	50439

*Source : 32nd Round National Sample Survey on Employment and Unemployment in Meghalaya and All India.*Directorate of Economic Statistics and Evaluation, Meghalaya, Shillong, 1984, p. 17.

Potentialities

Both for agricultural and industrial development, Meghalaya is potentially rich. Findings of Indian Council of Agricultural Research. suggest that all types of crops, from tropical to temperate, can be grown in the State because of its topography. It is also the primary and secondary home of the origin of many crops and the variability of genetic resources available in the area of such crops is the great assest to improve the crops (Borthakur,1979:8). With a suitable land use system, adequate technology and effective land reform measures, the State can very well forge ahead in agricultural growth.

In Meghalaya 36.12% of the total area is under forest. Before independence important items of border trade between the hills and the plains were forest produce. Various types of timber, bamboo, cane, root, medicinal plants, edible leaves etc. were such trade items. These are abundantly available in the State and can very well be used as industrial inputs. Forest experts also suggest that a planned forest development scheme can ensure that trees produced in 15 or 20 years are consumed by forest based industries like paper and pulp. (Rynjah,1976:155). Some trees like Eucalyptus, which is a fast growing tree and can easily be grown in Meghalaya, is usable as an industrial input.

But as in the case of agriculture and industry, in the case of forestry also, no clear cut policy is apparent. It is true that because of the lacunae in the currently practised customary land tenure and a clash of authority between the government and the District Councils, who are in the management of forests, the government finds difficulty in extending its area of operation in forest management. But there is an advantage in Meghalaya. With communal ownership of forests, the state provides an opportunity of growing of forests, the state provides an opportunity of growing trees by communities themselves (understood here as villagers of clusters called *raid* in the Khasi-Jaintia Hills and *akhing* in the Garo Hills). Forest experts believe if such programmes are undertaken a sustained annual yield becomes assured and the produce can successfully be used in forest based industries (Rynjah,1976:156). But then forestry is to be planned as part of agrarian programme which in Meghalaya requires urgent land reform measures to ensure true communal ownership that characterizes a tribal setting.

Mineral resources are equally rich in the State. Certain minerals are found in abundance such as limestone and sillimanite. A fairly continuous belt of limestone deposit exists along the southern slopes of Meghalaya. The richest deposit is, however, in south Cherrapunji in the Khasi Hills where at present there is a cement factory, the only one in the public sector. The Khasi limestone was one of the major trade items during the colonial rule. Sillimanite deposit is also found in large quantity in the Khasi Hills. There are also other important minerals such as Beryl, Shale, Corrundum, Kaolin and Dolomite.

The possibilities of industrial development are usually considered under two heads--the resource based industries and non-resource based industries. Development of backward areas like Meghalaya can be rapid by establishing resource-based industries, in view of the vast agricultural, forest and mineral resources. Agro-based and forest-based industries in particular can be developed with very little effort.

Coal deposit is also very large in Meghalaya. The total estimated quantity of coal in the State is about 1500 million tonnes. Coal from Khleriat in Jaintia Hills and Cherrapunji in Khasi Hills now form a major trade. But because of the uncertainty in the land system, as discussed above, it is difficult to ascertain who are the beneficiaries of this trade. One statement can, however, be safely made that neither the state nor the people derive the benefit. A major step for structural transformation of economy of the State would be to nationalise the coal industry in the State. A prior step for it would, however, be a scientific and progressive land reform determining the proper land rights by removing the confusions in the customary land tenure. This is necessary to determine ownership rights in the coal belt.

But all this seems to be a far cry. If the experience of last 15 years has anything to suggest then we can be sure of one distinct trend in the economic and political life of Meghalaya. There has not been any serious attempt so far to evolve a proper development strategy and planning. It might be that the political will was also lacking.

National Tribal Development Policy Questioned

The foregoing discussion leads us to an examination of hitherto followed national tribal development policy, particularly in the context of development in a predominantly tribal State like Meghalaya. This policy was initially based on the Panchsheel of tribal development enunciated by Jawaharlal Nehru under the inspiration of leading anthropologists of the country, particularly of Verrier Elwin. Experience suggests that Nehru-Elwin approach was nothing more than a 'Welfare approach' indicating a sympathy and concern for tribal welfare and development and the nation's readiness to provide funds for improving the conditions of tribal life. Very legitimately this policy is now criticized as inadequate for tribal development. In a recently held symposium at Shillong a tribal scholar has stated categorically that tribal development, to be truly effective, cannot depend on the charity of social welfare agencies. The emphasis should be on growth and self-reliance.

She further says that while this policy has led to the emergence of a new class of elite and a proliferation of political leaders with improved standards of life and status, it has not made significant impact on the majority of tribal population,most of whom live in abject poverty (Nongbri,1985).

Although it is admitted that the 'Welfare approach' might have been the appropriate one at the beginning of the 1950, it should now only play a subsidiary role to the integrated political, economic and social approach (Roy Burman, 1972:97). The development measures and the administrative arrangements for their implementation and the objective of hastening the establishment of schools, dispensaries and other paraphernalia of conventional five year plans have been very rightly questioned (Rustomji,1982). That the tribal population in the North-east finds safety in regionalism is also believed to be due to this still continuing policy (Jafa, 1982).

In fact, despite all the pious wishes of the policy framers inspired by the romantic tribal sanctuary scheme of Nehru and Elwin, the national tribal development policy till today could never shake off its paternalistic veneer. That this approach did not work satisfactorily is by and large admitted now supported by the evidences of socio-political tensions in the the tribal areas of the country. Unfortunately the development schemes and administrative arrangements could never inspire confidence among the tribal people.

Subsidy Approach

In the changed situation after 1970, particularly in north-east India with the establishment of States and Union Territories in the tribal areas a new 'subsidy approach' has only replaced the earlier 'welfare approach', retaining in most part the policy of paternalistic support without evolving a development policy under which development efforts could be generated from within. The tribal sub-Plans in the States where tribals are in the minority, are yet to be anything but welfare schemes. The tribal States of NE India, however, have their own State plan. But their revenue raising capacity being low they thrive by subsidy from the centre. The 1983-84 Meghalaya State budget shows in the Revenue Receipts the share of central taxes as Rupees 957 lakhs and the State tax is Rupees 659.47 lakhs. While the non-tax revenue of the State is Rupees

1174.47 lakhs, the central non-tax revenue amounts to Rupees 9524.46 lakhs (Meghalaya at a glance, 1983).

With so much dependence on central assistance, without any significant movements towards capital formation through industrialisation and revitalisation of agrarian sector with an emphasis on self-reliance the growth rate is sure to be low and a subsidized economy is bound to be counter productive with accelerating rate of unemployment and upward inflationary trend. The 'subsidy approach' is thus considered as much damaging as the 'Welfare approach' of earlier days. Any development policy and model under which the people are treated as beneficiaries of welfare doles without any direct involvement in the development process can bring anything but development.

Under this arrangement whatever growth takes place will be accrued mostly to political, bureaucratic, professional and landed elites. They will be the principal beneficiaries of the subsidy system. A group of construction contractors, transport operators and the like will emerge who will have control over and access to decision making process. It is true, in the initial phase, a section of the population will derive benefits of the subsidized economy through education, and employment in the service sector. A few of them will also form the construction contractors group for competing at different decision making levels. But without a process of self-sustaining growth from within rural poverty will be on the increase and urban employment potential will saturate and fail to match the fast growing unemployment problem.

In sum, the subsidy approach is a benefit for a tiny minority of power elites while the large majority of the population remains alienated. This approach can never generate a self-sustaining growth.

References

Blah, R. P. (1981) 'Past and Present Agrarian Social Structure', paper presented in a *Seminar on Land and Land Relations in the Hills of North East India* NEICSSR, Shillong (unpublished).

Borthakur, D. N. *et. al*.. (1976) 'Alternative Systems of Farming for increasing Productivity in Jhum Land', *Shifting Cultivation in North East India*, Ed. B. P. Pakem *et. al*. NEICSSR, Shillong.,

Borthakur, D. N. (1979) 'Problem of Agricultural development', *Agriculture in the Hills : A case Study of Mehgalaya* Ed. B. Datta Ray, NEICSSR, Shillong.

Chattopadhyay, K. P. (1948) 'Khasi Land ownership and Sale', *Eastern Anthropologist*, Vol. 2.

Chaudhury, Rabindra Kumar (1985) 'Nutrition in Meghalaya', *Point Counterpoint*', Vol. I No. 3. (Calcutta)

Dutta, B. B. (1981) 'Land Relation in Khasi Hills- A study in Ownership and Alienation', paper presented in a *Seminar on Land and Land Relation in the Hills of North East India*, NEICSSR, Shillong (unpublished)

.... (1983) 'Politics of Unemployment - A Case of Meghalaya, Paper presented in a *Seminar on Unemployment Problem in the North East*, Gauhati University (unpublished).

.... (1985) Issues of Tribal Development In N.E. India- A Case Study of Khasi-Jaintia Tribal Setting, Paper presented in a *Seminar on Tribal Demography and Development* North-Eastern Hill University (unpublished).

Government of Meghalaya (1974) *Report of the Land Reforms Commission for Khasi Hills*.

.... (1982) *Statistical Hand Book* (SHB) (Directorate of Economics, Statistics and Evaluation, Meghalaya, Shillong).

.... (1983) *Meghalaya At a Glance* (Directorate of Economics, Statistics and Evaluation, Meghalaya, Shillong).

.... (1984) *Report of National Sample Survey, 32nd Round* (NSS 32) (Directorate of Economics, Statistics and Evaluation, Meghlalaya, Shillong).

Jafa Jyoti (1982) 'Safety in Regionalism-Self Expression in the North-East', *The Statesman* (Calcutta, 19 November).

Kar, P. C. (1979) 'Land Relations and Changing Agricultural Practice', *Agriculture in the Hills: A Case Study of Meghalaya* Ed. B. Datta Ray (NEICSSR, Shillong).

.... (1981) 'Note on the Changing Land ownership Among the Garos of Meghalaya', Papers presented in a *Seminar on Land and Land Relations in the Hills of North East India* (NEICSSR, Shillong) unpublished.

Knongwir, S. D. (1979) 'Inaugural Address', *Seminar on Agriculture in the Hills : A Case Study of Meghalaya*, Ed. B. Datta Ray NEICSSR, Shillong.

Lahiri, Binoy, (1979) 'Land Relations and Changing Agricultural Practice, *Agriculture in the Hills: A Case*

Study of Meghalaya, Ed. B. Datta Ray NEICSSR, Shillong.

Meghalaya Legislative Assembly (1983) *Proceedings*, March 1973.

Nongbri, Tiplut, (1985) *Focus of the Symposium on Tribal Demography and Development* North Eastern Hill University.

Pakem, B. (1984) 'State Formation in Pre-Colonial Jaintia, *The NEHU Journal of social Sciences and Humanities*, Vol. II, No.3

Roy Burman, B. K. (1972) 'Integrated Area Approach to the Problems of the Hill Tribes of North East India', *Tribal Situation in India*, Ed. K. Suresh Singh IIAS, Simla.

Roy, David (1934) 'Land Tenure in the States', *Notes on Khasi Law*, K. Cantlie (A.S. Khongpai (Ed), Shillong).

Rustomji, Nari (1982) 'Frontier Blunder's', *The Statesman* (Calcutta), 25-26 October.

Rymbai, R. T. (1976) Land Reforms and Tribal Economy', *Proceedings of the Seminar on Tribal Economy* Ed. T. Mathew Department of Economics, NEHU, Shillong,Mimeographed.

Rynjah, .L. (1976) 'Role of Forest and Agriculture in Tribal Economy', *Proceedings of the Seminar on Tribal Economy* Ed. T. Mathew, Department of Economics, NEHU, Shillong Mimeographed.

Sarma, A.K. (1981) Land Use Under Permanent Plough Cultivation in Meghalaya, Paper presented in a *Seminar on land and Land Relations in the Hills of NE India* NEICSSR, Shillong. (unpublished).

Sen Soumen (1983) Election Manifestoes of Parties in Meghalaya, Paper presented in a *Seminar on Electoral Politics in NE India* NEICSSR, Shillong. (Unpublished)

.... (1984) Regionalism in the North-East and Regional Parties of Meghalaya, *Interdiscipline* Vol. 15, No. 2.

.... (1985) *Social and State Formation in Khasi-Jaintia Hills* B.R. Publishing Corporation, New Delhi.

..................(1985b) A Case Study of Khasi-Jaintia Customary Land Tenure, *Point Counterpoint* Calcutta Vol. 1. No. 1.

Sinha, K. K. (1976) The Problem of Shifting Cultivation in Meghalaya--Effort towards Solution, *Proceedings of the Seminar on Tribal Economy*, Ed. T. Mathew, Department of Economics, NEHU, Shillong Mimeographed.

Vincent, K. (1976) A Peasant Economy in a Tribal Area--A Case Study of Bhoilymbong Village in the Khasi Hills of Meghalaya, *Proceedings of the Seminar on Tribal Economy*, Ed.T. Mathew Department of Economics, NEHU Shillong Mimeographed.

CHAPTER 9

Strategies for Tribal Development in North-East India With Special Reference to Assam

B. N. Bordoloi

Introduction

When we speak of Tribal Development as a concept, it reminds us that sets of strategies are essential for the development of the tribal communities in India. Here one may raise some pertinent questions. Why are the strategies for development of the general people cannot be applied for the development of the tribal people? Why do we need separate strategies for the development of the tribal people? In what respects the tribals in India differ from the other people?

Answers to these questions are very much obvious. The tribal communities in India are regarded as the weakest section of the society although it is an admitted fact that a few Tribal Communities are at a far advanced stage of development.

The Dhebar Commission(1961) had divided the tribal communities in India into four broad layers or groups:

(i) at the bottom a class in an extremely under developed stage.

(ii) at the top-most level a class or layer which can afford to forge any further help and in between these two layers there are two more classes with varying degrees of acculturation and development.

Even today, after 23 years' of Dhebar Commission's Report, the situations have not changed much and still we can well demarcate four categories of tribal communities in India designating them as primitive, shifting-cultivators, transitional groups and advance groups.

Dr. L. P. Vidyarthi, however, has classified the tribal communities in India into six cultural types i.e. (i) Forest-hunting type, (2) Primitive Hill Cultivation type, (3) Plain Agricultural Type, (4) Simple Artisan Type, (5) Cattle herder Type and (6) Industrial-Urban Workers Type. All these categories need separate strategies for development. In formulating the development strategies for the tribal communities, their eco-system, ethnicity and other socio-cultural factors are given due importance.

DEVELOPMENT STRATEGIES FOR THE NORTH-EAST TRIBES DURING PRE-INDEPENDENCE PERIOD

The British Government did not formulate any rational policy for the development of the tribal communities of north-east India and as such they did not have any development strategies for them in the true sense of the term. The areas inhabited by the tribals were either excluded or partially excluded ones. The British Government allowed the tribals to manage their own affairs and did not interfere in their internal matters unless it was absolutely necessary. Their *Laissez faire* policy or policy of segregation and isolation paid them good dividend. The main intention of the British Government was to keep the tribal people as far as practicable at a long distance from the rest of the population. They followed this policy to suit the needs of the administration and found that it has been working well in serving their interest to the full.

Each tribal community is a distinctive unit with its own socio-cultural background and values. As a matter of fact the tribes differ from each other ethnically, linguistically and socio-culturally. Their problems differ from tribe to tribe and from region to region. Even among the members of the same tribe the local problems have different dimensions. Similarly the pace of development, not to speak of different tribes, is not at all uniform among the members of the same tribe inhabiting different regions. What, therefore, holds good in one case may not necessarily apply to other cases. Long years of isolation have made the matter worse.

Loss of basic resources like land or forest, prolonged exploitation in various forms, tapping of natural resources of tribal areas by external agencies, non-tribal cultural arrogance, a psychological feeling of being ignored or injured, low level of nutrition, illiteracy, and such other problems faced by the tribal communities have made it rather obligatory on the part of the Government to formulate separate development strategies for the tribal communities.

It would, however, be quite injustice to say that during the British days nothing had been done for the development of the tribal people in the north-east India because of the lack of a clear-cut policy of tribal development. But we shall have to remember that whatever development activities were performed by the British Government for the development of the tribal people of this region, they were undertaken not in the interest of the tribal people, but to serve the interests, both administrative and commercial of the rulers. New railway lines were opened to carry coals, timbers, oil, tea, etc., from this region to outside, roads were constructed to connect district and sub-divisional Headquarters so that soldiers and police personnel could be sent quickly as soon as some tribal uprisings were reported. To offer basic amenities to the Government employees serving especially at the district and sub-divisional headquarters opening up of educational institutions, hospitals and dispensaries, provision for drinking water supply, opening up of commercial establishments, trade centres, markets etc., considered absolutely essential. The tribal people living in the north-east region had reaped some of the benefits of development schemes primarily meant for providing basic amenities to the employees of the British rulers and other infrastructural facilities created for smooth running of the administration and also for serving the commercial interests of the rulers.

Under the patronage of the British rulers the Christian missionaries had done a yeoman's service in spreading education and offering medical and other social welfare facilities to the tribal people of north-east India. The high percentage of literacy amongst the tribes of north-east India can bc accounted for this.

To supply essential commodities and other consumption goods to the personnel connected with administration, maintenance of law and order, etc., the British rulers allowed traders and merchants mostly from outside the north-east India to make an inroad to the tribal areas. These people in course of time settled in the tribal areas permanently and started exploiting the people in various ways. They at the same time, tried to establish a bond of friendship with the tribal people and the trading community became their(tribals') friends, philosophers and guides in due course. By taking advantage of the tribal people's simplicity, truthfulness and ignorance, these traders exploited them to the highest possible extent.

The British rulers, however, kept a close contact with the tribal chiefs of the different ethnic groups in north-east India and through them dao tax and house tax were collected. These tribal chiefs who had a good command over their community members, were like petty kings with their small kingdoms and subjects. The British Government always tried their best to have a friendly relationship with these tribal chiefs by following the policy of least interference. But even then, during the early period of the British rule there were frequent uprisings against the British among the hill tribal communities of North-East India. Sometimes the entire British encampment was ravaged to the ground at night killing all the inmates. Thus to keep the tribes of North-East India under control was rather a grave problem for the British rulers as there had been a feeling of distrust between the rulers and the ruled. The British Government's approach towards the tribals to make them feel the impact of administration was very gradual and for fear of reprisal, no specific strategies for tribal development were enunciated. Although the Government of India Act, 1935, had envisaged some development strategies for the tribal communities in India, they were primarily meant for the tribes of Central India and not for the tribes of north-east India.

From the above we can conclude that the British Government did not have specific strategies for development of the tribal communities of north-east India.

DEVELOPMENT STRATEGIES FOR TRIBALS DURING POST-INDEPENDENCE PERIOD

(a) Constitutional Frame

Tribal development, as we understand today, has taken its root from the Constitution of India itself. Article 46 which is otherwise known as the Directive Principles of State Policy lays down that the State shall promote with special care the educational and economic interests of the weaker sections and in particular of the Scheduled Castes and Scheduled Tribes. The State shall also protect them from social injustice and all forms of exploitation. Article 244 empowers the President of India to declare an area as a Scheduled or Tribal Area under the Fifth Schedule and (or) the Sixth Schedule separately. It is also very interesting to note that the Sixth Schedule was created only for the hill tribal areas of Assam(undivided). Since the hill tribal communities of Assam had their own systems of administration through their traditional socio-political institutions, the founding fathers of the Constitution of India created this special provision with a view to allowing the Autonomous District Councils to manage their own affairs including the development aspects according to their likings.

Article 339 (2) lays down that the executive powers of the union extend to the giving of directions to a State as to the drawing up and execution of schemes for welfare of the Scheduled Tribes in the state.

Article 275 provides for financial assistance to the States for implementation of schemes of development of Scheduled Tribes and raising the level of administration in the Scheduled areas. The Constitution also makes a provision for appointment of a Commissioner for Scheduled Castes and Scheduled Tribes. He has to oversee whether the Constitutional guarantees have been properly implemented. He makes an Annual Report to the President and this report is presented to the Parliament so that its members can oversee the progress in the tribal areas.

The founding fathers of the Constitution of India under Article 339 provided for the setting up of a Commission at the end of 10 years of the commencement of the Constitution to review the tribal situations and recommend measures for their development. This Commission set up in 1961 under the Chairmanship of Shri U.N. Dhebar, made extensive recommendations. The Constitutional provisions refer to the tribal development strategies in an implicit way only. In July, 1958, our Late Prime MInister, Jawaharlal Nehru explicitly enunciated the strategies for tribal development in more clear terms summarising them in five fundamental principles which are commonly known as 'Panchasheel' for tribal development. They are quoted below :-

1. People should develop along the lines of their own genius and we should avoid imposing anything on them. We should try to encourage in every way their own traditional arts and culture.

2. Tribals rights to land and forests should be respected.

3. We should try to train and build up a team of their own people to do the work of administration and development. Some technical personnel from outside will, no doubt, be needed especially in the beginning. But we should avoid too many outsiders into tribal territory.

4. We should not overadminister these areas or overwhelm them with a multiplicity of schemes. We should rather work through, and not in rivalry to their own social and cultural institutions.

5. We should judge results, not by statistics or the amount of money spent, but the quality of human character that is evolved.

The above five principles may be regarded as an integrated approach to tribal development. The strategies and objectives laid down in different five year plans reflect the underlying idea of the Panchasheel for tribal development. But, however, the strategies and objectives very often become square pegs in round holes and do not suit the changing panorama of tribal situations. In other words, when these strategies are translated into actions they rather fail to deliver the goods. A resume is given below:-

(1) During the First Five Year Plan emphasis was on education and economic development, improvement of roads and communication and provision for medical and public health facilities. An extensive rural development programme commonly known as community development

programme, was launched in early fifties aiming at total development of the rural masses. It was considered to be people's programmes with government participation. As the community development was a flexible model, it was thought expedient to apply this model to the development of tribal areas also with slight modifications.

(II) Thus during the Second Five Year Plan, special Multipurpose Development Projects/Blocks numbering 43 were created on the same model as Community Development Block with a higher investment of Rs. 27 lakhs for each Project/Block. Emphasis was given on economic development like agriculture, cottage industries, forest, co-operatives, etc.

A Study Team headed by Dr. Verrier Elwin reviewed the working of these S.M.P.D. Blocks and recommended a comparatively less intensive programme for tribal development blocks but extensive in coverage.

The Scheduled Areas and Scheduled Tribes Commission (1961), popularly known as the Dhebar Commission, while endorsing the Panchasheel of tribal development enunciated by Late Jawaharlal Nehru observed that "The problem of problems is not to disturb the harmony of tribal life and simultaneously work for its advance; not to impose anything upon the tribals and simultaneously work for their integration as members and part of the Indian family."

During the 3rd Five Year Plan 489 Community Development Blocks where percentage of tribal population was 66 or above were converted into Tribal Development Blocks. Thus the Tribal Development Block Programme was rather an intensification of Community Development Programme with higher investment of resources. The T.D. Block programme was expected to take care of all the problems in the tribal areas. By the end of the 4th Five Year Plan the number of T.D. Blocks was increased to 504. Although a third stage of intensive development was added to the T.D. Blocks, this programme had failed to deliver the goods because of the few major factors. First, the budgets of the T.D. Blocks were so schematic and rigid that flexibility to suit the felt needs of the people was rather a difficult proposition. Secondly, a larger section of the population was left out of this programme although another stage of five years of intensive development was added without there being any geographical expansion. Thirdly, there had not been any integrated approach for tribal development. Fourthly, micro-level or grass-roots planning for tribal development was more or less absent. And lastly, and not the least, is the dearth of adequate trained personnel with missionary zeal.

A Study Team on Tribal Development headed by Mr.P. Shilu Ao(1969) comprehensively reviewed the T.D. Block programme. This team suggested that there should be no attempt to transform the tribal people who are at various stages of development (from food gatherers to advanced ones) overnight into carbon copies of sophisticated plainsmen, but by fostering all that is good and beautiful in their culture--their acesthetic sense, honesty, zest for life. The Study Team further suggested that there should be progressive advancement social as well as economic with a view to their integration with the rest of the community on a footing of equality within a reasonable distance of time. The period of time has necessarily to vary from tribe to tribe depending on the degree of advancement of the tribe.

Whatever development strategies were undertaken for the development of more than 250 tribal communities in India till 4th Five Year Plan the fact remains that due consideration was not given to treat each tribe separately basing on the fact that there has been a wide divergence in their socio-economic, cultural and technological milieu. That is why, we have witnessed loud voices of protests, dissent and divisive tendencies among some tribal communities in the north-east. Economic backwardness with fear-psychosis of losing ethnic or group identity has compelled them to think in terms of getting away from national polity.

THE NEW STRATEGY

A. Background:

The Renuka Roy Committee, even as early as 1959, emphasised integrated programmes based on agriculture, forestry, handicrafts and village industries, their degree of emphasis depending upon the systematic survey of needs and possibilities in each tribal area. The Dhebar Commission (1961) also stressed an integrated approach. The Shilu Ao Team(1969) suggested an integrated perspective for development of each tribal community.

The Expert Committee set up in 1972 headed by Prof. S.C. Dube to formulate new strategy for tribal development in the country during the 5th Five Year Plan has equated tribal development as social and economic development of the tribal people through fast and time bound area development and other programmes suiting the genius of the people, progressive elimination of all forces of exploitation and ensuring a move towards the goal of equality and justice.

5th Five Year Plan

On the basis of the recommendations of the Dube Committee mentioned in the above para, the new strategies for tribal development were spelt out in the 5th Five Year Plan document.

Two important strategies are:

(i) An integrated approach to tribal development with a view to bridging the gap between the level of development of tribal areas and other areas.

(ii) Improving the 'Quality of Life' of the tribal people.

Tribal sub-Plan

The strategy for integrated approach to tribal development led to the launching of the Tribal sub-Plan during the Fifth (5th) Five Year Plan period. The concept of Tribal sub-Plan is based on three fundamental facts.

Firstly, there are variations in social, political, cultural milieu among the Scheduled Tribes communities in India.

Secondly, these communities are concentrated in some parts of some States and dispersed in other States.

Thirdly, the most backward tribes or primitive tribes live in secluded regions.

The immediate objectives of the tribal sub-Plan have been envisaged as the elimination of exploitation, accelerating the pace of socio-economic development, building inner strength of the people and improving their organisation capability.

The compact areas where the percentage of tribal population is 50 or above has been demarcated and brought under tribal sub-Plan. As the basic unit of planning and execution Integrated Tribal Development Projects have been created to cover the entire sub-Plan Area. At present there are 180 I.T.D.Ps. in India and in the Tribal sub-Plan Areas of Assam there are 19 I.T.D.Ps For each I.T.D.P., a project Report has to be prepared where the perspective development schemes of various development departments for a span of 5 years are incorporated after proper co-ordination. The Report also contains *interalia* the topography of the region, natural resources and their exploitation, core problems of the people, profile of the tribal communities, special sub-Region, growth centres and so on.

Resources for Tribal sub-Plan are pooled together (i) by quantifying an amount from the divisible State plan outlay, (ii) Special Central Assistance from the Home Ministry, Government of India, (iii) Grants from the Central Ministries and (iv) Institutional finance.

In Assam, about 80% of the Scheduled Tribes (Plains) population are covered by tribal sub-Plan. The remaining 20% of the Scheduled Tribes (Plains) population are covered by backward sector plan.

The tribal sub-Plan concept is not applicable to States like Arunachal Pradesh, Nagaland, Mizoram and Meghalaya in North-East where the majority of the population belong to Scheduled Tribes. Whatever development schemes are meant for the States can, therefore, be regarded as tribal development programmes.

It may, however, be mentioned that during the 5th Five Year Plan while more emphasis was given on the infrastructural development in the tribal areas, in the 6th Plan the approach has been changed and more emphasis has been given on the family oriented schemes.

CROSSING OF POVERTY LINE

Now the most important tribal development strategy whether that of tribal sub-Plan or of point 7 of the 20 Point Programme of the Prime

Minister is to enable 50% of the tribal families below the poverty line to cross the poverty line with individual family oriented schemes during the 6th Plan period.

Although the Planning Commission has computed the adjusted poverty line at Rs. 75/-(Seventy-five) per capita per month at 1979-80 prices, for the north-eastern states 20% increase is allowed due to higher price index in this region and hence it would come to Rs. 90/-(Ninety) per capita per month.

Various family beneficiary schemes by different development departments under Tribal sub-Plan as well as Point 7 of the 20th Point Programme have already been launched vigorously to generate sufficient monetary income to arrive at the goal of crossing the poverty line by 50% Scheduled Tribes families who are below the poverty line at present.

The most important development strategy so far as the plains tribal areas of Assam is concerned in recent times is the creation of the Tribal Development Authority in September 1983 for the accelerated development of the tribal people. It is a corporate body with a perpetual succession. The main functions of this Authority are:-

1.(a) To prepare short-term and long-term plans for all round socio-economic development of the areas to which this Authority is applicable.

(b) To formulate schemes for the development of the area in the context and within the frame-work of the State Plans.

(c) To recommend such other measures as may be considered necessary for accelerating the development of the area.

(d) To review the schemes for the development of the area and their progress from time to time.

(e) To call for their reports relating to the implementation of the development programmes in the end to suggest measures for co-ordination and supervision of the schemes.

2. The Authority may with the approval of the State Government set up such agency at Sub-Divisional or Block level as it may consider necessary for the effective discharge of its functions.

All sums received from the State Government for the development of the plains tribal areas shall be credited to the "Tribal Development Authority Fund" which is non-lapseable. The Authority shall have the power to take loans from the State Government on such terms and conditions as may be agreed upon.

It is hoped that this Authority will be in a position to implement the schemes meant for the development of the plains tribes in a more effective way as the tribal people themselves will be fully associated in preparing short-term as well as long-term plans for their all round socio-economic development. It will go in a long way in fulfilling Late Prime Minister Nehru's desire that the tribals should be allowed to develop according to their own genius.

For effective implementation of the tribal development programmes proper monitoring and evaluation are most essential. But unfortunately in the North-East this aspect has not so far received due attention. Evaluation by independent machineries is highly essential.

Strategies for tribal development enunciated by the Government from time to time are well intended. They are translated into actions by the officers of various levels at different stages. Unless these functionaries are properly trained and motivated mere allotment of huge financial outlays for tribal development would serve no purpose.

CONCLUDING OBSERVATIONS

From the preceding discussion it has now become apparent that tribal development as such can no longer be treated piecemeal at the convenience of the multiplicity of development agents including the Central and State Governments. An integrated approach based on the felt needs and priorities is the need of the hour.

The involvement of the tribal people in the development process is most essential and these can only be achieved by strengthening their traditional institutions and assigning a progressively increasing role in modern democratic development activities.

It has already been mentioned that during the 6th Five Year Plan emphasis has been given on the family oriented schemes. But such programmes can take off effectively with the contributions from the financial institutions. But unfortunately the flow of institutional finance is quite inadequate.

Tribal communities of the north-east India are passing through transitional stages. Development always presupposes changes and changes create numerous problems some of which are psychological and some physical. While the physical problems are discrenible and, therefore, can be tackled to certain degrees, the psychological problems more or less remain unattended. Hence no final word can be said about tribal development. Those who are entrusted with the planning and execution of tribal development programmes must begin to think first from the tribals' point of view. And this is the need of the hour.

References

Bordoloi, B.N. (1982a) *Tribal Development and National Integration in North-East India with Special Reference t to Assam.* Paper presented at the Symposium held during the 7th Indian Social Science Congress in New Delhi in June, 1982.

......................(1982b) *Tribal Development in North-East India with Special reference to Assam* --Paper presented at the Seminar on Problems of Economic Development in North-East India organised by the Department of Economics, Dibrugarh University, in November, 1982.

Mehta, Om (1981) *Tribal Development - the New Strategy.*

Ministry of Home Affairs (1979a) *Occasional Papers on Tribal Development,* Xth International Congress of Anthropological and Ethnological Science and Tribal Development.

.....................(1979b) *Report of Group on Administrative Arrangements and Personnel Policies in Tribal Areas* - Government of India.

........................(1980) *Report on working Group on Tribal Development during Sixth Plan (1980-85),* Government of India.

n.d. *Planning Strategy for Tribal Development in Restrospect and Prospect,* Government of India.

Planning Commission (1981) *Report on Developments of Tribal Areas* - National Committee on the Development of Backward Areas.

Sharma, B.D. (1982) *Tribal Development - The New Strategy* (Paper presented in Eleventh Course on Tribal Development Administration - I.I.P.A., New Delhi).

CHAPTER 10

'Tribal' Development in Sikkim : A Tale of Unused Experiences

Tanka Bahadur Subba

Introduction

Sikkim, before the establishment of Namgyal dynasty in 1642, was an obscure Himalayan territory ruled by 'tribal' chiefs. The Lepchas, Limbus and the Mangars, who lived in and ruled different parts of it often fought amongst themselves, which paved the way for the non-Sikkimese to establish a formal political structure there. Though the Lepchas were also later given high administrative posts like *dzongpens* or district chiefs, they usually played the second fiddle. There is no record of the Mangars and the Limbus being placed in such high positions. In fact, they were identified with the later Napalese 'immigrants' and even granting of headmenships of the revenue blocks was normally denied to them.

When the Nepalese immigration grew prominent around the mid-nineteenth century, the lands which earlier belonged to the Lepchas were found passing into the hands of the Nepalese. No wonder the authors like Waddell, Gorer and Risley believed that the Lepchas were a dying race. Such a belief was a result of their submerging into the Buddhist social frame-work and intercommunity marriages with the Bhutias and the Nepalis including especially the Limbus. And to Waddell :

> "The real reason for their disappearance in British Sikkim, is the disappearance or "conservation" of their forests, which by cutting off in great measure their sources of food, forces them into the unreserved tracts of Bhotan and Nepal (1979:293)".

The clearing of the forests which sustained their life took place due mainly to the British policy of settling of the Nepalis in Sikkim. Thus if any party is to be held responsible for the Lepchas' 'dying out', it is the British. There were number of reasons for this. The Nepalese were considered not only the best soldiers in the world but were also found equally good as peasants in the hills and terrains of Sikkim (Basnet, 1974:42). So by settling them there the British would have soldiers within their territory (there were some difficulties in their recruiting the soldiers from Nepal for quite some time) and at the same time they would get some revenue out of this unproductive region. The need for cheap labour in their highly useful Indo-Tibet trade through Sikkim was another factor. One more reason was the erosion of goodwill and friendship between the rulers of Sikkim and the British after 1949 when Captain Lloyd and Joseph Hooker were imprisoned in Sikkim (Karan & Jenkins, 1963 : 59). The Nepalese population was expected to neutralize the anti-British feelings of the Tibetans.

It has also been recorded that the simple Lepcha peasants were exploited by the dominant Bhutias earlier. Under the Bhutia rule, many Lepchas left Sikkim and settled in Darjeeling and east Nepal. Most of the Lepchas who came to Darjeeling embraced Christianity while those who were left back remained intertwined with the Bhutia socio-cultural fabric. The Lepcha identity was therefore affected by many factors, leading many people to think that they were a 'dying race' (Basnet, 1974:68).

A brief political history of Sikkim

The first instance of the contact between the Sikkimese rulers and the British took place when the Raja of Sikkim (Chungphod Namgyal) sought the help of the British to restore the lands(comprising the whole of the present Darjeeling district excluding Kalimpong). Under the Treaty of Titaliya(1817), the British obliged the Raja of Sikkim but made it obligatory on him 'to refer to the arbitration of the British Government all disputes between his subjects and those of neighbouring States'.

The granting of 138 square miles of Darjeeling by the Raja of Sikkim to the East India Company in 1835 soured the relationship between Sikkim and Tibet. The offence was retaliated in the forms of restrictions on the Raja to visit Lhasa for 8 years and the grazing rights of the Sikkimese on Tibetan land. But by then, Sikkim had lost the confidence of the British too. This provoked the British to carry out a number of military expeditions to Sikkim between 1850 and 1860. Finally, following a peace treaty signed at Tumlong (the previous capital of Sikkim) on 28th March 1861, Sikkim became a British dependency(Sinha, 1975:16-17). In 1888, J.C. White was appointed the first political officer to Sikkim, and following the Anglo-Chinese Convention at Calcutta in March 1890 Sikkim lost all ties with Tibet and confirmed its dependency on the British. Sikkim remained a British protectorate from 1890 to 1947 and thenceforth an Indian protectorate till April 1975 when it was declared the 22nd State of India.

'Tribal' demography

Early accounts on the 'tribal' demography of Sikkim are not much authentic but give a rough picture anyway. The population of the Lepchas, according to Campbell's estimate was, 3,000 and that of the Bhutias, 2,000 in 1840 (Risley, 1972:259). Though Silliguri was still under Sikkim then(it was annexed only in 1850) we cannot expect the Lepchas to have settled in such a malarial terai, as it was then. Even if the strip of land annexed in 1835 is included, the difference would be negligible because when it was annexed in 1835 it had only 100 heads.

The first ever reliable Census of 1891 shows that the Lepcha population was 5,762 or 18.92 per cent, the Bhutias 4,894 or 18.07 per cent, the

Limbus 3,356 or 11.02 per cent and the Mangars 901 or 2.96 per cent (*ibid* : 27). The rest of the population comprised other Nepalese castes and 'tribes' including the troops. According to the 1931 census, the last with ethnic categories, shows that the figures on the Lepchas to be 13,060 or 11.89 per cent and 11,955 or 10.89 per cent for the Bhutias. The 1951 census recorded the total population of Bhudhists as 39,397 out of which the Lepchas were 13,625 or 9.89 per cent and the Bhutias 15,626 or 11.35 per cent (Sinha, 1975 : 10).

The steady fall in the percentage of the Lepchas to total population does not mean a fall in their absolute number as it does in the case of the Onges of Andaman islands. The fall in their percentage can be easily attributed to the factors pointed out above. The slight increase in the percentage of the Bhutias is probably due to the net decline in the number of 'immigrants from Nepal' after the Indian independence.

The total percentage of the Scheduled Tribes (referred to as STs henceforth) in Sikkim, according to 1981 Census, is 23.27%. The distribution of the STs population in the four districts of Sikkim is shown in the following table (Table 1).

Table 1

PERCENTAGE DISTRIBUTION OF THE STs IN SIKKIM, 1981

State/District	*Total STs Population*	*% age of the STs to total population in the State/District*
Sikkim	73,623	23.27
North	14,702	55.57
East	30,540	22.01
South	13,310	17.52
West	15,071	20.04

Source : Census of India 1981, Sikkim : 114

The above table shows that the total percentage of the STs in Sikkim is 23.27. It also shows that more than 50 per cent of the population in the North are ST's. The STs population in the South are 17.52 per cent only while the East and West have 22.01 and 20.04 per cent STs population respectively.

Though Sikkim is predominantly an agricultural area its urban region is fast sprawling, especially after 1950. Therefore, it is worthwhile to show the distribution of the ST population in urban and rural areas of Sikkim, with the help of the following table.

Table 2

PERCENTAGE DISTRIBUTION OF THE STs IN RURAL AND URBAN AREAS TO THE TOTAL POPULATION OF STs, 1981

State/District	*Rural*	*Urban*
Sikkim	85.06	14.94
North	98.35	1.65
East	66.76	33.24
South	97.14	2.86
West	98.49	1.51

Source : Census of India 1981, Sikkim : 113

It is clear from above that 85.06 per cent of the ST population in Sikkim is in the rural areas. Districtwise, the percentages of the ST population in urban areas are rather insignificant in the north, south and west but the east has quite a significant urban ST population (33.24). Though the census records do not show who among the STs dominate this percentage, it is observed that almost the whole of it is represented by the Bhutias and the Tibetans, who have taken to trade and business as their livelihood. That this high percentage of the ST population in the urban areas of the east is mainly due to Gangtok, and Rangpo and Singtam to a smaller extent, will be clearer from the following table(Table 3).

Table 3

TOWNWISE DISTRIBUTION OF STs IN SIKKIM

Town	Total Population	Total ST Population	Percentage
Mangan	780	243	31.15
Gangtok, M.C.	36,747	9,731	26.48
Singtam	4,043	287	7.10
Rangpo	2,452	133	5.42
Namchi	1,444	168	11.63
Jorethang	3,921	213	5.43
Gyalshing	745	161	21.61
Nayabazaar	952	66	6.93
Total	51,084	11,002	21.54

Source : Census of India 1981, Sikkim : 134

It is seen from above that the percentage of the urban ST population is 21.54 and townwise, the highest (31.15) in Mangan, followed by Gangtok Municipal Corporation (26.48) and Gyalshing (21.61). The share of the urban ST population of other towns is negligible. But while the percentage of the urban ST population is lower in Gangtok than in Mangan, the absolute figures clearly establish that the urban ST population is as high as 9,731; the next town to follow the order being Singtam but with 287 heads only. Therefore the earlier statement about Gangtok is firmly established.

An anomaly regarding the percentage of different communities is seen recently. The Nepalis, for instance, claim to form 75 per cent of the population in Sikkim. The administration, on the other hand says on the basis of voters' list that the Nepalis constitute about 53 per cent, the Lepcha-Bhutias 36 per cent, and the people from the plains 11 per cent of the voters of the States. This is quite possible because 30,000 Nepalis are reported not to have been granted voting right in Sikkim as yet. The following passage is interesting in this context:

> "The percentage issue is as complicated as all the other issues in this state. Although census operations were carried out in Sikkim every 10 years, as in India, these do not have any legal validity because they were not said to have been conducted in accordance with the 1948 Census Act. Apparently, the operations were carried out by the Chogyal's men in a perfunctory manner. A record of sorts was kept, however, and this showed that the Nepalese formed 62% of the population and the Lepcha Bhutias 38%. The distinction between the two communities was made on the basis of language and since it is not uncommon in Sikkim for a Nepali to speak a Bhutia Lepcha dialect and vice versa, the percentage is not accepted by all (Ganguli, 1979)"

The Scheduled Tribes : a rationale

The STs as listed in the Constitution (Sikkim) Scheduled Castes and Scheduled Tribes Order, 1978 [1] are:

1. *Bhutia* (including Chumbipa, Dopthapa, Dukpa, Kagatey, Sherpa, Tibetan, Tromopa, Yolmo), and

2.*Lepcha.*

The above list of the STs is subject to a few comments. Ethnically, the Bhutias do not include the Kagatey, Sherpa and the Yolmo though religionwise most of them are Buddhists. Historically, the 'Bhutias' are referred to as the earlier settlers of Sikkim and with a mixture of the Lepcha 'blood'; the 'Tibetans' as the recent immigrants from Tibet; the 'Dukpas' are said to hail from Bhutan, and the 'Sherpas' from Nepal. Socially, the 'Kagatey' and the 'Yolmo' are synonyms of the same group of people in the way the 'Subba' and the 'Limbu' or the 'Pradhan' and the 'Newar' are. And the names like the Chumbipa, Dopthapa and the Trimopa are the different sections of the Tibetan Bhutias hailing from different places of Tibet.

It may also be added that the names like 'Kagatey', 'Subba' and the 'Pradhan' initially referred to occupational or status groups and not castes as such. The 'Kagatey', for example, referred to those who made their living out of handmade paper; the 'Subbas' were headman and tax-collectors and the same is true of 'Pradhans'.

Before taking the discussion further, the Constitutional provisions regarding the STs may be seen. Article 342 of the Indian Constitution lays down :

1. The President (may with respect to any State or Union Territory, and where it is a State, after consultation with the Governor thereof) by public notification, specify the tribes or tribal communities or parts of or groups within tribes or tribal communities which shall for the purposes of this Constitution be deemed to be Scheduled Tribes in relation to that State(or Union Territory, as the case may be).

2. Parliament may by law include in or exclude from the list of Scheduled Tribes specified in a notification issued under clause (1) any tribe or tribal community or part of or group within any tribe or tribal community, but save as aforesaid a notification issued under the said clause shall not be varied by any subsequent notification.[2]

An article 371 F on the special provisions with respect to the State of Sikkim, notwithstanding anything in this Constitution, provides in sub-clause (g) (1976:154):

> "The Governor of Sikkim shall have special responsibility for peace and for an equitable arrangement for ensuring the social and economic advancement of different sections of the population of Sikkim and in the discharge of his responsibility under this clause, the Governor of Sikkim shall, subject to such directions as the President may from, time to time, deem fit to issue, act in his discretion"

Incidentally, the various groups of the Nepalese community like the Rai, Limbu, Tamang, Mangar, Gurung, Bhujel, Sunuwar and the Thami are not included in the list of the STs though, as we can see from above. And there is no logic why these communities are not included in the list of the various communities mentioned above, the Limbus are recognized as a 'Backward Class'. If the criterion for being included as an ST is the 'chronology' of settlement in Sikkim the Limbus and the Mangars should have been included too. On the other hand, the Tibetans and the Dukpas should not have got the ST status on this ground. Nor can there be any socio-economic ground for the discrepancy as far as I can see.

The intra-tribe socio-economic differences are true of all 'tribes' whether scheduled or non-scheduled. If their being 'Hinduised' is a silent disadvantage (for the STs are all Buddhists, at least officially) for them, at least the Tamangs should have been recognized as an ST. If the experts-in-charge had any valid reason to call the Lepchas and the Bhutias as 'tribes', I do not see any reason why they could not include the above mentioned 'tribes'. After all, the word 'tribe' has no unanimous meaning and the debate on this problem is on for the last couple of decades. Even the anthropologists to whom 'tribes' have remained the focus of attention for so many years have failed to convince the word what 'tribe' means exactly (Fried, 1975).

The only answer that I can visualize on behalf of the experts-in-charge is that they followed the example of the hill areas of West Bengal where the Lepchas, Bhutias and the Sherpas are STs. or in other words, it was repetition of the Indian experience on Sikkim, without taking into consideration the local conditions.

Socio-economic profiles of 'tribals' in Sikkim

The socio-economic status of the 'tribes' or 'castes' is very important ground for including them in the list of the STs or SCs. Therefore, in any development plan, it is imperative to have a fair idea of the socio-economic profile of the target people and place. Unfortunately, data covering all the socioeconomic aspects of the STs in Sikkim are not available. What follows is an assessment of the same with the help of a few indicators like education, class, occupation and landholding. All these taken together is expected to give a fair, *albeit* not total, picture of the STs in Sikkim.

To start with, the following table(Table 4) on literacy of the ST population in Sikkim is presented.

Table 4

SCHEDULED TRIBES AND LITERACY IN SIKKIM

State/ District	*Total ST Population*	*Literates*	*%*	*Male*	*%*	*Female*	*%*
Sikkim	73,623	24,389	33.13	16,469	67.53	7,920	32.47
North	14,702	4,455	30.30	3,172	71.20	1,283	28.80
East	30,540	12,272	40.18	7,938	64.68	4,334	35.32
South	13,310	4,157	31.23	2,808	67.55	1,349	32.45
West	15,071	3,505	23.26	2,551	72.78	954	27.22

Source : Census of India 1981, Sikkim : 132-133

This table reveals some interesting points. It is seen that literacy among the STs in Sikkim is 33.13 per cent which is quite satisfactory compared with all Indian standard, leave alone the State standard. The only district which has a poor literacy rate among the STs is the west but the same is true of this district's non-Scheduled Caste peoples. Sikkim has only one degree college and one law college(recently opened), which may lead many people to think that the Sikkimese, including the STs, have a lower percentage (compared to other states of India) of people with college and above education. The absence of adequate facilities for higher education has certainly lowered the percentage of people with higher education but quite a number of the Sikkimese students are found studying in Darjeeling district, Calcutta, Delhi, Chandigarh, Bombay, and other places. And, among those who are studying outside the State of Sikkim, not a few are STs.

The following table (Table 5) is also significant here.

Table 5

ETHNIC AFFILIATION OF THE SIKKIMESE ELITES

Ethnic Stock	*Number*	*Percentage*
1. Lepchas	18	14.10
2. Bhutias	25	19.10
3. Nepalesae	54	42.20
4. Tsongs	3	2.34
5. Others	27	21.06
6. No information	1	0.78
	128	99.58

Source : Sinha, 1975 : 65

Table 1 has shown that the total percentage of the STs in Sikkim is only 23.27 but the above table shows that the Lepcha-Bhutias alone constitute 33.20 per cent of the elites in Sikkim. The criterion of being elites here is the high positions in bureaucracy, trade and commerce and the sample is rather small for the State as a whole. It is also difficult to say if Sinha has included all the groups mentioned in the ST list. However, the percentage of their population at least analytically shows that their class position is satisfactory. On the other hand, the Nepalis who constitute(including the Tsongs) about 70 per cent of the total population, have only 44.54 per cent elites. The next in the row are the Lepcha-Bhutias, followed by the Nepalis.

In this context it is desirable to furnish the following table (Table 6) on the occupational distribution of the STs.

Table 6

STs AND OCCUPATION DISTRIBUTION IN SIKKIM OCCUPATIONAL CATEGORIES 3

State/District	*I*	*II*	*III*	*IV*	*V*	*VI*	*VII*
Sikkim	73,623	32,773	21,777	638	238	10,075	1,885
%	23.27	22.22	24.58	13.06	17.84	19.24	35.05
North	14,702	6,355	3,993	159	25	2,178	1,173
%	19.97	19.39	18.34	24.92	8.83	21.62	62.23
East	30,540	12,348	6,143	207	224	5,774	327
%	41.48	37.68	28.21	32.45	79.15	57.31	17.35
South	13,310	6,290	4,857	85	12	1,336	289
%	18.08	19.19	22.30	13.32	4.24	13.26	15.33
West	15.071	7,780	6,784	187	22	787	96
%	20.47	23.74	31.15	29.31	7.77	7.81	5.09

Source : Census of India 1981, Sikkim : 132-133.

This table shows that the percentage of total main workers among the STs in Sikkim is slightly lower(22.22) than the percentage of their population (23.27). But the same is very high among them in the East due again, mainly to the urban/industrial centre, Gangtok and partly Rangpo and Singtam in this district. For example, the percentage of the STs in category V in the East is 79.15. The percentage of the STs in the categories IV, V, VI are also less than their percentages of population. While this in the context of category IV can be as favourable picture, their lower percent age in categories V and VI cannot probably be taken as a positive sign. It shows that they have taken to non-agricultural occupations less than other communities. This may also be due to a relative abundance of land among them, which automatically inhibits them to go for non-agricultural occupations. It should be noted at the same time that the non-agricultural occupations fetch more than the agricultural occupations, especially in an ecological milieu like that of Sikkim. So it is quite plausible that despite their relative land abundance their income is lower than that of the non-scheduled communities.

The records of the Land Revenue Department, Government of Sikkim (1979) shows that the following variations in the number of holdings and the excess land likely to be acquired amongst the Lepchas, Bhutias and the Nepalis. The total number of excess holdings among the Lepchas is 60 and the excess land likely to be acquired is 645.40 acres; the Bhutias have 187 excess holdings and the excess land likely to be acquired is 2795.01 acres; and the Nepalis have 201 excess holding with 1352.83 acres excess lands. Thus the excess land per excess holding is 14.9 acres among the Bhutias, 10.8 acres among the Lepchas and only 6.7 acres among the Nepalis. This shows that the position of the STs regarding landholding is much better than that of the Nepalis.

Now, I shall present some of the findings of a socio-economic survey on the 'Lepchas of Dzongu' conducted during December 1981 - January 1982 and published by the Bureau of Economics & Statistics, Planning and Development, Government of Sikkim.

Dzongu is a 'reserved area' for the Lepchas, meaning that there is restriction on other tribes and communities to settle there. The percentage of Lepcha population there is 56. Educationally : the illiterates (excluding - 4 aged) among them constitute 51.51 per cent ; the literates 17.58 per cent ; the primary-level educated 21.25; the junior high school

6.18; the high schools 2.25; and the higher secondary and above 0.94 per cent. Among the illiterates, the bulk of them or 64.40 per cent are females 40.31 per cent males. Occupationally : 95 per cent of the households were found engaged in agriculture, 3.5 percent in government services and 1.5 in other works like construction(as contractors) etc. and priesthood(*as lamas*).

The average size of operational holding per cultivating household is 9.34 hectares whereas the State average is only 2.56 hectares as per 1976-77 Agricultural Census, and the district(north) average is 7.22 hectares. About 47 per cent of the population was found economically active in the age-group above 10. 38.67 per cent of the households have tin roofs, 58.62 per cent have thatched roofs and only 2.71 per cent have roofs of other materials such as tiles.

The average expenditure of a household with about 6 persons is Rs. 1053.46 per month, which shows affluence. But 73.13 per cent of the households had taken one or more loans : 41.25 per cent had one loan and 31.81 per cent had more than one loan. 64.30 per cent of the total loan is from the landlords, traders and money-lenders and the government loan constitute only 34.22 per cent of all loans. It was also found that in some cases, the rates of interest were as high as 60 per cent per year.

The statistics given above shows that the Lepchas have quite a satisfactory socio-economic status on the whole. But it should be remembered that Dzongu is a 'reserved area' for the Lepchas and even being so, they are not immune from the landlords, traders and money-lenders. Moreover, statistics and reality do not always correspond. Though statistically they have a satisfactory position, a close observation does create some doubts. Such doubts may be partly due to their 'cultural lag' and partly on account of economic backwardness itself.

Steps for 'tribal' development

This is perhaps why the British had adopted some 'protective' measures for the Lepchas and the Bhutias. The collection of rent in Sikkim used to be in kind till 1915 when Sir Charles Bell introduced a cash rent system. There were separate rates of interest for the Lepcha-Bhutias and the Nepalis. For example, the rent for the Nepalis for Class

I paddy field was Rs. 2.00 per acre but for the Lepcha-Bhutias, it was only Rs. 1.48 paise per acre; and for Class II paddy field the Nepalis had to pay Re. 1.48 paise per acre but the Lepcha-Bhutias only Re. 1.12 paise per acre[4]. It is clear therefore that the rent for paddy for both the classes lower for the Lepcha-Bhutias. However, this rate was in application only till the 1st Settlement Operation and proclamation of the Maharaja of Sikkim, 1956.

Later, Sikkim also came under the Five Year Plans of India but there was no separate notification for the STs in this State. The need for identifying a ST was emphasized soon after Sikkim became a part of India and the few 'tribes' mentioned above were declared STs in June 1978. A tribal sub-Plan was also prepared. But since the identified 'tribes' were scattered all over the State, there were chances of the plans not actually reaching the target people. Thus, certain areas such as the north district where the concentration of the STs was more, were selected for the purpose of the tribal sub-Plan (1979 : 1).

Like elsewhere in India, the Planning and Development Department, Government of Sikkim, has identified a number of sectors for development of the STs and allotted amounts for each sector, depending on the priority of development. A detailed picture of this is shown in the following table(Table 7).

Table 7

TRIBAL SUB-PLAN OUTLAY (RS. IN LAKHS) IN SIKKIM

Sector	*Divisible Out lay*	*%*	*Year 1980-85 Flow to Tribal sub-plan*	*%*
Agriculture	561.68	26.11	69.70	21.66
Animal Husbandry	229.35	10.66	60.25	18.72
Fisheries	9.00	0.42	2.25	0.70
Forests	39.00	1.81	28.50	8.86
Cooperation	76.05	3.54	8.69	2.70
Industries	93.00	4.32	30.28	9.40
Education	520.00	24.17	48.00	14.91
Medical & Public Health	312.00	14.50	33.00	10.25
Housing	130.00	6.04	18.02	5.60
Nutrition	181.00	8.41	23.15	7.19
	2,151.08		321.84	14.96

Source : *Sixth Five Year Plan 1980-85*, Draft Proposals from Govt. of Sikkim, Deptt. of Planning and Development, Govt. of Sikkim, Gangtok.

This table shows that the percentage of flow to tribal sub-Plan to the divisible outlay is 14.96. The sectors which have been more emphasized in the tribal sub-Plan are : animal husbandry, fisheries, forests and industries. These sectors are certainly vital to them but it is difficult to show, at this juncture, to what extent the sub-Plan is really going to help them. Animal husbandry among the north Sikkimese has as such been badly affected since the Sino-Indian disputes began in 1835, following the granting of Darjeeling to the East India Company by the Raja of Sikkim. Unless some viable alternative sources of fodder are brought in there is little hope in this front. The same is true about the industrial sector.

Conclusion

It is true that 'tribal' development programmes are not even a decade old in Sikkim and no evaluation of their impact is possible at this stage. However, the tribal sub-Plan does not appear that promising. By and large, it seems in some cases the same experiments which failed elsewhere, are being repeated. There is no adequate consideration of the historical, social and cultural/religious aspects of the Sikkimese society.

The 'tribes' of Sikkim have had certain psychological shocks during the last couple of centuries such as the fear of being completely swamped by the non-tribals, the change in the mode of economy due to demographic change and political developments. The problem of Sikkim does not end in developing her 'tribal' communities in the projected manner of the tribal sub-Plan but also includes the tricky question of instilling in them a 'sense of security' without aggravating the ethnic bitterness.

Notes

1. Census of India, 1981, Sikkim series 19, Part IIA and IIB, General Population Tables and Primary Census Abstract(Gangtok : Director of Census Operation). The above list does not take any cognizance of the religious background of the STs.
2. The Above list does not take any cognizance of the religious background of the STs.
3. Category I = Total ST Population
   Category II = Total Main Workers
   Category III = Cultivators
   Category IV = Agricultural Labourers
   Category V = Household industry, processing, manufacturing, servicing and repairs.

Category VI = Other Workers
Category VII = Marginal Workers
The above categories are defined in the Census only.

4. State Report on Agricultural Census 1976-77, Sikkim (Gangtok: Agricultural Census Unit, Govt. of Sikkim).

References

Basnet, L. B. (1974) — *Sikkim : A short Political History*, S.Chand, New Delhi.

Fried, M. H. (1975) — *The notions of Tribe*, California, Cummings Publication.

Ganguli, A. (1979) — *Plain Tales from the Hills*, The Statesman, September.

Karan, P. P. and W. M. Jenkins (1963) — *The Himalayan Kingdoms : Bhutan, Sikkim and Nepal*. London. D. Van Nostrand, London.

Planning & Development Department (1979) — *Tribal Sub-Plan For Sikkim State: A Proposal*, Govt. of Sikkim, Gangtok.

Risley, H. A. (1972) — *The Gazetteer of Sikkim*, New Delhi, Manjushri, New Delhi.

Sinha, A. C. (1975) — *Politics of Sikkim*, Thompson Press,

Waddell, L. A. (1979) — *Among the Himalayas*, Mittal Publishers, Delhi.

CHAPTER 11

Tribal Welfare and Development in West Bengal

A.K. Das

The list of Scheduled Tribes, as originally notified by the President of India in 1950 under Article 342 of the Constitution included only seven tribes for the State of West Bengal. Their population as per 1951 census was 11.65 lakhs. This list was subsequently amended to include nineteen more tribes for this State in accordance with the Scheduled Castes and Scheduled Tribes Orders (Amendment) Act, 1956. The total tribal population of these nineteen tribal communities according to 1951 census was 13,44,527. After the reorganization of the States, further modification was made in the lists of Scheduled Tribes and as a result of Scheduled Tribes (Modification) Order, 1956, twenty-two new tribes were included in the list of West Bengal Tribals concerning the transferred territories only. The total population of the forty-one tribal communities in the reconstituted State of West Bengal was 15.67 lakhs forming approximately 6 per cent of the total population of the State. This list was further modified as per the Scheduled Castes and Scheduled Tribes Orders (Amendment) Act, 1976. Altogether thirty eight tribal communities have been scheduled and with the removal of the area restriction these communities started receiving the status of Scheduled Tribes throughout the State of West Bengal, unlike the situation prevailing earlier when the area restriction. within the list of communities was a special characteristic. The total population of these thirty-eight communities, as per 1971 Census was 25,32,969 showing an increase of 23.31 per cent over the population recorded in 1961 census (20,54,081). As per 1981 Census, total population of these existing thirty-eight Scheduled Tribes is 30,70,672 showing a growth rate of 21.23 per cent during 1971-81 decade. The Scheduled Tribes of West Bengal Constitute 5.63 per cent of the total population of the State whereas their percentage of coverage in 1971 was 5.72. This state occupies thirteenth rank position (in 1981) as per tribal concentration whereas the position was eleven in 1971.

Numerically most dominant among the tribal communities of the State is the Santal, who share more than half of the tribal population of the State. The following nine communities jointly covered more than 90 per cent of the total Scheduled Tribes population of the State in 1971, (1981 Census figures for individual tribes are not yet available. But the trend is expected to reveal the same situation. The position was similar in earlier decades also).

Santal (54.35%), Oraon (11.49%), Munda (7.85%), Bhumij (6.69%) Kora (3.69%), Mahali (1.87%), Lodha/Kheria (1.81%), Bhutia (1.33%), Mal Pahariya (1.22%).

Out of sixteen districts of the State the following six districts cover more than 70 per cent of the total tribal population of the State as per 1981 Census.

Midnapur (17.55%), Jalpaiguri (16.02%), Purulia (11.34%), Bardwan (9.06%), West Dinajpur (8.47%), Bankura (8.16%).

The following five districts cover 25 per cent of the tribal population.

24 Parganas (6.16%), Malda (4.99%), Darjeeling (4.92%), Birbhum (4.73%), Hooghly (4.59%).

The remaining five districts share rest of the tribal population.

Nadia (1.82%), Murshidabad (1.47%), Cooch-Bihar (0.33%), Howrah (0.24%), Calcutta (0.14%).

The Scheduled Tribes of West Bengal may racially be divided into two broad categories--Proto-Australoid and Mongoloid. The plains area tribals (Santals, Oraons, Mundas, Bhumijas, Koras, Lodhas, Mahalis, Malpaharies, Nagesies etc.) in general possess Proto-Australoid and Mediterranean traits and mainly the North Bengal tribes such as, Lepchas, Bhutias, Rabhas, Meches, etc. have Mongoloid physical features and characteristics.

Linguistically, the tribals of West Bengal may be grouped into three broad categories.

The Santals, Mundas, Hos etc. belong to the Austric Speech family; the Oraons and Malpaharies to Dravidian Speech family, and the Lepchas, Bhutias, Meches, Rabhas etc. to the Tibeto-Chinese family of Languages.

The tribal people, more particularly the Santal, Oraon, Munda, Bhumij, Lodha, Mahali etc. have been living in the Western Districts of the State (Midnapur, Bankura, Birbhum, Purulia) adjacent to the Bihar and Orissa states for a pretty long time and these tribal folk in general and the Santals in more particular have a good deal of historical tradition in these districts. On account of growth of collieries in the western part of Bardwan District in the last century, the Santals migrated from Santal Parganas to work as colliery labourers. South-east part of Bardwan District and northern part of Hooghly District, were generally affected during the second half of the last century due to considerable deterioration of hygienic conditions. Round about 1860, these areas became largely depopulated due to the break out of "Bardwan fever" in severe epidemic form. At that time tribals of Midnapur and Bankura districts were encouraged by owners of land to come down and settle in the area. With the improvement of the condition the settlement of the tribals was gradually discontinued But every year, tribals from Midnapur, from Bankura Birbhum, Purulia, Santal Parganas etc. migrate to Bardwan to and Hooghly Districts seasonally to work in the agricultural land as labourers. But the intensity of these seasonal migrants are also gradually dwindling due to the improvement of situation in the places of their origin. In the district of 24 Parganas the tribals come down and settled since the beginning of nineteenth Century. They were mainly brought over to these areas to clear up the jungle tracts of the Sunderban and to bring the land under cultivation. Tribals in the northern fringe of 24 Parganas, Nadia and Murshidabad were brought a few generations ago to work as labourers in the indigo plantations. Santals of West Dinajpur, Malda and Murshidabad believe that their forefathers migrated to these areas after the Santal rebellion of 1855 which took place in Santal Parganas and Birbhum. After partition many tribals, from East Pakistan (now Bangladesh), who had been taken over there to clear up jungle tracts and to work in the indigo plantations, came over to India, and settled in Nadia and a few places in 24 Parganas and West Dinajpur Districts.

In North Bengal the history of settlement of the tribals follows a different course unlike the one described above. In Darjeeling District Lepchas and Bhutias are considered to be the earliest inhabitants. There are also a quite large number of Bhutia immigrants from Tibet, Sikkim and other sub-Himalayan regions. Meches and Rabhas are considered to be earliest inhabitants in Jalpaiguri District and parts of Cooch-Bihar district. They migrated to these areas of West Bengal in the historic past from the adjoining districts of Assam. The Garos of this area are considered to have migrated from Mymansingh District of Bangladesh. Tribal Communities like Oraons, Mundas, Santals, Kherias, Nagerias etc. are also found in Jalpaiguri and Darjeeling Districts where they migrated a few generations ago, as tea garden labourers.

It is thus seen that a considerable position of tribal population of the State of West Bengal has migrated from the neighbouring States of Bihar, Orissa, Assam and Sikkim and countries like Tibet, Bhutan, Nepal and Bangladesh during the last few generations. They cleared up the jungle tracts and made the land cultivable. They constitute a significant portion of the labour force of the State. In North Bengal there are a few tribal groups (Mech, Rabha, Garo) who settled there a long time ago. Through the Mongoloid tribal group of North Bengal Constitute only 3 per cent of the total tribal population of the State and their number is not quite large in comparison to other tribal groups still their importance from various aspects of socio-economic and cultural life of the State cannot be ignored.

II

Problems of the tribal people received special attention after Independence. During the British regime very little attention was given towards welfare and development of this very important section of the country. They were mainly kept aloof from the main current of the national life. However, there were certain administrative measures for safeguarding the interests of the tribal people, then known as the "aboriginals". With the attainment of independence the approach of 'Isolation' was discarded and instead of separatist outlook the policy of integration was adopted for ensuring national unity and healthy growth. Thus immediately after Independence, a Special Ministry for Aboriginals and Backward Classes was set up by the Government of West Bengal in January 1949. In 1952, a full fledged Department of Tribal Welfare replaced the Special Ministry to take over the administration of the different welfare measures and to meet constitutional obligations to the different sections of Backward Classes, particularly the Scheduled Tribes. In course of time the activities of the Department increased manifold and the part-time Minister and part-time officers were replaced by a full-fledged Department with a directorate and field officers of its own.

During pre-Plan Period the main function of the Ministry for Aboriginals and Backward Classes was to co-ordinate the activities of different departments in relation to the Backward Classes. The responsibility of administration of chapter VII A of the Bengal Tenancy Act was also taken over by the Ministry. It was also the look-out of the Ministry to protect the aboriginals against injustice and exploitation. In addition to the schemes implemented by the special Ministry a few schemes for the welfare of the Scheduled Tribes were implemented by various departments out of normal budget of their own. Five special Officers for Aboriginals were employed for ensuring protection of the tribal people from injustice and exploitation and to render all facilities which the law of the land permitted. They were also to enforce the provisions of Chapter VII A of the Bengal Tenancy Act, so that the poor aboriginals might not have their land snatched away from them by cleverer sections of the people. These Officers also encouraged cultural activities and rendered advice on all matters.

To enable the tribals to defend their just rights in the courts of Law a scheme for giving free legal aid was in operation since pre-Independence period. During the period 1947-51 an amount of Rs. 9,559 was spent on this account.

A sum of Rs.25,000 was sanctioned in 1950-51 and placed at the disposal of District Officers and Divisional Commissioners as special discretionary grants towards expenditure on small & urgent projects connected with the welfare of tribals and backward classes, in addition to ordinary discretionary grants.

For the advancement of education among the Tribes, Scheduled Castes and Backward Classes, a special Fund known as "Fund for the Promotion of Education among Backward Classes" was set apart for providing stipends, building grants, book grants and grants for examination fees, etc. to them. In 1948-49, the grant was to the tune of Rs.11,48,000 and in 1949-50 and 1950-51 these were Rs.11,37,000 and Rs. 11,58,000 respectively. The tribal people received their due share of benefit out of this fund. A college was run at Darjeeling for the Hill Tribes and a hostel for the Bhutias and Lepchas of the same district.

There was provision for remittance of the court fees chargeable on applications of the tribals under sections 49-F,H,J and M of the Bengal Tenancy Act and also on in the case of lawyers appointed by the Government for the tribals. Court fees had also been exempted on applications for new special license for home brewing country liquor.

An amount of Rs.4,000 in 1949-50 and Rs.10,000 in 1950-51 were provided to the tribals for special purposes such as payment of court's decrees and meeting the expenses for the necessities of life. The Government also relaxed the rules for grant of crop-loans to tribals who suffered from restrictions in the matter of mortgaging their lands and could not consequently avail themselves of these loans. One Multipurpose Co-operative Society was established for the Santals at Jhantipahari in the district of Bankura. In 1949 the society did business in controlled goods to the value of Rs.3,27,686 and earned a profit of Rs. 17,758. A number of minor irrigation schemes for improvement of backward areas were launched by the Irrigation Department of the Government. A sum of Rs. 1,63,645 was spent for this purpose up to 1950-51. The following institutions meant for the benefit of the tribal people were running under the Industries Department of the Government.

a) The Darjeeling Industrial School and Workshop at an estimated cost of Rs. 1,05,000 per year.

b) Five Peripatetic Weaving Schools in the districts of Bankura, Midnapur, Malda and Birbhum at an annual expenditure of Rs.32,000/-.

c) Three Palm-gur centres in Vishnupur sub-Division of Bankura District at a cost of Rs.1,500/-.

d) A Co-operative Wool Weaving Society at Kalimpong. The Department spent Rs. 1,500 annually on the demonstrators.

III

With the above facts in the background let us now examine the significant features and achievements in different plan periods. Under Article 275 (1) of the Constitution, special programmes for the welfare of Scheduled Tribes were launched from 1951-52 and this marks the beginning of the development programmes under First Plan. The administration of the Tribal Welfare activities was placed under the control of a full-fledged Tribal Welfare Department since June 1952.

At the beginning of the First Plan period various schemes for the welfare of Scheduled Tribes were implemented by the different departments of the State Government out of their own budget. A separate budget provision was made for the welfare schemes of Scheduled Tribes in 1954-55 and these schemes were included in the State Sector of the Plan as analogous schemes. The expenditure for the welfare of Scheduled Tribes were incurred under the following categories- (i) Expenditure out of State Plan provision (ii) Expenditure out of Central grant-in-aid, (iii) Expenditure out of normal budget of the State Government. In contrast to the First Plan period the mode of expenditure during the Second Plan Period was as follows:-(i) State Plan-The expenditure for each individual scheme was shared by Government of India on 50:50 basis, (ii) Centrally sponsored scheme--the entire cost was borne by Government of India, (iii) Committed expenditure--the entire cost of those schemes which started during First Plan Period and continued in Second Plan were met out of the normal budget of the State.

Since the beginning of the first plan the pace of development work has increased manifold as would be evident from the following facts.

During the First Plan Period an amount of Rs. 53.2 lakhs only was spent on specific schemes meant for the welfare of the Scheduled Tribes as against Rs. 149 lakhs during the Second Plan Period which increased to Rs. 231.5 lakhs during Third Plan Period. Various types of schemes under different sectors such as education, health, agriculture, cooperation, cottage industries miscellaneous etc. were taken up in different Plan Periods for an over-all development of the Scheduled Tribes. Educational schemes were given the first priority amongst the schemes of different sectors in this State. Expenditure during Second Plan in education sector was Rs. 36.5 lakhs which progressively increased to 87.69 lakhs during Third Plan. These figures do not include the amount spent for Post-Secondary Scholarships which was exhibited outside the Plan provision. Apart from free tuition facilities to all tribal students reading in secondary schools, the Government also provides boarding charges, book-grants, stipends etc. in deserving cases. During the First Plan book grants, boarding charges etc. were given to 2,312 students, 136 primary schools, 30 basic schools and one M.E. Schools were opened, 18 hostels were constructed. Whereas during the Second Plan book grants were given to about 7,000 tribal students involving an expenditure of Rs. 1.45 lakhs. The Third Plan provided book grants in 19,000 cases at the cost in Rs. 5.7 lakhs. Similarly, as against the provision of Rs. 21,000 for giving examination fees to 994 students, the Third Plan provision was for 2,500 students at a cost of Rs. 55,000. Under the Second Plan boarding charges were given to 4,200 students of secondary schools at a total cost of Rs. 5.62 lakhs as against a provision of Rs.22 lakhs during the Third Plan for the same purpose. Due to the impact of all these schemes the number of tribal students in the secondary schools increased from 3,500 in the year 1954-55 to 13,700 in 1961-62. The Tribal students were provided with scholarships in the post-secondary stage also. In addition to the schemes of above nature, schemes for upgrading of schools, construction and extension of school hostels were also continued during the Third Plan. During the Third Plan new schemes for providing ashram facilities for tribal students and another for providing coaching facilities to 2,000 meritorious students were introduced.

The schemes for economic uplift were given second place in order of priority in the plan for the welfare of Backward Classes. Under this head schemes in different sectors, e.g., agriculture, irrigation, cottage industries, cooperation etc. were taken up. Second Plan expenditure towards economic uplift for the Scheduled Tribes was to the tune of Rs. 35.62 lakhs as against provision of Rs.77.52 lakhs during Third Plan. During the First Plan period in the field of agriculture Rs. 25,000 worth of fodder, manures, seeds etc., were distributed, 89 demonstration centres were organised, two poultry farms were opened and 7,740 poultry birds were distributed at subsidized rates, 144 stud bulls were distributed for improvement of livestock in tribal areas. For irrrigational purposes altogether 87 small minor and major irrigation schemes were completed. In the field of cottage industries, five peripatetic weaving schools were started. Training facilities at Vishnupur Industrial school and at Cooch-Behar Industrial School and Workshop were expanded for the benefit of the tribal people, two Training-cum-production centres for seed lac were opened at Bankura and Murshidabad, two centres for manufacturing of jute and woollen goods were opened at Malda and West Dinajpur, a scheme for development of wool industry was introduced in Darjeeling District. Altogether more than 300 tribal boys were benefited by cottage industry schemes under the First Plan. In the field of Co-operation 30 Co-operative grain golas were opened in order to ensure easy availability of credit in rural areas. Four dairy societies and one co-operative weavingsociety were also established.

During the Second Plan Period, about 10,000 maunds of seeds were distributed at subsidized rates, about 3,000 demonstration plots were opened in cultivators holdings, 40 more stud bulls were distributed, one Poultry Multiplication centre was opened and 15,600 birds were distributed at subsidized rates. Two hundred and six goat-keeping, sheep rearing , pig-rearing blocks, each with one male and 20 female animals were set up. Grants were given to 6,400 families for encouragement of homestead vegetable-cum-fruit gardening. In the matter of training, 420 students were given stipends financially for getting training in vocational trade and crafts of whom 178 students were financially assisted, on completion of their training, to set up business of their own. Besides, six training-cum-production centres in different trades were started and 300 persons were trained. In the field of co-operation, in recognition of the importance of co-operative grain golas, the original target under the second Plan was revised upwards to open 117 new grain golas.

Arrangements were made for providing credit in cash as well as in grain and the societies were re-designated as grain gola-cum-credit societies. Besides, seven *creamery* societies were also opened to provide subsidiary means of livelihood, 530 families were supplied with improved dhenkis.

A scheme for bee-keeping and another one for development of lac cultivation were in tribal areas. Altogether, 1,170 persons were benefited by these schemes. At Kalimpong, a Wool Industries Centre was set up. A scheme for marketing of paddy and for providing storage facilities to the paddy growers of Sundarban areas were opened. Seventy three Toto families were rehabilitated in the district of Jalpaiguri and a scheme for settlement of 128 lend-lease tribals in agricultural colony was taken up. In addition 640 persons were given financial assistance for purchase of agricultural land and houses.

Apart from the maintenance of the schemes started under the First and Second Plan the Third Plan provided two training units in bee-keeping, on centre for development of lac cultivation, 130 goat keeping, sheep-rearing, pig-rearing blocks. A provision of Rs.19 lakhs was also earmarked for small and minor irrigation schemes for the benefit of tribal people.

Facilities to 1,250 Scheduled Tribe students in vocational trades and crafts were provided during the Third Plan. Schemes for development of non-mulberry Tasar Industry, training in sericulture, ericulture, spinning etc. were also provided. A provision of Rs. 60,000 was made for providing residential facilities to students receiving training in vocational trades and crafts. Rupees Two Lakhs were provided for giving financial assistance to Scheduled Tribe artisans in selected trades for setting up independent business. For purchase of agricultural land and house sites by the landless Scheduled Tribes, Rs.5 lakhs were provided as assistance. Provision of Rs. 10 lakhs was also made for reclamation and development of waste land for distribution of such land to landless tribal people and those with uneconomic holdings. The number of multi-purpose co-operative for dispensing credit in cash and kind was further strengthened by 300 new societies with a provision of 22.20 lakhs. At the end of 1961-62, the total number of grain golas functioning stood at 197. A provision of Rs. 1.50 lakhs was made in the Third Plan for organizing 17 Labourers, cooperatives. Provision of Rs. 50 thousand was also made for providing supervisory cost to industrial co-operatives to be formed by ex-trainees of vocational trades and crafts.

Apart from these schemes of educational advancement and economic uplift, other miscellaneous schemes covering the different sectors such as health, housing, roads, etc., were also undertaken for the welfare of the Scheduled Tribes. Under the First Plan, 8 beds were reserved in TB Hospitals for tribal patients, 148 dispensaries were given grant for supply of costly medicines to poor tribal patients free of charges. Six Health Centres and eleven Leprosy clinics were opened in tribal areas. For removing the scarcity of water supply in tribal areas, 7,700 new sources of water supply were constructed. For opening of communication in the interior tribal areas, 41 miles of roads and 29 small village roads were constructed. For the amelioration of the condition of the tribal forest villagers 217 forest villagers, huts were constructed and arrangements were made for supply of drinking water to these huts by providing 68 new sources of water supply. Six welfare centres were started in tribal areas and 12 non-official organisations were given grants for welfare work among the Scheduled Tribes & Castes.

Under the Second Plan schemes of general nature were continued. Three Hundred sixty five dispensaries were given grant, 30 additional beds were reserved for treatment of tribal T.B. patients, 2,158 new sources of drinking water were constructed, 2,160 tribal families were given grant for construction of houses. Three Leprosy clinics were started and one mobile Dispensary-cum-V.D. unit were opened in North Bengal. Seventy miles roads and about two culverts, bridges and cause ways were constructed. Grants were given to forest villagers for construction of 212 huts and for providing 106 water supply sources. Thirty three new welfare centres were opened and non-official organisations numbering about 14 were given grants for carrying out various welfare works in tribal areas. One hundred and twenty eight Bhutia and Lepcha Monasteries were given grant for preservation and development of their culture. Besides, grants were given to adult education centres, night schools, exhibitions and for the purpose of other cultural and recreational activities. Rewards and prizes were given for outstanding welfare work. The total expenditure on such miscellaneous schemes came to Rs. 134.44 lakhs during the second plan period.

A provision of 66.24 lakhs was made under the Third Plan for schemes of similar nature. This amount included provision of Rs. 20 lakhs for giving grant to about 4,000 families for purchase of house sites and construction of houses, Rs. 10 lakhs for providing about 1000 sources of water supply in tribal areas. A provision of Rs. 5 lakhs was also made for setting up two mobile T.B. Units for preventive and curative purposes and two Health units for curative purposes in unreserved tribal areas. There was also a provision of Rs. 2 lakhs for giving grant to a few selected non-official organisations for carrying out tribal welfare work. Besides, grants were given to institutions, organisations etc. for cultural, recreational and social activities.

During the Third Plan there was a provision of Rs. 3.14 lakhs for the welfare measures of the Denotified Tribes. The measures included scheme of rehabilitation and housing of 100 ex-criminal tribe families. Provision was also made for providing Ashram facilities to Denotified tribes in basic schools. Under the scheme three hostels were set up attached to basic schools each IV with accommodation for 20 students.

After the Third Five Year Plan there was a recess in the continuity of Five Year Plans during the period 1966-69, when annual Plans were in operation.

The pattern of schemes was almost similar during these annual Plans as in the case of earlier Five Year Plan Periods, excepting a few variations. An employment oriented scheme known as General Duty Attendants Training Scheme for Tribal girls was introduced during 1966-67. The scheme envisaged setting up of a training Centre in Bankura in cooperation with Medical College and Hospital there, to give training to the selected tribal girls in elementary nursing and other hospital duties so that they could be employed as General Duty attendants, in different hospitals on completion of training. One of the main policies of Government was to distribute the surplus vested land to the Scheduled Tribe persons possessing no or less than two acres of land. With the introduction of the West Bengal Land Reforms Act in which a new chapter (chapter II A) was inserted by way of Amendment in 1965, the old Bengal Tenancy Act stood repealed. All the provisions of chapter VII A of the B.T. Act governing the alienation of Land by tribals were incorporated in the new Act with some additions and changes to the benefit of the tribals. Like land, forests also play an important part in the daily life of the tribals. The sub-committee of the representatives of the Forests, Co-operation and Tribal Welfare Departments appointed by the Ministers level co-ordination committee in 1965 made some recommendations in the matter of granting certain rights and privileges to tribals in Forests and in information of forest Co-operatives.

In addition, during the year (1965) decisions were taken to examine the practicability and feasibility of setting up two residential secondary schools for tribal students in the State with diversified courses. Government orders were also issued for reservation of 5% and 15% of seats for Scheduled Tribes and Scheduled Castes respectively in Engineering College and Technical Institutes of the State. The order also provided for relaxation of upper age-limit for seeking admission.

Another important decision was to plan for intensive development of tribal packets with ad-hoc assistance from Central Government. The Central Government so long denied to this State any assistance for establishment of Tribal Development Blocks on the ground that the prescribed criteria for the purpose do not obtain in any part of West Bengal. The Department had all along been pressing forward the view point that some special consideration should be shown to West Bengal for the Welfare and development of 2 millions of Scheduled Tribes living in the State. The Central Government finally accepted the justness of the argument and agreed to give full assistance for the implementation of the schemes of the development of the tribal concentrated pockets in lieu of Tribal Development Blocks. Accordingly, sixteen sub-blocks in nine districts (Malda, Jalpaiguri, Darjeeling, West Dinajpur, Hoogly, Bankura, Birbhum, Midnapore and Purulia) were taken up during the year. A provision of Rs.10 lakhs was made in the first year against which a sum of Rs. 8.58 lakhs was spent.

During the Annual Plan of 1966-67 of the State an amount of Rs.32.87 lakhs was spent for schemes meant for educational advancement (23.63 lakhs), economic uplift (6.01 lakhs) and Health, Housing and other schemes (3.23 lakhs).

Under centrally sponsored programme an amount of Rs. 15.87 lakhs was spent towards schemes under education sector (3.85 lakhs), economic sector (3.37 lakhs) and health, housing and other schemes (8.65 lakhs).

Most of the schemes of the Third Plan Period remained in operation during the year barring a few which were discontinued. In this year, about 72% of the total expenditure under the State Plan were made for the educational schemes. Five Primary Schools were constructed at a total cost of Rs. 20,000 in Scheduled Tribe areas; four new Ashram Hostels were constructed at a cost of Rs.80,000; the existing Ashram Hostels were maintained at an expenditure of Rs. 61,000; tuition fees were provided to 20,394 students (9.90 lakhs), book grants given to 4,262 students (0.83 lakh); boarding charges were provided to 4,549 students (9.78 lakhs); special stipends were given to 1,163 students (1.08 lakh) and 0.13 lakh was spent towards examination fees of 639 students; one new school attached to school was constructed at a cost of Rs. 20,000 and two existing hostel buildings were extended at a cost of Rs. 24,000; Rs. 47,000 were spent for reading coaching facilities to students reading in Class IX,X and XI. Under the centrally sponsored programme Rs. 92,000 were granted for construction of four school hostels for Scheduled Tribe girls; major portion of the fund was spent for giving postmatric scholarships to 58 students (Rs. 2.94 lakhs).

More than 18% of the total expenditure for Scheduled Tribes in the State Sector were spent on the schemes of economic uplift. Financial assistance were provided to 267 Scheduled Tribe families for purchasing of plough cattle, agricultural implements and for reclamation of waste land and expenditure incurred thereon was Rs.40,000; 92 minor irrigation schemes were executed at a cost of Rs.3.22 lakhs; 144 families were provided with financial assistance for purchase of house-site and agricultural land at an expenditure of Rs. 33,000; 544 pigs were distributed in 16 selected blocks in the year at a cost of Rs. 37,000; training in vocational trades and crafts were given to 132 Scheduled Tribes at a cost of Rs.28,000 and residential facilities were made available to 102 trainees for which an amount of Rs. 12,000 was incurred; financial assistance to the tune of Rs. 28,000 were given to 271 trainees who successfully came out of the Training-cum-Production Centres of the Department for setting up their own trade and also to traditional and trained artisans.

Under the Centrally Sponsored Programme, the most important scheme for economic uplift was development of co-operatives. During the year 28 new societies were established at a total cost of Rs.2.87 lakhs in addition to the 399 established during preceding years; six labour

Co-operative societies were established during the year at a total cost of Rs. 50,000; 9 Scheduled Tribe Candidates received training in Five Junior Level Co-operative Training Institutes. In addition sub-Block scheme was run under centrally sponsored programme.

During the year Rs. 1.92 lakhs were spent to create 157 new sources of potable water like tube-wells, masonry wells, R.C.C. Wells, pipe lines etc. in tribal areas; 7 leprosy clinics started during first and second Plan periods were maintained so also two mobile units for treatment of V.D. patients and 50 beds reserved for tribal T.B. patients in various hospitals; 168 Scheduled Tribe families were given grants for purchase of house-sites and housing materials at a cost of Rs.50,000. To promote drive for literacy and recreational activities, 68 clubs, libraries and other Institutions of the Scheduled Tribes were given grants at a total cost of Rs. 9,000. Seven non-official voluntary agencies were provided grants to the tune of Rs. 34,000 for doing welfare work among the Scheduled Tribes.

Two Ashram hostels started earlier for the students of the denotified communities were maintained at a cost of Rs.29,000 out of centrally sponsored schemes.

During 1967-68, an amount of Rs. 38.36 lakhs out of State Sector provision and Rs. 12.32 lakhs under central sector were spent towards welfare of Scheduled Tribes. In addition, an amount of Rs.0.20 lakh was spent for the welfare of the Denotified Tribes. During this year also main stress was given on educational programmes. The following chart will provide information in details about different schemes implemented during the year 1967-68 together with the expenditure incurred and physical targets achieved.

S. No.	*Name of the schemes*	*Expenditure (Rs.in lakhs).*	*Achievements/ Beneficiaries.*
A.	Education		
1.	Payment of Tuition fee	11.19	24,033 students
2.	Book grants to tribal students reading in Secondary Schools.	0.94	5,262 students
3.	Coaching arrangements in Secondary Schools.	0.31	861 students
4.	Examination fees for students appearing at the S. F. Examination and H. S. Examination.	0.16	725 Students

S. No.	Name of the Schemes.	Expenditure (Rs.in lakhs).	Achievements/ Beneficiaries.
5.	Special stipend to poor meritorious students in selected secondary schools.	0.37	454 students
6.	Provision for Ashram facilities in Basic schools.	0.46	2 Hostels run and 4 Hostels Buildings constructed.
7.	Extension of existing School hostels.	0.28	2 Hostels extended.
8.	Construction of new hostel buildings	0.50	3 Hostels
9.	Boarding charge for students of Secondary Schools.	13.72	5,464 students
10.	Provision for hostel facilities for students reading in Post-Secondary Institutions in Calcutta	0.12	Preliminaries done but scheme postponed.
11.	Grants for construction of Primary Schools.	0.37	8 schools
II.	Centrally Sponsored Programme.		
1.	Scholarship to students reading in Post-secondary Schools.	3.52	696
2.	Construction of hostels for girls students.	0.40	3 Hostels.
B. ECONOMIC UPLIFT			
I.	State Plan.		
1.	Motor Mechanism and and Motor Driving	0.07	16 persons.
2.	Pig rearing as a subsidiary means of livelihood.	0.05	Old blocks maintained.
3.	Minor Irrigation	3.56	45 schemes
4.	Training facilities in vocational trades and crafts.	0.30	127 Trainees.
5.	Development of non-mulberry Tassar Industry.	0.35	125 Trainees.
6.	Residential facilities to students receiving training in vocational trades crafts.	0.10	69 Students.
7.	Scheme for spinning & Weaving.	0.36	17 Trainees.
8.	Financial assistance to artisans in selected Trades.	0.20	199 Persons.
9.	Provision for purchase of agricultural lands and House sites.	-	
10.	Reclamation & Development of waste land	-	

S. No.	Name of the Schemes.	Expenditure (Rs.in lakhs).	Achievements/ Beneficiaries.
11.	Provision of wooden bridges and masonry culverts.	0.05	2 Culverts.
12.	Improvement of Kutcha Village Roads.	0.15	2 Roads.
13.	Scheme for Training Centre for Carpentry	0.12	13 Trainees.
II	Centrally sponsored Programme.		
1.	Co-operation (Grain golas, Labourers and forest Co-operatives).	0.52	1 new grain gola and maintenance of 28 grain golas, 2 new laboures Co-operatives and maintenance of 6 old co-operatives.
2.	Ad-hoc assistance for pocket of tribal concentration (various welfare schemes).	7.20	Water sources 29, primary schools 3, Road-10, Co-operative Society-6, Minor Irrigation 5, Land reclaimed 81.79 areas, Housing-48 families, Wooden bridge 4, Community Hall Teachers quarters-2, Settlement in 360 acres of land.
C.	HEALTH, HOUSING AND OTHER SCHEMES.		
I.	State Plan.		
1.	General Duty attendant training	0.29	30 Persons.
2.	Aid to voluntary agencies	0.48	10 Organisations.
3.	Grants to Institutions and Organisations for Cultural, Recreational and Social activities and the like.	0.15	144 Organisations & Institutions.
4.	Field staff & Supervisory staff,	3.19	348 Sources
5.	Recreational & Development of waste land and rehabilitation	0.51	Field staff strengthened.
6.	Water Supply.	2.72	135 sources.
II.	Centrally Sponsored Programme.		
I.	Tribal Research and Training. Welfare Denotified Tribes. Education (Centrally Sponsored Programme).		
1.	Ashram & Hostel facilities to denotified community students in Basic School.	0.20	1 Hostal, maintenance of two existing Ashram hostels.

V

West Bengal with its per capita plan outlay of Rs.243 during the 18 years (1951-69) occupied 12th position amongst the States in respect of per capita plan outlay. The position of Scheduled Tribe population of this State was certainly much low. The sectoral flow was almost negligible and the Scheduled Tribes mostly depended on the programmes under Backward Classes Sector. During Fourth Plan the expenditure under this sector for the Scheduled Tribe population was Rs. 38,712.13 lakhs, which was 0.32 per cent only.

The normal schemes, which were usually executed up to Fourth Plan period for the Welfare of the Scheduled Tribes under Backward Classes Sector were mainly relating to educational grant schemes, schemes for construction of houses for poor and deserving Scheduled Tribes, scheme for suply of potable dirinking water, minor irrigation schemes, rehabilitation scheme for the denotified Scheduled Tribes, scheme for giving ad-hoc assistance to pockets of tribal concentration, scheme for constructions of Primary school buildings, hostel buildings attached to schools and colleges, roads, bridges and culverts and economic support schemes like establishing grain gola, labourers and forest Co-operative and training-cum-production centres. Some progress was achieved in promoting education in Secondary and post-Secondary stages, in other fields the coverage was extremely poor. Due to lack of any integrated approach whatever benefits that accrued to the tribal people could not be substantiated in real terms subsequently.

The State of West Bengal could not satisfy the criteria of having 2/3rd or more tribal population, an area of 150-200 squares miles viability to function as an administrative unit and a population of about 25,00 for opening of the tribal development blocks since second Plan period. It was also not possible to carve out any Tribal Development Block even on the basis of reduced criteria of 50 per cent, tribal concentration for the Fourth Plan. Because of dispersed tribal population in the State even the scheme of sub-Blocks on the criteria of i) an area of 60-100 sq. miles ii) total population of 10,000; iii) tribals concentration of atleast 50 per cent could not be operated in this State. Accordingly, since 1966-67 an ad hoc assistance of Rs. 10 lakhs was approved yearly from the central sector for special schemes in the pockets of tribal concentration where at least 45 per cent of the population must be tribals.

Under the scheme for giving ad-hoc assistance about 750 villages were covered during the period from 1966-67 to 1972-73 (Since annual plans for three years to the last year of the Fourth Plan period) in 14 districts under 62 sub-blocks. In these villages about Rs. 61 lakhs were spent on schemes like water supply, housing construction of Primary Schools, Roads, bridges, supply of plough-cattle, land development and minor irrigation schemes, live stock and poultry schemes etc. During this period entire sum of Rs. 61 lakhs was spent with a total tribal population coverage of 2.41 lakhs, which means that on an average a sum of Rs. 3.60 was spent per head per annum. Actually, the figure will be less as the benefits had also reached the rest of the population living in the area. This scheme suffered from lack of continuity and follow-up action, limitations in building up necessary infrastructure for area development and absence of any administrative machinery for supervision.

At the end of Fourth Five Year Plan it was felt necessary to review the performances so far achieved through these years. Prior to this, in 1961 a review of tribal Development was made in the Report of a Commission for Scheduled Areas & Scheduled Tribes under the chairmanship of Shri U.N. Dhebar. It was pointed out that many of the evils to which tribals were subjected were still there. Indebtedness, land alienation, bonded labour system and cunning operation of the money lenders, contractors and traders were playing their roles unchecked. Later on, in 1969 the study Team on Tribal Development Programmes headed by Shilu Ao made similar observations and it was pointed out that the result of the planning was not impressive, rather the progress of development was checked in certain areas and perceptible imbalance occurred in between different regions and communities. It was thought that programmes for general development would also automatically help the tribals living in backward areas but it was not so and the same was mainly due to non-appreciation of special problems of the tribals and drawing up suitable programmes to solve the same. An expert committee was set up in 1972 under the chairmanship of Dr. S.C. Dube for advising the formulation of a new, strategy during the Fifth Five Year Plan. The Committee observed "some of the tribal communities have remained completely untouched by the process of development and some have even been adversely affected by it. This cannot be allowed to continue. It is proposed, therefore, to take a fresh look at the tribal situation in the country, review the strategy of development and define the total needed national effort with a view to making tribal communities equal partners in all spheres of national life as early as possible..."

The committee defined the task of tribal development "as social and economic development of the tribal people through fast and time bound integrated area development and other programmes suiting the genius of the people, progressive elimination of all forms of exploitation and ensuring a move towards the goal of equality and justice". The corner stone of their recommendations was that "tribal development could no long be left" to be tackled piecemeal at the convenience of multiplicity of organisations, subject to the availability of men and material and to the vagaries of out of context policy decision. Tribal development should be treated as an integral part of social and economic development for which a purposive leadership should come from the national level".

Although West Bengal had the seventh highest tribal population of the country, the programmes for the welfare and development of tribal people in this State have had little coverage in the earlier Plan Periods as the State could not satisfy most of the criteria of Tribal Development Block approach. In the Fifth Five Year Plan, the Government of India and the Planning Commission envisaged Tribal Sub-Plan approach. The Guidelines for preparation of Sub-Plan and on Preparation of Integrated Tribal Development Project for Tribal Areas elaborated the outline as follows:-

i) All districts with 50 per cent or more tribal population.

ii) All taluks/tehsils/police stations not included in (i) above with more than 50 per cent tribal population and (iii) All development Blocks not included in (i) and (ii) above having more than 50 per cent tribal population.

There are only three Blocks in Jalpaiguri and Purulia Districts of West Bengal which could come under the purview of the above guidelines. As the majority of the tribal population would be left out under these guidelines, West Bengal adopted a different pattern of identifying mini-micro project areas, by grouping one or more contiguous C.D. Blocks, having a good number of single-unit or cluster of mouzas with

50 per cent or more Scheduled Tribe population as per 1961 Census. This got the approval of the Planning Commission in 1973 and the Ministry of Home Affairs in 1974. In other words in view of the special tribal demographic situation of the State, the Planning Commission adopted separate approach for demarcating the tribal population and with contiguity in boundaries were considered for constitution of a unit for Integrated Tribal Development Project (I.T.D.P.).

In West Bengal out of 16 districts, twelve districts (Purulia, Bankura, Birbhum, Midnapore, Hooghly, 24-Parganas, Burdwan, Murshidabad, Malda, Jalpaiguri, Darjeeling and West Dinajpore) were selected for this project considering the numerical strength of the population. As per the criteria 33 I.T.D.P. areas(sub-Plan areas) were identified in these 12 Project Districts. Of the total tribal population (25,32,969) of the State as per 1971 Census, 38.80 per cent (9,82,958) resided in these 33 mini-micro areas which were under 114 C.D. Blocks and 98 Police Stations. Total mouzas covered in these I.T.D.P. areas number 4,389 with a population of 15,24,487 of whom 64.48 per cent (9,82,958) were tribal people. The area in 12 districts under consideration was 78,963.0 Sq. km. out of which 8633.11 km. were covered under Tribal Sub-Plan.

According to the Planning Commission, the long term objectives of the Sub-Plan are i) to narrow the gap in the levels of development tribal and other areas and ii) to improve the quality of life of the tribal communities. The question of tribal development during the Fifth Five Year Plan was broadly divided into the following two parts:- (a) areas of tribal concentrations and (b) dispersed tribals population.

A concept of "area development with focus on the development of tribal communities" has been evolved for the tribal areas. Where the tribal population was predominant, investment on infrastructural development also becomes an elemant in tribal development.

The case of dispersed tribals is on a different footing. Infrastructural development in areas with dispersed tribals has to be part of the general developmental programme. The focus of attention here has to be on the individual and the group. The development has to be planned taking community or family as a unit.

In addition, a third category namely, primitive tribal communities has been identified--Communities largely depending on food gathering and hunting, having pre-agricultural level of technology with small population size and pre-literate have been taken into consideration for the purpose. In their case a very flexible approach of development (keeping in view the condition of individual, group or community) has been adopted.

In accordance with the above principles on the eve of the Fifth Plan, a comprehensive programme of development was prepared, in the first stage of areas of Tribal concentration. Side by side, programme of primitive tribal communities was also given high prioriy and specific schemes were drawn up for them. It was decided to take up the task of intensive development of dispersed tribal communities at the second phase, during the Sixth Plan Period.

The Tribal sub-Plan which represent total development effort in the tribal region comprise the following four elements: i) Investment for State Plans, ii) Investment for Central Plans, iii) Special Central Assistance for Tribal Development and iv) Institutional finance.

It was shown in the draft sub-Plan that an investment to the minimum extent of Rs. 158 crores would be necessary for the tribal areas of West Bengal. The State Plan outlays for these areas were worked out as Rs. 40 crores. At the instance of the State Planning Board and the Planning Commission the demand for Special Central Assistance were scaled down to 37 crores for additive programmes to the sub-Plan. The balance amount was from Central Ministries' allocation and institutional finance. Financial outlays in different sectoral programmes during Fifth Five Year Plan period under State Plan and Central Assistance Programme are given below :-

Sector State Plan for Sub-Plan areas.	*Outlay*	*Special Central Assistance.*	*Remarks.*
1. Agriculture	389.00	1,120.00	15% of the expenditure on revisional
2. Marketing	70.00	97.70	settlement
3. Irrigation	1,289.00	500.00	operation
4. Land and Land Utilisation.	10.82		were for tribals & backward
5. Forests	115.00	300.00	areas.
6. Animal Husbandry and Veterinary services	69.80	298.39	
7. Education	247.96	20.00	

Sector State Plan for Sub-Plan areas.	*Outlay*	*Special Central Assistance.*	*Remarks.*
8. Health & Public Health	206.00	200.00	
9. Cottage & Small Scale Industries.	33.00	100.00	
10. Communication	480.00	320.00	
11. Cooperation	26.61	200.00	
12. Social Welfare(Special Nutrition Programme).	86	1.27	
13. Backward Classes Sector			
a) Welfare Programmes.	179.90	170.75	
b) Special development programmes for the under-developed tribes.	2.50	88.25	
c) Project Organisation.	-	40.00	
d) Creation of Propaganda Cell for promotion of temperance.	-	1.00	
	4,050.04	3,666.91	

The State Planning Board observed that the maximum emphasis should be given on production oriented schemes to attain viability and for proper integration of all schemes. The Planning Commission also commented that economic development programme could be based mainly on agriculture and allied activities. Emphasis has been laid on creation of additional employment potential through encouragement of cottage and small scale industries both based on agro and minor forest, as well as by encouraging poultry keeping, duck and goat rearing; and these activities should be supported by training programmes and credit facilities. The strategy to tackle the problems of exploitation of tribal people should receive some package deal from the State Government.

In the sub-Plan the main stress has been given on setting up LAMPS (Large Sized Multipurpose Co-operative Societies), one each for 10,000 population to be located in the most concentrated tribal pockets in the ITDP Areas. These were considered the main instrument in the Project Areas to fight all evils of exploitation and for generating sustained economic growth. These are designed to cater the needs of the tribal people from a single point by arranging marketing of their agricultural, industrial and forest produce, supplying of essential commodities and production inputs, arranging flow of credit, providing credit for consumption and social purposees, providing credit for redemption of all debts and post-debt relief care. An apex body of the LAMPS, named as West Bengal Tribal Development Co-operative Corporation (WBTDCC) pressed into service for coordinating and assisting the working of the LAMPS. The LAMPS are also required to provide the loan component of these agricultural and animal husbandry schemes where granting of graded subsidy has been proposed.

The Agriculture Department indicated their outlays under special State Plan Programme for tribal areas and also such other area development programmes like SFDA/MFAL/DPAP etc. Some schemes like training of tribal farmers, restructuring of cropping pattern, construction of small dug-wells, soil conservation schemes etc. were also included.

Forestry programmes in sub-Plan Areas included afforestation, soil conservation, production of minor forest produce, mixed plantation on community lands, cultivation of host plants, training, etc. The medium Irrigation projects in Tribal sub-Plan Areas were expected to cover 150 thousand hectares at the end of the Fifth Five Year Plan, average benefit cost ratio being 1.38 to 2.56. The special schemes on animal husbandry included setting up pig farm, goat farm for supply of requisite species of animals at subsidised rate to tribals. There were also cattle and poultry development schemes and some veterinary schemes like establishment of aid centres, clinic van etc. To increase the employment potential in tribal areas training of tribal youths in cottage industries, in animal husbandry and in forestry was included. The scope for employment of both skilled and unskilled hands were opened up with the increased developmental activities in the areas in Agriculture Sector, Irrigation Sector, Forestry Sector, Road Sector etc. Under Education Sector, to raise the enrolment percentage of tribal children from 58.5 per cent to 71 per cent under general plan expenditure and up to 78 per cent in tribal areas with some additive programmes. There were programmes for better health coverage by suitably integrating programmes under State Plan for opening of health centres, clinics for prevention of V.D., Leprosy and T.B., rural water supply and nutrition programme. There was also provision for certain infrastructural facilities like regulated markets, approach roads to markets, power connection etc. The sub-Plan also envisaged undertaking certain socio-cultural programmes like establishment of welfare centres, promotion of tribal art, language & culture, mass communication etc. for the promotion of the quality of their social and cultural life.

VI

The following accounts from the documents on "Tribals Sub-Plan of West Bengal for 1980-85 and 1981-82" of the Scheduled Castes and Tribes Welfare Department will provide some facts relating to the achievement during the Fifth Five Year Plan Period as well as the Programmes for the Sixth Plan Period for the Scheduled Tribes. The total State Plan outlay for 1980-85 was Rs. 3,660 lakh, out of which flow to Tribal Sub-Plan was Rs. 183.00 lakh, forming 5% of the total State Plan outlay. The sub-Plan caters to 40% of the total Scheduled Tribe population of the State i.e. 2.30% of the total population of the State. The Scheduled Tribes of West Bengal mainly depend on agriculture sector (80 per cent) and on livestock, forestry, fishing etc. (11 per cent). Very small percentage of the workers are engaged in other types of occupations like mining, quarrying, household industry, construction, transport, communication, service etc. Dependancy on rural economy and non-acceptance of urban-type industrial occupation made the tribals least mobile.

The percentages of agricultural labourers among the tribal working population in 12 ITDPs of the State varies from 17 to 73.55, average being above 50. The percentages of cultivators also ranges between 17 to 74, more than 60 per cent of whom possess less than 1 hectare of land with minimum fertility and minimum scope for irrigation. The Scheduled Tribe Bargadars recorded till 31.12.80 stood at 1,80,357; 2,32,695 Scheculed Tribe persons were assigned with vested lands till 31.12.80. Only a small percentage of Scheduled Tribe workers eke out their living from house-hold industry.

In most of the project areas, 50/70 per cent of the total tribal families possessed land and of them 20 to 30 per cent had land below one acre. About 20 to 37 per cent of the tribal land owning families had land between 1 to 2.5 acres, 10 to 20 per cent between 2.5 to 5 acres only 2 to 5 per cent of the families possessed land above 5 acres. A good majority of the tribal workers were engaged as share croppers. Most of them worked as cultivator-cum-share-cropper or as cultivator-cum-agricultural labourer.

More than 75 per cent of the tribal families earned below Rs. 2500 per annum, of whom 44 per cent of the families had annual income below Rs.1000. Due to the low income and small landholding a significant percentage of the tribal families were in debt. The debt range varied between Rs. 135 to Rs. 540 per family.

It was presumed that two-thirds i.e., 4.2 lakhs of them had income below the poverty-line. As about 70% of Scheduled Tribe population lived below the poverty line, it was assumed that 1.78 lakhs Scheduled Tribe families lived below the poverty line, which came to almost 4.2 lakhs working population among the Scheduled Tribes of sub-Plan Areas. The objective being to raise the income level of 50% of these families about 90,000 Scheduled Tribe families were required to be brought directly under various ITDP programmes during 1980-85 ensuring income generation at the desired pace.

Educational achievement was not very significant in the tribal societies. Particularly, due to lack of educational facilities in the sub-Plan areas the literacy rate was very low. In different project districts this percentage varied between 7.8 to 24. Highest was recorded in Bankura district and lowest in Hooghly.

The educational programmes as included in the Tribal sub-Plan for 1981-82 and 1980-85 gave emphasis on increasing enrolment of Scheduled Tribe students at the primary and secondary stages, on non-formal education and literacy programme.

The State Government have made education free for all up to secondry stage. Besides, there are specific programmes for granting hostel charges to the Scheduled Tribe hostellers within some income group level. Separate hostel buildings and Ashram hostels are also constructed for their accommodation. A scheme for granting maintenance charges at Rs. 20 per month was continuing since last year of the Plan. Book grants, examination fees etc. are also provided. The scheme for coaching also aimed at making quantitative changes among Scheduled Tribe students. The Scheme for Ashram hostels being a very popular one was capable of attracting students belonging to Scheduled Tribe including the primitive tribes.

Programmes for development of roads, markets and credit-cum-marketing institutions were also taken up as far as practicable. The Tribes Advisory Council of this State took decision to approach Government of India for a special grant for construction of quite a good number of connecting roads in the Tribal Areas.

The State Government also took necessary steps consolidating and improving the protective measures adopted in the tribal areas to eliminate exploitation of tribals in the fields of alienation of land, money lending, debt bondage, trade, excise, forest etc.

(a) Forest Policy

Dependence of tribals on forests for their livelihood is well known. In certain areas the tribals had customary usage of gathering brushwood/ fuel wood, leaves, flowers, fruits and seeds of certain trees from the forest free of cost. That apart, occasionally under the erstwhile private forest they could take wood for making ploughs or rafter of the houses from forests. With the vesting of the forests in the State and their subsequent conversion to Reserve/Protected forests the customary usage ceased to exist. Discontinuance of this usage had adversely affected the life of the tribals dependent on forest.

It was recognised that protection of forests can only be ensured with the willing participation of the population whose life is dependent on forestry. It was also recognised that without forests the life of the population dependent on forestry would be adversely affected. Hence, a balance between the national need for protection and development of forests and the customary usages on which the life style of the tribals depend was thought worth while for the healthy growth and development of tribal life.

In view of this the Government decided to allow the tribals free of charge-

i) to collect brushwood/jhanti domestic use head-load per individual and cart load per group.

ii) to gather leaves, flowers, fruits and seeds of trees like Mohua, Peasal, Kendu, Sal etc;

iii) to have one pole per tribal household per annum for being used as plough, and three poles per tribal household for house construction every five years; and

iv) to assign any tree in the forest as Jaher Than for the purpose of offering prayers and worship by tribals.

The Government also decided not to recognise any occupier of forest land who had encroached upon such land after August, 1977. About those who had been in occupation of the Reserve/Protected forest land prior to August, 1977 for a pretty long time, a screening was planned to find out who would be eligible under the criteria laid down in section 49 of the West Bengal Land Reforms Act giving due priority to people belonging to Scheduled Tribes and Scheduled Castes. Those found eligible were assigned Pattas up to an area not exceeding one acre per household. In cases where persons settled deep inside the forest it was thought worth-while to make attempt to persuade them to move to the periphery where they would be assigned similar type of land up to aforesaid limit. Attempts should invariably be made to sort out problems amicably through persuasion as far as practicable.

For increasing employment potential, Government desired that downstream activities for processing of the forest produce to the extent possible, should be undertaken departmentally either by the Forest Directorate or by the Scheduled Castes and Tribal Welfare Department or by the existing Large Sized Multipurpose Cooperative Societies (LAMPS). Simillarly, attempts were made for large scale afforestation under the Draught Prone Area Programme (DPAP) departmentally.

As a follow up measure of the New Directive Forest Management in Tribal Areas, the West Bengal Tribal Development Co-operative Corporation Ltd., the Forest Development Corporation, the minor Forest Produce Division of the Forest Department and the LAMPS are taking up various down-stream activities. These include establishment of expeller units, saw mill, rope making, distillation plant, bidi making etc. The West Bengal Tribal Development Co-operative Corporation Ltd was also trying to introduce manually-operated hand crushers in collaboration with the Mechanical Engineering Department of Jadavpur University.

It was desired that the Coupe operations should be given to Labour Co-operatives/Societies/LAMPS of tribals to the extent possible. Forest Directorate employed as casual/temporary workers whether directly or through contractors mainly from amongst the Scheduled Tribes households situated in and around the forest.

As a policy for associating tribal people more and more in forest management the tribal people were given greater participatory role starting from wage-earners, watcher, supervisors, collectors etc. to Directors of LAMPS.

In order to train up these people in the forestry affairs and to build up a closer rapport between the tribal people and the forest officials steps were taken to induct foresters in the tribal development programmes.

Extension of Social Forestry on Government fallow lands or non-agricultural lands identified for community plantation, degraded forests, resumed tea-garden areas was taken involving the land-less and poor Scheduled Tribe persons in the raising of nursery, plantation and nursing of the plants allowing incentives at the rate of Rs. 1 per plant per month.

The West Bengal Tribal Development Co-operative Corporation Ltd. was strengthened with the creating of a marketing wing, consumers' business wing and a development section. Four Range Offices were also opened with officers from the Home Department, Cooperation Department and Forest Department.

(b) Land Reforms Measures

The two main objectives of the Land Reforms programmes of the State of West Bengal are -

i) prompt recording of the names of the share-croppers.

ii) identification of land held beyond ceiling, vesting thereof and distribution of vested land amongst the weaker section of the community.

As a part of the 'Land Reforms' measures in this Sate a sizeable number of Bargadars have been recorded in the record of rights known as preparation throughout the State mostly through process known as "OPERATION BARGA". The level of achievement has been spectacular. Up to the end of March 1980 it was possible to record the names of 8.55 lakh share-croppers, i.e. Bargadars in the record of rights, of which the Scheduled Tribe components was 1.26 lakhs. It was possible to distribute agricultural lands to as many as 11.28 lakh beneficiaries up to the end of June, 1980 out of which the number of beneficiaries belonging to the Scheduled Tribes stood at 2.20 lakhs.

The average size of the holding in each case was one acre. Out of 11.97 lakh acre of land vested with the State, 6.50 lakhs acres of land had so far been distributed. More than 1.78 lakh acres of land were hit by injunction and there were more than 3.68 lakh acres of land still available for distribution. Most of the lands settled with the assignees of vested land were fallow and needed development through such measures as land preparation, soil making, levelling, application of soil conditioners etc.

In order to bring tribal people out from the clutches of the vested interests and make them economically self-reliant, the State Government had tried to help them through institutional finance from the Nationalised Banks.

In 1979 Kharif season, about 52,000 Bargadars and assignees were given bank loan. During the Rabi season, over 7,000 bank accounts were opened mainly for the assignees. It was expected that about 1.60 lakh of beneficiaries would be brought under this bank financing programme during 1980. Among the manifold works undertaken under tribal sub-Plan mention may be made of the following schemes relating to land reforms measures affecting the tribal people.

i) updating of land records of the tribal people of those areas,

ii) confirment of land rights on the tribal people of those areas.

iii) restricting alienations of tribal lands.

iv) restoration of tribal lands illegally appropriated by others, and

v) giving free legal aids to the tribal people.

Under Chapter II A of the West Bengal Land Reforms Act, 1955 restrictions have been imposed on alienation of land belonging to Scheduled Tribes. Following is the year-wise figures of land alienated and restored.

Year	*Quantum of land alienated (in acres).*	*Quantum of land restored (in acres).*
1960-61	933.66	Nil
1961-62	1494.60	4.32
1962-63	774.93	Nil
1963-64	961.65	2.91
1964-65	1154.64	20.88
1965-66	1140.88	10.14
1966-67	1138.55	15.15
1967-68	836.74	16.15
1968-69	1115.04	10.55
1969-70	1400.99	21.18
1970-71	1269.29	12.03
1971-72	925.79	11.65
1972-73	900.75	13.17
1973-74	1249.75	6.06
1974-75	1465.75	299.98
1975-76	196.70	25.33
1976-77	49.85	368.08
1977-78	48.43	730.44
1978-79	69.54	181.64
1979-80	19.00	32.00
1980-81	218.00	45.00

The records show that the quantum of land alienated by registered deeds of transfer has come down from 1495 acres in 1961-62 to 48.43 acres in 1977-78. This apparent decrease in land alienation cases, however does not reveal the actual position in the field. The poor tribals are being dispossessed of their lands either by illegal transfers or by transfer of their physical possession in the land. The State Government have also drawn up one programme of purchasing all lands of tribals by Government which are required to be sold out for meeting some emergent needs of the tribal owners and where tribal purchasers will not be available. Some fees legal aid to the tribal people of these areas are given to meet the legal expensees in connection with restoration of illegally alienated lands to them.

(c) Credit-cum-Marketing Structure

In order to streamline credit-cum-marketing structure in the Tribal Areas the Policy for setting up a number of LAMPS under the Apex organisation of the West Bengal Triabl Development Co-operative Corporation Ltd. was taken in the Fifth Plan Period. Till 1979-80, 52

LAMPS were set up and 25 more LAMPS were proposed to be set up during 1980-81 and 1981-82. The target of setting up 100 LAMPS in all was proposed to be achieved by the end of 1984-85.

The Tribal Development Co-operative Corporation and the LAMPS are designed to undertake various functions with the help of other secondry level cooperative institutions, apex bodies and Banks. These include both credit and non-credit activities. In the matter of short term loan for agricultural operation the LAMPS are linked with the Central Cooperative Banks and other sponsoring institutions. Though in principle the LAMPS are supposed to get financial assistance from the Banks or Cooperative institutions for mid-term loan as well as for short term loan for various non-agricultural purposes, the Tribal Development Cooperative Corporation and the LAMPS often have to come forward to finance the credit needs of the tribal members in such cases where credit is not made available from those Banking Institutions.

In order to make an assessment of the working of the LAMPS a study was undertaken by the Cuttural Research Institute of the Scheduled Castes and Tribes Welfare Department. Of the 33 LAMPS studied so far the toal number of beneficiaries were 4,42,931, the tribal beneficiaries being 3,43,020 i.e. 77.44%. Total number of enrolled members in 1979 were 28,211 of which 23,470, i.e. 83.2% were tribals. Till 1979, 9,528 (40.6%) tribal members were granted short term loan of which2,582, i.e., 27.10% were defaulters. Out of 1,245 tribal members, who were granted mid-term loan, 27.46%, i.e., 419 were defaulters. Consumption loan was advanced to 735 tribal members of which 371, i.e., 50.48% did not pay even single instalment. Artisan loan was paid to 137 tribal members and out of them 99, i.e., 72.26% were defaulters. Twenty-five LAMPS started consumers' business dealing in various articles like cereals and pulses, edible oil, clothing, stationaries, agri implements, and cattle feed. Percentage of tribal buyers ranged from 50 to 100 varying from LAMPS to LAMPS. In the business of forest products 3,92,177 persons were benefited till 1979 of which 2,99,220, i.e. 76% were tribals. The Banks had in general shown their eagerness to route credit at (Differential Rates of Interest) DRI through the Tribal Development Co-operative Corporation (TDCC) and LAMPS for financing eligible individual cases. With the amendment of the West Bengal Scheduled Castes and Scheduled Tribes Development and Finance Corporation Act, the Scheduled Tribe people were also covered under the loaning operations of the Corporation. This benefited individual Scheduled Tribe entrepreneurs in undertaking economic activities.

In the marketing of the forest produces the LAMPS and Tribal Development Co-operative Corporation had still to depend largely on the existing business overcomes. The constitution of TRIFED, a Federation of Tribal Development Corporations and Forest Development Corporations, is expected to answer the long-felt need in this respect.

d) Excise Policy Relating to Tribal Areas in West Bengal

The Excise Policy of this State in tribal areas are as follows:-

i) no new liquor shops in predominantly tribal areas (that is *mouzas*) should be opened;

ii) existing CS shops located in tribal concentrated *mouzas* would be gradually shifted outside,

iii) *pachwai* shops may be retained or set up in tribal *mouzas* only if they are run by tribals accordingly other *pachwai* shops in tribal *mouzas* may be abolished; and

iv) Home-brewing *pachwai* licences may instead be issued in adequate numbers.

In pursuance of the above decisions no new CS *pachwai* licence has been granted in areas predominantly inhabited by tribals. The State Government's decision to arrange for gradual shifting of existing CS shopsnow located in tribal concentrated *mouzas* to outside was communicated to districts. The process of shifting is continuing. Out of 33 country liquor shops situated in tribal concentrated areas, 3 shops were shifted and attempts were made to shift the remaining shops from tribal areas. The delay in shifting the existing shops from the tribal areas was, however, mainly due to non-availability of suitable objection-free sites to which these shops might be shifted.

According tothe State Government's Excise policy in tribal areas relating to *pachwai*, the district officers have been requested to issue home-brewing pachwai licences in adequate number in tribal areas for traditional needs of the tribal people and on special occasions such as marriage, death and religious festival.

The Tribal sub-Plan approach adopted for the ITDP Areas continued during the Sixth Plan Period also. It was observed during implementation of earlier sub-Plan programmes that in spite of higher rate of investment in the sub-Plan Areas the resultant accrual of benefit to the tribal people and response of the tribal people to these programmes were not commensurate with the pace. Accordingly in the formulation of the Sixth Plan document care was taken to ensure that the sub-Plan mechanism really caters to the needs of the poorer sections of the Scheduled Tribe people and involve them intimately in the programmes of the ITDP. The programmes were accordingly reoriented.

The programmes started during Fifth Five Year Plan also continued and where necessary intensified and added during the Sixth Plan Period i.e., 1980-85. The percentages of flow of fund of State Plan to sub-Plan during 1980-81, 81-82, and 80-85 were 3.4%, 3.4% and 3.5% respectively. For better monitoring of accrual of Plan provisions in the Tribal sub-Plan Areas, it was felt necessary to open a separate demand for tribal sub-Plan Areas pooling all the sectoral provision in that demand.

VII

The document on the "Tribal Sub-Plan of West Bengal: 1985-90 and 1985-86" presents the following facts.

The geographical area covered by 33 micro ITDP areas in 12 ITDP Districts (Jalpaiguri, West-Dinajpur, Malda, Murshidabad, 24-Parganas, Burdwan, Birbhum, Bankura, Midnapore, Purulia, Hooghly, Darjeeling) is 8,84,55,273 hectares. This area is spread over 4,492 *mouzas* in 101 Police Stations.

Till the end of the Sixth Five-Year Plan no special development programme could be drawn to benefit 61.20 tribal population of the State.

On the eve of the Seventh Five-Year Plan Government of India proposed for a higher coverage with the adoption of cluster approach, each cluster having 5000 or above total population with ST concentration of 50% or more. It has been found that such cluster approach will not be suitable for this State. Accordingly with the approval of the Government of India an alternative approach has been adopted in this State. With this alternative approach the Tribal sub-Plan concept can be extended to 3187 neighbouring *mouzas* covering additional 7,10,351 tribal population. According to this new strategy in all 17,25,285 ST population can be brought under Tribal sub-Plan, constituting 68.11 per cent of the total tribal population of the State.

There will be 13 ITDP Districts in place of existing 12 with the inclusion of Nadia District.

Only individual family approach should be adopted for these 31.89% left out ST families. In order to pay special attention to them a new scheme, namely, Special Development Programmes for the ST population living outside ITDP has been introduced under the Backward Classes sector from 1985-86. The financial provisions proposed for 1985-86 and 1986-87 under this scheme are Rs. 58 lakhs and Rs. 100 lakh approximately.

The Totos, the Birhors and the Lodha/Kherias have been classified as 'Primitive Tribes' in this State. The State Government have further proposed for inclusion of the Forest Rabhas and the Lepchas among the primitive tribes of this State in view of their subsistence level of economy, non-agricultural occupation, secluded habitat etc. In consideration of the urgency to speed up development of the Rabhas the State Government have proposed for undertaking special programme for them during the Seventh Five-Year Plan.

During Sixth Plan period Government of India provided Rs. 72.19 lakhs for the development of identified primitive tribes. During 1985-86 the Govt. of India agreed to fund to the tune of Rs. 24.85 lakhs. The fund was utilised mainly on housing, education, water-supply, small irrigation, soil conservation, horticulture, animal husbandry and small trades and crafts. The tribal people living in the three hill sub-Divisions of Darjeeling District are not getting benefit of Tribal sub-Plan. Originally one ITDP area was demarcated in the Kalimpong Sub-division to cater to the needs of the tribal people of that area. In view of the fact that the area falls within Hillls Areas Development Plan, the Planning Commission did not allow any ITDP for this area. Various Tribal Councils of the Hill areas are not, however, happy with this arrangement, as the treatment they could have received under the Tribal sub-Plan is lacking in the Hill Affairs Plan. During 1985-86 the TSP outlay was proposed as Rs. 2771.64 lakhs which was 3.7% of the total State Plan of Rs. 75000.00 lakhs proposed for 1985-86. The 7th Plan proposed for the TSP is Rs. 19005.67 lakhs.

During the decade 1971-1981 the literacy rate among the Scheduled Tribes of this State has registered a rise from 8.92% to 13.21%. The male ST literacy rate in 1981 was 21.16% and the female literacy rate was 5.01% in comparison to general male literacy rate of 50.67% and female general literacy rate of 30.25%. Thus in spite of so much educational development programmes undertaken for the STs the gap still continues rather widely. The literacy position in the ITDP Areas separately is not available from the 1981 Census data. In the up-dated Project Report of Hooghly ITDP a finding has been arrived at on the basis of socio-economic survey conducted in 1983. According to this sample survey the literacy rate among the tribals was 26.6%, 39.9% being among the males and 12.5% among the females. This is not perhaps a representative figure as the tribal literacy in Hooghly ITDP according to Bench Mark Survey, 1977 was only 6.84%.

According to the undated Project Reports of Malda and Hooghly ITDP prepared by the Agricultural Finance Corporation Ltd (AFC) the position of tribal students in relation to total enrolment at various levels of education are as follows:-

Primary	Malda ITDP 1982-83	Total enrolment	10,655
		ST enrolment	3,920
		PC of ST to Total.	36.78%
		ST Boys	38.05%
		ST Girls	34.49%
Middle	Hooghly ITDP 1982-83	Total enrolment	2,676
		ST enrolment	119
		PC of ST to Total	4.4%
		ST Girls	nil.
High	Hooghly ITDP 1982-83	Total Enrolment	26,171
		ST enrolment	925
		PC of ST Total	3.5%

Enrolment position of ST students in primary and secondary schools and the targets proposed for the Seventh Plan and 1985-86 may be seen from the following table:-

Item	*Sixth Plan Target.*	*Achievement*			*Seventh Plan Target.*	
		1980-83	*1983-84*	*1984-85*	*1985-90*	*1985-86*
Classes I-V						
i) Age Group 6-11 years.						
Boys	259	193	195	210	258	216
Girls	140	77	83	95	172	107
Total	399	270	278	305	430	323
ii) Percentage to age-group.						
Boys	104.00	81.10	80.00	84.30	91.81	85.04
Girls	58.50	33.47	33.24	39.70	63.47	43.50
Total	83.70	57.70	57.61	62.50	77.90	64.50
b) Classes VI-VIII.						
i) Age group 11-14 years						
Boys	39	32	33	34	68	36
Girls	17	11	12	13	36	14
Total	56	43	45	47	104	50
ii) Percentage to Age group						
Boys	30.00	26.23	23.80	26.15	46.26	27.06
Girls	13.49	9.16	9.75	10.31	25.17	10.85
Total	21.87	17.76	18.07	18.36	35.86	19.08

To achieve the above targets, programme has been taken to establish additional 200 primary schools during the Seventh Plan. The 1980-85 target was 984. The quota for establishment of new schools in tribal areas during Seventh Plan and 1985-86 represent 20% and 30% of total State programme respectively. The additional enrollment target for the age group 11-14 has also been proposed to be achieved through opening of 250 new Junior High Schools every year, benefits from which will also flow to Tribal Area. While stagnation in primary classes has been eliminated through introduction of no-detention policy up to class V, the major programmes relied upon to reduce drop-out rates has been the incentive including provision of free text books, provision of uniform to all Scheduled Tribe students, provision of sports facilities, provision of attendance scholarship for girls for the group 11-14 etc. The seventh Plan proposed target is to cover the entire target group among the STs in primary/junior Basic stage under these programmes. The Mid-day Meal programme, which constitute another important incentive programmes aims at taking care of the entire rural primary school children during the Seventh Plan Period. Primary school buildings in Tribal Areas are mostly in deplorable condition. It has been proposed to take up construction of 3,000 primary school buildings in each year for all the areas including Tribal Areas. To bring about unschooled children and drop-outs under the fold of non-formal education, new Non-formal Education Centres have been proposed to be opened in Tribal Areas under two centrally sponsored programmes. The non-formal education programme for youths in the age group 15-25 is continued during the Seventh Plan with emphasis on the obligatory training of Instructors, supply of teaching and learning materials, fuel etc. for the success of the programme. A policy decision has been taken in regard to adoption of '01-Chiki' script in the preparation of primers in Santali Language at the primary stage for teaching through their mother tongue in Santali inhabited primary schools. Books printed in '01-Chiki' by the Education Department have been distributed to concerned Districts.

The schemes implemented under Backward Classes sector for the ST students reading in secondary and post-secondary stages are continued during Seventh Five-Year Plan also with such refinements as are needed for their better implementation. The levels achieved in 1984-85 and the proposed targets are indicated below:-

Scheme	*1984-85 level*	*1985-86 target (Additional)*	*Seventh Plan target (Additional)*
i) Book grants & examination fees	57,343 students	32,428 awards	1,38,571 awards
ii) Hostel charges	25,379 "	7,500 "	59,833 "
iii) Maintenance	33,000 "	4,186 "	33,334 "
iv) Post matric	4,000 "	4,400 "	N.A.

Hostel facilities are extended through construction of Hostel buildings and Ashram hostels. Provision has also been kept for completion/ repair of incomplete hostel buildings and to provide maintenance cost for superintendent and cook. Government managed central hostels for boys have also been proposed to be run at the Headquarters, sub-Division and in some cases at Block level. The residential school for Tribal girls in the Tribal Areas of Belpahari Midnapore district is now a full-fledged Higher Secondary Institution. The number of students during 1985 academic year was 360.

According to 1981 Census 12,73,768 ST persons constituting 41.48% of total ST population are main workers. Out of them 8,34,302 are male, which is 53.51% of total ST male population of 15,54,268 and 4,39,466 are female, which is 29.08% of total ST female population of 15,11,384. Year-wise and category-wise distribution of ST workers are indicated below :-

	1971		1981	
Industrial Category	*Number*	*% to total workers.*	*Number of workers.*	*% to total*
i) Cultivators	2,96,661	31.18	3,95,358	31.04
ii) Agricultural Labourers.	4,65,700	48.91	6,20,743	48.73
iii) House-hold Industry, manufacturing, processing, servicing, repairs etc.	9,651	1.02	13,377	1.05
iv) Other workers	1,79,446	18.89	2,44,290	19.18
Total	9,51,458	100.00	12,73,768	100.00

During the decade 1971-81 there has not been any appreciable improvement either in occupational diversification or in achieving any favourable ratio between cultivators and agricultural labourers among the STs. According to Socio-economic Survey of Hooghly ITDP conducted in 1983 the percentage of agricultural workers and cultivators are 58.3% and 38.3% respectively, which are above the State averages as per 1981 census. According to updated Project Reports of Malda and Hooghly ITDP the number of working days per agricultural labourer and marginal workers in the ITDP Areas are as follows:-

	Malda	*Hooghly*
i) Agricultural worker	254	180
ii) Marginal worker	208	192

Accepting this as two sample representative cases of mandays of employment in ITDP Areas of North Bengal and South Bengal, the average mandays of employment of total ITDP comes to 244 and 200 respectively for agricultural workers and marginal workers. In Malda ITDP Areas, 72.69% of tribal families hold land with average size of 1.66 ha per small farmer and 0.51 ha per marginal farmer and 20.84% of the cultivated lands is under irrigation. In Hooghly ITDP areas however, 15.29% only hold land with average holding of 0.44 ha. Thus on an average not even 50% of ST families within ITDP areas possess lands and their average holding is not even 1 ha. These lands being mostly non-irrigated and lateritic or fallow, the tribal holdings are mostly uneconomic.

The socio-economic surveys conducted recently by AFC in Hooghly and Malda ITDPs give an idea of the per capita income of a tribal family, their rates of expenditure, indebtedness etc. Form the sample households it has been found that the STs in general suffer from financial deficits at varying rates as follows:-

ITDP	*Income*	*Expenditure*
Malda		
Average	Rs. 3,643	Rs. 3,674
Hooghly		
Agricultural labourer.	Rs. 3,949	Rs. 4,301
Marginal Farmer	Rs. 4,081	Rs. 4,554
Small Farmer	Rs. 6,906	Rs. 7,194

In Malda ITDP, the money lenders still predominate contributing 7[illegible]% of their total loan requirements followed by 16.74% from commercial Banks and 12.09% from co-operative Banks. Out of total loan taken 61.39% was used for consumption purposes, 36.75% for cultivation and 1.86% for other development purposes, average amount of loan per borrower being Rs. 261 for consumption and Rs. 605 for cultivation. In Hooghly again village money-lenders provided 51.3% of the total loan followed by commercial Banks to the extent of 44.16% and co-operatives to the extent of 4.53%. Amount of loan per borrower family was Rs. 644. It is thus apparent that though the tribals are gradually gaining banking habits the money-lenders still vouch for major share of their loan particularly to meet their consumption and other immediate requirements.

a) Land Reforms

In order to plug the loopholes in the existing law, a few additional provisions were inserted in Chapter II A of the West Bengal Land Reforms Act, 1955 by the West Bengal Land Reforms (Amendment)

Bill, 1981. During the period 1980-81 to 1983-84 permission for transfer of 273.47 acres of land only was given and that too against purchase of suitable alternate land from non-tribals or for investment on own lands. In the matter of restoration of alienated tribal lands, 336 cases involving 594.05 acres of land were detected as unauthorized occupation or transfer. Out of these 155 cases have so far been restored to tribals under law involving 272.86 acres of land. There are cases of malafide and illegal transfers made at the cost of a simple tribal, a good number of which are still avoiding detection.

There is budget provision under the Backward Classes Sector for purchasing tribal lands sold in distress or to meet urgent commitments, where tribal purchasers will not be available, and to distribute the same among landless tribals.

One important aspect of land reforms measure effecting the tribal people is updating of land records of the tribal people and conferment of land rights on them. Up to the end of September, 1985, it was possible to record the names of 13.23 lakhs share croppers i.e. Bargada's in the record of rights, of which the Scheduled tribe component was 1.61 (12%). Despite numerous legal hurdles, it was possible to distribute agricultural lands to as many as 16.27 lakhs beneficiaries upto the end of September, 1985 out of which the number of beneficiaries belonging to the Scheduled Tribes stood at 3.16 lakhs (20%).

During the years 1982-83, 1983-84 and 1984-85, ST share croppers and assignees of vested lands numbering about 60,000, 55,500 and 46,000 respectively were provided with financial assistance. Out of 65,000 ST share croppers and assignees of vested lands to be covered in 1986-87 40,000 would be new and 25,000 old cases.

Considerable progress has also been made in the matter of implementation of the West Bengal Land Acquisition of Homestead Land for Agricultural Labourers, Artiṣans and Fishermen Act, 1975. Till 31.12.84, 37,589 Scheduled Tribe persons were allotted with homestead plot which was 19.6% of total allottees of 1,91,330.

A centrally sponsored scheme for providing financial assistance to the assisgnees of vested lands has been introduced during 1985-86 for development of their lands through such measures as land shaping, land levelling, contour bunding, small irrigation including hand tubewell, dug-well, shallow wells, field channels, etc. according to the local needs and resources. Out of total share croppers and assignees of vested land (recorded up to 31.12.84), 1,90,235 persons were covered under Barga financing scheme involving government subsidy, margin money of West Bengal Scheduled Castes & Tribes Development & Finance Corporation and institutional finances from Nationalized & Co-operative Banks.

In places where large blocks of land have been allotted to different individuals under the land distribution programme attempts will be taken to group them together into a corporate body like a society so as to enable them to seek development assistance and services of technical personnel for collective development of the entire blocks of land.

b) Excise Policy

The present policy of the Govt. to allow continuance of the tribal-owned *panchwai* shops in tribal Areas was objected by the West Bengal Tribes Advisory Council on the ground that the non-tribals were doing '*bename*' business very often in the name of the tribals. Pending enunciation of any policy in this regard the Excise Directorate impressed upon the district authorities to follow strictly the above decisions in letter and spirit so that the pachawi shops are run only by the tribals in Tribal areas and to ensure that no *pachawi* shop in the Tribal Areas is run by persons not belonging to the Scheduled Tribe either in their own name or in the name of tribals.

Annual home-brewing licences are granted at fees varying from Rs. 1 to Rs. 2 in Darjeeling, Jalpaiguri, West Dinajpur, Malda, Purulia and certain other areas for manufacture of Pachawi for domestic consumption. Licenses for the manufacture of Pachwai for domestic consumption up to such limits as may be prescribed by the occasions like marriage, deaths and minor religious festivals are granted in Darjeeling. Dooars portion of Jalpaiguri, Purulia and rural areas of the districts of Birbhum, Bankura, Midnapore, West Dinajpur and Malda at a fee varying from 25 paise to 50 paise per license per occasion. Tribal and other allied people in the above mentioned districts are further given the facility of exemption from the provisions of the Bengal Excise Act relating to manufactures and possession of Pachwai for home consumption and not for sale during 'Banda' festival and other fixed festivals as may be notified by the collectors.

As regards the upto-date achievements for implementation of the excise policy, it is stated that--i) No new liquor shop in predominantly tribal mouzas should be opened; and ii) Home brewing Pachwai licences in large numbers. It may be stated that brewing of Pachawi is slowly being replaced by drinking of distilled alcohol. Socio-economic changes in the country have contributed to some extent to this change of drinking habit among the tribal people.

Actions are being taken for shifting of Country Spirit shops and Pachwai shops form tribal mouzas to non-tribal mouzas. But the process is slow mainly for the reason of non-availability of suitable sites in such non-tribal areas. Moreover the existing licences are reluctant to shift their shop from the existing sites and in fact certain writ petitions were filed by the licenses. Excise Dept. is examining the question of framing necessary rules in this regard.

c) Forest Policy

In order to ensure that the tribal collectors get remunerative prices of their collections and the role of contractors is eliminated, the West Bengal Tribal Development Co-operative Corporation Ltd. (WBTDCC) and the LAMPS have been trading on Kendu leaves and sal seeds on monopoly basis. Besides, the State Govt. have also introduced a price support scheme through the WBTDCC for collection of other Minor Forest Produce like Myrobalan, Neem, Mahua, Karanja, Jusum, Sabai grass etc. with a view to stopping exploitation of the tribal collectors by unscrupulous traders. Position of collection, sale and generation of employment during the calendar years 1981, 1982 and 1983 in respect of Kendu leaf and Sal seed is indicated as follows :

Year	*Total Collection*		*Total Sale value (lakh Rs) Kendu leaf/salseed.*		*Total mandays created.*
	Kendu leaf	*Sal seed*			
1981	20,00,000 kg	1981 MT	Rs.16.00	Rs.31.00	8.6 lakh
1982	16,00,000 kg	1660 MT	Rs.40.00	Rs.23.00	9 lakh
1983	14,50,000 kg	4100 MT	Rs.51.00	Rs.66.00	10.10 lakh.

The WBTDCC and its affiliated bodies have taken up some processing units like sal-leaf plate making, lime manufacture, stone crushing, rope making etc. The WBTDCC and some LAMPS are also going ahead in taking up some value-addition projects like mini-solvent extraction, oil expeller, khair plant, mini paper plant, cotton (simul) spinning mill etc.

There are as many as 164 forest villages in the districts of Jalpaiguri and Darjeeling distributed in five forest Divisions as follows:-

Division villages.	*No.of forest*	*Tribal Population*	*Non-tribal population*	*Total population.*
i) Baikanthapur	4	1,250	-	1,250
ii) Jalpaiguri	24	3,388	834	4,231
iii) Buxa	29	8,532	241	9,274
iv) Cooch-Behar	18	6,268	2,842	6,509
v) Karseong	26	462	7,460	3,304
vi) Darjeeling Kalimpong	63	2,119		9,579
	164	22,019	12,128	34,147

Of them the first 4 Divisions are mostly under ITDP. The population as estimated in 1980 comprise mostly of Scheduled Tribe which is more than 2/3rds in the ITDP area only the percentage of ST population will be more than 90%. These forest villagers were allowed homestead land and enjoyed free firewood, free grazing, free building materials, fodder etc. and in return they had to give free labour to raise 0.40 ha.of plantations and tend an equivalent area of one year old plantation. This 'begar' system was abolished in 1969 and the forest villagers are entitled to get wages for forestry work. A policy decision has been taken to change this age old concept by conferring lease-hold rights on them in order to make them eligible to get institutional finance and enjoy various development programmes for improving their economic conditions. Only one hectare of land will be leased out to each forest villager, the lease area in respect of hill sub-Divisions of Darjeeling District being 0.60 hectares.

As per policy adopted to eliminate contractors from timber operation gradually, the Forest Department and Forest Development Corporation are coming up in a big way for departmental operation of wood lot. The LAMPS are also being given forest coupe operation and supply of wood to Tea gardens of North Bengal.

The New Directives on Forest Management in Tribal Areas have been followed by granting monopoly rights of collection of minor forest produce like Kendu leaves, sal seeds, etc. to the WBTDCC and LAMPS. As against annual changeable royalty of Rs. 8 lakh approximately the Forest Department has agreed to charge Rs. 2.50 lakh only.

A large section of tribal people including tribal women have been involved in the manufacturing of Sal-leaf plates through semi-mechanised process. Rope making has also been introduced. The West Bengal Forest Development Corporation has started one Khoir-making plant in Jalpaiguri. The WBTDCC is also going for a mini-paper plant in that District. These are expected to provide additional returns to the tribal people engaged in the collection of raw materials. Suitable schemes are also being thought out for extraction of oil from the oil seeds of tree origin.

The Forest Department has further allowed the WBTDCC to undertake tree felling operation in the southern districts of South Bengal through LAMPS by replacing private contractors. The LAMPS which are also designed to take up forest labour contract jobs, will associate tribal members in the felling, debunking, cutting, carriage operations both for wood lot and fire wood. The entire operation during 1985-86 generally covered forest area of 650 hectares with an average expected yield of 30 cu.m. per hectare. As per approved rate, cost per cu.m. operation has been estimated to Rs. 86.33 of which labour component will be Rs. 61.30. In North Bengal the LAMPS will continue undertaking peel operation for supplying fire wood to Tea gardens.

A massive developmental programme has also been taken in hand in the forest villages with the assistance provided by the Government of India under Article 275 (1)- Ist proviso.

Credit cum Marketing out of 100 LAMPS targeted to be set up by the end of the 6th Five Year Plan 66 LAMPS were organized till December 1984. A special drive was taken to organize as many LAMPS as possible within 1984-85 for which 36 probable centres were identified in the ITDP areas. It has been contemplated to set up in all 130

LAMPS by the end of the Seventh Plan. The existing membership of the 66 LAMPS is 66.0000 out which 56,000 are tribals. It is anticipated that at the rate of 2000 ST members per LAMPS total ST membership in LAMPS will be 2,70,000 by the end of Seventh Plan. It is expected that by the end of the Seventh Plan the entire ST population of ITDP Areas can be brought within the fold of LAMPS.

Flow of cooperative credit to the tribal members through LAMPS and PACS has made appreciable impact. From 1981-82 to 1984-85 around a sum of Rs.20.5 crores was advanced to about 4.25 lakh share-croppers and assignees of vested lands under Bargo financial scheme out of which 75% belonged to SC and ST. Against the 6th Plan target of channelising 6% of the short-term production credit among the STs the achievement has been 5%. The Seventh Plan target has also been kept at 6% of the total ST credit. Long-term credit flow to ST members is also expected to increase with the enactment of the new West Bengal Cooperative Societies Act which will enable the land Development Banks to dispense investment credit without insisting on landed security and to participate in implementation of IRDP (Integrated Rural Development Programmes) in a more significant manner. During the Sixth Plan period around Rs. 105.72 lakhs was advanced as consumption credit, Medium Term (MT) loan etc. and Rs. 75 lakhs was advanced annually on an average for forestry operations. Till 1983-84 both the short-term and medium-term projects were covered under the margin money scheme of West Bengal Scheduled Castes & Scheduled Tribes Development and Finance Corporation (WBSCSTDFC). The margin money component against short term schemes was withdrawn during 1984-85 requiring the Banks to enhance their credit flow to cover this component.

The WBTDCC has introduced a scheme for providing interest subsidy to ST members of LAMPS for their borrowing from Banks and LAMPS so that they are not required to pay interest at a rate not more than 4%. In the marketing of minor forest produces the WBTDCC and the LAMPS often face difficulty as the ultimate market is controlled by private traders and manufacturing concerns. Immediate steps will be taken to affiliate the WBTDCC Ltd with TRIFED to (i) avail of the TRIFED's financial-cumtechnological package, (ii) derive benefit from its marketing set up, and (iii) fetch other benefits. The LAMPS through their 70 outlets have been distributing essential commodities to the tribals of the respective areas. During the year 1984-85, the Corporation alone supplied for distribution of consumer goods worth Rs. 60 lakhs. The LAMPS supplied Consumer Goods in tribal areas of the State worth about Rs.300 lakhs. The total target for supply of Consumer goods in Tribal areas of the State in 1984-85 Rs. 250 lakhs.

The WBTDCC Ltd. has been supplying since 1980-81 essential consumer goods like controlled cloth, Janata cloth, cheap variety winter garments, napkin, lungi, genji, soap, torch light, battery, exercise books, etc. to the LAMPS throughout the State for distribution in their respective areas through a number of outlets at reasonable rate. During 1985-86 consumer goods valued Rs.100 lakhs were expected to be supplied.

The Government of India's scheme for subsidized distribution of wheat and common rice to all people living in ITDP Areas has been introduced in this State with effect from 30.12.85. The beneficiaries were supplied with wheat at Rs. 1.50 per kg and common rice at Rs.1.85 per kg. from the Ration Shops in Modified Rationing Areas against production of ration cards.

Out of 130 LAMPS to be set up the end of Seventh Plan till date 69 LAMPS have been organized and in 1986-87 target is 20 new LAMPS.

Family Oriented Programmes

The Planning Commission objective to give more thrust on family oriented schemes during the Sixth Plan received priority attention in the implementation of Tribal Sub-Plan (TSP) programmes in this State. The targets and achievement of ST families assisted to enable them to cross the poverty line during Sixth Plan period are indicated as follows:

Year	*Target*	*Achievement*
1981-82	25,423	41,447
1982-83	57,364	90,549
1983-84	70,980	72,867
1984-85 (Till Jan. '85)	74,500	53,357

The families were assisted with Govt. subsidy, margin money of WBSCTDFC and Bank loan. Besides Barga-financing schemes, which is implemented for agricultural development, the Scheduled Tribe families were motivated to accept other subsidiary occupations under various medium-term financing schemes. The target groups among the ST working population belong to agricultural labourer, share-cropper, assignees of vested lands, small and marginal farmers, small artisans etc. The schemes are so designed as to improve upon the efficiency of their primary occupation and also to attempt diversification of occupations. Main thrust in this regard is provided under Integrated Rural Development Programmes (IRDP) and under Barga Financing scheme followed by other sectoral programmes under TSP. Necessary tie-up arrangement has been made with the financing institutions for ensuring requisite flow of institutional credit against these programmes to link govt. assistance. The WBSCTDFC acts as catalyst in attracting institutional finance through its margin money scheme.

According to the assessment of the Working Group on Tribal Development during Seventh Plan an investment of Rs. 10,000 per family has been estimated to be the average requirement per family for bringing it above the poverty-line. A capsule of small units and capacity of the man should be made available to the agricultural labourers.

Group and Community Schemes as well as some infrastructural development schemes were also implemented under TSP both with State Plan outlays and Special Central Assistance. Schemes with 100% subsidy in order to give them some support in their economic activities.

VIII

During the Sixth Plan period following amounts under State Plan and Special Central Assistance (SCA) were estimated to have been incurred under TSP. Both in respect of State Plan and Special Central Assistance the allocations have been reduced than what were proposed in the plan documents.

In the implementation of TSP programmes the SC & ST members of various Panchayat Raj bodies have been closely associated. According to the new set up of Welfare Committees for the Blocks and

Districts on Sch. Castes and Sch. Tribes as SC/ST members of each Gram Panchayat is represented in the Block Level Welfare Committee, which has been constituted with Sabhapati, Panchayat Samity, as Chair-

(Rs. in lakhs)

Year	State Plan		Special Central Assistance	
	Outlay	Expenditure	Allocation	Expenditure
1980-81	2021.79	1332.85	364.58	366.16
1981-82	2620.22	1568.27	366.00	370.89
1982-83	1922.10	16.35.72	410.00	407.01
1983-84	1921.37	1659.18	475.15	502.19
1984.85 (anticipated)	2718.43	2543.12	524.60	524.60

man, BDO as Secretary and other SC/ST members of Panchayat Samity. District Welfare Committees are headed by the Sabhadhipati, Zila Parishad with District Magistrate/Deputy Commissioner, Additional Magistrate, SC/ST MLA/MP, Special Officer, Sch. Castes & Tribes welfare and one SC/ST representative of each constituent Block welfare Committee as members. Project Officer, ITDP is the Secretary of these Committee at the District level. The Project Officer utilizes this forum to coordinate and supervise implementation of ITDP, monitoring and on the spot evaluation of ITDP schemes are done through Blocks and the 33 Project Area offices set up in the ITDP each with one Inspector and three social workers.

The guidelines laid down by the Planning Commission in the Approach to the Seventh Five Year Plan relating to the development of Scheduled Tribes stress that "the planning process in tribal areas will have to be a mix of beneficiary-oriented, infrastructure and human resource development programmes". It has been emphasized that 50% of the ST families should be assisted to cross the poverty line. The Ministry of Home Affairs has fixed a target of 2,56,100 ST families for this State, who are to be assisted to cross the poverty line during 1985-90.

During 1985-86 the TSP outlay was Rs. 2771.64 lakhs, which was 3.7% of the total State Plan of Rs. 75,000 lakhs proposed for 1985-86.

The Seventh Plan proposal for the TSP is Rs. 19005.67 lakhs. The Central Government of India have tentatively earmarked an allocation of Rs.534.69 lakhs as Special Central Assistance for TSP and Rs. 3.96 lakhs for pockets of tribal concentration. Allocation for primitive Tribe will be fixed later. Requirement of Special Central Assistance for the Seventh Plan has been estimated to be Rs. 5,000 lakhs on the basis of proposed size of State Plan for TSP. During the Sixth Plan following amounts were utilized for implementation of development programme for the Primitive Tribes, namely, the Lodha/Kerias, the Birhors and the Totos out of special central assistance provide specifically for them.

1981-82	-Rs. 11.85 lakhs
1982-83	- Rs. 11.18 lakhs
1983-84	-Rs. 24.85 lakhs
1984-85	-Rs. 24.91 lakhs
	-Rs. 72.79 lakhs

Special Central Assistance, for this purpose, was utilized to provide grants on 100% basis. In undertaking development programmes for them emphasis was given towards development of their traditional occupation as well as for diversification of occupations in other areas. Emphasis was also given on housing, water supply, primary education and other minimum needs programme. Development of their age-old culture was also looked into. In the matter of implementation of these programmes assistance of Panchayat, Voluntary Organisations like Bharat Sevasram Sangha, Ramkrishna Mission, Seva Bharati etc. and specialized govt. agencies like District Science Centre, Purulia, Comprehensive Area Development Corporation etc. have been taken.

The programmes implemented so far during 1980-84 included construction of 134 houses, sinking of 125 wells, shallow etc., excavation and re-excavation of 63 tanks, soil conservation 297.88 hectares, reclamation of waste land 33.60 hectares, purchase/repair of 7 pump sets, sabai grass plantation 50 acres, live-stock & poultry 1156 units, distribution of 856 minikits and 832 agriculture implements, various industrial schemes like 250 mat-making, 36 Bidi making, 7 rope-making, 7 sal plate machine, 1 horn industry, 3 other industries etc., assistance to 6 groups with fishing nets, 4 market stalls, 1 community centre, 1 hospital room, 10 ashram hostels etc.

The Project organization in the ITDP Districts is headed by Project officer, ITDP, who is assisted by one Sub-Assistant Engineer and other staff. There are at present 6 posts of Assistant Engineers attached to 12 Project Offices on sharing basis. There are 33 project area offices corresponding to 33 mini-ITDP Areas, each with one Project Inspector and 3 Social Workers.

ITDP works of respective Deptts. are implemented through their district level officers and BDOs. The Panchayat members belonging to SC and ST and the Panchayat Raj bodies are closely associated in the work of ITDP. The Project Officer coordinated the activities of these agencies through the forum of District Welfare Committee and District Project Coordination Committee.

The demands for infrastructural facilities in selected tribal villages being high it has been decided to confine present activities in the following fields mainly. These would yield benefit to both government employees and the public.

i) Construction of important connecting roads and bridges.

ii) Construction of community centres with facilities for literacy programmes, Ayurvedic/Homeopathic dispensaries and rest rooms for inspecting personnel.

iii) Construction/repair of primary school buildings and drinking water wells.

In selecting the village mainly following cariteria are followed :-

a) Villages which are geographically isolated because of hills, rivers and forests like Totopara in Jalpaiguri District, Ranga on Ajodhya Hills of Purulia District Ranibundh PS of Bankura District across Kangasabati, gram Panchayats of Binpur PD of Midnapur District across Kangsabati etc.,

b) Villages with population of 1000 and above and lacking in infrastructural facilities:

c) Tribal growth centres requiring infrastructural support; and

d) Village in Tribal Areas indicating low level of development as standard indicators.

IX

Labour and Employment

NREP-- There is no separate TSP outlay under NREP. As per guideline, at least 10 per cent of the resources have to be spent on schemes directly benefiting the SC/ST. The mandays generated during last few year is shown below:-

	Mandays generated in lakhs		
Year	*Total*	*ST*	*%*
1982-83	360.22	29.78	8.27
1983-84	287.78	24.85	8.64
1984-85	211.87	24.49	11.56
1985-86 (Up to Nov., 1985).	65.22	8.81	13.51

RLEGP --In earmarking fund under this programme 25 per cent is meant for SC/ST population in rural areas. Other than housing project for SC/ST, no other project is meant exclusively for their benefit. Care is, however, taken to see that the number of SC/ST beneficiaries in each project is not below the prescribed 10 per cent. During 1984-85 and 1985-86 (upto Dec. 85) 9.81 and 11 lakh mandays of employment were created for the ST population only.

DPAP --The Drought Prone Area Programme is now being implemented in 20 blocks of Purulia,7 blocks in Midnapore and 7 blocks in Bankura, all in ITDP, giving priority on schemes which will ensure maximization of employment and income of poor and backward farmers with emphasis on areas mainly inhabited by SC and ST.

Labour Intensive Programmes

In the Forestry and other works programme the tribal labour constitute main working force. In the minor forest produce operation through the WBTDCC more than 9 lakh mandays of employment were created during 1985-86. This is likely to go up with the undertaking of forest felling operation. The provisions of Minimum Wages Act are enforced as far as practicable to ensure better wage return. The trend of migratory labour among ST is not that acute due to local employment scope.

SESRU -- The Self-Employment Scheme for Registered Unemployeds has been introduced in this State to enable the unemployed youth validly registered with Employment Exchange in the State over a long period of time, to secure financial assistance from the Bank at low rate of interest for embanking on economically meaningful projects.

AEP -- The Additional Employment Programme introduced in the State as a Central Sector Scheme with 100 per cent central assistance will be continued for promoting self-generating employment schemes in the field of industries, commerce and service through various concerns/societies and also for providing assistance to unemployed persons for the purpose of creating additional employment according to the prescribed yardstick which lays down that there should be employment of at least one person for every Rs. 2500 of margin money. Special attention is paid to the members of the SC and ST.

Poverty Alleviation Programmes.

During the Sixth Plan 2,77,418 ST families were assisted with various poverty alleviation schemes and the target for the Seventh Plan was proposed as 2,82,582 ST families. The target for 1985-86, as approved by the Planning Commission, was 79,809. Till January, 1986, 53,130 ST families could be covered, which was 66.6 per cent of the total target. The target for 1986-87 is 77,515 ST families which will include also those families who require second dose of assistance.

A brief discussion of the important programmes for the purpose is given below:-

Integrated Rural Development Programme (IRDP)

The target groups under this programme are small and marginal farmers, landless labourers, rural artisans etc. and those belonging to SC and ST. During 1984-85 the State achievement was 137.02 per cent of the State target. During 1986-87, the targeted number of families to be covered per Block is estimated to be 600 including old beneficiaries requiring second dose of assistance. The proposed outlay for 1986-87 is Rs.1700 lakhs, out of which Rs.170 lakhs, being 10 per cent of the total outlay, is proposed under TSP. The coverage of ST families has been estimated to be 20,000 during 1986-87.

The IRDP is implemented through the Panchayat Samities in all the 341 Blocks of the State under the supervision and guidance of respective district DRDA. The percentage of ST population during the last two years of the Sixth Plan were as follows:-

1983-84 - 13,363 ST families, which is 5.6% of total
1984-85 - 11,093 ST families, which is 6.2% of total
(upto Feb., 1985.).

The Seventh Plan proposals for the State and TSP are Rs.15,000 lakhs and Rs. 1500 lakhs respectively. The number of ST beneficiaries targeted for the Seventh Plan and 1985-86 is 1,25,000 and 25,000 respectively. The Scheduled Castes & Tribes Development and Finance Corporation is primarily concerned with economic uplift of the target group families through formulation of income generation schemes for providing adequate income for these families. The schemes will be formulated with the already accepted funding patterns of 20% margin money of this Corporation of soft loan basis, 30% institutional finance and 50% as subsidy under different government funds.

The Corporation proposed to implement schemes for 2 lakh 36 thousand beneficiary families during the Seventh Plan Period.

Since October, 1985 the margin money component against IRDP schemes have been delinked requiring the banks to increase their credit flow to substitute this component.

During 1982-83, 1983-84 and 1984-85 there has been progressive improvement in the investment trend in the financing of ST cases with margin money of the Corporation. The achievements during those periods were 3,074; 9,430 and 13,886 ST families respectively.

It is with this aim that the Corporation has drawn up a programme for covering 35,400 ST families during 1986-87 involving government subsidy of Rs. 6.90 crores, bank loan of Rs. 4.14 crores ; and margin money of Rs. 2.76 crores.

Development Schemes under Article 275 (1) of the Constitution of India:

Under provision of Article 275(1) first proviso of the Constitution of India, Government of India accorded administrative approval worth Rs.1009 lakhs to the project on development of forest villages and released Rs. 143 lakhs during 1985-86.

The Project has been taken in hand for implementation through the West Bengal Forest Development Corporation.

Eighth Finance Commission Award:

The Eighth Finance Commission has given award relating to upgradation of the standards of administration in Tribal areas for the period 1984-85.

The infrastructural facilities in the selected tribal villages has been proposed to be confined to following terms:

i) Construction of important connecting roads and bridges.

ii) Construction and repair of school buildings and spot for drinking water supply; and

iii) Construction of community centres with facilities for literacy programmes, Ayurvedic/Homeopathic dispensaries and mass communication.

Special Central Assistance :

Bulk of Central Assistance provided by the Govt.of India as additive to TSP is mainly utilized in implementing family oriented schemes and income generating schemes through LAMPS. ST families assisted during the Sixth Five Year Plan and requiring second dose or back-up assistance for enabling them to cross the poverty line may be supported with another family-oriented scheme provided that the total project cost of all the family oriented schemes granted to each should not exceed Rs. 12,000 per family.

As far as practicable, the family oriented schemes should be implemented in conjunction with State Plan outlays in cluster of villages selected for specific occupational groups like agricultural workers, leather workers, weavers, other rural artisans, share-croppers, assignees of vested lands, fishermen, scavengers, etc. or for specific agricultural developmental programmes for small and marginal farmers. The packages of schemes devised for individual families in a cluster should be projectised taking into account all aspects relevant to the successful implementation of the schemes.

The family oriented schemes should be implemented on loan-cum-subsidy basis as per tie-up arrangements existing or to be introduced in this regard.

Implementation of group community or cooperative schemes should be taken up only when normal family benefiting approach cannot be adopted to bring the individual ST families above the poverty line. It should further be ensured that each constituent ST member of the group community or cooperative is assured of his due and adequate share of income not as a wage earner but as an active partner to enable him to go above the poverty line. Role of intermediaries in any form should be completely abolished.

Women's Programme

The programme of development of women and children in Rural Areas under IRDP is new being implemented in the district of Bankura and Purulia which are very much accustomed to migratory labour. Some other sectoral programmes especially in the field of animal husbandry, making of fishing nets, paddy to rice scheme, bidi-making, weaving etc. are being implemented with the involvement of tribal women.

Programme for economic development through group efforts has been found to be successful in the district of Bankura, where Mahila Samities of tribal women organized the Centre for Women's' Development Studies, were financially assisted for undertaking sericulture, animal husbandry and leaf-plate making.

III FINANCIAL AND PHYSICAL ACHIEVEMENTS UNDER TPS DURING 1984-85, 1985-86 AND 1986-87.

State Plan Flow			*Special Central Assistance (Rs. in lakhs)*			
Year	*Outlay*	*Expenditure (anticipated)*	*Allocation*	*Expenditure (anticipated)*	*Beneficiaries No.*	
					Target	*Achievement.*
1984-85	2718.43	2543.12	524.60	524.69	75,000	72,555
1985-86	2492.78	2339.03	616.27	617.15	79,809	74,228
1986-87	2983.97	634.30*	629.20 ***	238.16*	** 78,000	17,241

* Figure up to 31.8.86

** Reduced targets yet to be accepted are 2,73,975 SC and 59,857 ST families.

*** Till date Rs. 918.93 lakhs and Rs. 314.60 lakhs received as Spl. Central Assistance from the Governement of India under S.C.P. and T.S.P. respectively.

OUTLAYS UNDER TRIBAL SUB-PLAN OF WEST BENGAL DURING 1980-85 AND 1985-90

S. I. No.	*Head of Development*	*Sixth Plan (1980-85)*		*Seventh Plan (1985-90) Proposed outlay*	
		State Plan Outlay (Divisible)	*Flow to TSP*	*State Plan Outlay (Divisible)*	*Flow to TSP*
I.	*Agriculture and allied Services.*				
1.	Agriculture	7886.25	1503.50	6711.94	1047.60
2.	Minor Irrigation	8976.70	657.70	25000.00	980.00
3.	Land Reforms	4600.00	702.00	6500.00	954.00
4.	Animal Husbandry and Vety. Services.	2776.00	186.34	5728.00	345.37
5.	Fisheries	2800.00	115.00	8000.00	400.00
6.	Forests	2971.43	716.78	9715.00	1673.00
7.	Comm. Dev. & Panchayat	600.00	132.00	950.00	52.00
8.	IRDP	3800.00	380.00	1500.00	1500.00
9.	Dev. of Backward . areas Jahargram	360.00	170.00	400.00	188.00
	Total	34770.38	4563.32	78004.94	7139.97

II.	*Co-operation*	2339.49	158.44	5595.88	418.92
10.	Co-operation				
III.	*Water and Power Development,*				
11.	Irrigation & Flood Control.				
12.	Power(Rural electrification)	20631.88	2779.58	55367.00	5664.31
IV	*Industries & Minerals*				
13.	Village Industries	994.41	274.65	4060.00	420.62
V.	*Transport & Communication.*				
14.	Road Bridges	9000.00	1100.00	10500.00	1120.00
VI.	*Social & Community Services.*				
15.	Education	14718.76	1366.11	30510.10	2011.80
16.	Health & Family Welfare.	11700.00	586.00	24502.00	1225.00
17.	Rural Housing(CRD)	1200.00	264.00	950.00	52.00
18.	Social Welfare	1172.00	134.00	2803.55	94.95
19.	Youth Welfare	812.77	174.30	870.00	162.00
	Total	30265.53	2820.41	61698.15	4391.45
	Grand Total	98001.69	11696.40	215225.97	19155.27

II OUTLAY UNDER TRIBAL SUB-PLAN OF WEST BENGAL DURING 1985-86 AND 1986-87

(Rs. in lakh)

Sl. No.	*Department/Sector*	*Total State Plan Outlay(Divisible Sector).*		*Flow to T.S.P.*		*Percentage*	
		1985-1986	*1986-87*	*1985-86*	*1986-87*	*1985-86*	*'86-87'*
1.	Agriculture	2375.00	2723.00	142.66	163.25	6.00	5.99
2.	Minor Irrigation	2550.00	3100.00	189.00	193.08	7.41	6.23
3.	Land Reforms	690.00	800.00	103.50	109.50	15.00	13.69
4.	A.H. & V.S.	725.00	700.00	51.07	33.80	7.12	4.83
5.	Fisheries	750.00	810.00	28.00	38.00	3.73	4.69
6.	Forest	1025.00	1065.00	22.50	241.05	21.70	22.63
7.	CDR Panchayat	181.00	190.00	4.85	7.56	2.69	3.98

8.	IRDP	181.00	190.00	4.85	7.56	2.68	3.98
9.	NREP	-	1775.00	-	N.A.	-	-
10.	District Plan (Dev. Dept).	1890.00	2400.00	155.70	144.00	8.24	6.00
11.	Jhargram Dev.	50.00	59.00	23.50	47.00	47.00	47.47
12.	Sundarban Dev.	410.00	847.00	-	-	-	-
13.	Cooperation	700.00	735.00	21.03	44.90	3.00	6.11
14.	Irrigation and Waterways.	5000.00	5500.00	406.34	558.94	8.13	10.16
15.	Rural Electri-fication	6400.00	18700.00	135.00	135.00	2.11	0.72
16.	Village Industries	1425.00	1600.00	47.97	46.54	3.36	2.91
17.	Roads	1000.00	1440.00	60.00	86.40	6.00	6.00
18.	Education	4598.00	4830.00	192.41	194.00	4.18	4.02
19.	Medical & Public Health	2250.00	2500.00	154.60	184.90	6.87	5.1
20.	Rural Water Supply(PHE)	900.00	1450.00	54.00	49.25	6.00	3.4
21.	Rural Housing (CDE)	90.40	168.00	4.00	5.70	4.42	3.39
22.	Social Welfare	369.00	475.00	33.15	47.85	8.98	10.07
23.	Youth Service	150.00	165.00	15.25	16.00	10.17	9.70
24.	Backward Classes Welfare(SC & TW).	1061.00	1162.00	247.72	558.30	23.45	48.03
25.	Urban Dev.	1075.00	1675.00	-	-	-	-
26.	Labour	-	295.00	-	5.00	-	1.69
27.	Metropolitian Dev.	-	4680.00	-	-	-	
28.	Commerce Industry.	-	3750.00	-	4.90	-	0.13
	Total Relevant Sector	35664.40	65334.00	2492.25	3084.92	16.9	4.7
	Total State Plan Allocation.	67500.00	75000.00	2492.78	3084.92	3.7	4.1

IV SPECIAL CENTRAL ASSISTANCE TO TRIBAL SUB-PLAN UNDER SEVENTH PLAN 1985-90 & ANNUAL PLAN 1985-86--PROPOSED OUTLAYS

(Rs. in lakhs)

Head of Development and Sector	*Expenditure during Sixth Plan(1980-85)*	*Proposed outlay*	
		Seventh Plan (1985-90)	*Annual Plan (1985-86).*
1. Agriculture	319.59	600.00	60.00
2. Minor Irrigation	224.17	400.00	60.00
3. Land Reforms	568.88	920.00	155.40
4. Animal Husbandry and Vety, Services.	171.02	400.00	60.00

5.	Fisheries	64.99	125.00	25.00
6.	Forests	317.49	300.00	40.00
7.	Co-operation	206.55	1104.60	231.92
8.	Village Industries (including Trade & Business).	90.20	450.00	77.00
9.	Roads & Bridges	96.82	250.00	25.00
10.	Education	12.44	30.00	5.00
11.	Medical	3.20	20.00	5.00
12.	Water Supply	49.69	200.00	25.00
13.	Admn. & other charges	46.79	200.40	30.68
14.	Primitive Tribes	60.92	(To be assessed later-on)	
Total :		2262.75	5000.00	800.00

Evaluation and Monitoring

Family-monitoring cards have been introduced in the schemes sponsored through West Bengal Scheduled Castes & Scheduled Tribes Development and Finance Corporation. In respect of TSP schemes, however, no systematic monitoring mechanism could be evolved.

References

1. Tribal Welfare Department(Government of West Bengal), 1958. *Report on Social Welfare and Welfare of Backward Classes in West Bengal*, Pp.49.
2. Ministry of Education(Government of India), 1959. *List of Other Backward Classes recognised for Government of India Scholarships*, Pp.48.
3. Tribal Welfare Department(Government of West Bengal), 1960. *A Report on Tribal Welfare in West Bengal*, Pp.36.
4. --------, 1962. *Welfare of Backward Classes in West Bengal*, Pp.6.
5. --------, 1964. *Annual Administrative Report for 1961-62*, Pp.26.
6. --------, 1964. *Annual Administrative Report for 1961-62*, Pp.26.
   --------, 1964. *Annual Administrative Report for 1962-63*, Pp.25.
7. --------, 1967. *Annual Administrative Report for 1965-66*, Pp.26.
8. --------, 1969. *Annual Administrative Report for 1966-67*, Pp.53.
9. --------, 1972. *Annual Administrative Report for 1967-68*, Pp.22.
10. Scheduled Casetes & Tribes Welfare Department(Government of West Bengal), 1975. *Sub-Plan for the Tribal Areas of West Bengal*, Pp. 270.
11. ------, 1975. *Tribal Sub-Plan of West Bengal at a glance*, Pp.13.
12. Sing, Bhupinder, 1980. *Planning Strategy for Tribal Development in Retrospect and Prospect: A Mid Term Appraisal*, Ministry of Home Affairs, Government of India, occasional paper on Tribal Development No. 29, Pp.31.
13. Scheduled Castes & Tribes Welfare Department(Government of West Bengal) 1980. *Tribal Sub-Plan for 1980-85 & 1981-82*, Pp.220.
14. ----------, 1981. *Tribal Sub-Plan for 1980-85 and 1981-82 Addendum*, Pp.25.

15. Das, A.K.and others, 1982. *Planning for the Scheduled Tribes and Scheduled Castes:- A West Bengal Perspective*, Bulletin of the Cultural Research Institue, Spl. Series No.27, Pp. 198.
16. Ministry of Home Affaires(Government of India), 1984. *Report of the Working Group on Development of Scheduled Tribes during Seventh Five Year Plan(1985-90)*, Pp. 278.
17. ------, 1985. *Tribal Development - A Statistical Profile*, Background paper on Tribal Development, No.12, Pp. 126.
18. Scheduled Castes & Tribes Welfare Department(Government of West Bengal), 1985. *Tribal Sub-Plan for 1985-90 and 1985-86*, Pp. 186.
19. --------, 1986. *Tribal Sub-Plan for 1986-87*, Pp.117

CHAPTER 12

Socio-Cultural Factors in Development of Tribal Areas

K.Mohan Rao

The socio-cultural matrix of tribal communities in our country which is at different levels of development exhibits distinct systems and traditions. Some tribal groups living in North-Eastern part of our country are at present very progressive educationally and economically. There are certain groups like Chenchus of Andhra Pradesh who still remain more or less at food gathering stage of economy . The Kolams, Porjas of Andhra Pradesh and Bondos of Orissa are isolated primitive groups. There are certain communities like Gonds and Banjaras who by and large continue to be as pastoral communities. Tribals living in forest and mountainous tracts like Khonds, Savaras, Kotias, Konda Reddies subsist on shifting cultivation.

Among the tribal communities, traditional values and social ethos play an important role and significance of socio-cultural factors cannot be ignored in formulating schemes for their all-round development.

---

* Reproduced by the permission of the authority of 'Man and Life' and Institute of Social Research and Applied Anthropology, Calcutta from 'Man and Life', 9 (3+4): 157-168, 1983.

The planners somehow missed to take cognizance of these different stages of economy of tribals, causing practical difficulties in implementation. Agricultural schemes introduced among Chenchus of Andhra Pradesh who are more or less at food collection stage, could not make headway as the schemes could not cater to the exact needs of this group and in hundreds of cases forest cultivable lands as assigned to Chenchus at Bairluti, Nagaluti, Pecheruvu and Narapareddy Kunta in Kurnool District, are left fallow. The social and economic levels of the tribal communities, are not homogeneous. But they are at different levels of socio-economic spectrum. In view of this wide socio-cultural variability, tribal development cannot be uniform.

The development schemes have to be devised in the light of socio-cultural factors and economic needs of the tribals in each region.

The developmental functionary working among different communities with different socio-cultural background, should guard himself from the prejudices arising out of ethnocentrism. Generally one views 'alien groups' and their cultures on one's own standards and is likely to project his superiority. When the culture of a particular group is analysed in the context of its own habitat, the cultural patterns are found to suit the local conditions, and the native genius.

Social Factors And Development

Family is the basic social institution which largely influences the behaviour of the individual. The composition of family in tribal areas is largely based on economic and social factors. Woman is very industrious in tribal communities when compared to man and she is an economic asset. If a man has more land, he marries more than one wife, as all his wives could assist him in all kinds of agricultural operations in addition to their regular household duties. Among the rich Raj Gonds and Bagathas of Andhra-Pradesh who are settled agriculturists, polygynous families are found. The second factor responsible for plural wives is due to social custom called levirate type of marriage prevalent among most of the tribes of India. It is the customary duty of younger brother to marry the widow of the deceased elder brother. The younger not only marries the widow, but also inherits the property and children of his deceased brother. This levirate marriage takes place only with the consent of the widow. The plural wives in a family maintain harmonious relations and attend to their domestic as well as other agricultural activities with perfect understanding.

A Chenchu, a primitive tribe of Andhra Pradesh, is highly suspicious of his brothers because of levirate custom. Therefore he prefers to live in the company of his affinal kins rather than his consanguineous kins soonafter marriage. One of the reasons for failure of housing colonies at Nagaluti, Kurnool district of Andhra Pradesh, during Second Five Year Plan was due to settlement of different persons at one place without consideration of local housing patterns and kinship relationship. A Chenchu in his arduous task of exploitation of honey combs from the top of cliffs takes with him his brothers-in-law and not his brothers. He believes that his life will be secure in the hands of his brothers-in-law rather than his own brothers.

The Community Irrigation Wells and Oil Engines given during Fifth Plan Period under D.P.A.P./I.T.D.A. schemes to Chenchus are not properly utilised. The Community Irrigation wells and Oil Engines given at Chenchugudem, Uma Maheswara Chenchu Colony, Mannanur of Mahboobnagar District are not being utilised properly. The group of Chenchus whom community irrigation well was sanctioned at above villages, are at loggerheads in sharing the cost of operation and benefits. But in cases where Chenchus are affinal kins, the Community Irrigation Wells are successful. The Chenchu farmers at Macharam and Venkatswara Bavi who are affinal kins are utilising to the maximum extent possible the irrigation wells and they are growing commercial crops under irrigated conditions. Thus it is evident that whenever housing colonies or cooperative societies or community irrigation wells and oil engines ar sanctioned the kinship patterns and associated behaviour patterns of local tribals have to be taken into consideration.

The marriage patterns of tribals also are relevant in scheming development of education of tribal girls. Marriage by capture is a socially accepted way of acquiring mates in the tribal societies. The girls in Ashram Schools of Tribal Areas of Vizag District who attain puberty are captured by parties of aged boys and marriage are solemnised. In view of their social customs the education of a tribal girl is discontinued by the parents as the girl attains puberty. Numerous such instances recorded from the Gannela Ashram School in Araku Panchayat Samithy of Visakhapatnam district have established this among girls belonging to Scheduled Tribes. In order to develop education among the girls, the Educational Planners have to think of separate schools exclusively for girls preferably away from their habitats at upper primary and secondary levels of education.

Social Institutions And Exploitation

In view of simplicity of tribal people the shrewd non-tribals have been exploiting the tribals by managing to enter somehow into their social institutions. The following illustration reveals how the local social institutions are manipulated for exploitation.

The tribal communities of Srikakulam, Visakhapatnam and East Godavari districts have preserved vital social institution called 'Nes-tam' or Institutionalised Friendship. In Srikakulam tribal areas this friendship is known as 'Sangato or Tonagotta'. In tribal areas of Visakhapatnam, it is known as 'Goth Band' Bar and in East Godavari it is known as 'Nestam'. Even though the traditional friendship is known with different names in different parts, the main rituals, practices and conventions observed are the same. The tribals, irrespective of community, sect, creed, or sex enter into this diminutive association by exchanging gifts. The main objective of this friendship is to promote the welfare of each other and they never think or tolerate ill of their 'friends'. This social association is perpetuated from generation to generation. The shrewd and selfishly motivated non-tribals are found to enter into his institutionalised friendship with influential tribal leaders with an ulterior motive to purchase the fertile lands. These lands are registered in the names of their tribal friends in order to circumvent the protective legislation. Further they secure all kinds of agricultural inputs and benefits through these tribal friends free of cost from development agencies. Thus this traditional friendship of these tribals in the changed context deprives them of their lands and the modern inputs provided by the Government agencies. Ultimately they are also cornered by the new settlers in their own areas. During investigation about the implementation of protective legislation the tribal never reveal that the lands registered in their names are virtually cultivated by non-tribals in view of the oath they took at the time of entering into institutionalised friendship.

The landlords and money - lenders devised another dubious method by means of which they develop spurious marital relations with tribal women folk to purchase the lands in their names as the regulation does not prohibit transfer of land from one tribal to the other. All these non-tribals, though already married, enter into wedlock with a tribal woman in order to acquire lands without any legal complications. Such cases of acquiring land through marital relations are rampant in tribal areas adjacent to the plain areas like Koyyuru Samithi of Visakhapatnam district and Rajavolmmangi, Addatheegala Panchayat Samithis of East Godavari and Polavaram and Buttayaguden Panchayat Samithis of West Godavari District. In the names of tribal wives the landlords enjoy all modern inputs from development agencies free of cost or at subsidised rates. The officials are not able to implement fully the provisions of protective legislation as several non-tribal landlords and *Sowcars* are breaking these protections by entering into the social fabric of tribal communities. The developmental functionaries should also study the local social institutions, customs and practices in order to plug the cunning ways of exploiters.

Totemism and Development

Generally the tribal societies are based on totemic clans. The totem objects, whether they are plants, flowers, birds or animals are revered as their mythological ancestors. For example, the Kolam tribe of Andhra Pradesh like Gonds are organised on the basis of four phratries *viz.* (1) Seven divine kin group (*Yodu Dayaluker*), (2) Six divine kin group (*Arudayalker*), (3) Five Divine kin group (*Iduday-alker*) (4) Four divine kin group (*Nalidayalker*). These four phratries are further divided into totemic clans. In five divine kin group phratry, there is a clan namely 'Dadanja Kumra' whose totem symbol is goat. These clan members claim mythical affinity to goat and eating of flesh of goat and even domestication is tabooed by the members of the clan people. Therefore the Development functionaries have to scrupulously study the intricacies of social organisation of tribals and schemes of distribution of social organisation of tribals and schemes of distribution of animals or birds can be successful only when the totemic affiliations are also considered.

Cultural Values, Practices and Habits

In all kinds of agricultural operations right from selection of seeds to harvesting, the tribal communities observe severe rituals which affect the adoption of exotic seeds and new practices. In Araku valley of

Visakhapatnam district the tribal would not sow the seeds unless they are charmed through certain rituals. These rituals are performed during Chaitra festival which falls during March and April months. All varieties of seeds are brought from the house of the village headman to the shrine of the village deity called 'Nisanidevata' on an auspicious day with beating of drums and blowing of trumpets. The village headman and priest observe fast on that day. All the villagers assemble at this place and the priest (Pujari) sacrifices a red cock and mixes the seeds with its blood. The village priest takes a handful of the seeds and sow them in front of the shrine of the village deity. The village's headman (Nayudu) takes these charmed seeds and throws them five times on the assembled persons from the elevated platform. Each villager catches the seed in his upper cloth held between the hands. The tribal believes that the seeds which are ordained to fall in his cloth are capable of providing him good harvest in the ensuing year. Tribals carry home these charmed seeds and mix them with the stock of seeds in their houses and preserve them until the onset of monsoon. The tribals hesitate to sow uncharmed seeds supplied after performance of this ritual. The hybrid maize seeds supplied to tribals in the Araku Panchayat Samithi in the past were cooked and eaten by most of the tribals as they were not charmed. Late supply of seeds, not charming them in the rituals of Chaitra festival, and several similar factors rendered hybrid maize not so popular in the Scheduled Area of Visakhapatnam district.

The local maize is generally sown alongwith pumpkin seeds. Tribals carry out cultivation in small plots either in their backyard or in their fields which are in close proximity to their households. The tribals do not favour cultivation of maize in distant fields for fear of destruction from the menace of wild animals, foxes and birds and the loss due to thefts. That is why the maize is cultivated either in the backyards or in plots nearer to their households to enable them to constantly watch the crop.

The pumpkin seeds are invariably sown along with the maize. Besides, the pumpkins being the choicest item of tribal food. The entire pumpkin creeper is very useful to the tribals. No only the boiled pumpkin but also the boiled leaves and shoots are used as food. During pumpkins season the tribals are assured of enough food. One pumpkin is sufficient for the entire family for one time. They preserve pumpkins for consumption in times of scarcity and also to be exchanged as gifts with relatives. So pumpkins play a very significant role in the social life of tribals. When pumpkin seeds are sown along with local maize, the maize as well as pumpkin thrive well. As the local maize grows shorter than hybrid variety the pumpkin creepers also get enough sunshine and thrive well simultaneously with native variety of maize. But if pumpkin seeds are sown along with the hybrid maize, the hybrid maize grows taller denying sunshine to the pumpkin crop and it will not thrive along with the tall hybrid maize. Further, the local maize crop could be harvested a month or two earlier than that of the hybrid variety and come to their rescue earlier.

The tribal complain that the hybrid maize corn would be harder for digestion as compared with native variety. On the other hand, the local maize corn would be soft and easily digestible.The tribal cultivators are convinced of the higher yields and higher profit from the hybrid maize, but they cannot forego certain of their advantages mentioned above. That is why some of the tribals still prefer to cultivate local variety of maize in half of his land for domestic consumption. They don't mind cultivating hybrid maize in another half of the plot as this would fetch him better income. They preserve local maize for domestic consumption and sell away hybrid maize crop in weekly markets. Thus the hybrid variety of maize is not so popular in tribal areas of Visakhapatnam district.

Banjaras in Andhra Pradesh celebrate an agricultural festival called Teej in the month of June. It is a festival of fertility. The maidens in the village fill the new baskets with earth and manure. The young boys of the village fill the new baskets. These baskets with seeds are kept on an elevated platform in the centre of the village. For seven days the maidens water the baskets and make all kinds of merriments. On the seventh day the baskets with germinating seeds are brought down and all the villagers worship the baskets. If there is good germination in the baskets they all feel happy and they believe that they are going to get bumper harvest. Thus the potency of the seeds is tested through this ritual before they start sowing operations. The seeds supplied after completion of these rituals are not generally accepted for sowing purposes. The extension workers have to consider the ritual calendar of the local tribals and introduce the improved seeds at appropriate time to enable them to test the fertility of the seeds through their ceremonial sowing.

Kolams are another isolated primitive tribal community found predominantly in Adilabad district of Andhra Pradesh. Jowar is their staple food. They invariably prefer to cultivate their local jowar only and are reluctant to cultivate hybrid variety. The local jowar is known as 'Tekadari Personna' in their dialect and this crop is of six months' duration. They cultivate another variety of local jowar called 'Samasonna' which is of 3 months' duration. Hybrid jowar is not popular among Kolams in spite of persuasion by local extension workers for the last several years. Local tribals are refusing to sow hybrid jowar. Kolams complain that 'Roti' or the bread prepared of flour of hybrid jowar is hard to eat and digest. Further the hybrid jowar stalk is not fit to be good fodder as the leaves are scant on it. For this reason this hybrid jowar stalk is not relished by the cattle also. The tribal farmer is accustomed to scrupulously utilise every bit of his jowar produce. He does not want to forego his culinary habits in favour of higher production.

Generally tribals do not eat new varieties of good grains, new fruits etc., until they are offered first to their gods, as eating of new foodgrains and first fruits, is a taboo. Among the tribal communities it is usually forbidden to eat crops or fruit until they are ceremoniously offered to their respective gods and goddesses. These taboos connected with harvesting may appear superstitious to the modern man, but there are some inherent intrinsic values in these taboos. The rituals are observed generally when crops or fruits reach ripening stage. Indirectly by this taboo the tribals are prevented from using premature crops and fruits due to their impatience or poverty. Hence this practice oblige them to wait till the complete ripening of the crop so that they can achieve greater produce.

Tribals of Srikakulam and Visakhapatnam districts are not in the habit of milching cattle even though the cow population is enormous in these tribal areas. They believe that just as the mother's milk for the child among human beings, so also the cow's milk is meant for the calf. On the other hand they argue that if calves are fed on cow's milk they would grow to be strong and useful bullocks for agricultural operations.

It is observed that tribals are not altogether averse to milch cows and buffaloes provided they are properly motivated about the importance of nutrition and economic benefits accruing therefrom. The Girijan Development Agency in previous years and Integrated Development Agency in modern times have successfully introduced milch buffaloes in tribal areas. The tribals are learning the skills of milching and cattle management on scientific lines and able to augment their income by selling the milk in nearby towns. Because of their better management and supply of fodder they are able to look after their cattle well.

Customs and Needs

The proposed change or innovation in Tribal Areas should be relevant to the immediate needs, local practices and habits. Introduction of changes without taking cognizance of local habits and practices would generally result in failure of a scheme.

Introduction of sewing machines in Mahila Mandals of tribal areas were not successful and tribals are not able to utilise the sewing machines as in the Mahila Mandal classes the sewing instructors generally teach cutting and stitching of blouses. The ladies in tribal areas of Visakhapatnam district generally do not wear the blouses. A tribal lady in this area ties the sari in traditional style so as to cover herself decently. Instead of imparting skills in tailoring and embroidery which are not at all useful to their immediate needs, the tribal women folk can be taught skills regarding stitching Adda Leaves into leaf plates used as dining plates and deseeding of tamarind fruit before it is sold away to Girijan Cooperating Corporation enabling them to get better price of their produce. The Mahila Mandals in tribal area may introduce schemes for cottage industries for which raw material is readily available in their areas. Such schemes serve their immediate needs and aspirations better than stereotyped activities which have no purpose to serve ultimately.

Local Dialects and Development Worker

Most of the hill tribals speak their own dialects and development functionary should learn local dialects in order to build good rapport with tribals among whom he is working. Knowledge of tribal dialects facilitates not only intimate contacts and easy communication, but also enhances the credibility of worker among tribals. In case the development worker ignores this fact it may be difficult for him to work among tribals and especially among women folk who are monolingual. Sometimes it may result in repulsive attitude when certain words which convey different meanings in different dialects of languages are spoken. Jatapus, who are also known as Khonds or Samanthas are predominantly found in forest and hilly areas of Srikakulaṁ, Vijayangaram and Visakhapatnam districts. They call themselves as "Kuvinga" or "Doralu" among themselves. They speak a dialect called 'Kui' which can be included in Dravidian linguistic family. Their habitation are found in the interior places. The womenfolk used to go to medical dispensaries, or primary health centres either for treatment for themselves or for their kids. The Doctor concerned in few cases wanted to give injections to either to children or to mothers. When Doctor said that he wanted to give particular injection on buttock (Pirra in Telugu) womenfolk took their children and ran away due to shyness or anger. The Telugu word for buttock is `Pirr' and the same word in Kuli dialect stands for female genital organ. As Doctors are not aware about this type of subtle meaning, they could not avoid uttering these "Vulgar"words in presence of tribal womenfolk and because of this situation womenfolk developed aversion to hospitals. The womenfolk are reluctant to go to hospitals even if their children are sick. They insist that only their households should take their children to hospitals. If the doctor is also familiar with local dialects he can avoid such awkward situations and on the contrary all the people including womenfolk can be attracted to dispensaries and primary health centres situated in tribal areas.

The Role of Change Agent

The village functionaries and other workers among tribal communities may sometimes land in difficulties if they are not familiar with native customs and practices. The following interesting case study of a village functionary illustrates this point.

A Village Development Officer has been working in tribal village predominantly inhabited by Jatapus in Bhadragiri Block of Vijayanagaram district. Among Jatapus 'Ceremonial Capture' is one of the socially accepted ways of acquiring mates. In this method if any young man who catches the arm of particular girl of his liking, she has to accept the marriage with him. During Chaitra festival which generally falls in the months of March-April all men go to the forest for hunting womenfolk remain in their village and make all kinds of merriments. If any male member of the village were to remain in the village, womenfolk join together and throw water mixed with cowdung at him compelling him to leave the village for hunting. The local Village Development Officer who was not familiar with local customs and practices did not leave the village along with the hunting party. Consequently tribal womenfolk gathered around him and started throwing cowdung at him. In this fair the village Development Officer by a momentary impulse, caught hold of the arm of an unmarried girl. This particular girl informed the village elders and her parents about his 'ceremonial capture'. The village elders in turn compelled him to marry that particular girl or pay a penalty of Rs. 200/- in lieu of a broken promise for marriage with that particular girl whose arm he caught hold of unintentionally. The village Development Officer was obliged to pay a penalty of Rs. 200/- to the village elders and thus got himself exonerated. This illustration highlights the force of traditional values among tribals. The planning will be missing the vital content of implementability of impact if such traditional values are ignored in fixing up the role of a development functionary.

The modern technological advances and scientific methods can promote the well- being of the tribal societies when they are planned carefully keeping in view the cultural values, local beliefs, customs and conditions.

But certain customs and habits which are considered detrimental the prosperity and welfare of the tribal communities in changing circumstances, have to be gradually discouraged. For example, habits like drinking illicit liquor frequently, celebrating festivals for long periods, lethargic attitude towards work especially in tribal men have to be gradually discouraged so as to facilitate for their fuller participation in nation building activities.

It has been my endeavour to focus the public attention on the need to take cognizance of the traditional values and practices of tribals while formulating schemes for their development. My idea is not that we should succumb to the superstitions of tribals, but to realise the need to take advantage of their deep rooted traditional values in the present stage of transition and development for gaining momentum in our planning activities.

References

Bhowmick, P.K. (1982) *Some Aspects of Indian Anthropology.* Calcutta.

Batten, T.R. (1957) *Communities and their Development*, Oxford University Press, London.

Dube, S.C. (1958) *India's Changing Villages*, Routledge & Kegan Paul, London.

Epstein, T.S. (1962) *Economic Development & Social Change in South India*, Manchester University Press.

Foster, George. M(1962) *Traditional culture & Impact ofTechnological change*, Harper and Row, London

Hoogvelt Ankie M. M. (1976) *Sociology of Developing Societies*, Macmilian Press, London.

Madan, G.R, (1964) *Changing Pattern of Indian Villages*, S.Chand, New Delhi.

Majumdar D.N. & Madan, T.N. (1962) *Introduction to Social Anthropology*, Asia Publishing House, Bombay.

Mead, M. (ed) (1963) *Cultural Pattern & Technical Change*, reprinted as a mentor book by arrangement with the Unesco - a mentor book - the new American Library.

Singh, Baljit & Singh, V.B. (1967) *Social & economic change*, Allied Publishers, Bombay.

CHAPTER 13

The Andaman Tribals : Problem of Survival

P.C. Coomar
M.K. Raha

The problem of depopulation among the Negrito tribes of Andamans created great concern to many scientists and scholars since long as these tribal groups of the Union Territory of Andaman and Nicobar Islands are declining at a rapid pace at least since the occupation of these islands by the colonial power(Mann, 1976; Verma, 1976; Awaradi, 1976). The same problem could possibly be present in case with some other groups of our country or countries outside. But the problem is undoubtedly grave for the Andaman tribals and requires sincere attention. Out of the six tribal groups of these islands, four Negrito and two Mongoloid, the Andaman group of islands have given shelter to all the four Negrito groups(the Andamanese, Onge, Jarawa and the Sentinelese) and the Nicobar group of islands the two Mongoloid ones (the Nicobarese and the Shompen). It is not factually known if the Jarawa, the Sentinelese and the Shompen (the Nicobarese are increasing) are also declining ones as we do not have any idea about their population figures in the past. But we can definitely say that the other two Negrito groups, the Andamanese presently settled in the Strait Island and the Onge inhabiting in two camps at Little Andaman are diminishing quite rapidly. Even a century back they were in a big number. But now they are only a few. They are facing the grave problem of survival. Probably the Jarawa, the Sentinelese and the Shompen are also facing the same problem of survival. The question is whether these tribal people will survive in the coming twenty-first century? In the following pages we have discussed this problem particularly of the Andamanese and the Onge. We have discussed different reasons behind their rapid decline and a hint towards their future.

Out of four Negrito tribes of Andaman namely the Jarawa, the Sentinelese, the Onge and the Great Andamanese no demographic information is available on the former two groups due to lack of sufficient and necessary contact with them. As a result we have in this paper, to concentrate our discussion on the other two tribes, i.e. the Great Andamanese and the Onge. Before the penal settlement was established in 1958 the estimated population of the Negrito tribes were 5000 to 8000 (Malhotra, 1981 : 12). But due to their encounter with the colonial administration by the British Government and also with the Japanese a large number of them were killed. The effect of the Second World War and the arrival of the people from outside had affected their population which was decreased to about 500 within a span of 200 years (Malhotra 1981 : 12-13). During the Japanese occupation the aboriginal tribals severely suffered economically, socially and psychologically. Due to their depopulation their sex-ratio has also been affected, and this leads to the non-availability of their marriageable partners (Table-I)

If we go through the demographic figures of two Negrito tribes namely the Great Andamanese and the Onge from 1901 to 1971, we will find that within this time span the Great Andamanese had been reduced to 4.16% of their population as existed in 1901. Among the Onge identically the rate of decrease of the population during this time span (1901 - 1971) was also quite high; in 1971 it was 14.58% of population as existed in 1901 though not as high as the Great Andamanese. The 1901 Census ascertained that at that time the Great Andamanese were 625 souls, about 13% of the total Great Andamanese population(estimated) existing in 1858. Although their population is decreasing, but they have maintained their sex-ratio throughout the entire span, except 1931 and 1961 when their sex-ratio was 137 and 138 females per 100 males respectively. Likewise among the Onge in 1921 and 1931 the sex-ratio

Table-1

SEX-WISE TOTAL POPULATION OF GREAT ANDAMANESE AND ONGE FROM 1901 TO 1981

Year	1901			1911			1921			1931			1951			1961			1971			1981		
	Male	Female	Total	Male	Female	Total	Male	Female	Total	Male	Female	Total	Male	Female	Total	Male	Female	Total	Male	Female	Total	Male	Female	Total
Great Anda-manese	335	290	625	221	234	455	104	105	209	38	52	90	11	12	23	8	11	19	15	9	24	14	12	26
Sex-Ratio			86.57			105.88			100.06			136.84			109.09			137.50			60.00			85.71
Onge	336	306	672	301	330	631	204	142	346	147	103	250	-	-	150*	59	70	129	59	53	112	49	49	98
Sex-Ratio			83.61			109.63			69.61			70.07						118.64			89.83			100.00

Ref. Malhotra, R. 1981. Some Demographic Studies in Andaman. Anthropological Survey of India, Port Blair, (Unpublished).
* Sex-wise figures not available.

Table - II

DECADAL VARIATION IN POPULATION FROM 1901 TO 1981

	1901-1911			*1911-1921*			*1921-1931*			*1931-1951*			*1951-1961*			*1961-1971*			*1971-1981*			*Net variation from 1901 to 1981*		
	Male	*Female*	*Total*	*Male*	*Female*	*Total*	*Male*	*Female*	*Total*	*Male*	*Female*	*Total*	*Male*	*Female*	*Total*	*Male*	*Female*	*Total*	*Male*	*Female*	*Total*	*Male*	*Female*	*Total*
Great	114	56	170	117	129	246	66	53	119	27	40	67	3	1	4	7	2	9	1	3	4	321	278	599
Anda-manese	(-)	(-)	(-)	(-)	(-)	(-)	(-)	(-)	(-)	(-)	(-)	(-)	(-)	(-)	(-)	(-)	(+)	(-)	(+)	(+)	(-)	(-)	(-)	(-)
Percentage decrease/increase			(-) 27.20%			(-) 54.07%			(-) 56.94%			(-) 74.44%			(-) 17.30%			(+) 26.32%			(+) 8.33%			(-) 95.84%
Onge	65	24	41	97	188	285	57	39	96	-	-	100	-	-	21	0	17	17	10	4	14	317	257	574
	(-)	(+)	(-)	(-)	(-)	(-)	(-)	(-)	(-)	(-)	(-)	(-)	(-)	(-)	(-)	(-)	(-)	(-)	(-)	(-)	(-)	(-)	(-)	(-)
Percentage decrease/increase			(-) 6.10%			(-) 45.17%			(-) 27.75%			(-) 40.00%			(-) 14.00%			(-) 13.18%			(-) 12.50%			(-) 85.42%

Ref. Malhotra, R. 1961. Some Demographic Studies in Andaman. Anthropological Survey of India, Port Blair (Unpublished).

was 70 and in 1961 it was 199 females per 100 males. From the Table-II it is observed that though the population of these two tribes in 1901 was more or less same, the rate of decline is more among the Great Andamanese comparable to the Onge. The probable reason may be that the Great Andamanese came in contact with the outsiders earlier i.e. in 1858 than the Onges (in 1886). At that time the Great Andamanese were distributed in North, Middle and South Andaman, where the penal settlement and refugee rehabilitation were made. But the Onges were at that time living in the Little Andaman, which was relatively isolated area; there they were less affected by the outside culture unlike the Great Andamanese. Among the Great Andamanese maximum reduction in population was recorded between 1931-1951, which is 74.44%, when their number was reduced from 90 to 23. It was because at that time, particularly during the Japanese occupation (1942-1945), many of them were killed (Malhotra, 1981 : 17-18). The Onge were decreased during 1911-21 and 1931-51. The probable cause may be that during 1911-21 for the first time they came in contact with the outside culture, which compelled their population to decrease rapidly (Malhotra, 1981 : 17-18).

From the Table -II, it is also revealed that initially the males reduced faster then the females. Malhotra is of opinion that men interact more with the outsiders and have less resistance power while women have the better resistance power 'Homeorrhesis' against the diseases as they have low interaction (1981 : 18).

Mann pointed out another factor for the decrease of the Great Andamanese population and that was the higher rate of the infant mortality among them. This is due to the presence of syphilis and other different types of diseases, which was introduced through contact with the outsiders in the Andamans Home around the year 1864 built by the British administration (1976:43). Mathur mentions that :

> "There was a great deal of sickness and many deaths among the Andamanese in the forests in June, 1866. Out of the fifteen births that occurred in the Andamans Home from August 1866 to October 1866 not a single child survived. The year 1867 and 1868 were also a period of sickness among the Andamanese (1968:96).

Infant and child mortality is not due to congenital disorder. Swaminathan and others (1971) reported that among the Onge infant and child mortality is 40%. 42.1% women among them are also sterile (c.f. Whitaker, 1985:12). Mann stated that "The Bronchio-pulmonary infection in 1968 took an epidemic form and sapped the existence of many tribals" (1976:43). It is reported that the presence of syphilis is considered as one of the reasons for the decline of the Great Andamanese, but the medical examination among 50% Onges do not show the existence of such disease, congenital or otherwise(c.f. Whitaker, 1985 : 12). Mann in one of his papers, has commented that the Andamanese are sterile, which is the outcome of syphilis and rate of fertility is therefore very poor (1976 : 42). The introduction of venereal disease in a small community has an adverse effect which leads to the low fertility and high rate of fatal death which ultimately causes and decline in population (Verma, 1976:20).

Mann (1932) has also pointed out that after the contact with the outsiders these primitive tribes were affected with some diseases like venereal disease, tuberculosis, measles and other contagious disease(c.f. Malhotra, 1981:13). In 1868, Bronchio-pulmonary disease spread as an epidemic form which caused the loss of many tribal lives. Radcliffe-Brown in his book The Andaman Islands states,

> "In March, 1877 an epidemic of measles broke out among the Andamanese, introduced with a batch of convicts from Madras, and spread rapidly from one end of the Great Andaman to the other. In six weeks 51 out of 184 cases treated in hospital proved fatal. It is almost certain that the proportion of deaths was much greater in the case of those, the vast majority, to whom medical aid could be given"(1964:17).

Similarly in 1886 the Andamanese were affected with epidemic mumps and influenza which took away a considerable number of lives (Mann 1976:43). Malhotra has explained that these various types. of diseases and their addiction to opium, liquor, tobacco have led to lower birth rate, and high rate of abortions, miscarriage and infant mortality. After their contact with the outsiders these tribal people were addicted to alcohol and opium, and this is also an important demographic cause of their depopulation (1981:13). Cipriani(1966) is of opinion that the opium was introduced among Onges through the Chinese and the Burmese smugglers. It was also rep ted that the Karen people supplied the opium to the Andamanese as a bribe for the sexual relation with the tribal women (c.f. Mann, 1976 : 42).

After their contact with the civilized people both Onge males and females got addicted to tea and tobacco. Both the tea and tobacco are not good for health. Nicotine hampers the blood flow which has a negative sign for the full sexual excitement (Awaradi:1978:6). Baker and Dubin (1977) have pointed out that smoking might lead to the blockage of vascular passage (c.f. Awaradi, 1978:6).

Different types of diseases introduced have resulted in their depopulation. As pointed out by Pandit and Bose (1975) the Onges have been suffering from fungal infection and ring worm. Awaradi has recorded cases of tuberculosis in one Onge family where all the three members were suffering from tuberculosis which is confirmed by the doctor. (1978:6). Palchoudhury (n.d) has mention in his paper about the high incidence of pulmonary tuberculosis among the Onges. In a recent Medical Survey among Onge by Jain *et al* (1981) it is reported that some diseases like skin infection, malaria, vitamin-A deficiency, anemia etc. are also the causes for their weak health. But Cipriani (1953) did not find any case of tuberculosis, cancer, stomach trouble or any hereditary diseases(c.f. Awaradi, 1978:6).

The other probable reason for the depopulation of the Onge is the incompatibility of marriageable age between the husband and wife. It is observed that a young man may have to marry an aged lady as she is expert in collection of foods from the forest and also in other household activities. On the other hand, there is also a number of examples where the aged man married a young girl. The reason for this type of marriage is that as they belong to the hunting, gathering and fishing community, it is not possible for the aged persons to lead an economically independent life. For this reason they like to marry a young girl who will look after him in his old age. Due to this incompatible marriage age the women cannot utilize her reproductive age in some cases as her aged husband become unproductive or sterile. So the fertile woman cannot utilize her reproductive span. On the contrary, young man also leads to the unproductive marriage as his wife is in the menopause age. So in some cases it is found that both young men and women complete their life span without any offspring. The main reason for incompatibility of marriage age is due to non-availability of suitable marriageable spouses (Awaradi,

1978:8). So the young men marry older widows. The another interesting point is that the older widowers choose young girls as their marriage partner. For this reason also in majority of the cases the young men do not get young women for marriage. So they marry older widows. This is one of the factor for their low fertility rate. In this connection Malhotra points out,

> "Due to the smallness of population, there are more possibility of homozygotes coming together rendering low genetic viability of the individual. This is because the lethal genes whose harmful effects are suppressed by their dominant alleles in heterozygotes, manifest fully in homozygotes. Sentinelese and Jarawa are the best example to elucidate this example in spite of their being not disturbed by outsiders; they are declining in number"(1981:34-35).

> Cipriani(1953) also mentions"Civilisation hasperhaps accused herself unjustly of causing the decline of the primitive races, whereas she in fact only hastened the disappearance of groups already heading for demographic decadence as a result of physiological factors which lie within the group itself. The intrinsic damage done by civilization as such has been exaggerated in some quarters. Biological senscence of a race is brought about by their total isolation for thousand of years exacerbated by being broken in to small endogamous groups"(c.f.Verma,1976:19).

The physical features of the Andaman Negritos like steatopygia, dwarfism, infantilism etc. have impact on the fertility as these are associated with the endocrine glands. In the past the Onges were fully dependent on the forest and sea for food. Their food items consisted of various types of wild fruits, roots, tubers, honey and different species of marine products and also wildpig etc. which have high nutritive value. But for the last several years they are getting free ration which includes rice, wheat, oil, spices etc. from the Government. So they are now habituated of taking these types of food. For this reason now-a-days they do not go to the forest regularly as they did in the past. Hunting is a good physical exercise for fitness of the body. It mav be due to the change in food habit from protein rich to carbohydrate rich food and also gradual reduction of body fitness may be the important causes for their weak health and reduction in the reproductive power. Choudhury (1967) and De (1976) have also narrated that the cause of depopulation of these tribes is the supply of limited food to them. Due to the introduction of new types of food sometimes they suffer from various diseases which are new to them. Due to regular supply of the above types of new food now they have become less active and also quite lazy. This habit also invites different types of diseases like indigestion, which were not known to them earlier (c.f.Malhotra, 1981:37).

Till today the Onges are not fully conscious about the health and hygiene. To pass the urine and latrine they go to nearby places within their settlement. They are not giving up this unhygienic habit. This also have adverse effect in their life, because majority of them now live in the permanent settlement constructed by the Andaman & Nicobar Administration. Previously when they were fully nomadic they did not stay in a particular place for a long time. At that time this habit had little adverse effect on their health.

Majumdar(1958) reported that among the Onges, 38.2% married couples were sterile (c.f.Mann, 1976:42). Cipriani(1966) also mentions that Onge women rarely became pregnant before 28 years. Even after 28 years there is only a hope of fertility, which ceases around the age of 48. Two explanations are available on the delayed fertility among the Andamanese women. One attributes the delayed appearance of fertility to a general biological condition fostered by vagina acidity content, while the other ascribes to the Onge sterility to the *naquineghe* - the grass like apron worn by women. This garment leads to copulation from the rear reducing the chances of fecundation (c.f. Mann 1976:42).

Awaradi has explained that at present the Onges are wearing modern dress, which has disadvantage in their life. In this tropical climatic condition, their body sweats too much which is not good for health. Awaradi states that during the rainy seasons the clothes covering the genital portion remain wet and it may dry up due to heat of fire, which have a negative effect on sexual activity (1978:9).

Rivers (1922) is of the opinion that the lack of interest is also a reason for depopulation among the Melanesians (c.f.Mann, 1976:44). This could be true for these two tribal groups, the Great Andamanese and the Onge, at least for the former one if not the latter one.

Mann thinks that certain wrong and unintelligent approach has deprived the aborigines of certain institutions, practices and customs which gave them interest in the life, which in turn reflected adversely upon their desire to live. Further new diseases resulted into high mortality rate (Mann, 1976:44).

After the penal settlement was established in 1858 the aboriginal population had lost part of their land due to the rehabilitation of convict and settler population. Now the Onges are confined to 110 sq. km. reserve area. Previously they used to visit the nearby islands for hunting, fishing and for other economic activities (Whitaker, 1985:11). Allen (1975) points out, "Probably the most destructive impact of development on forest peoples is loss of land" (c.f. Whitaker 1985:11). This is also true for the Great Andamanese. In the past the Great Andamanese were distributed throughout the Great Andaman Group of islands, but at present they are confined to 603 hectare area in Strait Island.

In the year 1975 Mrs. Indira Gandhi said in a public meeting that

> "Neither resettlement nor development should be made an excuse to uproot tribal groups or cut down forests. The tribals are original inhabitants and any disturbance may threaten their survival" (c.f.Whitaker, 1985:11).

Like the Negrito tribes of Andaman, some other aboriginal population of the world are also rapidly declining. J. W. Page has pointed out that the Yahgans of Tierra del Fuego were reduced to 50 from 2500 within a period of sixty years. The reasons of declination were the drowning and diseases. The Onge are also facing decline due to the disease, warfare and difficulty of obtaining food. In 1870, the native population of Polynesia was 690,000 but after sixty years in 1930 they were reduced to 200,000. Similarly the Melanesians and Micronesians have also been decreased from 3000,000 to 2000,000 and from 273,000 to less than 90,000 respectively (1938:127, 137, 263). W.H.R. Rivers has described the rapid degeneration of native population in Sandwich island and some areas in New Hebrides(1922:84, 90, 94). Evans (1937) in his book, "The Negritos of Malaya" reported that the Semang and the Pangan of Sakai also faced the problem of depopulation. The reasons of their decline was some epidemic diseases (c.f. Mann, 1976:40). This view has also been supported by Rivers. He has stated the causes of depopulation of the Melanesians as the pulmonary diseases like pneumonia, influenza, tuberculosis which also exist among these primitive tribes like the Great Andamanese and the Onge. Table-3 gives information about the rate of declination of the aboriginal population in some other parts of the world.

Table 3

POPULATION WHEN CONTACTED

Tribe and place	*Date*	*by civilization*	*Present Population*
Txikao, Brazil	1960	400	50
Nambikwara, Brazil	1850	20,000	700
Yahgan, Chile	1850	3,000	extinct
Tasmanians, Australia	1820	200	extinct (1870)
Arunta, Australia	1900	2,000	nearly extinct.

Ref. "Into the Primitive Environment", Robert Brain(c.f. Whitaker, 1985:7).

The same thing is also noticed among the Australian aborigines. As Chopra has rightly pointed out in one of his recent articles that the aborigines were cornered in their original inhabitant areas, when the British people came to settle in their area. At that time many of them were either killed or poisoned by the newcomers. Due to the population pressure of the outsiders they were exiled from their forest based land, where they hunted animals for food. Due to the non-availability of sufficient food the aboriginals started starving. Some of those who were friendly were engaged as labourers by the Britisheres. The insufficient food supplied by the white men made them sick and poorly nourished. The diseases like V.D.,Cholera and smallpox etc. which were introduced by the newcomers also took the toll of a huge number of lives. The death and diseases were so violent that the British Government were to set up a reserve area for the aborigines. Later on most of them were handed over to the Christian Missionaries for the supervision and welfare works. But the Christian missionaries considered these primitives a dying community. For this reason they did not take much attention and interest in them. As a result in Tasmania they were completely vanished. The last Tasmanian died in 1876. But in the mainland they somehow survived. Today their population is about 1% of the total country's population, which is about 1.7 lakh (1988:19)

Possibly it was true for all such places where colonial rule was imposed. Like Tasmania where the colonial rule could successfully wipe out the aborigines in Australian mainland the story was similarly true.

> "yes a genocide was perpetrated here too. The estimated 7,50,000 aboriginal population in 1788 had dwindled to around 60,000 by 1888. They were dispossessed, their culture and way of life destroyed.(Chopra, 1988:17).

It happened in Australia where the Aborigines did not allow the white people to occupy their land and reign over them so easily. The result was obvious. "There were a few pitched battles in which at least 20,000 Aborigines were killed(Chopra, 1988:19)." In Andaman also same history was repeated. In the battle of Aberdeen the British bullets took so many innocent lives of the Great Andamanese. Besides there were so many small conflicts those took so many lives. The Jarawas often sacrificed their life to the bullets of those who came to administrate them and take these islands into modernity.

From the above discussion it is revealed that the two primitiveNegrito tribes of Andaman and Nicobar Islands e.g. the Great Andamanese and the Onges are declining. Various reasons have been put forward for this decline. The Great Andamanese are now addicted to opium and alcohol. The smoking of tobacco leaves is now popular among the Onges. As discussed earlier the addiction to these bad habits has adverse effect on the health; so necessary measures should be taken to check these habits. Due to introduction of new types of food and also for their contact with the outsiders, they are now afflicted with some disease like indigestion, tuberculosis, venereal diseases; so it is almost necessary to have their thorough medical check up by the medical specialists and find out the remedy. The other reason of the depopulation of these tribes is low fertility rate, high rate of infant mortality, sterility, etc. In this regard a detailed multidisciplinary study is required to be undertaken without any delay to find out the remedy in case of Onges due to the rehabilitation of the refugee and other mainland people now they are not confined in a limited area and some time they are facing the problem of non-availability of their required food. The authority will give proper attention to stop the encroachment of the tribal land, loss of interest in life. Trained social worker who knows every close corner of their lives and customs, rites and rituals, should encourage them to continue their traditional norms and practices. Before implementing any development measure, we should minutely examine all the pros and cons as which will not affect the type of these sensitive tribes.

The analysis of their degeneration amply shows that what their own environment,-- ethnic, social and physical, -- could not do, ours, the advanced men's new imposed environment could do that. Much greater damage was done to these helpless peaceful souls by the modern men's will to reign over them. No doubt modern men's bullets did much harm to them, but modern men's sympathetic hospitality did much more damage. Our contribution in this regard is quite great. The modern men made them addicted to so many vices so long unknown to them. They contributed diseases, hunger, poverty, pains and what not and all these not only pushed them to degeneration but also compelled them to forget many of the valuable cultural elements of those surviving. But the most important among these is that these have wiped out the most valuable aspect of human life from them, the means of life and desire to live.

Thus we have positive reasons to believe that the tribal people of these islands barring the Nicobarese, particularly the Andamanese and the Onges are declining. The reasons are manifold. Once they were many but now they are a few. The great Andamanese are 28 and the Onge, about 100. The Jarawa may be between 150 - 200 and the Sentinelese 100 - 150. The Shompen, though they are Mongoloid are also as unfortunate in this regard as the Negritos of Andamans are. They are about 200 or so. But no doubt they were numerically much stronger earlier. They have come down from their glorious past to the unfortunate present. Could be that even in the precolonial era the unhealthy and hostile environment and isolation were not-congenial to them and compelling them to degenerate slowly; but we the advanced and modern people, cannot strike our own responsibility in wiping out these lively souls at very rapid space, from this beautiful earth. If we do not become sensible even now and stretch our helping hand to save these poor helpless souls, the day will soon come when we will only read about them in the pages of books and articles and recognise them through photographs as we do now about the Tasmanians and the Yahgan.

References

Awaradi, S. A. (1976) *Decadence of Onges. The Demogenetic Aspects*. Paper presented in Seminar on Genetical Demography held at Calcutta 16th - 18th January 1978.

Chopra, P. (1988) *From the Penael past to hedonism,* The Hindu January 24, pp - 17, 19

Jain, T. S. (1981) Recommendations of Research on *"Action Oriented Research of Primitive Tribal Communities in A & N Islands."* (Unpublished).

Malhotra, R. (1981) *Some Demographic Studies in Andaman.* Anthropological Survey of India, Port Blair (Unpublished)

Man, E. H. (1932) *On the Aboriginal Inhabitants of the Andaman Islands,* Royal Anthropological Institute, London.

Mann, R. S. (1976) *Depopulation among Andaman Aborigines: An Analysis* Journal of Social Research Vol. XIX No. II, pp. 37-50

Mathur, L. P. (1968) *History of the Andaman and Nicobar Islands,* Sterling Publishers Ltd. Delhi.

Page, J. W. (1938) *Primitive Races of Today.* George G. Harrap and Co. Ltd.

Palchoudhury, N. C. (n. d.) *Incidence of Pulmonary Tuberculosis among the Onges* (Unpublished).

Pandit T. N. and D. K. Bose (1975) *The Onge of Little Andaman*, paper presented in the Workshop on Primitive Tribal communities, January 16-17, 1975. Ministry of Home Affairs, New Delhi.

Radcliffe-Brown, A. R. (1948) *The Andaman Islanders.* The Free Press, Illinois.

Rivers, W. H. R. (1922) *Essays on the Depopulation of Melanesia.* University Press Cambridge.

Verma, I. C. (1976) *Health Problems of Tribal Communities in Andaman & Nicobar Islands.* Journal of Social Research. Vol. XIX No. II. pp. 16-24.

Whitaker, R. (1985) *Endangered Andamans.* Environmental Service Group. World wild life Fund -India & MAB India. Department of Environment.

Index

TRIBAL INDIA

PROBLEM DEVELOPMENT PROSPECT

(Vol. II)

TRIBAL INDIA
PROBLEM DEVELOPMENT PROSPECT
(IN TWO VOLUMES)

Edited by
MANIS KUMAR RAHA

Associate in Editing work
PALASH CHANDRA COOMAR

VOL. II

GIAN PUBLISHING HOUSE
NEW DELHI - 110002

Gian Publishing House
4348, Madan Mohan Street,
4C Ansari Road
New Delhi-110002

ISBN 81-212-0275-2 Set
ISBN 81-212-0273-6 Vol-II

Printed in India
Published by : Mrs. Gayatri Garg for
Gian Publishing House, New Delhi 110002.
Laser Typeset by :
Shiva Shakti Laser Printing Works
4379/4B, Ansari Road, Daryaganj,
New Delhi-110002.
Printed at Goyal Offset Printers,
Shahzada Bagh, Daya Basti, Delhi.

The view, if any, expressed in any article of this book, is of the author and not of the Editors. The Editors are in no way responsible for the same.

In Memory of Late

J. K. BOSE

PREFACE

We have already mentioned in Volume One the objective of this book. This book deals with various problems the inhabitants of Tribal India encounter in their day-to-day life. Besides the policies adopted by the Government, time to time, towards the welfare of the tribal people of our country, this book also has articles covering various measures taken by the Governments, both the Central and the States, to promote the socio-economic conditions and also the educational standards of the Scheduled Tribes. Articles on different other issues concerning their life and activities have also been incorporated in the two volumes of this book. While Volume One includes articles specifically on the general policies of the tribal welfare and the problems and welfare of the Scheduled Tribes in the State and Union Territory level, Volume Two incorporates articles on the problems of the tribal people created due to different economic situations and also different other issues concerning their way of life.

We have also mentioned in Volume One that we have dedicated this book in the memory of Runu (Late Sarita Bhowmick) a talented but young scholar and anthropologist who met an untimely accidental death on her way to attend a seminar on 'Tribal Problem and Development' organised by the Institute of Social Research and Applied Anthropology at Bidisa in the district of Midnapur, West Bengal on June 12, 1982. Many eminent anthropologists and scholars assembled at Bidisa to participate in the seminar. Like many others we were also present in the seminar. The news of the accident and the sad demise of Runu came as a big shock and made us dumbfounded. When the sad incident along with associated rites were all over, we thought of doing something that would very much be befitting to the memory of Runu. So as a token of our love for Runu we thought of dedicating a book on tribal welfare and development, a topic on which she had enough interest. The outcome of this desire of ours is this book.

Preface

The Volume Two of the book is being dedicated to late Prof.J.K. Bose who was travelling in the same car in which Sarita Bhowmick travelled, and also like her met an accidental death. We cherish his memory as well as his contribution to the understanding of the problems of the tribals. This dedication is a token of our great regards for Prof.Bose.

To give different dimensions to this book we have selected twenty nine articles. These articles have been written by eminent scholars many of whom were/are actively connected with the welfare of the Scheduled Tribes. While we could incorporate thirteen articles in Volume One of this book, the rest of the sixteen articles have got their place in Volume Two. This volume has dealt with various issues concerning the life and activities of the Scheduled Tribes, the varied problems and troubles they face at every step and the impact of these problems and troubles on their life. We firmly believe that like Volume One, this volume will also be of immense help to the administrators, planners, social workers, academicians and others who take interest for the tribal people and help them in solving their problems, their backwardness, their miseries and their poverty. This book will particularly help them in carrying out their activities towards the welfare of the Scheduled Tribes.

We will feel our objectives achieved if this book directly or indirectly helps in solving at least some of the basic problems of our tribal brethren, and to enable them to improve their socio-economic conditions.

M. K. RAHA

ACKNOWLEDGEMENT

It is my discipline, Anthropology and my profession which are responsible for generating interest in me to know the problems of the tribal people of our country and to look into the welfare of the tribal people. This interest was further strengthened when I served in the Cultural Research Institute, Scheduled Castes & Tribes Welfare Department, Government of West Bengal, at the beginning of my service career. Thereafter my profession took me to different parts of our country to know our tribal brethren and understand their problems. I also got some opportunity to evaluate some of the development projects meant for them and also to see whether these actually benefit them and if so how much. At this juncture Prof. P.K. Bhowmick of the Department of Anthropology, University of Calcutta and Honorary Secretary, Institute of Social Research and Applied Anthropology, requested me to edit this book. It is undoubtedly a great privilege and honour he bestowed on me. I offer my deep sense of gratitude to Prof. Bhowmick.I am also grateful to the authorities of the Institute of Social Research and Applied Anthropology for their kind permission and encouragement to edit and publish this book. I am really thankful to the authorities of the Institute of Social Research and Applied Anthropology and also of the journal, *Man and Life* for permitting me to incorporate some of the articles in this book which are already published in the journal, *Man and Life*.

My sincere thanks are due to all the contributors who are scholars in their respective fields. Without their active co-operation this project of mine could not have been successful. To Shri D. Banerjee, Mrs. Vimla, Miss Geeta, Shri E Pitambaru and Shri Anand Minz my sincere thanks as they took much pain to type out the manuscripts whenever required. I am also thankful to all of my colleagues in the Andaman and Nicobar Regional Office of the Anthropological Survey of India, Port Blair and also others for their kind co-operation and assistance in one way or other.

Finally I express my gratitute to my publisher, M/s Gian Publishing House, New Delhi. Their active co-operation, experience and skill have made the publication of this book possible at a very short period.

CONTRIBUTORS

Professor P.K. Bhowmick	Department of Anthropology, Calcutta University, Calcutta, West Bengal.
Dr. Sukumar Benerjee	Superintending Anthropologist (Retd.), Anthropological Survey of India, Calcutta, West Bengal.
Dr.R.K. Kar	Reader, Department of Anthropology, Dibrugarh University, Dibrugarh, Assam.
Dr. Suman Sao	Department of Architecture and Planning, Indian Institute of Technology, Kharagpur, West Bengal
Dr. S.K. Mishra	Department of Architecture and Planning, Indian Institute of Technology, Kharagpur, West Bengal.
Dr. R.K. Chattopadhyay	Department of Architecture and Planning, Indian Institute of Technology, Kharagpur, West Bengal.
Professor G.P. Reddy	Professor, Department of Anthropology Sri Venkateswara University, Tirupati, Andhra Pradesh.

Dr. M.K. Raha	Deputy Director, Anthropological Survey of India, Central Region, Nagpur.
Professor L.R.N.Srivastava	Head, Scheduled Caste & Scheduled Tribe Education Unit, National Council of Educational Research and Training, New Delhi.
Shri T.K. Sanyal	Senior Research Officer, Department of Development and Planning, Govt. of West Bengal, Calcutta, West Bengal.
Shri P.N. Das Gupta	Senior Research Officer, Department of Development and Planning, Govt. of West Bengal, Calcutta, West Bengal.
Dr. A. Joseph	Joint Director (Retd), Tribal Cultural Research and Training Institute, Govt. of Andhra Pradesh, Hyderabad.
Dr.N.N. Vyas	Director, M.L.V. Tribal Research and Training Institute, Govt. of Rajasthan, Udaipur.
Dr. Shyamlal	Head, Post Graduate Department of Sociology, Govt. College, Banswara, Rajasthan.
Shri Swapan K. De	Assistant Planner, Cultural Research Institute, Govt. of West Bengal, Culcatta, West Bengal.
Dr. Atul Chandra	Department of Museology, Calcutta University, Calcutta, West Bengal.

Dr. A.K. Danda	Director, Anthropological Survey of India, Indian Museum, 27, Jawaharlal Nehru Road, Calcutta.
Dr. P.R.G. Mathur	Director, Kerala Institute for Research, Training and Development Studies of Scheduled Castes and Scheduled Tribes, Govt. of Kerala Kozhikode, Kerala.

CONTENTS

PART ONE : ECONOMIC ISSUES

PART TWO : OTHER ISSUES

INTRODUCTION

INTRODUCTION

In the Preface as also in the Introduction of the First Volume of this book we have already mentioned that this book would be in two volumes. In Part I of Volume One we have dealt with the development among the tribals in India in general, the related problems these people face and also the policies concerning the tribal welfare. We have devoted Part II of Volume One to cover the issues concerning the welfare of tribal people in different States and Union Territories. In Volume One we have included thirteen articles of which six are in Part One and rest are in the Part Two. This is the Second Volume. We have dealt in two parts of this Volume the economic issues of the tribals and problems emerged out of these and also various other issues concerning the tribal way of life. While Part I of this Volume deals with the economic issues and economic problems of the tribals, Part II covers multifarious issues connected with the tribal life. In the Introduction of Volume One we have already mentioned that we have selected twenty-nine articles for this book and distributed these articles intwo volumes.While Volume I is satisfied with thirteen articles, the rest of the sixteen articles have got their place in Volume Two. The inclusion of sixteen articles in Volume Two was felt essential to make it more comprehensive and interesting and also to focus various facets of tribal life and multifarious problems they deal with in their day-to-day life.

The tribals have their problems of varied types in their original habitats as all human beings have. But when they migrate to such places quite new to them, or when they are taken and put to a new situation and environment quite different from what they were experiencing so long in their homeland, or when they come across a new social environment and face different social norms and problems or when they are put to as new economic order and forced to adopt it, and when they in course of their migration reach to such new socio-economic and ethnic situation, they no doubt, face problems quite new from what they were so long encountering. These new problems emerged out of the new situations lead sometimes to maladjustment among them and make many of them bewildered at the beginning. But gradually when they become somewhat successful in adjusting themselves with these new situations, they start thinking these places as their own and cope with the problems.

With the industrial development in our country, a large number of the tribal people from different parts of India, particularly from Eastern and Central India, migrated to many large industrial units as labourers, and settled there. Similarly for the development of tea industry big labour force was felt necessary, and to cope with this large labour force thousands of tribal people of both sexes from different parts of our country were recruited.

Mines and collieries also attracted a large number of tribal people as labourers. As agricultural labourers a good many of the tribal people have also found their place in different parts of India. And in all these places, the industrial belts, tea industry, collieries and mines etc., when they go and get settled they encounter some new socio-economic and ethnic environments; and these new environments, in a natural way, create many new problems to them as these environments are quite different from what existed in their homeland. In Part I of this volume three articles deal with such tribal situations and problems arose out of these situations which tribals there face.

The article on the impact of industrialization on the tribals of West Bengal by Professor P.K. Bhowmick begins with the critical review of research works on the same topic and then assesses the impact of industrialization on these people.

As already said a large number of the tribal people work in the collieries as labourers. Here the condition of the Santal labourers working in the coal mines of Jharia-Ranigunge area, has been vividly described by Dr. Sukumar Banerjee. He has also shown the problems faced by the tribal labourers there.

The tea industry in Assam and West Bengal is one of the largest employers of the tribal labour force. The tribal labourers on coming to the tea estates, face some peculiar problems quite different from those present in other industrial estates and mines. Dr. R.K. Kar has in his article, discussed about the conditions of the tribal labourers employed in the tea estates of Assam, their unique problems and also the facilities they get from these estates.

Besides agriculture and labour a good number of the tribals also have other occupations. Rope making is one of these. The article of Suman Sao, S.K. Mishra and R.N. Chattopadhyay has analysed the functioning and viability of rope making industry and identified factors for formulating policy decisions towards its development. They have also prescribed a set of proposals for the development of this industry so that the tribals get more benefit out of it.

Many of the tribals are agriculturists. But again, many of them are not. Some of the tribal people are still in the hunting and food gathering stage. But because of the constitutional safeguards and facilities granted to them to improve their lot, a number of measures were taken for their welfare. As a measure to improve their economic conditions agriculture was introduced among some non-agriculturist tribal groups. While some of these tribal groups could adopt agriculture to some extent, among some this scheme has utterly failed, Professor G.P. Reddy through his article has tried to show how agriculture which was introduced among the Chenchus a hunting-gathering and pre-literate tribal group of the Eastern Ghat in Andhra Pradesh as a welfare measure, has resulted in utter failure. He has also highlighted the reasons of such failure.

Part Two of this Volume begins with the problems of the denotified tribal people. The erstwhile criminal tribes of the British period have a new nomenclature as the Denotified Tribes. These tribal groups had unique problems.

They also created problems through their activities during the colonial administration. Though after independence almost all of them have stopped their criminal habits (if we could actually call their activities and their way of life as 'criminal') yet they are often looked upon with suspicion. As a result these denotified tribes encounter with various problems even these days when they have already given up their past activities. Even today people living around them are suspicious of their activities and some people particularly some mahajans are taking advantage of this condition. As a result some of these people are becoming victims of the situation. The Government is taking steps to improve their socio-economic condition and is also taking measures to save them from unwarranted exploitation. Professor P.K. Bhowmick in his very intresting article, has narrated the condition of such a tribe inhabiting amidst such a situation. He has also discussed the problems they are facing and divulged the approaches of the Government towards these denotified tribes laying particular stress on the impact of these approaches on these people.

Right to education is nowadays considered the birth right. People of all walks of life irrespective of caste, creed, religion, sex and age, have equal right over education. The Scheduled Tribes in a similar way have all rights to become literate and to get education. But actually what we see is something very different and miserable picture so far as the tribal education is concerned.

One of the most crucial and important problems in the tribal India is the presence of a very low modern education standard. The rate of literacy is very low among them. The lack of proper education among most of them is one of the major contributory factors for their backwardness. In spite of taking a number of measures no significant development is seen in their education. The paper by the editor reveals the rate of progress in literacy among the tribal people of India and the related problems hindering the progress of education among them.

One of the main reasons that hinders the progress of education among the Scheduled Tribes is the absence of proper curricula for the tribal students. The tribal students are unable to cope with such a situation. Dr. L.R.N. Srivastava feels the need to develop a particular curriculum suitable to the tribal students which he thinks, is essential for the promotion of the education among the tribal people among whom educational standard is notably low.

The tribal manpower is growing every year and their demand for employment is also on the increase. Shri T.K. Sanyal and Shri P.N. DasGupta, through their article on tribal manpower have assessed the manpower available among the tribal people of West Bengal with particular reference to their employment situation and socio-economic status.

The leadership is undoubtedly a sure indicator for the progress made by a society or an area. That means the progress often depends on the influences of the leader and influence of the leader depends on how powerful he is politically. The problem of leadership brings socio-economic crisis and hinders progress. But sometimes conflict between traditional and modern leadership beget serious problems particularly in a tribal situation. Dr. A. Joseph's paper is on the leadership problem in the tribal areas of Andhra Pradesh and the situation arose due to introduction of the statutory panchayat system in the tribal areas admidst the traditional village council. He also carefully assessed the situation and the problems and stated the same very clearly through his article.

In the post-independence period India saw a massive and multifarious constructional and developmental activities. A large number of factories, heavy industrial units, power stations, dams etc. were constructed inorder to move India forward to achieve economic prosperity and also self-reliance and to get leadership among the developing countries. These development measures, no doubt, have become boon to majority of the Indians, but sometime in some cases, these have brought miseries to some at least temporarily. These wretched people are those who have been displaced from their cradle land for the construction of some industries, factories, dams etc. Dr. N.N. Vyas has, in his article, described that such situation arose out of a construction of a dam in a tribal area which has forced the tribals there to leave. The paper has analysed the various social processes among the indigenous population that are taking place as result of the emerging displacement situation.

The proper and extensive measures to uplift the existing condition of the tribal people were taken by the national Government after India achieved freedom from the hands of colonial rulers. As a result the tribal people have harvested many benefits which definitely have improved their lot considerably. And it is also true that the British administration in this country thought very little about the tribals whom they primarily kept in isolation.

Whatever benefits the tribal people in the pre-independence period could get, they got from the Christian missionaries who relentlessly worked among these people for their upliftment with a motive to baptizing them. The paper by Dr. Shyamlal discusses the various welfare programmes, such as educational, medical, agricultural etc. which induced the Bhils to accept Christianity and as a result of which significant changes have come in their culture which distinguish them from the traditional Bhils.

As already said that the independence was a boon to the tribal people of our country who saw a large number of development and welfare measures implemented for them by the Government after India won freedom. These developments and welfare measures were and are meant for the overall improvement of the existing condition of the tribal people who so long remained in the sea of poverty and remained mum and dumb and probably cursed their own fate. But smile shined on their face when they could taste the fruits of welfare though it is true that many of the welfare projects were not successful and could not fetch good results. LAMP (Large Sized Multipurpose Co-operative Society) is such a measure meant for making these people co-operative minded and to instill in them the idea of self-help. But not always and everywhere the true spirit of this project was realised by the tribal people thus leading to a big failure of this project in some cases. Shri Swapan Kumar De has dealt in his article the activities of LAMP in West Bengal and success and failure of this project.

Drink is the integral part of the tribal life. It is intimately interwoven with their culture. In any crises of life, be it birth of a new baby, marriage of a child or death of a person, drink becomes a must. In all worships it is offered to the deities and spirits. In festivities the males and females, young and old, cannot dream of singing and dancing without this. Though some have advocated for banning or prohibiting drinks among the tribals, it remains as important as it was in the past. Dr. Atul Chandra Bhowmick has highlighted the importance of drinks in the tribal life, its rich food value, its tribal method of preparation etc. through his paper.

Anthropology, though deals with biological and cultural aspects of the man both modern and primitive, yet it has always given emphasis on the primitive or tribal groups. The anthropologists are also partisan about the tribal studies. They have shown keen interest on the biological and cultural aspects of the tribal people and assessed the nature and extent of the problems which cripple the tribal life. The basic principle of the Applied Anthropology is to unearth the basic problems of the tribal people and recommend solutions for these

Dr. A.K. Danda through his article, has shown the role of anthropology in ascertaining the tribal problems and prescribed solution of these through welfare works.

In the concluding article, Dr. P.R.G. Mathur has analysed the role of applied anthropology and trained anthropologists in the developmental tasks in India, especially for the tribals. Besides he also examines the theoretical concept of "applied anthropology" and cites opinions of well-known authorities on this issue.

Thus we have tried to incorporate various issues concerning the tribal life. These issues have raised different problems the tribals encounter in their day-to-day life both in their homeland and in the places where they have migrated in search of the livelihood. The problems are varied and difficult, the solution is even more difficult. The scholars who have contributed these articles, have critically examined the different situations in which these tribals are placed and the problems developed due to the interaction of the tribals with these situations. The scholars who have long standing experience with tribal situation of our country, have brought out the truth and the realities of such situations.

There cannot be any doubt that both Union and the State Governments are doing their best for the welfare of the Scheduled Tribes. The authorities have planned a number of welfare measures and implemented those. But in spite of these sincere and best efforts of the Government, the real benefits of these schemes are not reaching the tribals in the fullest extent. Sometimes these people are not getting even partial benefits of these. As a result there remains a big gap between the expected and the actual results. The tribals are not gaining in the same proportion from these welfare works as they should have. The probable reasons for this gap is the lack of awareness among the tribal people about their right over such benefits, partial lack of interest, devotion and missionary zeal among the implementing agencies, the influence of the vested habitations, interest, remoteness and inaccessibility of the tribal politics with their poverty, etc. If we sincerely want to upgrade the present standard of living of our tribal brethren and take them at least above the poverty level by uplifting their economic condition and raising the standard of their literacy, thereby bringing them near the mainstream if not at par, we need to overcome all the above hindrances and to do justice to the cause of the downtrodden with a zeal of the missionary. If we are not in a position to do it even now, it may be too late to rescue these poor souls from sinking deep into the sea of misery and oppression.

Dr. A.K. Das through his article has shown the role of anthropology in ascertaining the tribal problems and the solution of these through welfare work.

In the concluding article, Dr. [illegible] has analysed the role of applied anthropology and role of anthropologists in the development of India, especially for the tribals. Besides, he also examines the theoretical concept of "applied anthropology" and cites opinions of well known authorities on this issue.

Thus we have tried to incorporate various issues concerning the tribal life. These issues have raised different problems the tribals encounter in their day-to-day life both in their homeland and in the places where they have migrated in search of their livelihood. The problems are varied and difficult, the solution is even more difficult. The scholars who have contributed these articles, have critically examined the different situations in which these tribals are placed and the problems developed due to the interaction of the tribals with these situations. The scholars who have long standing experience [illegible] of our country, have brought out the truth and the realities of such situations.

There cannot be any doubt that the [illegible] and the State Governments are doing their best for the welfare of the Scheduled Tribes. The authorities have planned a number of [illegible] and implemented these. But in spite of these since [illegible] of the Government the real benefits of these schemes [illegible] the tribals in the full measure. [illegible] these people [illegible] partial benefits of these. As a result there remains [illegible] the expected and the actual results. The tribals are not [illegible] in the large proportion from these welfare works as they should [illegible]. The reasons for this [illegible] of awareness [illegible] their rights, partial lack of [illegible] among the implementing agencies [illegible] the vested interests, [illegible] etc. If we make [illegible] the present situation of [illegible] of our tribal brethren [illegible] the [illegible] of their [illegible] the [illegible] their history, their [illegible] if not [illegible] of the above [illegible] justice to the [illegible] interaction with [illegible]. If we are not [illegible]

Part One : Economic Issues

CHAPTER 1

Impact of Industrialization on the Tribes: A Background Situation in West Bengal

*P. K. Bhowmick**

I

Introduction

Industrialization is the change in the productive technology related to the process of economic development on a national level. Through it, extensive use of inanimate sources of power, minerals and other raw materials are made for economic production on a large scale. In the realm of technology, it is nothing but a change from simple, traditionalized techniques to the application of scientific knowledge and modern techniques. It is also related to the aggregation and ratio of power-driven machinery employed for augmenting production and monetary return on the unit of investment by selling manufactured products through a network of exchange relations. "It is also capable of exercising

* Reproduced by the permission of the authority of 'Man and Life" and Institute of Social Research and Applied Anthropology, Calcutta from 'Man and Life', 7(3+4): 105-121, 1981.

control over the total resource of a society to be applied to its economic build-up.'' (Hoselitz: 1968).

It, with the multiple new demands and interests, interacts largely with the traditional behaviour of social groups engaged in this sector. Thus we find gradual erosion of old values, incorporation of new ones into the matrix of the old, ecological and demographic imbalance through migration, along with functional diffusion of economic activities, sometimes leading to disorganised state of society through exploitation, deprivation, frustration, value-conflict and loss of emotional security. Change is inevitable and universal and people have to adjust themselves with all the changing situations for living a better life. Through effective planning and successful implementation of programmes, many ills and adverse effects of these processes can be avoided.

More than 5 crores of Indian people belong to Tribal Communities, who are in various stages of economic development. A good many of them are still found to live in the remote inaccessible rugged and hostile regions of our country. The British Administration in our country tried to keep them in isolation from other people. There had been little interaction between tribals and its mainstream of Indian culture. As a result these people were deprived from all common amenities and remained backward and, developed as a result, a peculiar mental breeding with queer angularities in their psycho-social aspects of life. With timidity and coynees, they silently bore exploitation and deprivation by a large section of other privileged classes of population. Though after independence, the situation has changed to an appreciable extent still we find that these tribal people are being still exploited the same way by their so-called advanced neighbours, taking advantage of their illiteracy and ignorance; their simplicity and less understanding of the total situation brought about by industrialization, and limited world-views. Together with these, lack of aspiration level due to less contact with the development situations are potent causes of suffering of these tribals.

It is to be noted here that important mineral zones are mostly located in the harsh terrain and where the tribals are concentrated. The British Administration did not utilise these resources for the development of this country. Industrial policy of Free India was first envisaged in 1948, through planned development of basic industries in successive phased plan-programmes. Though there were private undertakings in some industrial sectors, Government had to review and r these for better and useful exploitation of all available resources and work these up to their installed capacity for a quicker and balanced industrial development.

Keeping this in view, fresh outline of India's Industrial Policy was fixed and announced by the Government in April 1956. Since then attempts are being made by the government for proper utilization of the resources of the country, for a balanced development of large and small industries simultaneously and proper regional distribution of industries to boost the national economy. All the provisions of this new Industrial Development Act with modifications from time to time according to needs and experience, are now being enforced for overall industrial development of this country, and also setting up Development Corporations for specific industries, along with foreign participation for obtaining technical 'know-how' and technical assistance, so that the existing man-power and resources of the country could be best utilised. As a result, the tribals have been drawn into many industrial enterprises. Impact of industrialization on the cultures and societies of the tribals in general, is profound. It leads the individual or the society to a process of adjustment from settled agriculture to an industrial way of life either integrating the involving groups into a harmonious situation or leading them to hostile segments. As a result, many social scientists and administrators have been attracted very recently to study the process of industrialization. It is to be noted that more industrialization means more development, so country must go ahead through industry where technological sophistication will provide new employment opportunities.

II

Impact Situations Studied

Major focus has been cast in this paper to examine the factors leading to the exploitation and deprivation of the tribals in various industrial situations in different mines and factories and other fields in West Bengal. In the recent past, attempts have been made by some scholars to study such problems from different aspects.

'Impact of Industrialization on the life of the tribals of West Bengal' by Das and Banerjee (1962) published by the Cultural Research Institute, Scheduled Castes and Tribes Welfare Dept; is a pioneering work in this respect. It describes in brief in the context of industrialization, human mobility and shifting occupations through three generations. It also emphasised the impact of industrialization on social life, family, clan, marriage, education, etc. with more emphasis on psychological milieu. These are all related to the factory workers of tribal communities at Chittaranjan Locomotive Works, Hindusthan Cable Factory, Jhimary Colliery, Kanchrapara Locomotive Works and Haringhata Milk Factory. In all these cases (600), the major tribal groups are the Santals and the next are the Mundas. Most of them are Class IV workers, with a small percentage of Class III staff.

This study is limited in its scope and, as such, some simple observations were made like more earning than agriculture, preference of younger generation towards industry along with contrasting hankering for land by the older generations, though they earn more and spend more in the new industrial environments. More generalisations were made in respect of social life like, growth of nuclear type of families, weakening of traditional leadership, incidence of marriage in the same clan, weakening of traditional religiosity on the one hand, widening of the world-view on the other. In respect of psychological aspects, the authors observed the oscillating mind of the tribal workers for land and money in factory. Rigid routine work is intervened by their agrarian 'go-slow' habit and, as such, less output in production results. They are also interested in forming Labor Union etc. They also noticed frequent absenteeism and suggested some remedial measures by way of conclusion.

Dr. Dasgupta's work on 'Impact of Industrialization on Tribal Life' (1964) is related to Chittaranjan Locomotive Works. His work was concentrted in six villages namely Amladahi, Bormudi, Uparkesia, Durgadi, Fatehpur, and Sundarpahari. In course of establishing the Industrial Complex, 520 families were uprooted in 1948, of whom 330 families are Santal and 7 families are Kol. Though compensation for the land was given to them, these were not properly utilised by these people. Before the installation of the industry, about 97% of the villagers were agriculturist. At the time of survey, Dasgupta referred that in 1962, there were 8,801 workers in CLW, of whom 203 persons i.e. 3.3% were tribals. A fraction of them were Oraon and Munda who came from the Ranchi area. All the tribal employees were unskilled and semi-skilled within a pay range of Rs. 70/-, Rs. 80/-. But there were a good number of casual labourers , of whom, in a sample of 440 people, 151 were Santals who subsisted by other activities and came to the workshop from within a radius of 7 miles. Among them, women constituted a large number.

In discussing other problems, Dasgupta referred to the degradation of the moral of the Santal girls while working in the factory and this also created a tension in their traditional panchayat organisation. Naturally, there were cases of marriage in violation of tribal customs. There were little changes in family life, food habit and cultural composition though new recreational facilities were extended to them. The Santal Medicine-man was still found to be in his occupation although there were some registered physicians in the area. Dr. Dasgupta also stated that economic development through technological change could have changed the various aspects of socio-politico - religious life of these people. But these are not so pronounced, as the Industrial Complex was set up only 12 years ago. Some superficial changes were obviously noticed. Some people still practise agriculture and also do industrial work and thus have made a compromise with loyalty to their traditions. No problems or remedial measures were suggested by him.

Dr. Sukumar Banerjee's work on 'Impact of Industrialization on the tribal population of Jharia-Ranigunj Coal Field Areas' (1981) is somewhat significant. As a scholar from ASI, he conducted his survey in six collieries, but two collieries (1) Bhowra (Jharia Coal-field) and (2) Moira (Ranigunj Coal-field were studied indepth. To note the changes, he compared traditional Santal life with that of the colliery Santals. He contacted the colliery personnel, as well as the village leaders to supplement his views. But entire materials refer to the time when all these collieries were not nationalised (1973). In his study, the life of the Santals have been pin-pointed, as they represent the major tribal group. The Table 1 shows the ratio of tribal workers in the six collieries during the period 1969-72.

Dr. Banerjee refers to mixed economy. In his sample study of one village he noticed that 71% are workers in agricultural field, and 27% work in colliery, because they possess uneconomic holdings. He mentioned that the total Santals have very carefully adjusted themselves with the mining-life without much disturbance. In Bhowra Coalfield he stated that out of 143 Santals (male), 60 are in mining, and out of 150

Table 1

WORKERS AND TRIBAL

Coal field	*Name of the collieries*	*No. of total workers*	*Santal*	*%*
Jharia	1) Bhowra	4,363	272	8.1%
	2) Central Tisra	300	20	7%
Ranigunge	3) Saltore	1,034	101	10%
	4) Madhujore	1,200	240	20%
	5) Moira	1,600	56	3.2%
	6) Rangakal	280	116 (Casual)	41.4%

females, 26 are engaged in mining, with a total of 32.08%. Banerjee described in details the types of work categorically along with pay-scale of the employees. In his survey piece-rated employees constituted 60%, while time-rated workers constituted 40%..In all the cases, education was very low. He also found migrant Santals in the colliery areas.

Dispossession of land is causing such migration. In respect of traditional life, they have not much deviated, as they keep regular contact with the Santals of the surrounding areas. In respect of performing some village festivals, he observed that most of the festivals have been simplified now. Migrant Santals are also found in the Ranigunge Coalfield areas. Banerjee pointed out some problems like,-excessive drinking, absenteeism among them, whereas absenteeism is less in case of other labourers. Problem of housing is also acute among them. Many of the Santal workers are regularly exploited or deprived, as they do not know the rules and regulations of the factory. This is done by not giving them their due bonus as well as due remuneration, by not giving them the fraction in coins. The authorities have been found to favour non-tribal labourers in allotting shift-duties etc. As a result, in a few cases, Santal labourers have left the collieries. Though there are Trade Unions and one or two other Unions, but Santals are not fully involved with these organisations. Bringing of non-tribals from different parts of Bihar and U.P. has created a lot of problems and generated frustration among them. Ultimately they have to leave occasionally and try their lot elsewhere. Thus a systematic retreat from the coalfield as a result of influx of up-country labours is a dominant feature, as observed by Banerjee, as the up-country labours have better social proximity with the management.

Mohammad Mohsin in his doctoral dissertation on '*Chittaranjan: A Study in Urban Sociology*' (1964) has described very lucidly the aspects of urbanization. He has already mentioned that how eight Santal villages gave way to Chittaranjan complex completely uprooting the tribals who were mainly Santals. He further noted the rehabilitation of only a few families in nearby villages of Gaidoba, Bhaga and Sinjuri. Tension in time of eviction was strongly noted by him (p. 156) :

> "Particularly the Santals of the erstwhile Fatehpur village took strong exception to the construction of artificial lake in the area. A group of them armed with spears, bows and arrows attacked the personnel deputed to carry out the undertaking. Armed constabulary had to be called in to quell the unrest in which both the parties suffered casualties."

In course of discussing the nature of impact in the life of the tribals especially among the Santals he stated (p. 159) :

"The presence of the township and factory amidst them have, in no way, improved their material conditions. Very few Santals have succeeded so far to get into the workshop as Khalasis..... Besides the nature of work and the policy of recruitment as pursued by the contractors, have considerably affected and undermined the morals of these Santals. As female labour is comparatively cheaper, we find that a large number of these Santals who are working as casual labourers are often females. They get one and a quarter rupees as against one and a half rupees paid to their male counterparts for an eight-hour-day work. As most of the labourers have to commute the distance from their villages to the work site and back on foot,from the greater part of the day, they are out of supervision of their elders. The frank, free and easy disposition of the Santal women have made them vulnerable to sexual exploitation by the non-Santals of the township. I have come across many cases where Santal belles are living with the non-Santals as mistresses."

Dr. Mohsin, has not studied in depth of this contact situation but his statements have been endorsed by his Santal interpreters and guides like

Hupna Manjhi of Gajdoba, Haripada, Marandi and Jyotin Marandi of Amel of the locality. The distressing picture of un-controlled urbo-industrial contact undoubtedly demand thorough probe into the matter. It is reflected that lure of an easy life has resulted in the elopement of quite a few Santal women from the neighbouring villages with non-Santals who are alleged to be selling them later to brothels. Anyway, if this observation is considered true, then it is suggested that appropriate authority would take care of this situation and to suggest remedial alternatives for this problem.

Another book '*Urban Complex of an Industrial City*' by Jugendra Sahai (Allahabad: 1979) describes in depth urbanism and urban complex of planned city Durgapur of West Bengal. In his dissertation Dr. Sahai described the ecology of the city and details of economic back-ground of the immigrants as well as occupational structure of the city. His main thrust was to analyze and find out the relationship between urban growth and social and economic development in India with reference to developing societies. He observed meaningfully the main tendencies emerging out of the process of urban growth in India. The pull factor is operating here to attract outsider with requisite qualifi-cation for better job.

It has been reported that the deterioration of the residential villages of Khoirasol, Muchipara and Faridpur into slums and a state of conges-tion and unhealthy environs in the otherwise flourishing bazar areas of Durgapur and Benachiti. Dr. Sahai did not emphasise the impact of urbanization as he was more serious to study the network of relationship in the city through occupation and relationship.

These are the published materials related to the tribals in industrial situation of West Bengal. Tea Industry along with many other ancillary industries (Paper mill in Jhargram and some other industries at Khar-agpur in Midnapur) have not been covered till now, and in most of the cases, real problems have not been covered till now, and in most of the cases, real problems have not been pin-pointed except the depiction of tribal life and its departure from the traditions.

Displacement of the tribals in D.V.C., Kansabati and Mayurakshi projects along with Farakka barrage project require also a full depth study in respect of tribal situation. Besides, at Santaldihi where thermal project is operating in Purulia, the impact of it on the tribals yet to be examined.

In a dynamic society, many factors are playing their roles and even in non-industrial areas also, such changes are observed. Prof. Vidyarthi's work at Ranchi situations has been referred by Dr. Banerjee, where tribals are mostly involved and they faced the problem of land acquisition along with rehabilitation of uprooted families. Influx of migrants and their interaction with the traditional tribal societies are also significant. There are problems of housing and other civic amenities everywhere, though after the Government take-over it has abruptly changed, making these more difficult.

Now the entire Coal Mines have been nationalised (Oct. 1971): Coking Coal; Jan. 1973 : Non-Coking). The Heavy Industries are also under Government management. So we can expect a more fair deal for the employees. Naturally the problems have to be realised in different contexts and as such, a reconnoitre tour was made in some places of Burdwan-Durgapur-Chittaranjan and Coal Mines of Assansol-Ranigunj area including Jamuria and Domohani. Dr. R. M. Sarkar has also surveyed a few collieries, but his report is yet to be analysed. Altogether 14 collieries in West Bengal (Eastern Coalfield: Area VI & VII) i.e. near the southern portion of Ranigunj Field have been covered, where out of 850 families depending on mining, 417 are Santal and other tribals. Among them there are local Santals as well as migrants from Palasthali (Bihar-7 miles away from West Bengal) areas. Among the total tribals, Santals constitute 83%, Koras 13% and Oraons 4%. In some other areas there are, Ho, Oraon, Munda, Kora from Orissa. The important changes found are that traditional housewives have become wagon-loaders neglecting their children. Thus the tribals are gradually losing their traditional life.

III

Industrial Infra-structure in West Bengal

West Bengal occupies the second place after Bihar in the production of minerals, of which coal is the most important item. Of the output of coal in India, West Bengal produce 30%. The first coal mine area in Ranigunj was opened in 1820, and the first Railway line between

Ranigunj and Calcutta was opened in 1853 during the time of Lord Dalhousie and this opened up a new chapter in the industrial history of West Bengal. History of mineral-based industries in West Bengal dates back to 1774, when in Birbhum attempt was made to make iron from ore. There was slow progress in this field and individual enterprises like, the Bengal Iron and Steel Company Ltd., grew up at this stage. Blast Furnaces were installed by this Company at Kulti (1875). Shortly thereafter, the Indian Iron & Steel Co. Ltd. amalgamated with the Bengal Iron and Steel Co. Later on two centres one at Burnpur and the other at Durgapur were engaged in production of steel and iron. Engineering industries began to function not only at Hooghly belt, but also at Ranigunj Coal Mining Area. The Locomotive manufacturing workshop for the Indian Railways has been started at Chittaranjan (1948) in the district of Burdwan. Simultaneously with the establishment of DVC (1947), a number of projects in the Public Sector accelerated industrialization in these areas. Development of a aluminium industry at Jaykay Nagar, the Cable Factory at Rupnarayanpur and many other small scale ancillary industries in different parts of coalmine area have changed the industrial landscape of West Bengal. As a result, Ranigunj area (600 sq. miles) holds a great promise for the development of various industrial activities. Thus Kulti-Burnpur, Chittaranjan form the core of industrial complex. The 1961 Report in respect of occupations, especially in Asansol subdivision stated that 17.95% people depend on agriculture, whereas mining accounts for 32.80%, manufacturing 20.19%, trade and commerce 7.18%, transport 5.03%. Durgapur Industrial (Steel) Complex appeared in the Industrial Map of the world in 1959. This is a planned town with all facilities.

It is to be noted here that all these Industrial Complexes, especially located in the district of Burdwan have over-lapped other districts like, Birbhum, Bankura, Purulia and the adjoining regions of Bihar. These areas represent lateritic rugged and harsh terrain of undulations, where a good number of tribals are found to live. During the British Administration in India, this area was known as 'Jungle Mahal', or the land of the so-called aboriginal groups of people, Peterson (Bengal District Gazetteer, Burdwan: 1910) observes:

> "For centuries this area had been a sort of debatable land between the Jharkhand or great Western forest, inhabited by the aboriginal tribes... at the end of the eighteenth century it was the

> haunt and refuge of hordes of broken outlawed men who, taking advantage of the unsettled state of land, ravaged and plundered the countryside."

However, due to various historical factors and technological changes and urbanization, we find a changing cultural landscape that dotted the entire tribal region, which was inaccessible once upon a time.

After the installation of the industries, we find gradual push-back of some indigenous population on the one hand; and penetration of the migrants of varied ethnic and cultural entities on the other by constructing of temporary hutments, liquor and tea stalls, market centres, and places of socio-political gathering cradled slowly in these landscape. These created new demands in the local ecological arrangements. Tradition-oriented pattern of social actions began to conform to the canons of purposive rationality. Pre-independence period with limited industrial establishments was dominated by profit making motive in industrial norms, leading to economic exploitation of the working classes. But intervention of government as custodian, of economic advancement for welfare of the general people has brought a corresponding change in the total industrial scene. Naturally, these prolonged historical processes have witnessed many such interactions, contrasts, conflicts and compromise of different nature, along with the establishment of monetary exchange and extension of marketing organisation. Some of these aspects have been explained in detail in the subsequent section.

IV

The industrial landscape of West Bengal with special reference to tribal involvement is fast changing. It is to be noted here that before independence, the entire industrial policy was of different nature, which was more related to maximization of profit, at the cost of all other developmental aspects. But after independence, the picture has changed. As India is a welfare State and some of the population are treated as weaker sections: i.e., Scheduled Castes/Scheduled Tribes, their problems have been reviewed with special care under Constitutional Provisions and many of their interests have been safeguarded and various financial assistances are extended to them for their general development. Naturally, the entire situations regarding different industries, as well as, human involvement aspects, are not neglected now.

In this connection, it can be said that the Public Undertakings/Govt. Sponsored Projects are all well-planned, i.e. after creating all possible infrastructures in areas like Durgapur and Chittaranjan the plants began to function. Naturally many cautious measures were taken for staving varied and possible deterrents that might affect these planned industries. Industrial development needed large investment in the industrial sector,which creates many other associated opportunities like, extension of transport and communication, installation of ware-house, educational facilities, health-hygiene measures, providing accommodation for the workers etc. The Coal Industries have a bit different set of approaches, in which some urbanised sectors became enclaves within non-industrial environment. But in both the cases, we find that some demographic composition has been changed. People go out when their land is acquired by the Project and variegated sets of people from outside come for employment and functioning of the project. So migration is common in such cases, which gives rise to new contacts and interactions,accelerating social, economic and cultural transformation. Change not only occurs in the ecology and environment, but also in the institutional order, giving rise to a new order to fill the vacuum. So careful handling of the situation will help to overcome many of the constraints or impediments, stemming from the attitude of the people involved in the changed situation. In Durgapur and its neighbourhood, a good many ancillary/auxiliary industries like, Durgapur Cement Works, Thomas Monjit etc. utilise the rejected iron-scraps; Civil Construction Firms, Automobile Industry etc. have been set up to use the by-products along with many other related institutions, Transport Companies, where both local and migrant labourers are employed. In the Coalmine areas also new townships (Pandaveshwar, Barakar) are developing though a few collieries are not being utilised after nationalization.

This urbo-industrialization has affected spatial dimensions, i.e. non-industrial sectors also. As urban-industrial sectors always require agricultural surplus, it demands reorganisation of agriculture to yield these surplus. Isolation, self-sufficiency of the neighbouring villages, along with traditional community organisations, thus begin to erode. Consequently in the elements of social system, functional interdependency develops for making the necessary adjustments.

With this background we have to visualize the problems of the tribals in particular and suggest the means of their solution.

It has been pointed out that the tribals in most of the cases were compelled to vacate the Project Areas and were not paid the assessed compensation. They got money in instalments and could not, as such, use this for other productive purposes, both for lack of experience and aspiration. Besides, there was provision that the owners of the three acres of land who had to shift for acquisition, will have employment in these projects, but in actuality, the tribals have been virtually deprived, losing their land and getting no employment in most cases. A proper verification of these aspects will enable us to devise a number of alternative measures for their employment.

Among the Management Personnel in the collieries, a preference is being made to recruit tribals from Orissa and Bihar (constituting, Ho, Kol, Munda, Santal and Oraon groups). They consider that the local tribals (Santal) are not upto their need of competency for mining works. Besides, prevalence of non-tribal labour, especially from Bilaspuri-peasants locally known as up-country labour in the operational level is dominant here. This is because the migrant peasants as well as tribals are basically more serious and sincere in their assigned work and do it more efficiently. There is also less a absenteeism among them. So, this preference for migrant labour is justified so far as production process is concerned. But this has created little inter-ethnic disharmony leading to occasional conflicts. It is very very dominant in the colliery situation.

These migrants along with surplus floating man-power have also created the problem of housing. They live in hutments and slums (dhowarahs) where hygienic condition and sanitation are completely lacking. Though recently the Coal India Limited (CIL) has built-up hygienic brick-built labour quarters, but these are not at all sufficient. Transport facilities are not available to all the workers. So it poses difficulty in inner transportation.

Water supply is a serious problem. Hospital facilities and schooling for the children are also inadequate. Fewer children attend the schools due to their distant location. The housewives do the work of wagon-loaders creating a serious domestic problem, for whom a good number of creches for taking care of their babies in their absence are necessary. It has been found at the time of enquiry that younger boys or girls have to look after the kiddies and youngsters, while their parents are engaged in their jobs. Obviously this needs arrangements for schools for the children and creches for the working women in this area to solve the tribal needs. These regions are saddled with rich coal mines and a good number of tribals working in this mines earn a lot. A family of husband and wife together earn at least Rs. 1500/- p.m. But there is a scope for exploitation of these workers. Firstly the tribals are not in the habit of counting the coins or notes to verify their dues. An agent/cashier, as reported, always pay their dues in a round figure retaining the fractional part of the coins, thus making a deduction from their actual dues. In this way, exploitation continues. In respect of allotting overtime and shift duties, granting bonus, etc. it was reported that the tribals are being cheated in this respect also. For such duties are only given to them who pay the agents or the staff concerned, a percentage of their earning as bribe. It is also reported that the filling of the empty mines are not done properly as a result the surface land has no capacity to sustain moisture. Thus lands are going to be useless, unfit for agriculture. Certain measures to be taken to check up all these disadvantages created by the contractors. Hence, now a common proverb for functioning of the ECL has emerged which interpret its name as "Eating, Cheating and Looting". It is found that a good number of sweetmeat shops, restaurants, tea stalls have sprung up here. On the salary days they prepare many items to allure the poor tribal workers, who get a good amount of cash in hand on the pay days. They also do not hesitate to spend money lavishly to enjoy such treats. There is also a strong tendency of alcoholism among them and they spend a lot of money for this. Practically they do not have any control on this bad habit. This is another type of exploitation of the tribals by non-tribals who run the wineshops. Alcoholism has also generated the associated vices in the locality. Quarrelling is very common in the Dowrahas i.e. the bustees where the tribals workers live in their own hutments. Government has permitted the tribals to consume liquor with continence and it has also created a bad effect. Non tribals too come and join them and commit many other vices aggravating the local law and order situation. It has also affected the non-tribal population. So the entire social atmosphere is almost vicious. Wagon looting, removing tonnes of coal and reporting them falsely to the authority as 'fire-case', have become a common practice among them and this mentality has percolated also among the tribals who were basically sincere and honest.

It has become very common, now, for a group of young men to collect subscriptions on various issues and this has become a large scale practice during CPI(M) regime more. This has become intolerable to the tribals.

There are some approved Trade Unions in this area, especially at DSP. These Trade Unions have protested many times against the mal-administration, anti-labour policies of the authority by calling bunds or strikes, i.e. cease work to compel them to mend their ways. In 1980-81 there were altogether 254 such incidents. Serious nature strikes are as follows:

CITU - called 24 strikes/cease work
INTUC - called 20 strikes/cease work
AITUC - called 5 strikes/cease work
BCKU - called 3 strikes/cease work
UTUC - called 1 strike/cease work
CPI(ML) - called 2 strikes/cease work

In the same way ECL has experienced 164 strikes which wasted 3,21,257 man-days affecting its production by a large extent in the establishment. Besides these unions, there aresome other unions exclusively organised and meant for the SC/ST workers. There is also 'the Jharkhand Majdur Sabha' controlled by both tribals and non-tribals. This is also non-recognised union. It has been also reported that before the nationalization of the coal mines, the tribals used to get more work. But it has been restricted due to quota system if their proportionate representation now introduced.

> "According to an expert study, nearly eight to ten million tonnes of coal production are lost due to labour and power problem. In fact the law and order problem in Bengal-Bihar belt has seriously affected total production because this belt accounts for 60 per cent of India's coal output". (Krishnan: 1982).

By way of conclusion, based on field study it can be said that most of the tribals hold very lower categories of jobs in the industrial sectors, where stratification has widened the group distance and no alternative arrangement to overcome this situation has been made. Some elite section of the tribals also exploit the poorer tribals. This is closely related to their occupational prestige and so it will create a lot of tension in near future in the pulling down the tribal population into the gorge of ethnocentrism in desperation. Along with these, over population created a problem where threads of immigration have weaved an intriguing web. Loss of emotional security in this contrasting environment has an adverse impact in the mind of the tribals.

We cannot ignore the value conflict between the groups concerned that have emanated now, for this would clearly show how migration has severed the kinship bondages and obligations, disrupting familial links in some cases, in the pressing situation of industrial formalities. Ideology of maintaining family ties slowly vanishes and reshaping the people's mind and value senses into new without proper beneficial supplementation. Industrialization largely confronts with economic and social difficulties and how unknowingly the money is diverted rather sucked for many other tangential matters like paying subscription, consuming liquor, eating new type of food etc. It was also found that many of the tribals have been pushed back from the jobs by non-tribal peasant competitors in the field through the machination of the administrative personnel. Another baneful aspect was noted during the survey. The Bilaspuri or 'upcountry' peasant labours returning from their work spend their time leisurely by singing 'Rama hai' a chorus with beating of their musical drums in a group, whereas a casual observer will see the vacant look of the Adivasi worker with on full dose of liquor sitting alone in the courtyard of his Dhowrah or at the street side. Naturally an urgent need of social-engineering is needed for tackling this degenerating situation for mending the morals of these eroded communities.

V

Suggestions

Based on field study, the following measures are considered to be essential for relief and overall development of the tribal workers especially at industrial situations. The State Tribal Welfare Department should extend their ITDP in the adjoining areas or some arrangements for these marginal people should be made providing minimum housing, health and sanitation facilities and supply of drinking water so that they may be able to live in a healthy condition which will enhance their working capacity and skill contributing to larger proportion. Facilities for adult education, recreation, creche for the youngster are also necessary to create in them a sense of confidence and to free the women labours from mental anxiety and back-pull for their kiddies. Encouragement for establishing new manufacturing organisation for meeting the local needs and demands, is also necessary for supply of consumer items. For cultural integration, as was observed, they pay subscription for Kalipuja, open-air theatres and operas but they cannot enjoy for restricted participation or for ignorance of the subject matter of the plays, language difficulties and difference in traditions. It should also be examined how far they make full use of their leisure in enjoying some of their traditional games and festivities. If it is found interested, these should be given facilities for encouragement and participation. The Tribal Development Cell meant for industrial areas should be structured and reorganized on some specific aspects (apprenticeship in industries etc.) and they will devise the means to supplement the vacuum in social interaction arising out of conflict, confrontation and frustration among the tribal workers for their proper uplift.

Appendix 1

CONCENTRATION OF TRIBALS IN ITDP AREAS

1	*2*	*3*	*4*	*5*
District	*No. of ITDP*	*Total population*	*Tribal population*	*% of col. 4 to col. 3*
1. Purulia	6	2,43,367	1,71,876	70.21
2. Bankura	3	1,45,509	1,07,486	73.87
3. Burdwan	2	29,500	25,590	86.75
4. Birbhum	4	34,123	46,714	55.53

Note: Most of the mines and industrial belts are located in those areas where tribals are concentrated.

References

Banerjee, Sukumar (1981) — Impact of Industrialization on the Tribal Population of Jharia Raniganj Coal Field Areas. ASI, Calcutta.

Bhowmick, P. K. (1981) — *Some Aspects of Indian Anthropology,* Calcutta.

Bose, A. (1961) — Population growth and industrialization, Urban Process in India, Man in India, 41: 255-275.

Bose, N. K. (1961)	Impact of changing Technology on Society. Economic Weekly, 23: 473-474.
Chatterjee A. B. Mukhopadhyay P. K. & Gupta, A. (1970)	West Bengal, Calcutta.
Chowdhury. M. R. (1971)	*The Industrial Landscape of West Bengal,* Oxford & IBH, Calcutta.
Das, M. (1947)	Rural Uplift through Industrialization, Indian Review, 48: 298-300.
Das and Banerjee (1964)	*Impact of Industrialization on the Life of the Tribals of West Bengal,* CRI Special Series 4, Calcutta.
Dasgupta, P. K. (1964)	*Impact of Industrialization on the Tribal Life. Bule, ASI,* Calcutta.
Dutta-Majumdar (1955)	*The Santals, ASI,* Calcutta.
Krishnan, R. (1982)	Problems of Power and Coal Industries Yojana, Vol. XXVI, New Delhi.
Mohsin, M. (1964)	*Chittaranjan: A Study in Urban Sociology,* Bombay.
Peterson, J.C.K. (1910)	Bengal District Gazetteer, Burdwan, Calcutta.
Ray, U. K., Das, A. K., Chowdhury, M.K. (1982)	Planning for the Scheduled Tribes and Scheduled Castes, Calcutta.
Roy Chowdury, K. P. (1957)	*Technical Education for Tribals, Tanyajati,* pp. 87-93.
Sahai, J. (1980)	*Urban Complex of an Industrial City,* Allahabad.
Sinha, D. N. (1960-61)	Social and Behavioural Problems in Industry, Indian Journal of Social Work, 21: 235-246.
Vidyarthi, L. P. (1970)	*Socio-Cultural implication of industrialization in India; A case study of Tribal Bihar,* New Delhi.

CHAPTER 2

Santal Coal-Miners

Sukumar Banerjee

Modern industry not only requires a large capital and an efficient management, it also needs the machine technology for increasing production. Due consideration is given in appointing highly technical hands for organising the work but the same kind of technicalities is not observed in recruiting the lower categories of workers. It is for this reason that the teeming millions of our country enter the various industrial units as labourers.

The productive organisation in Indian rural society is carried out in the basis of division of labour. The farmers and artisans are in especial relationship of inter-dependence which is not only limited to economic aspects, but has pervaded in other spheres of life. (The tribal groups are not exceptions to this feature as they have been brought within the sphere of Hindu economic organization). Indian society is, therefore, a compromise body in which various constituents are in a network of relationship for an organized social life. This is the position in the pre-industrial phase when the process of social change may not have proceeded in a desired pace. This belief is shared by many scholars for in their views the workers who visit the industrial centres, are not in a position to internalise the values appropriate to industrial society on account of the link with the traditional social structure and to their territory (village).

The tribals are also placed in a similar position. Having been drawn from agriculture sector, the tribal labourers are found to be least skilled. The legacy of traditions based on mechanical solidarity has not only turned them as kin-oriented with a nexus to their original territory but it has enabled them to develop a world-view distinct from those of the rural peasantry. It is natural that the contact between the two in an industrial setting not only present a unique situation as a characteristic feature of a developing country but also an interaction between the simple people as working hands and arranged industrial organization.

In conducting the study on the impact of coal-mining complex in Jharia-Raniganj area, the Santal tribe forming the largest tribal group among the various immigrants that came to this region, was placed not only in a new cycle of work but also in a multi-ethnic arena of interaction. So it was considered necessary to know how the Santal miners had adjusted to the mining situation in respect of their various aspects of culture. Apart from these, whether the problem of absenteeism, social disorganization, and the exploitation by a section of industrial workers are in any way responsible for affecting the quality of their labour commitment. While these Santal labourers are not irrelevant in the mining situation on which we are focussing our attention in this paper, the material of which were collected during my earlier work on the Santals coal miners in the Jharia-Raniganj coal field area in the year 1971-72. (Banerjee, 1981).

The Santals are the main tribal group involved in this industry and constituted 7.4% of the total strength in this region (2,81,001) as mentioned in the Census of India (1961). Having arrived from immediate hinterland, they bore the main brunt of coal-mining as pick miners at early phase of mining industry. But they failed to move up in the scale of industrial employment and have almost been 'pushed' out of the mining situation, turning themselves in abject minority.

Historical Account

In earlier period, the Santal workers were found all over the coal field. But most of them, have withdrawn to the places that are not very far from the hinterland from where they migrated. Though the availability of land was the prime factor for settlement at these places, their selection was made in consideration of the location of the colliery where they can work as daily commuters over and above the facilities of continuous interaction with their original villages. Finding the Santal workers to be most suitable for having imbibed the manual orientation of their agricultural pursuits, the colliery managements 'pulled' a large number of the Santals from the adjoining districts of Birbhum, Santal Parganas, Hazaribagh, Purulia and Bankura.

The coal industry came into existence in early part of nineteenth century but it is difficult to say about the exact point of time of the Santals' arrival into this region. After undergoing a slow pace of growth in this period, the industry received sudden drive round about 1900 A.D. It was at this time that the bulk of their influx was reported to have taken place in response to a great demand for labour. Taking advantage of higher wage for piece-rated jobs, a Santal miner used to earn an appreciable amount by working in a team when loading of coal tubs used to be done by his wife or by other woman members of his house. The prevailing working arrangements was in keeping with the demand of the Santal miners. In order to maintain their link with the village, they took advantage of the prevailing situation and thronged at the pick-miners job. For this reason the other caste groups (Kurmi, Mahato, Bauri, Dom, Turi, Napit, Muchi and others) were employed in other occupations of this industry. It was for this reason that some sort of occupational specialization occurred in this industry enabling the different ethnic groups to involve in different jobs of mining work. But this flexible nature of coal industry did not last long for the management began to initiate necessary changes in the organization to conform to the modern industrial system.

Layout of the Work force

On my initial exposure to the field situation, I came to know about the existence of two types of enterprises. The first included those units that were small in organization, owned by private individuals or run under the system of partnership where the mining operations were mostly hand-operated. The second type belongs to various industrial managements, having mechanized units setting up the organization on a three tier basis--resembling a pyramidal structure, the single owned firms or proprietors occupied the topmost level being the decision-making when the mining engineers (supervisors) and workers constituted the next two orders. Starting in the fashion, the pattern of organization emerged as a proto-type as the various industrial managements organised their units on the same line. For business purpose, the respective managements of the collieries studied had their headquarters at Calcutta from where the Executive body through their colliery departments, exercised necessary control in regard to the production and sale of coal in their respective units. Though variation existed in the administrative set-up, we may leave aside this part as it is not directly concerned with our problem.

The account of supervisory level mostly related to the different grades of mining officials appointed on the basis of their technical qualification and practical experience for conducting the duties the coal-mines in the sphere of maintenance, safety and production. With this nature of their background, it will be in vain to expect the tribal people to get these positions. The workers in the colliery perform their duties either on the surface (above ground) or underground. The division of labour as reflected from thirty types of job present among them, was due to the introduction of various machines for effecting large scale production. Extending this arrangement among the underground workers who were found in no less than thirty five categories of jobs, it was observed that these were classified broadly into two divisions relating to maintenance and production.

Santal's place in the working level

Having so much scope to enlarge their area of involvement in the coal mining industry the Santal coal miners preferred to concentrate in the piece rated jobs engaging themselves mostly as pick miners. A shift in the occupation to that of 'Loaders' was not acceptable to them for it would fetch less wage besides the overall supervision of other officials. Secondly they considered it a job more suited to woman workers. A high frequency of absenteeism was prevalent on account of working either in the village farm during the sowing and harvest seasons drinking heavily after the weeks' work in the mines due to sickness caused as a result of strains being a peasant miner.

On finding no improvements in the matter of attendance on the part of the Santals the management had to make alternate arrangements.

In a bid to maintain the tempo of the production in the coal mining industry especially during the Second World War period, the Government came to their rescue by diverting a section of their labour to work in the coal mining establishments, recruiting them through Gorakhpur Labour Organization.

The Santals being more adept in their agricultural pursuits, as in earth cutting jobs, found it comparatively easy to acquire the skill within a few days' apprenticeship under their experienced miner brethren. All the levels of mining officials held a very good opinion about their performances. They all agree that the requisite qualifications of a miner were inherent in each and every Santal worker. Their workmanship was fine and better than up-country labours and apart from being diligent, obliging and expert, their output was much more than those of other non-tribals. The officials of the collieries regretted for finding the Santal workers not picking up in all earnest the norms of industrial economy. They find that the Santal are loosing interest in spite of their being fine workers.

CLASSIFICATION OF THE SANTAL MINERS

(1) *Commuters:-* Three different categories of the Santal coal miners have emerged in this coal field area. The first category consisted of commuters who came to work daily from their villages. The proximity of colliery from the Santal villages was the main factor for turning a miner either as commuter or to settle down as temporary resident in the mining situation. In the early phase of the industry, the Santal miners were simply 'pulled' from immediate hinterland through various recruiting agents. But the situation had changed in the village where pressure on land, created the problem of surplus labour. Gradually they were 'pushed' out of the farms which did not allow them to maintain their subsistence. As there was no regularity of getting agricultural labour, they tried to seek extra-income from daily wages from these economic resources .

(ii) *Permanent settlers-* The second category of the Santal miners resided within the mining situation. As original inhabitants of a village, that has become a colliery site for the accidental discovery of coal there, they had turned themselves as permanent settlers in an industrial site. It may not be understood that the presence of the Santal settlements in the coal field area indicated the location of the colliery in the tribal tract. But it happened to coincide with the farthest extension in this part of the country where they arrived at some point of time in search of fresh lands. They were carrying on with their traditional economy as owners cultivators or share croppers or as peasant miners. Generally these Santal families had adequate man-power to look after their cultivation. Even then, the peasant miner was not free from it, for he devoted his labour when he was free from his mining work. The gradual fragmentation of holding at every incidence of partition between brothers had created pressure on land compelling the owner to augment his income from an external source. The trend for switching over to the mining work accelerated as a result of their land being taken over by the colliery management for the expansion and development.

It was in the colliery situation that one might have noticed some occupational diversification among the Santal miners. Except for one or two miners who reached the lowest rung of supervisory level, (Mining Sardar) evidences of shift from pick-miner to loader, and other technical jobs in time-rated scale were perceptible in addition to a sense of partial commitment in the mining work as compared to other categories of the Santal workers.

(iii) *Migrant Santals:* The third category was constituted by migrant labourers, who were mostly found near about the collieries of Ranigunj coal field, about seventy and eighty miles from their respective tribal areas. Recruited at one time, from immediate hinterland, they preferred to settle down in this area for some advantage, not because of their living near an economic resource but due to opportunity of carrying on their traditional occupation by procuring land through various arrangements.

The story of the migrant Santals around the collieries on the eastern borders of the Ranigunj coal field was more or less the same with the difference that they agreed to settle down in a village when each of them had already roamed a couple of coal mines in their field. They are dissatisfied with the conditions of the mines for these were in the process of mechanization. As they were accustomed to carry on the work of pick-mining as prevalent then, they flocked to nearby coal-mines still being run in an indigenous fashion. In the course of their movement they went farther from their hinterland. While working in various adjacent collieries, these Santal migrants were also in difficulty about their accommodation allotted by their respective managements. As they did not prefer the quarters made by the authorities, the Santal miners belonging to same district or those who belonged to West Bengal region, formed their own settlements by taking land from local caste Hindus. This arrangements was convenient to them economically as they got an opportunity to cultivate land as a subsidiary occupation. A good number of roaming Santal miners settled down by forming small hamlets of a village occupied by various caste groups with all the essential prerequisites of an incipient Santal village. They instructed their respective agnates and affinals to cultivate the farms in the original villages. In this way, they maintained their traditional form of living. The Santal hamlets of different villages were drawn in a network of matrimonial relationship paying occasional visits to their original homes located in tribal territory.

Another common feature noticed among all the Santal miners was their ethnic isolation from other non-tribal coal miners brought from Bihar, Orissa and Madhya Pradesh. Here they not only kept themselves aloof and isolated from the up-country labourers but they also practised intra group aloofness even among themselves. Sharma (1962) has also observed similar social phenomena among the unskilled labourers of working in M/s Tisco, Jamshedpur who are mainly the Santals and the Kols. Describing it as tribal tendency of social segregation, he has not mentioned whether any such tendency was perceptible not only between the Kols and the Santals but even among themselves as a case of extreme segregation as observed by me in the coal mining industry of this region.

Having given an account of various categories of the Santal miners, we may now present a brief ethnographic adjustment account of each of these groups with a view to knowing their process of adjustment as a result of their involvement in coal-mining industry.

Commuters:

It would be appropriate to begin with an account of commuters who came to work in the colliery from the neighbouring villages situated at a distance of no less than five to six miles from the mining situation. This will help in giving a comparative picture of the Santal commuters with their brethren living permanently in the mining situation.

In the village, selected for study, there was altogether twenty -eight families with a population of 185 (males 83, females 102). Taking up the case of male workers (N=83). I found two distinct types of occupation namely agriculture and mining, representing 36% and 27% respectively. Analysing the data further, it was revealed that 77% of the total Santal miners is belonging to the village, were daily commuters who worked mostly in the two neighbouring collieries, while 23% returned to village at every week and resume their duties either on Mondays or Tuesdays. It was also revealed that 59% of the industrial workers had taken up the job of pick mining whereas 18% were working in different jobs like loaders, trammers and truck loaders under various contractors.

While 14% of the Santal families depended entirely on agriculture the remaining 86% had turned peasant miners. On being asked to state the reasons for such a drift in their occupation they said that the total yield of their respective farms was not sufficient for their subsistence for the whole year. On a detailed enquiry in a few domiciles, it came to my notice that the families having less than six bighas (two acres) of arable land, found themselves in great difficulty to pull on with their cultivation. In the early phase of the coal mining industry, the Santal, were no doubt pulled from its hinterland to work in the collieries as pick-miners but the situation changed since then, when they were gradually pushed out to seek labour elsewhere. Keeping these points in view, we may now examine the nature of adjustments made by the Santal villagers in their life, working as coal-miners.

Observing their settlement pattern, arrangement of their domiciles, household equipments, various items of food, and also their normal attire (dress) what I noticed was that these still showed many of the typical features as prevalent in their society.

In social organization, the Santal did show some evidences of stress and strain. In the course of my survey in the village under study I came across the prevalence of equal frequencies of simple and extended families, but the present trend showed the transformation of simple to complex type in incorporating new members belonging either to their maternal house or affinals too. These people indirectly give security in exchange for the facility offered for working as commuters from the village. Due to variable size of their holdings, all the Santals were not recipient of appropriate quantum of the proceeds from their land. Instead of depending on their subsidiary occupation, for these works could be undertaken by women and children, many of them preferred to make up their shortage by enlisting themselves as wage-earners in nearby mines. As the Santals of the village situation liked to remain in their own social system, there has not been any significant change in their economic life. Whatever variation was noticed in this aspect, it was more or less marginal. The variation noticed in their rite-de-passage and in their rituals, was in the form of adjustment to their mining work giving scope to emphasise some of the secular aspects. Even then they adhered to the main contents of their culture as reflected from the adjustments made in their village organization.

Finding the work of mining to be important for meeting both ends, they delegated some of the essential roles relating to village organization and rituals to their brethren who did not have any link with the mining situation for these people depend entirely on their agricultural pursuits. Participation of the Santal labourers was enlisted by adjusting the timings of various activities either on holidays or Sundays. Some sort of freedom was also given to them on the process of individualization as reflected from their kinship bahaviour. That is why, the kinship narrowed down in order to free from normal obligations with a view to adjusting with the work of new occupation.

It may not be out of place to mention here that a few changes occurred as a result of diachronic factors without the influence of this process of industrialization. But my focus of study was to observe these changes that helped the miners to adjust with the industrial situation.

Permanent Settlers

Among the ten ethnic groups living in the mining site of the colliery, the Santal families (N=56) form 25% of the total number of domiciles. Being concerned with this tribal groups, I found the Santal permanent settlers to be 21% of the total population of the settlements found within the mining site (N=1336). Examining the data, one would find some interesting variation from that of the village setting, particularly about complete reversal in occupational pattern among the permanent settlers.

If we leave aside the non-workers (38.35%) among the men we found 12% of them, depending exclusively on agriculture, when the corresponding figure for the village was 37%. Excluding the occupational categories like teacher and tailors being very few in number, the rest of the Santal men engaged themselves as industrial., workers in the colliery constituting 48% of their total population (N=143) when the corresponding figure in this respect in the village situation was 27%. Considering this matter on the basis of total population in the mining situation. We found the respective concentration in the occupation of agriculture and mining site were 58 and 32. The latter can be classified again as peasant miner and miners. Numerically, the proportion of these two groups of people were almost equal (48:46) but the former section (peasant miner) predominates in village situation.

Comparing the figures in family units, we noticed excess of agricultural families in the village (14%) as against 1.7% in the mining situation. The other Santal families living in the colliery did not depend on the wage income only but supplement their income from cultivation too. No less than 60% of the families living in colliery were peasant miners, and the rest had turned miners for being dispossessed of their lands for expansion and development of colliery initially by the present management in 1955. Engaged as pick miners since the early phase of this industry, the present trend among the Santal workers was to secure time rated jobs.

Material culture

Two old villages located within the jurisdiction of the mining site, had all the important elements to consider them as the typical Santal settlements. Arranging the domiciles in their linear fashion, each ethnic group had its own row of houses parallel to one another. Owing to frequent shifting of the Santal families at the time of expansion and development their domiciles in the new settlement did not find a place in the row meant for the tribal people but got mixed up along with other caste groups. As they desire to live in modern fashion many of the owners had turned their living room (ora) as 'pucca'. Replacing the mud walls by bricks, many of them had built reinforced concrete over it.

A close look at the household equipments, will at once indicate their economy to be on subsistence level. Though the bulk of these specimens was in no way different from what had been observed in the house of their brethren in the village situation, they got hold of many new articles due to cash wage from the mining industry. In spite of their being permanent workers in the collieries which was close to the urban areas, they preferred to take their normal pattern of diet. Comparing with the Santal commuters, the contents of their meals did show considerable variety particularly at week ends because they buy meat or fish out of their wages. But the prosperity to spend more on drinking was the usual fashion and there was hardly any Santal who was free from this habit.

Social Organization

The Santals of mining situation were found to be traditional in regard to their marriage customs by observing very strictly the rules of village and clan-exogamy. Like the Santals of hinterland, they held on to their social institution in a more rigid fashion for its adherence indicated tribal identity. So far, the help and co-operation were concerned the Santals apart from siblings, look forward to their maternal kins and affinals to a greater extent. As a result of this new orientation towards them, the Santals equate their own lineage members under the general category of *bhaiyyad*. The relationship having got blurred without any proper distinction between members constituting lineage of co-operation and lineage of recognition (Mayer,1960).' The Santals find more scope in releasing themselves from various kinship obligation and take recourse to the process of individualization.

We find that the Santals living in mining situation were subjected to greater pressure of industrial economy as it is reflected from progressive increase in the frequency of simple families (57%). Apart from usual extensions (lateral and vertical) we have a few evidences of new extensions made through other kins. Finding the collection as on economic resource, many Santal workers got easy accommodation in their wife's parental house. We find extensions through sister and even affinals (Wi El Si So) who came to form as additional members of the family. In spite of a good number of members being present in the house it had not inflected the average size of the family in the mining situation. It was only 5.05 when the corresponding figure in the village situation was 6.61.

With the establishment of the colliery in 1900 A.D. the Santals workers tried their level best to remain within their own system by undertaking a series of adjustments in their life. But they had to encounter tremendous obstacles when the management initiated the programme of shifting the population of the mining site to safer zones. As this arrangement compelled them to hand over their homestead as also cultivable lands to the colliery authorities, they rehabilitated themselves by procuring available space for living. Consequently the land found an entry into the market. Managing the work of their cultivation with their own available man-power, or by engaging daily labourers the Santal families not only conducted their economic transactions on the basis of market principle but also got further scope in individualization. As the village situation reflects a slight preponderance of reciprocity in economic transactions, the colliery situation showed a little more flexibility. Barring the cases leading contractual relationship of barber and mid-wife, and to some extent with blacksmith, complete, shift had taken place with whom they had their service relationship. Their services were exchanged on caste basis, land they had started to practise it as an attempt on their part to adjust with a new economy.

Secondly, the village secular and sacred headmen were not free like their counterparts in the village. In the changed situation they had to opt for mining work too. It was for this reason that they lost all authoritative control over the members and had given rise to the process of individualization and secularization of socio-religious aspects. The Santal permanent settlers like those of commuters, were found to be very traditional in some aspect of their life. The reason was that if they retained their link with their own system they would be able to maintain their tribal identity. The same trend was observed in their village festivals. They had simplified the process of various rituals in response to the demand of a new economy . The ultimate result was that the Santals without having any constraint from their culture, adjust with the work-cycle in a more committed manner than their brethren commuters living in the neighbouring village.

Migrant Santals

Forming at one time, the bulk of the work force, the Santals gradually receded from this field with the introduction of mechanization. As the blasting process of extracting coal left the roof of the coal-seams somewhat loose which may bring about some accidents, the management of the collieries engaged them as 'Dressers' to do the needful in making the roof safe.

While the number of jobs working as Dressers was insignificant, forty -one Santal miners (79%) were found to be occupying in the labour quarters when 21% were commuters from the adjoining Santal settlements. Enquiring the Dressers living in company quarters as to why they were working when most of them were owner-cultivators or share-croppers in their original villages in Santal Parganas, they all appraised the writer of the low productivity of their holdings. In spite of the fact they have gained wide popularity being an expert in the work of 'Dressing', I found that they still maintain their link with their home in Santal Parganas. As they considered themselves members of their own villages where they usually conducted their important function of social life, I had to divert my attention to a study of their brethren living in adjoining settlements, that came to be formed in the vicinity of the collieries on the establishment of the coal-mining industry in this area. Though the following account relates to one of the Santal settlements, I had supplemented my data from adjoining village too.

After roaming about a number of indigenous type of collieries the Santal migrant workers arrived here to work as pick-miners. As they found the scope of pick-mining being reduced on account of gradual mechanization and being asked to shift elsewhere enabling the management to execute the work of expansion, one of the Sardars of pick-miners took the initiative in settling up their own settlement. Being a person from Purulia District, the Sardar was able to collect 75% of the total families (N=20) from his own area while the other families came from Santal Parganas and Bankura districts. Analysing the data on occupational basis, we found that a good chunk of the Santal population (50%) had turned their attention to cultivation. Leaving aside the two women who worked as daily-labourer, all other women (N=41) were mainly engaged in the domestic work. The Santal men, were divided into two broad categories i.e. farmers (28) and miners or dressers (19).

In keeping with their usual dwelling complex, the only difference noticed by me is the absence of threshing floor as the same work conducted in the house of their respective patrons (owner or landlord). Pulling on with limited household equipments, it was observed that they still adhered to their usual diet which often got enriched with more nutritious items on account of wages in their possession. The most effective social unit was family. Though functioning as an economic unit it has developed a tendency to split up into nuclear families. As a result of their dependency on share-cropping and agricultural labourers the families incorporated extra hands by inviting a few affinal members to work either cow-boy for grazing the cattles or to work as agricultural labour. Their inclusion in the simple family changed its composition from simple to complex.

In order to get the facilities for working as peasant miner a migrant Santal preferred to stay in his own tribal settlement instead of occupying the quarters provided by the management of colliery. It was observed in the place of study at Ranigunj field that after obtaining a little compensation from the colliery authorities on account of dismantling their domiciles for purpose of expansion, these migrant Santals purchased homestead land from local caste-groups, or agreed to pay an annual rent for a piece of homestead land to work as share-croppers or agricultural labourers.

These Santals were not subjected to same sort of inter-ethnic relationship as observed in the Jharia field. As they were dependent more on local peasants, they had not considered it necessary to invite the artisan groups to settle down in their hamlets. They availed of their services as and when required paying usual fee for their professional services. Similar changes occurred in other aspects of their life as a result of entering into new economy. They rounded off the various rituals observed during the various stages of their life-cycle by highlighting the secular aspects. They conducted their rituals at the *'manjhithan'* instead of *jaher* (Sacred Grove) serving as a minimum cultural base to lead a cohesive life in a new situation. Except the main core represented by the clan organization whose maintenance was essential to assort their tribal identity all categories of the Santal miners tried to adapt to the demands of the industrial economy.

Commitment to labour

Having given the account of various categories of the Santal miners about the manner of adjustments to coal mining industry we may now consider the problem from another dimension related to labour.

At the initial phase of coal-mining industry, the Santal miners were not required to conform to its essential requirements. As they were accustomed to work three or four days a week, the mine owners used to employ them. To work for long hours in the mine. Due to hard labour and hazardous life coupled with the loss of status and prestige as inherent in the life of a cultivator the Santal miners resorted to excessive drinking while there has occurred considerable change in the working pattern. The Royal Commission on Labour in India (1931) have also observed about the indiscriminate use of labour among the aboriginal tribe in the coal fields. It was probable that the present lack of discipline as reflected from the high rate of absenteeism may be due to this habit of drinking which survived as a tradition. As a result of these habits and the consequent exploitation by a section of industrial workers they formed not only an unfavourable attitude towards managements, but responsible for bringing an erosion in the level of commitments to this industry. In spite of their commendable performance in the coal mining industry as opined by various grades of supervisory officers, the management failed to attune the Santal miners to the rhythm of the industrial norm. The employers were compelled to devise an alternative method to invite up-country labourers for bringing some stability in the work force. Comparing the study conducted among the Gautemalan community of Cantel (Nash, 1958), the smooth accommodation of Cantalenes, into local textile industry, have been achieved not only for extraneous elements selectively incorporated into their culture to promote industrialization, but it may be the phenomenon in keeping with a situation dominated by ethnic homogeneity. The variation in the adjustment as observed among the Santal miners may be due to their involvement in an arena of multiethnic interaction.

It may be recalled that one of the reasons for making their conditions difficult in the collieries was due to the general introduction of the strict rules and industrial legislations. The arrival of up-country labourers in the sphere of mining industry suddenly brought some complexity in the situation, which was bound to affect the process of adaptation of these tribal people. So far the pick-mining is concerned, the up-country labourers were not found to be efficient as the Santal miners. But the management utilized them in a different capacity (leaders') by introducing the system of mechanization which completely altered the conditions of the indigenous mines. The Santal miners could not adjust to such a situation for possessing less adaptability and skill (Royal Commission on Labour in India, 1931), they got further set back in finding the scope of pick-mining being reduced gradually. In view of the circumstances the Santal miners could find any other alternative than to protect their identity in this new environment and for this reason they preferred to isolate themselves from other ethnic groups and lived in their own social world.

Finding themselves in such a situation, the Santals were not in a position to decide about the steps to be taken to retrieve their position. While a section of tribal workers were impelled to recede from their field the Santal miners who had no alternative, re-organised themselves by extending their social horizon as an attempt on their part to adjust with the mining situation.

Not prepared to lose anymore through victimization in view of their subservient position in the coal mining organization the Santal did not like to form a body or trade union pattern. They had realised that so long as the Santal workers were not made conscious of their plight there was no way out. They thought it proper to set their house in order by disciplining themselves properly so that they could act as a united body to get some footing in the mining situation. Being related with the response from their brethren, the Santal leaders preferred to initiate their work in social field by organizing a body which was given name 'Sanot Santal Samaj'. Thus the vacuum created in the Santal Society owing to loss of their centralized structure (like the Paragana system) was taken up by this new organization, which was on arrangement to adjust their life in the industrial milieu. They expected also that necessary steps would be taken to counteract the discriminative move of the management with a view to securing the lost ground leading to increased commitment.

A situation as this where the Santals having a background of tribal organization characterised by 'mechanical solidarity' came into contact with the non-tribal labourers drawn from complex peasant society with a notion of superiority over tribes. The world-view of the Santals reflected a subservient position vis-a-vis the non-Santal workers and management. The pattern of interaction in the totality of the situation kept them on the fringe of industrial organization. Their aspiration remained limited as compared to others involved in this industry and partly responsible for the lack of commitment.

It is clear from the foregoing account that the Colliery situations are the meeting place of two different socio-cultural systems. The non-tribal people came to possess certain features of larger society (caste system, endogamy division of labour, occupational specialization and hierarchy) which gave rise to differentiation of roles. This was in marked contrast to the tribal heritage as that of the Santals.

So we find that no real impediment to attune the Santal industrial life comes from their own traditional structure. So it seemed that the programmes and policies adopted by the management (Morris, 1965) particularly the opportunities offered to the up-country labourers may be considered the main cause for inhabiting the growth of a disciplined labour force among the Santals.

References

Banerjee, S. (1981) — *Impact of industrialization on the Tribal Population of Jharia Ranigunj Coal Field Areas*, Anth. Survey of India, Memoir No. 52.

Govt. of India (1931) — Report of the Royal Commission on Labour in India, Calcutta.

Mayer, A.C. (1960) — *Caste and Kinship in Central India*, Routledge and Kegan Paul, London.

Morris, D. Morris (1965) — *The Emergence of Industrial Labour Force in India. A Study of Bombay Cotton Mills* (1854-1947), Univ. of California Press / Oxford Univ. Press.

Nash, M. (1965) — *Machine Age Maya: The Industrialization of a Guatemalan Community*, Illinois, The Free Press of Glenco Memoir 87. Univ. of California Press/ Oxford Univ. Press.

Ray, B. (1966) — District Census Hand Book - BURDWAN *Census of India, 1961.* Supdt. Govt. Prtg. Press. Calcutta.

Sharma, T.R. (1962) — A Tribal Community in an Industrial context: A case study in Jamshedpur city, Jr. Soc. Res. Vol. V, No. 1., pp. 114-123.

CHAPTER 3

Tea Industry in Assam and Tribal Labour : An Appraisal

R.K. Kar

Introduction

Tea labour in Assam consists mostly of the tribal communities (castes in lesser number) drawn from different parts of the country. They started migrating to Assam tea plantations since about the middle of 19th century.

In the present paper, an appraisal has been made of the general conditions of life of the tea labour, the changes that have occurred in their traditional way of life, their commitment to the industry, and the problems they confront sometimes because of tradition and sometimes because of emerging pattern of social structure.

Data were collected from different tea plantations in Upper Assam at different periods from 1973 to 1982. General statements have occasionally been substantiated by factual information collected from some of the plantations.

Tea industry in Assam

The natural home of tea plant is the monsoon lands of S.E. Asia, where the cool or cold weather is fairly dry with a marked temperature fall. The principal tea producing countries in the world are India, Sri Lanka, China, Indonesia, Japan, Kenya, and Uganda, etc.

India's place in the world tea market is unquestionably very high. She occupies the largest area under tea and also produces the largest amount in the world. The leading provinces in respect of tea industry in India are Assam and West Bengal. In Assam 1,92,427 hectares of land was under tea in 1978. This was distributed in some 750 and odd number of tea gardens (Statistical Hand Book of Assam, 1980).

In fact, cultivation of tea is practically restricted to the table land of Assam with its two adjacent districts, Darjeeling and Jalpaiguri of West Bengal and to the elevated regions of Malabar coast and Nilgiri regions of South India.

Detailed literatures discussing the origin and stages of development of tea industry in India are not available. Nevertheless, an overall idea of the history and growth of this industry in the country, with special reference to Assam can be obtained from the writings of Crawford (1924), Das (1931), Bhuiyan (1960), Mukherjee (1961), Kapur (1961), Danda (1962), Desai (1962), Banerjee (1963), Barua (1963), Das and Banerjee (1964), Harler (1964), Kidwai (1964), Griffiths (1967) and Kar (1981 a, b). Besides, there are some relevant publications by the Tea Board and Census Department, Government of India.

The origin of tea plantation in India can be traced as back as to 1774 when Warren Hastings was the Governor-General. Experimental commercial production in Assam, however, did not start before 1837. In that year the seeds from China were planted experimentally in Botanical Gardens in Calcutta, in Nainital, and at a site some 25 km from Dibrugarh in Assam. The site was named cha-bua (place where tea was planted).

By 1839 there were nurseries planted with China seeds at places like Jaipur, Chabua, Chota Tingri, Hukan Pukhuri, Jorhat, Nazira, and Gavru. In the beginning help was taken from some Chinese workers to open the gardens, to pluck the leaves and to manufacture finished tea.

At that time all the stages were worked with hand and no factory developed.

Till 1853 tea plantation was confined to Sibsagar and Dibrugarh districts only. Private gardens were also started by 1850-51. Tea cultivation in Cachar and Karimganj Districts (Borak Valley) was started in 1855 or 1856.

Recruitment of labour

Tea industry is a labour-intensive industry, and in 1975, the average number of labourers employed in Assam tea plantations in a day was more than 0.40 million.

In the beginning acute labour scarcity stood on the way to expand tea industry in Assam. In the first half of the 19th century, in the clearings of the lands now occupied by the Assam tea plantations, the local peoples were reluctant to take employment, probably because (i) they enjoyed an almost self-sufficient economy, and (ii) their socio-cultural background impeded them to work as tea labourer. Besides, the British planters might also have been reluctant to employ the local willing peoples. Because the uprooted labour was obviously far more easy to control and exploit.

Consequently, the labourers were recruited from various cultural, linguistic and ethnic heritages from other provinces. Different groups were recruited from different places, for example, the Munda and the Gonda from Bihar; Santal, Tanti and the Bhumij from Bengal, Orissa and Madhya Pradesh; the Lohar from Bihar, Orissa, Madhya Pradesh and Uttar Pradesh, the Khond from Andhra Pradesh, and the Boya from Tamil Nadu.

Ecological factors seem to have been the main reasons for this large scale migration. In their original habitats the people had been facing acute poverty because of infertility of soil, crude technology, recurrent flood, drought and famine, and the ruthless exploitation by the land-lords and money-lenders. Besides, many people lived in a perpetual state of insecurity because of frequent fatal attack by the deep forest animals.

All these peoples were branded as 'Coolie', and the world at large recognises them accordingly, and not by their group affiliation. The word 'Coolie' is, however now considered derogatory and has been replaced in official documents by the term Mazdoor, i.e., labourer.

The labour force in a plantation is usually composed of people belonging to various ethnic groups. An idea of the extent of ethnic heterogenity of a labour community may be had from Table 1. In the table are presented the ethnic compositions of labour forces in 4 tea plantations, namely, Mancotta, Rajgarh, Hilika (in Dibrugarh district), and Monabarie (in Sonitpur district) in Assam.

In the beginning, a good number of people suffered from maladjustment, some of them died, others went back home after the expiry of the contracted period, and still others fled away before the expiry of that period. A major section of the groups, however, survived that stage and had gradually settled in the new habitat, in a new economy, in a new neighbourhood, and far remote from their original home.

Recruitment of labourers from other provinces through various means continued from 1841, till 1953. In 1953 the question of recruitment of labour in Assam was raised from a wholly different angle. The Government of Assam, seriously perturbed at the growth of unemployment and at the shortage of food stuffs, suggested that recruitment of labour from outside the state should be curtailed or discontinued, and that attempts should be made to induce labour from over-laboured estates to transfer to estates requiring additional labour. The Indian Tea Association, while not sanguine as to the results of such a scheme, shared the Goverment's wishes and offered to cooperate in it. But, it was soon realised that there was a big gap between demand and supply from within the state. The Government therefore, permitted the recruitment of some 11,000 laboures in 1955. By about 1959 recruitment from outside Assam had been reduced to almost negligible proportions, and in 1960 recruitment from out side was discontinued. By then, a huge, number of tribal labourers from other sites retired from tea-garden job and settled in Assam forming a part of the peasantry here. By 1962 some 600,000 ex-tea garden labourers had been able to settle on Government land.

Categories of labour

The labourers in a tea garden are classified into a number of categories depending on various criteria, e.g., age, sex, resident/non-resident status and nature of appointment. Broadly, the following categories may be identified:

Men *(Mota)* --	Male workers in the age-range 18 to 60 years belong to this category,
Women *(Maiki)* --	It includes female workers between 18 and 60 years of age.
Children --	Age of this group ranges from 14 years to 18 years. A male child is locally called *chukra*, and a female child *chukri*.

On the basis of terms of appointment we have 'Permanent' and 'Temporary' *(faltu)* categories. Besides, in some plantation different terms are used to indicate resident and non-resident status of the worker. Thus *permanent faltu* refers to a labourer appointed permanently but not resident of the labour *lines* in the plantation. A temporary (casual) appointment is limited to a maximum of 150 working days.

Minimum wages of labour vary with age and sex, whereas the fringe and social security benefits vary with the nature of appointment. During June-July, 1983, the minimum wage rates (per day) were as follows:

Men - Rs. 9.65, Women - Rs. 9.47, Child - Rs. 4.79.

The present practice of recruitment of new labourers in a tea plantation is mostly informal. Often the workers themselves introduce their relatives and friends to find them jobs. The industry, it seems, has a standing agreement to maintain the level of employment of permanent workers obtaining as on January 1, 1969 by replacing old workers by an eligible substitute preferably from the family of the outgoing worker (Phukan, 1979: 77).

A worker who is no longer fit for work, but who cannot be retired because he has not reached the retirement age or because no retirement age is laid down in the terms of employment may thus be persuaded to retire if he knows that his son or one of his nearer relatives will be employed in his place.

Temporary workers are employed by the management to meet the periodic needs of the plantation. This is done from within the garden population as well as from the people of the neighbouring villages. The workers from the villages belong mostly to ex-tea garden labour group.

Barring the *Budli* (substitute for a permanent worker from his/her immediate family), the selection is done mostly on subjective considerations. When the workers from 'Children' category attain adulthood, they approach the management for promoting them to *mota/maiki* status. In that case, practical test is taken by allotting them a prescribed amount of task *(nirikh)* in pruning to be completed within a stipulated time. The successful workers are granted adult status.

Conditions of work including social security benefits

The earliest recruiting of labour for Assam tea gardens was done by contractors. Since there was no restriction upon the contractors, the system became known as the free contractor's system. It led, however, to some gross abuses, such as deception in recruitment, unsanitary conditions at the depot and on steamers and countryboats, and heavy mortality on the way to labour districts. "Contractors collected coolies by the hundred on false promises of high pay and light work and dispatched them to the tea districts without taking any sanitary precautions for their welfare on the journey; the result was shocking mortality on the voyage up, while many of the immigrants were of caste or constitution which precluded all hope of their surviving many months in the jungles of Assam" (Report of Assam Labour Enquiry Committee, 1906).

In 1861, an Enquiry Committee was formed by the Government of Bengal to investigate into the unsatisfactory state of affairs in labour recruitment. It was found that mortality on the voyage to Assam commonly reached 10% to 12%. While on one occasion it had been as high as 50%, and as the contractors seem to have been paid in full even when the labourers died on the way, most of them made no attempt to secure cleanliness or provide satisfactory food.

Besides, the health condition prevailing at that time in the newly cleared plantation was also extremely bad. The report of the Commissioner for the year 1962 shows that in some tea plantations of Nowgong, the death rate was as high as 413.33 per thousand. It is, therefore, quite expected that the labourers were not always very enthusiastic about their new situations.

The first Inland Emigration Act, Bengal Act III of 1863, was passed to control emigration to Assam. The Act provided that all recruiters should be licensed, that every intending emigrant should be produced before the magistrate of his own district, should be examined as to his willingness and physical fitness to migrate, and then should be sent to a central depot, where he was put under contract (not exceeding a period of four years).

But, the Act did not protect the labourer after his arrival on the garden. The Act was in fact, soon found to be inadequate, particularly when the tea mania of the early sixties temporarily attracted to the tea industry a low and often unscrupulous type of European, against whom the labourer clearly needed protection.

Bengal Act III of 1863 was amended to Bengal Act VI in 1865. It prescribed minimum wages, limited hours of work (9 hours per day, and 6 days per week), and laid down that contracts with immigrant labour must not extend beyond three years. Every estate was required to maintain a hospital. A protector and an Inspector of labour were appointed and empowered to visit gardens to supervise everything including the authority - labour relation.

In the Independent India, a number of legislations were enacted from time to time to regulate the conditions of work of the labourers in tea plantation.

In 1948, the Minimum Wage Act was promulgated. Its operation was extended to the tea estates.

The Plantation Labour Act, 1951 has defined many conditions of labour employment in clear terms, e.g., (i) Clause 30 of this Act provided that every worker shall be allowed leave with wages at the following rate,

(a) One day for every twenty- two working days for adult

(b) One day for every fifteen working days for minor.

(c) in the case of sickness, sickness allowance, and

(d) in case of woman worker maternity allowances are provided by this clause.

(ii) Under clause 8, in every plantation effective arrangements shall be made by the employer to provide and maintain sufficient supply of drinking water for all workers.

(iii) Clause 9(1): There shall be provided separately for males and females in every plantation a sufficient number of latrines and urinals of prescribed types.

(iv) Clause 10 (1): In every plantation there shall be provided and maintained free medical facilities for the workers and their families.

(v) Clause 15 : The employer is to provide and maintain for every worker and his family residing in the plantation necessary housing accommodation.

(vi) Section 12: The employer should provide creches for the children (below six years) of working mothers.

(vii) Section 14: Facilities for education be provided to children below 12 years of age.

(viii) Section 13: Employer should make provision in his plantation of recreational facilities for workers and their children.

The Act also provides that an employer shall provide the workers with umbrellas, blankets, rain coats or other like amenities for the protection of workers from rain or cold.

Field data collected from a number of plantations in Dibrugarh and Sonitpur districts in Assam during 1973-82 reveal that the labourers working on different tea plantations are provided, other than wages, with the following benefits:

(i) Rent-free accommodation: The floor space covered by each standard type of house is 425 sq. ft., while the total area of the campus is 3000 sq. ft. As per plantation Act, 1968, the specifications for a twin quarter are as follows: campus area- 5,000 sq. ft., floor space - 894 sq. ft.

(ii) Provision of paddy land subject to availability.

(iii) Contributory provident fund at the rate of 8% of wage. No provident fund accrues during the probation period (6 months).

(iv) Free medical attention. In each plantation there is a hospital with its own attending staff.

(v) Leave with wages.

(vi) Sick allowances.

(vii) Provision of fire wood: 228 cft per year per family, 114 cft per year per bachelor (1 cft = 8' x 6' x 4' x 9')

(viii) Subsidized ration and free tea leaf : 500 gm. rice/atta per head per day @ Rs. 20.00/ maund, and lb tea leaf per month per family.

(ix) Free cinema shows: 1 show in a month plus 4 shows during Durga/ Kali Puja.,

(x) Bonus: Minimum is 8.33% of the wage

(xi) Gratuity.

(xii) Drinking water.

(xiii) Creche.

(xiv) Recreation club.

(xv) Miscellaneous: (a) one apron in 2 years, (b) one pair of chappal in 2 years, (c) one umbrella in 2 years, (d) one blanket in 2 years and (e) sunglass, gum-boot, jersey and hand glove for sprayers of pesticides and insecticides.

Temporary workers are not entitled to the benefits (i) (ii), (iii), (vii), and (xi).

Candidates are present in not more than 25% of the plantations. Further, the canteens which exist are no better than such tea stalls as are commonly found in bazar and other trade centres in the state.

Socio-economic life

It has been noted earlier that a good number of tribes (and castes also) who migrated from different parts of the country some generations ago have now become fully settled in Assam tea plantations. Most of these peoples were landless cultivators with no security of jobs and food for every day throughout the year. The nature of job in a tea plantation is quite akin to agriculture to which they were familiar for generations. In the present setting they have, however, been put to a cash economy with close and constant interaction on both social and economic levels with peoples of varied cultures and heritages. Members belonging to both the sexes including the minors work in the plantation and earn independently. The routine of life here is quite different from that in agricultural economy. In brief, the major influences that have been at work since the people's immigration in the present environment are: (i) Contact with numerous other groups belonging to various tribes (castes) working in the same industry, (ii) Contact with the garden officials with varied cultural and urban background, (iii) Contact with the heterogeneous local people living in the neighbourhood, (iv) Involvement in a cash economy, (v) Urban contacts (personal and impersonal), (vi) education, (vii) Welfare activities sponsored by the garden authorities, and (viii) Association in the various activities of labour union in different capacities.

All these factors, in the process of their adaptation to the new setting seem to have influenced the peoples' socio-economic and socio-religious life to a remarkable degree. In certain areas they have adapted very effectively resulting into some re-organization of their traditional ways of life (Kar 1981: 407-19). In some areas, however, the tradition yet seems to work as an inhibiting factor in their successful adaptation. Degree of adaptation seems to vary with generation also.

In a tea plantation, for example, facilities for free modern medical attention is readily available. But, it has been observed that the people, initially take recourse to their traditional remedies in the form of magical rites and propitiation of the malevolent spirits, and natural and/or supernatural indigenous medicine. Very often modern medical attention is sought quite late. Most of the medical officers are of the opinion that mortality rate among the tribal labour could have been reduced if they would have sought medical attention in time. In case of child-birth also, it has been found that about 85% of the births take place in labour quarters and are attended by elderly women or dhai (midwife without formal training). In most of the groups there are certain socially prescribed practices with regard to the disposal of the placenta. In case of hospital births these practices cannot be observed. On the other hand the trained mid-wife/nurse of the hospital does not attend the parturient mother in the labour quarters. This may be considered to be an important factor for the relatively high still birth and infant mortality rate among them. Table 2 records the still birth and infant mortality rate for 3 years in the labour population in Monabarie tea plantation. It will be seen from the table that the still birth ranges from 56.14 to 111.11, and infant mortality rate from 60.66 to 123.07. The picture in other plantations is also similar.

Similarly some of the welfare schemes, e.g., distribution of free milk to children and imparting social education on hygiene and health, tried, by some gardens could not be continued sometimes for reasons of tradition and sometimes for reasons of vested interest., Thus, in 1977 a programme was undertaken by the management of Monabarie tea estate to provide milk to the labour children below 2 years of age in the satellite creche. But, the programme failed because of the non-cooperation of the labour. They were reluctant to bring their babies for feeding milk. The most important of the reasons was that their children were not used to artificial milk by custom. The programme was ultimately given up. In 1982, in Rajgarh an attempt was made to organize a Night School to impart social education to the labour community. It did not receive active support and co-operation of the labour leaders apparently for fulfilling their own vested interests. It will be discussed later on that the leadership in the labour community as a whole cuts across their ethnic affiliation and depends on some achieved traits.

The economy of the people is mainly based on the cash income derived from employment in the tea industry. Besides, in many plantations, a good number of workers enjoy the benefit of ownership of agricultural land that is provided by the plantation management. This constitutes the secondary source of their income, and it continues to remain so, as long as at least one member of the family remains in garden employment.

In a tea plantation there are broadly 2 types of activities (i) activities connected with the growing and collection of tea leaves, and (ii) those connected with processing of tea leaves. Plucking is better suited to women, while the other activities are mostly done by men.

Besides the regular phases of work directly connected with the growing and processing of tea leaves, there is a good number of essential services in the plantation that may or may not be directly related with the production. Each labour line (residential cluster) has one chowkidar who acts as the liaison agent between the management and the residents of the particular line, each establishment (office, factory, hospital, bungalows of the executives etc.) has a chowkidar who works as a caretaker. There are sardars who are gang leaders and supervise the works of the labour force in the garden, there are employees in various cadres in school, hospital and office; there are drivers, carpenters, and people for preparing and repairing fences in the plantation, and some labourers are engaged in distributing drinking water and raw tea liquor to the labour force at work. Further, there are sweepers, peons and bearers etc. in different units of the plantation.

The various categories of job within the industry are not equally looked upon by the people themselves. Barring the few skilled and semi-skilled hands, the posts of line chowkidars and sardar are the aspirations of many people. These appointments are made from among the permanent workers on the basis of efficiency and satisfactory service records. This is, however, decided subjectively and ethnic affiliation of the labourer does not play any role. These two posts are included in the 'sub-staff' grade and they receive monthly salary. Many young and some middle-aged people seem to give preference to factory jobs (even unskilled). It appears that their physical association with modern paraphernalia in the factory is considered to be more prestigeous as compared the others.

Recently, with the acquiring of formal education by a few, it has been observed that some changes in the major occupation have been taking place among the people. This is taking place both for reluctance in the tea garden job of a group of semi-educated youths, and also due to the increasing unemployment of the people in the tea industry. Many people feel that they can achieve higher status and better prestige within their own society, and also outside it by being employed in some government or private organizations other than tea garden. A good number of youths undermine or at least believe that their neighbours (Rural Assamese People) undermine the job of a tea garden labourer (Kar, 1979: 783-84).

The wage-rate, at regular interval is negotiated with the representatives of the labour union. Similarly, the bonus for each year is settled on the negotiation table. During plucking season the earning is proportional to the amount of leaves plucked.

About 80% of the families have 2 or more earning members. The average per-capita income of the people is at par with that of the rural Assam, and 20% to 40% of the families live below the poverty line (Kar, 1981: 131). But, most of the families seem to be very quick to spend whatever they earn in consumer goods. Many workers spend a substantial amount sometimes at the cost of basic needs, for country liquor. Many members of the younger generation have been found to spend a major amount for purchasing non-traditional consumer and capital goods like fashionable clothes, wrist-watch, bicycle, radio, sewing machine etc. "A change of dress often means a new psychology, a scorn of the traditions of the one's group, a sense of being ashamed of it" (Elwin, 1958: 145). On the other hand, a numerically small group has realized the value and necessity of money, and some of them have resorted to the habit of regular savings with some savings organizations.

Mostly because of their expenditure habit, one observes a tragic picture of indebtedness in many people. Money-lending business which was originally controlled by the Kabuliwallas has now in some plantations been taken up by the local rural people, and in some cases by their own relatively rich people. The total amount of debt and its various implications make it obvious that the magnitude of the problem is enormous. It has various aspects- psychological, social and economic. It is difficult to estimate the psychological burden; for some at least, all happiness and peace of mind is lost, while others so burdened seem to sink into a dull and hopeless apathy. Generally speaking, a major section of the group appears to have accepted indebtedness as a normal, almost inescapable aspect of their existence. While taking loan, many of them do not seem to believe in the law of limitation.

In July 1982, one money lender in Rajgarh was interviewed on this point. Rajgarh is a medium size (235.77 hectare under tea) tea plantation with a permanent labour strength of 724 (men-198, women-333 and children-193). During peak plucking season it reaches to around 1160 (1982 figure). Sherkhan, aged about 50 years has been living in Rajgarh since 1960s. He has married a labour girl, and has settled down at Rajgarh market with his wife and children. He lends money on interest and deals in cloth (mostly on credit). His business is confined to the labour of Rajgarh, Longboi and Borobam tea gardens. The three plantations form a neighbourhood. On 3.7.82, the outstanding amount of accumulated loan (including interest) was approximately as follows:

Rajgarh	--	Rs. 20,000.00
Longboi	--	Rs. 6,000.00
Borbam	--	Rs. 6,000.00

The approximate number of borrowers in Rajgarh was 300. The rate of interest is exorbitantly high. At the time of interview it was Rs. 4.00 for a principal of Rs. 10.00 and for a period of two weeks (recovery is made on payment day). Thus it is 80% per month. In 1974 it was Rs. 2.00 for a principal of Rs. 20.00 for two weeks, i.e. 20% per month. Besides, there are other forms of loan; they purchase clothes and grocery goods on credit, and sometimes borrow money for a longer period, and give paddy in return after harvesting is done. This last term of borrowing reminds one of the observations made by Elwin,

> "In many tribal areas, as in Madhya Pradesh, Orissa and Tripura, the crop is invariably mortgaged in advance. In Tripura and parts of West Bengal, according to the 'Dadan' system, it is a condition for the advance of a loan that the crop has to be sold to the money-lender at harvest time' (1963:77).

Thus in the plantation labour in Assam we observe the emergence of two new and distinct economic groups: the relatively 'rich' and the relatively 'poor'. The 'affluent' group of people have very often been found to show a tendency to exploit the weaker section to their own advantage.

The emergence of the new economic groups, coupled with occupational hierarchy and elected membership to the garden unit of the Labour Union *(Mazdoor Sangha)* has caused some obvious and significant variations in the socio-political plane of the community. The all-purpose leadership of the community as a whole is vested in the *line* chowkidars, *sardars*, on the people enjoying better economic status and also on those who achieved some figures in the *Mazdoor Sangha*.

Commitment to the industry

The concept of labour commitment is said to involve not only performance but also the acceptance of the relevant norms of the modern industrial life by the workers and orienting their behaviour in accordance with them (Mehrotra, 1975: 9). Life in an industry, demands an intelligent and rational outlook on work and life. Willingness to accept the routine, authority,discipline and even the monotony of the work is the first and foremost qualification.

Participation in union activities is also a measure of degree of commitment, while absenteeism can be a meaningful indicator of the lack of commitment.

An organized trade union activity on a sustained basis started in Assam for the first time in 1939, when in the whole of Assam it was the only trade union. Its Chairman was Shri A.K. Chanda and Vice-Chairman, Shri Sanat Kr. Ahir. Both of them were members of the Assam Legislative Assembly.

In May 1945, five individual garden unions and one Assam Tea Labourers Association consisting of them had been formed in Sibsagar district through the efforts of Prof. P. N. Sarwan of Jorhat. He was the member of a labourer family.

After Second World War the labour movement spread rapidly among the tea garden workers. In 1947, a branch of Indian National

Trade Union Congress was formed among the labourers. All India Trade Union Congress (INTUC) also had its unit functioning among the tea garden labourers.

At present, there are the following trade unions among the tea plantation labourers of Assam.

1. Assam Cha Mazdoor Sangha.

2. Assam Cha Mazdoor Union.

3. Assam Tea Labourers Association.

4. Assam Cha Mazdoor Sramik Sangha.

5. Assam Cha Mazdoor Parishad.

Various unions are controlled by various national political parties. Normally one union works in one garden. In each tea plantation, a garden unit of the Union is constituted. Its activities are confined within the particular garden, and it looks into the minor disputes and differences between the labour community and the management. It also looks into the demands, e.g., an individual who has been working as a casual labour since long but has not been made permanent, when a worker who had been receiving child-wage, aspires for adult wage, improvement of the physical standard of living by improving the provision of sanitation and to raise the standard of garden school, canteen and club.

When an issue cannot be settled by the garden unit it seeks the intervention of the circle or the central body.

Detailed investigation into the participation of general labour in union activities reveal that in almost all the gardens it is being controlled by few labourers. The office bearers and executive members in many units continue to remain in their offices even after the term is over. In some plantation it is observed that the general meeting of the garden unit has not been convened for more than one year. The general labourers, irrespective of their ethnic affiliation, however, do not seem to have any involvement with the affairs of the union. Many of them openly criticize the office-bearers and the executive members for their inefficiency, indifference, and sometimes self-keeping tendency in most of the matters. Sometimes specific allegations have been brought against the office bearers of corrupt practices. In 1982 some one from a plantation complained that the medium pruning for which wages were high were written in the name of the Secretary's son, though he did not do medium pruning. Further, he approached with some of his personal grievances; he was given *chokra nirikh* (child wage), but he was doing the job of spraying pesticides, carrying tea leaf baskets from field on the tractor, and again unloading at the withering trough, which in other gardens are done by men *(mota)*. The Secretary, he complained did not pay any heed to these personal problems.

Ethnic considerations do not seem to influence the election of office bearers, but in reality a garden unit of labour union is usually controlled by the numerically dominant group. Thus, the Savaras and the Tantis control the unions in Mancotta and Rajgarh because of their numerical dominance in the respective gardens.

The management of most of the plantations is sceptic about the commitment of the labour as a whole. Very often they make a correlation of commitment and ethnic affiliation which again varies from garden to garden. Thus the Oraon, Munda; Santal, Porja, Chick and the Tanti are considered to be more committed by some whereas the Savara and the Munda are considered to be less committed by some others. The Christian converts and the women workers are admitted to be relatively more conformist to the industrial way of life. In substantiating their contention the management speaks of the incidence of stealing of fencing, nursery shades, fertile tea bush (to use as firewood), in subordination, indifference to routine of work and absenteeism. The author, in course of his investigation, however, could not identify any such correlation.

Some factual data on the rate of absenteeism were collected from some plantations. Table 3 and 4 present the same for Monabarie and Rajgarh for one year. The average monthly rate of absenteeism is around 13.1%. It has been observed that the rate of absenteeism in Indian industries is considerably high. Ghosh (1966:187) observes that in the cotton mill industry the rate of absenteeism is 11.8% in Bombay, 8% in Ahmedabad, 18.3% in Sholapur, 26.4% in Mysore and 15.3% in Kanpur. In the engineering industry the rate of absenteeism is 13.4% in

Bombay, 12.9% in West Bengal and 12.4% in Mysore. In the coal fields, overall rate of absenteeism for India in the corresponding year (1963) is 12.6%. In the plantation of Mysore the rate of absenteeism is 20.4%. Ghosh further observes that the rate of absenteeism has increased in general since 1969.

Das Gupta (1978: 49) studied the workers of Chaibasa Cement Works located at Singhbhum in Bihar. For the year 1969, he reported that the rate of absenteeism among the daily-rated workers of the works was 16.8%. The corresponding figure among the piece-rate and time-rate workers of the Quarry was 22.6%. In the year 1968, the quarterly rates of absenteeism in the Quarry was 24.1% (January-March), 20.6% (April-June), 20.7% (July-Sept) and 20.5% (Oct.-Dec.).

Das Gupta (1978:49) also observes that absenteeism is more among the workers who are non-resident in the industrial area, who are attached to agriculture and whose level of literacy is relatively low.

Absenteeism rate in tea labour is thus more or less at par with the Indian standard. Male workers show a higher tendency towards habitual absenteeism. Higher rate is also observed during agriculture season and on the following day of the payment of wage. Residential workers in general show a higher rate of absenteeism than the non-resident ones. Relatively rationalized incentive schemes seem to reduce absenteeism rate to some extent.

Habitual absenteeism among the people has been found to be frequent. Among various reasons contemplated by various executives, addiction to liquor and indifference to work seem to be common.

To deal with the problem, the existing practice is that a worker is served with a warning/show-cause notice if he remains absent for 3 days in a week without giving any information to the management. After being served with 3 such notices, and the worker being still irregular, the management is at liberty to exercise the discretion of firing the person. But, in practice dismissal for habitual absenteeism does not take place unless the case is an extreme one.

100 men and 100 women respondents were interviewed in Monabarie in this respect. The results are presented in Table 5. It will be seen

from the table that during 1981, 35 men and 17 women have been served with notices for absenteeism. Out of them 14 men and 8 women workers received more than 3 notices, and there were at least 2 male respondents who were served with 10 notices during the year. In Rajgarh one worker remained absent for 66 days during the period January to June (January 10 days, February 7, March 11, April 16, May 7, June 15) in 1981. In some cases the workers abstain from plantation duty for doing some other economically more gainful casual works, e.g., fishing and working on agriculture land.

Table 6 records the total lay-off (name cut/dismissal) with reasons for the year 1979, 1980 and 1981 in Monabarie. It will be seen from the table that 9 (16.1%) out of 56 lay-off took place because of absenteeism. Out of the total of 9 workers 7 were men and 2 women. It may also be relevantly noted from the table that 35 (62.5%) individuals (men-18, women - 17) effected voluntary name-cut *(namekota)*. It is interesting to note that many workers approach the authority to get their names cut from the pay-roll, and insist for taking some member of his/her immediate family as *budli*. In case of women, it occurs mostly on genuine health ground. But, in case of men barring one or two cases, name-cut is effected just like that. Ostensibly all of them plead their cases on the ground of health. But, in fact most of them do it because of a very resigned attitude towards life and work. Besides, in doing so, they can encash the provident fund and gratuity money which they enjoy ruthlessly and also in a hurry. Generally this happens with the worker who is badly addicted to liquor and whose wife is a member of the work force. In 1981, one worker in Rajgarh being unsuccessful to convince the management of his ill health attempted to bribe to get his name cut.

Most of the habitual absentees appear to be pessimistic about life's chances and are very much concerned with the satisfaction of day-to-day immediate desires. This may be the reason why they tend to spend whatever they earn very fast in consumer goods.

Concluding remarks

The heterogeneity in the ethnic composition of the tea labour is not reflected in their socio-political, economic, and even sometimes in religious life. Conforming changes in their way of life are uneven in terms of generations as well as in terms of social domains. Tradition sometimes inhibit the acceptance of modern elements. A small group of people irrespective of ethnic heritages have taken the leadership of the community as a whole. This group seems to have a relatively more effective adaptation with the present way of life. But, the other members of the lot seem to have very low occupational and educational aspirations, and feel that they have little control over their destiny.

Addiction to country liquor and indebtedness have taken an acute magnitude in them. Many of them are being exploited by the traditional money - lenders, and also sometimes by their fellow members. Their participation in the general affairs of the community is negligible. Thus, two distinct trends are observed among the people; one section is inclined to participate with others in social gains and in potential mobility, while the other section is not similarly inclined.*

* The author is thankful to the University Grants Commission for granting financial support to take up the projects.

Table - 1

ETHNIC COMPOSITION OF THE LABOUR FORCE WORKING ON MANCOTTA, RAJGARH, HILIKA AND MONABARIE TEA PLANTATIONS

Sl. No.	*Ethnic Group*	*Percentage of families*			
		Mancotta	*Rajgarh*	*Hilika*	*Monabarie*
1	2	3	4	5	6
1	Baraik	-	-	7.00	
2	Bauri	4.00	9.00	2.00	
3	Bhakta	1.00	-	2.00	
4	Bhuinhar	-	-	1.00	
5	Bhuiyan	1.00	-	5.00	
6	Bhumij	3.00	-	13.00	
7	Birhor	-	-	-	4.00
8	Dosadh	1.00	-	-	
9	Ghasi	-	2.00	-	-
10	Ghatwal	-	-	-	
11	Goala	2.00	4.00	3.00	2.00
12	Gonjhu	1.00	-	-	2.00
13	Gond	1.00	-	4.00	3.00
14	Karmakar	4.00	-	23.00	
15	Kharia	1.00	4.00	6.00	
16	Kishan	-	2.00	1.00	
17	Kond	-	3.00	-	
18	Kumar	-	-	3.00	3.00
19	Kurmi	1.00	-	1.00	
20	Lohar	4.00	2.00	-	
21	Mahar		-	1.00	
22	Mahato	-	-	1.00	
23	Mahili	1.00	-	2.00	
24	Munda	7.00	14.00	-	9.00
25	Murmu	1.00	-	-	
26	Nagbangshi	-	-	1.00	
27	Nayek	4.00	6.00	1.00	
28	Oraon	3.00	8.00	5.00	
29	Santhal	6.00	8.00	12.00	
30	Savara	50.00	-	1.00	14.00
31	Tanti	1.00	35.00	2.00	44.00
32	Others	3.00	3.00	3.00	19.00
	Total	100.00	100.00	100.00	100.00

Table - 2

RATE OF STILL BIRTH AND INFANT MORTALITY IN THE LABOUR POPULATION IN MONABARIE (1978-80)

Year	*Still birth rate*	*Infant mortality rate*
1	*2*	*3*
1978	56.14	123.07
1979	111.11	72.45
1980	80.88	60.66

Table - 3

AN ACCOUNT OF THE TOTAL MANDAYS LOST IN MONABARIE (1981-82)

Sl. No.	*Month*	*Mandays lost due to*				*Total*	
		Absenteeism	*Maternity*	*Others**	*Total*	*Productive mandays*	*mandays*
1	2	3	4	5	6	7	8
1	June (81)	7617 (11.80)	681 (1.05)	7166 (11.10)	15464 (23.95)	49112 (76.05)	64576 (100.00)
2	July	6893 (10.28)	673 (1.00)	7633 (11.40)	15199 (22.68)	51830 (77.32)	67029 (100.00)
3	August	8444 (13.06)	729 (1.13)	11251 (17.40)	20242 (31.59)	44224 (68.41)	64648 (100.00)
4	Sept.	9706 (15.03)	839 (1.30)	8030 (12.44)	18575 (28.77)	46000 (71.23)	64575 (100.00)
5	Oct.	8976 (13,40)	991 (1.48)	11761 (17.55)	21728 (32.43)	45275 (67.75)	67003 (100.00)
6	Nov.	8287 (13.32)	851 (1.37)	5807 (9.31)	14945 (24.00)	47344 (76.00)	62289 (100.00)
7	Dec	8492 (12.72)	974 (1.46)	5293 (10.97)	16759 (25.11)	49989 (74.89)	66748 (100.00)
8	Jan.(82)	4359 (6.76)	951 (1.47)	11509 (17.84)	16819 (26.07)	47702 (73.93)	64521 (100.00)
9	Feb.	4529 (7.64)	1015 (1.71)	21874 (37.58)	27418 (46.93)	31459 (53.07)	59277 (100.00)
10	March	7473 (11.66)	1020 (1.59)	11497 (17.94)	19990 (31.19)	44095 (68.81)	64085 (100.00)
11	April	7505 (11..71)	650 (1.01)	8864 (13.85)	17019 (26.57)	47040 (73.43)	64059 (100.00)
12	May	7314 (11.23)	471 (0.73)	8752 (13.58)	16537 (25.54)	48218 (74.46)	64755 (100.00)
13	Grand Total	89595 (11.59)	9881 (1.28)	121801 (15.75)	221277 (28.62)	552288 (71.38)	773565 (100.00)
14	Average per month	7466.25 (11.58)	823.42 (1.28)	10150.83 (15.75)	18439.75 (28.61)	46024 (71.39)	64463.75 (100.00)*

Others include : sickness (paid), sickness (unpaid) leave without wage, leave with wage, holiday with pay.

* Figures within parentheses indicate percentage.

Table - 4

AN ACCOUNT OF THE TOTAL MANDAYS LOST IN RAJGARH (1981)

Sl. No.	*Month*	*Mandays lost due to*					
		Absenteeism	*Maternity*	*Others**	*Total*	*Productive mandays*	*Total mandays*
1	2	3	4	5	6	7	8
1	Jan.	3510 (17.9)	540 (2.3)	1944 (9.9)	5994 (30.1)	13554 (69.9)	19548 (100.00)
2	Feb.	1440 (8.7)	456 (2.6)	5904 (33.09)	7800 (45.2)	9576 (54.8)	17376 (100.00)
3	March	2943 (15.1)	351 (1.8)	4698 (24.0)	7992 (40.9)	11556 (59.1)	19548 (100.00)
4	April	2054 (7.7)	286 (1.1)	3276 (12.1)	5616 (20.9)	21398 (79.1)	27014 (100.00)
5	May	6345 (20.1)	162 (0.5)	1998 (6.3)	8505 (26.9)	22950 (73.1)	31455 (100.00)
6	June	1976 (6.3)	338 (1.0)	4550 (14.3)	6864 (21.6)	25662 (78.4)	32526 (100.00)
7	July	4131 (13.4)	405 (1.3)	2781 (9.0)	7317 (23.7)	23598 (76.3)	30915 (100.00)
8	Aug.	4860 (15.9)	405 (1.3)	2160 (7.0)	7425 (23.2)	23220 (76.8)	30645 (100.00)
9	Sept.	4134 (13.7)	416 (1.4)	3484 (11.6)	8034 (26.7)	22100 (73.3)	30134 (100.00)
10	Oct.	5481 (17.5)	513 (1.7)	2295 (7.3)	8289 (26.5)	23004 (73.5)	31293 (100.00)
11	Nov.	6898 (23.6)	442 (1.5)	2228 (7.4)	9568 (32.5)	20566 (67.5)	30134 (100.00)
12	Dec	2565 (13.6)	432 (2.2)	405 (2.1)	3402 (17.9)	16146 (82.1)	19548 (100.00)
13	Grand Total	46337 (14.5)	4746 (1.5)	35723 (11.1)	86806 (27.1)	233330 (72.9)	320136 (100.00)
14	Average per month	3861.41 (14.5)	393.81 (1.5)	2976.91 (11.2)	7233.81 (27.2)	19444.21 (72.8)	26678 (100.00)

Table - 5

AN ACCOUNT OF ABSENTEEISM NOTICES FOR 200 (100 MEN, 100 WOMEN) RESPONDENTS IN MONABARIE (1981)

Number of notices served	No. of respondents Male	Female	Total
1	2	3	4
1	-	1	1
2	13	7	20
3	3	1	4
4	5	3	8
5	3	3	6
6	1	2	3
7	2	-	2
8	-	-	-
9	1	-	1
10	2	-	2
Grand Total	30	17	47

Table -6

AN ACCOUNT OF TOTAL LAY OFF WITH REASONS IN MONABARIE (1979-81)

Sl. No.	*Reasons*	*YEAR 1979* *Male (M)*	*Female (F)*	*Total (T)*	*1980* *M*	*F*	*T*	*1981* *M*	*F*	*T*	*Grand Total*
1	*2*	*3*	*4*	*5*	*6*	*7*	*8*	*9*	*10*	*11*	*12*
1	Absenteeism	-	2	2	3	-	3	4	-	4	9
2	Own wish	10	11	21	5	2	7	3	4	7	35
3	Medical	-	1	1	1	4	5	-	-	-	6
4	Domestic affair	-	-	-	1	-	1	-	-	-	1
5	Misconduct	4	-	4	1	-	1	-	-	-	5
6	Total	14	14	28	11	6	17	7	4	11	56

References

Banerjee, B. (1963) History of tea plantation in India. Observer. Students' Geographic Association, Calcutta University.

Barua, R. (1963) Seuji Pator Kahini: Chapala Sahitya Sadan, Shillong.

Bhuiyan, N.C. (1960) Cha bagichar banua, Assam Sahitya Sabha, Jorhat.

Crawford, T. O. (1924) Hand book of castes and tribes employed on the tea-estates in North East India, Indian Tea Association, Calcutta.

Danda, A.K. (1962) A study on reference group among the plantation labourers of Jalpaiguri district, Bulletin of the Cultural Research Institute, West Bengal, Vol. 1, No. 2.

Das, A. K. and H. R. Banerjee (1964) Impact of tea industry on the life of the tribals of West Bengal, Tribal Welfare Department, Govt. of West Bengal, Calcutta.

Das, R.K. (1931) Plantation labour in India, Calcutta.

Das Gupta, P.K. (1978) Impact of industrialisation on a tribe in South Bihar, Anthropological Survey of India, Calcutta.

Desai, M. (1962) Aid to tea industry. The Tea, Vol. 12, No. 6.

Elwin, V. (1958) Myths of North- East Frontier of India, Shillong.

--(1963) A new deal for tribal India, Ministry of Home Affairs, New Delhi.

Ghosh, Subratesh (1966) *Indian labour in the phase of industrialisation,* New Age Publishers Private Ltd., New Delhi.

Griffiths, P. (1967) *The history of Indian tea industry,* Weldenfeld and Nicolson, London.

Harler, C. R. (1964) (Third edition). *The Culture and marketing of tea,* Oxford University Press.

Kapur, B. N. (1961) *Indian tea industry in 1960 retrospect,* The Tea, Vol. II, No. 6.

Kar, R. K. (1979). A migrant tribe in a tea plantation in India: economic profile, Anthropos, 74: 770-784.

1981 Tea Social change in a tea plantation tribe in Assam, India. Acta ethnographica, 30: 407-419.

--(1981) Tea industry in Assam: a chronological account, Man and Life, 7:131-150.

--(1981) *The Savaras of Mancotta: a study on the effect of tea industry on the tribal life,* Cosmo publications, New Delhi.

Kidwai, K. M. (1964) Tea is a dweller of the plains too, Indian Farming, Vol. XIII. No. 10.

Mehrotra, Gopal Naresh. (1975) *Studies in industrial sociology,* Atma Ram and Sons, Delhi.

Mukherjee, S. R. (1961) Tea labour in West Bengal: some of their problems, The Tea, Vol.II.

Phukan, A. C. (1979) *Personnel administration in the tea industry of Assam,* Archita Publication, Jorhat.

CHAPTER 4

A Model of Tribal Industrial Growth : Case Study of Rope-Making

Suman Sao, S. K. Mishra and R. N. Chattopadhyay

Tribals of Chotanagpur Plateau practice various crafts as important means of their livelihood[1]. Though some of the artisan goods serve their own purposes, yet the major portions of the products are marketed in the nearby Hats. Among many tribal household industries like carpentry, blacksmithy, iron smelting, bamboo-works, tasar rearing and weaving, stone works etc., the rope-making occupies a prominent position.

This paper aims at analysing the functioning and viability of Rope-Making industry and identifies the relevant factors for formulating policy decisions towards its development. Based on these policies a set of proposals for the development of the Industry has also been put forward.

Study Area

The study is based on the survey of 40 households practising Rope Making in Singhbhum District of Bihar as full-time or part-time occupation. The households mainly belong to Birhor and Ho tribal communities, though some of the Oraon and Munda households practising this craft have also been surveyed. The survey has been conducted first by selecting several typical Birhor and Ho villages in the blocks of Sadar, Monoharpur and Goilkera and then picking up households randomly from there keeping in mind that at least 10% of such tribal households practising Rope Making in a village has been included.

Characteristics of-Rope Making Industry

While analysing the economy of this informal industrial sector several characteristic features stand out in bold relief. These can be summarised as follows :

i) Though the units have small number of full-time workers, with the inclusion of part-time workers about 85% of them exhibit employment between 3 to 5 persons.
ii) A look at the sex distribution of employment of Rope Making Industry reveals the predominance of male workers (64.56%).
iii) Out of total workers, 72.55% are skilled, 21.57% partly skilled and rest 5.88 are unskilled workers.
iv) 64.56% of the total workers are in the age group of 15 to 45 and this percentage is equally divided between two age groups 15 to 30 and 30 to 45. Majority of the workers who are less than 15 years old, are part-time workers. While 62.7% of the total full-time workers are having experience above 10 years, the same percentage of part-time workers are engaged in the industry for less than 10 years.
v) Average Value Added by Manufacture per unit is Rs. 921.38[2] which is very low compared to that of other household industries. 92.5% of the total Rope Making units surveyed have Value Added by Manufacture less than Rs. 1500 while in basketry 4.88%, blacksmithy 13.33%, carpentry 24% and in weaving and stone works 22% of units fall in the same bracket. None of the units of Rope Making industry has Value Added more than Rs. 3000. This marked deviation in economic term compared to other tribal household industries however could be due to the fact that Rope Making is principally a subsidiary economic activity of the households surveyed. This is evident from the fact that only 31.8% of the total income of the households surveyed is contributed by this activity.

vi) Average Value Added per unit of fixed-capital is as high as Rs. 14.98. Tools used for this industry are mainly for the collection of raw materials. Apart from that no other implement is used for manufacturing and all the operations are carried out manually. In fact during the life of operation, production has generally remained unchanged and so has production methods.

vii) Value Added per unit of working capital[3] is also high (Rs. 14.72) and it is slightly lower than Value Added per unit of fixed capital. This could be due to the fact that majority of Birhor workers collect raw materials free of cost after paying nominal tax for collection of minor jungle products and thus working capital requirement for Birhor workers is low. On the contrary, most of the Ho workers practising Rope Making purchase more than 75% of the needed raw materials from nearby Hats. This diverse situation accounts for the high intra-industry deviation in Value Added per unit of working capital.

viii) Majority of the units meet their need of fixed and operating capital with home saving rather than from any external sources.

ix) The units have hardly any backward or forward linkage. They purchase the raw materials (e.g. sabai grass) or collect it themselves and sell their outputs to customers consisting of households and other small traders or middlemen.

Briefly, the results of the analysis seem to pin-point that majority of the units covered in the survey suffered from low-productivity, displayed slow or no growth of productions and exhibited no diversification in production system. In fact, they suffered from non-availability of credit, financed their capital needs including day-to-day operation from home generated savings and of crucial importance, they had no transactions with Govt. or formal sector except tax payment for collection of raw materials which is considered by them a restrictive measure.

Mechanism of Productivity Growth in the Sector : Theoretical Model

Having described the characteristics of Rope Making units in the tribal household industrial sector we now proceed to examine which of these characteristics have a bearing on the units' productivity. On the basis of a prior reasoning we would expect some economic, human and institutional characteristics as possible explanatory variables for changes in the productivity, the dependent variable[4]. The objective is of course to frame some policies, through the instrumental variables to bear on the dependent variables in order to achieve desired changes in them.

For production one can hypothesize relationship between output on the one hand and various inputs on the other hand and cast this relationship in the form of a production function either of the Cobb Douglas or constant elasticity of substitution type. The assumption that units of household industrial sector are not straight forward profit maximizer firms, their output should be affected by various factors including characteristics of the mainworkers and part-time workers and of the unit's itself in addition to labour and capital uses in traditional production function analysis.

Productivity in household industrial sector is an involved process accounted for the actions and reactions of numerous economic and behavioural factors. Some of these are direct determinant of productivity while some others operate indirectly. These factors are again closely interconnected with each other and a change in one is reciprocated by the others. Thus the system in which productivity is determined comprises several interdependent sub-systems each involving several variables.

The important factors determining productivity should be related either with the efficiency of the labour, e.g., percentage of skilled workers, experience of workers, percentage of finished products sold to customers or with the extent of utilisation and employment of main and auxiliary workers, e.g., capacity utilisation of all workers, mandays worked and percentage share of work by part time workers. However, these relationships are mainly confined to the characteristics of labour and are not exhaustive. The factors related to capital, especially fixed capital assets, should also play a positive role in determining productivity as one may expect that efficient and sufficient number of tools will facilitate workers to produce better both qualitatively and quantitatively.

Further it may be expected that larger distance covered for collection of raw materials which is usually either because of procurement of better or cheaper quality product, should also help in enhancing net profit and thus labour productivity. Apart from these one may postulate that spatial distance covered for sale may determine productivity positively as larger distances covered for sale is associated with sale in Hats and naturally with bulk sale to customers who pay relatively higher price for the goods than what mahajans or middlemen pay for the same good.

The attempt so far made has been pointed towards identification of factors that determine the productivity rather directly. However, one may postulate that apart from the factors enumerated above some of the factors are in turn determined by several other factors and also interact with each other.

To look into these aspects a query may be made as to what are the factors that determine the percentage of skilled workers per unit. In this concern it may be held that the variable is collectively determined by size of the unit, age of the workers and experience of workers. While the first factor will determine the need for optimal mix of skill categories among workers, the last two variables will indicate the quality of labour force and if they are of higher value they will naturally influence the dependent variable positively.

Value of fixed capital should be related to the size of the unit and finance mobilisation capability of the unit determining the need for capital and efficiency to enhance capital in due course respectively. Naturally the said dependent variable should be the increasing function of the above mentioned explanatory variables.

Capacity utilisation, likewise, may be significantly affected by factors like value added per unit, focusing on the role of substitution between labour utilization and income, if any, and percentage of skilled workers and unapproachable market demand presented by the percentage of goods sold to Mahajans.

Working capital and hours of daily operation have no direct relation to productivity but they are themselves determined by some of the variables like value added per unit, finance mobilisation capability of the unit, and so on while the latter ones, in turn, interact with each other also. For comprehensiveness, thus, both the variables are included in the productivity mechanism model.

The Model

The factors(endogenous in nature) determining the productivity may be symbolically presented as follows :-

Y_1 = value added per unit as defined by total revenue from sale minus cost of goods and services bought in Rs.
Y_2 = percentage of skilled workers out of total workers per unit.
Y_3 = value of fixed assets in Rs.
Y_4 = weekly capacity utilization rate of all workers as defined by (hours of weekly operation/hours the unit should have operated in optimal condition) x 100.
Y_5 = hours of daily operation per unit.
Y_6 = value of working capital per unit in Rs.

The above variables (yi'i = 1,6) are determined by several other factors, exogenous in nature. The list of such variables as mentioned earlier are hypothetically selected and are given below.

X_1 = distance covered for collection of raw materials in metres.
X_2 = distance covered for sale of finished products in metres.
X_3 = standard mandays as defined by total man-hours worked/8 (taking as standard shift hour).
X_4 = percentage share of work by part-time workers, defined as : (total hours worked by part-time workers/total hours worked by full-time and part-time workers) x 100.
X_5 = years of experience of workers in code.
X_6 = percentage of finished products sold to customers.
X_7 = Size of the unit in terms of employment.
X_8 = age of the workers in code.
X_9 = finance mobilisation capability in code.
X_{10} = percentage of finished products sold to Mahajans and Middle men.

Using the convenient algebraic symbols for the factors as defined above, the relationship among different factors determining productivity of the units may be summarised in the following notational form.

$$Y_1 = f(Y_2, Y_3, Y_4, X_1, X_2, X_3, X_4, X_5, X_6) \quad .... (1)$$

$$Y_2 = f(X_5, X_7, X_8) \quad ....(2)$$

$Y_3 = f(X_7, X_9)$ ...(3)

$Y_4 = f(Y_1, Y_2, X_{10})$ ....(4)

$Y_5 = f(Y_6, X_7)$ ... (5)

$Y_6 = f(Y_1, Y_5, X_9)$ ....(6)

The above notational form may be considered a schematic model of mechanism through which productivity of the units is determined. Structure of the schematic model as formulated above indicates simultaneity in relation. Regarding functional relation of the equations it has been assumed that the relationships are linear and stochistic in nature[5]. The analytical form of the model has been specified as follows :

$$Y_1 = a_{11} Y_2 + a_{12} Y_3 + a_{13} Y_4 + a_{14} x_1 + a_{15} x_2 + a_1 x_3 + a_{17} x_4 + a_{18} x_5 + a_{19} x_6 + a_{10} + c_1 \quad \text{... (1a)}$$

$$Y_2 = a_{21} x_5 + a_{22} x_7 + a_{23} x_8 + a_{30} + c_2 \quad \text{.... (2a)}$$

$$Y_3 = a_{31} x + a_{32} x_9 + a_{30} + c_3 \quad \text{... (3a)}$$

$$Y_4 = a_{41} Y_1 + a_{42} Y_2 + a_{48} x_{10} + a_{40} + c_4 \quad \text{.... (4a)}$$

$$Y_5 = a_{51} Y_6 + a_{52} x_7 + a_{50} + c_5 \quad \text{.... (5a)}$$

$$Y_6 = a_{61} Y_1 + a_{62} Y_5 + a_{63} x_9 + a_{60} + c_6 \quad \text{... (6a)}$$

In these equations a_{ij} (# 0) stand for coefficients, a_{io} for constants c_i for errors.

Empirical Estimation of the Model and its Parameters

The model developed above characterised a set of simultaneous equations. Using the data collected on variables from the primary sources the model has been estimated by the technique of two stages least squares. The technique of two least squares yields a set of equations at its first stage and another set of equations at the second stage. In first stage, each of the endogenous variables is regressed on all exogenous variables to obtain a single reduced form equation for each of the endogenous variables. These reduced form equations represent the overall strength of exogenous variables in expelling the endogenous variables. Reduced form equations are used for estimating the overall changes in the endogenous variables in response to change in any exogenous variables. In the second state, in each of the equations, the right hand side (explanatory) endogenous variables are replaced by the expected values of endogenous variables, estimated by reduced from equations. However, the left hand side endogenous variables are the original ones, inclusive of error. Once again each of the endogenous variables is regressed on the set of relevant estimated endogenous variables and exogenous variables to obtain structural equations. These structural equations are more meaningful as they are relatively more unbiased linear estimators of the structural relationships among dependent and independent variables[6].

Structural equations obtained from two stage least squares analysis are as follows:

$$Y_1'' = \underset{(3.88)}{0.272Y_2'^{*}} - \underset{(4.62)}{0.348Y_3'^{*}} + \underset{(3.55)}{0.252Y_4^{*}} + \underset{(4.42)}{0.028x_1^{*}} + \underset{(4.01)}{0.016x_2^{*}}$$

$$+ \underset{(8.64)}{1.420x_3^{*}} - \underset{(3.90)}{0.480x_4^{*}} + \underset{(4.13)}{0.0004x_5} + \underset{(3.88)}{0.192x_6} + \underset{(25.20)}{0.000002x^{*}} \quad \ldots (1b)$$

$$R^{-2} = 0.877$$

$$Y_2'' = \underset{(1.64)}{1590x_5^{***}} - \underset{(5.43)}{20.700x_7^{*}} + \underset{(2.27)}{2.130x_8} + \underset{(15.30)}{95.900^{*}} \quad \ldots (2b)$$

$$R^{-2} = 0.665$$

$$Y_3'' = \underset{(3.44)}{31.100x_7^{*}} - \underset{(1.26)}{15.500x_9} + \underset{(071)}{24.500} \quad \ldots (3b)$$

$$R^{-2} = 0.242$$

$$Y_4'' = \underset{(3.71)}{-0.22Y_1^{*}} + \underset{(13.30)}{0.969Y_2} + \underset{(1.91)}{0.248x_{10}^{***}} + \underset{(0.09)}{0.029} \quad \ldots\ldots(4b)$$

$$R^{-2} = 0.764$$

$$Y_5'' = \underset{(5.44)}{0.0099Y_6^{*}} + \underset{(10.20)}{2330x_{17}^{*}} + \underset{(8.70)}{0.56^{*}} \quad \ldots\ldots(5b)$$

$$R^{-2} = 0.91$$

$$Y_6 \text{``} = 119.000Y_1 \text{'*} - 15.500Y_5 \text{'} - 57.300x_9 - 832.000^{**} \quad \ldots (6b)$$
$$(6.87) \qquad (1.08) \qquad (0.67) \qquad (2.65)$$
$$R^{-2} = 0.603$$

Figures in parentheses are the computed student's values. *,** and *** indicate t values significant at 1%, 5% and 10% level respectively for (n-p-1) degree of freedom where n represents the number of explanatory variables R^{-2} refers to corrected R^{-2} in view of the degree of freedom.

Empirical Findings

The structural equations obtained empirically have revealed the following relationships :

Productivity per Unit (y_1)

Reported R^{-2} for this equation (1b) is high and indicates the explanatory efficiency of the right hand side variables. It is interesting to note that the variables (along with constant) conceived to have influence on productivity are all statistically significant. Turning to the significance of each variable it can be concluded that productivity in Rope Making industry is the increasing function of ·percentage of skilled workers (y_2), capacity utilisation of all workers (y_4), distance covered for collection of raw materials (x_1) distance covered for sale of finished products (x_2), mandays worked (x_3), experience of worker (x_5), and percentage of finished products sold to customers (x_6). It is influenced negatively by fixed capital (Y_3) and percentage share of work by part-time workers (x_4). While the sign of first seven variables are in conformity with our maintained hypothesis, it is quite amazing to detect that productivity is influenced adversely by increase in fixed capital. In fact higher fixed capital will facilitate a firm to product more in a given time with minimal increase in labour force. But high fixed capital certainly does not mean higher demand for the product and does not guarantee resultant increase in productivity. The negative contribution of x_4 may be due to the fact that part-time workers usually help only in the collection of raw materials while weaving of rope is a tedious and time consuming job which is carried on by the skilled workers only.

Percentage of Skilled workers per Unit (Y_2)

The percentage of skilled workers per unit determine the efficiency, and thus, income of the units and hence has been regressed on experience of workers (x_5), size of the unit (x_7) and age of the workers (x_8) R^{-2} being 0.655 depicts that eplanatory variables are capable of explaining variation in concerned dependent variable. All the coefficient related to respective explanatory variable are statistically significant. Experience of workers which in most of the cases is a related factor of age and the age of workers itself influence the dependent variable positively. This could be due to the fact that it is customary among artisans to initiate younger generation to pick up the skill of operation informally from quite an early age, so that with the increase of age the workers are experienced and become better skilled. Percentage of skilled workers per unit is affected negatively by the size of the unit. This might be due to the fact that the size of the unit and percentage of supplementary workers are highly related to ($r = 0.706$) and most of the part-time workers who help only in the collection of raw materials are unskilled.

Fixed Capital per Unit (Y_3)

As per hypothesis fixed capital is an increasing function of size of the unit (x_7) and the coefficient of finance mobilisation capability (x_9) is statistically not significant. R^{-2} is significant but explains only 24% of the total variation in dependent variable.

Capacity Utilisation of all workers (y_4)

Capacity utilisation of all workers is an increasing function of percentage of skilled workers (y_2) and percentage of finished products sold to mahajans and middlemen (x_{10}) while it is negatively controlled by productivity of the unit. All the above mentioned variables are statistically significant and R^{-2} being 0.764 depicts that the variables have provided a good fit for the relevant dependent variable. While Y_2 and x_{10} bear positive signs for obvious reasons negative influence of productivity needs explanation. This clearly points out the behaviours of the tribals who live for present only. If the income is sufficient to meet the weekly needs they will never go for higher production to earn more with savings motive.

Duration of Daily Operation (y_5)

Duration of daily operation in the firm has been regressed on two variables namely working capital (Y_6) and size of the unit (x_7). The dependent variable is a positive function of both the above mentioned explanatory variable and they are statistically significant. High working capital is due to more expenditure on raw materials (out of total working capital 89.01% is spent on raw materials) and as all the units produce same product under conditions of same technology more expenditure on raw materials will naturally increase hours of operation. Size of the unit influences duration of daily operation positively for obvious reasons.

Working Capital per Unit (y_6)

Value of working capital per unit has been regressed on three variables : Value Added per unit (y_1), duration of daily operation in the firm (y_5) and finance mobilisation capability of the unit (x_9). R^{-2} is high (0.69) and therefore, it is observed that the explanatory variables are capable of explaining the variations of working capitals in artisan activities. Working capital is a positive function of productivity and the related coefficient in statistically significant. It is negatively influenced by the rest of variables.

Planning Implication of Reduced form Equations

Reduced form equations represent the overall and final response of endogenous variables to changes in exogenous variables. These equations are thus very important. Therefore, the reduced form equations are constructed to assess the impact of changes in the levels of exogenous variables on endogenous variables. Planning implications of these equations are that the reduced form equations have been used for designing the alternative projects or set of proposals for development of the said sector. Result of reduced form equations are given in Table no. 1 and they form the basic elements for policy formulation.

Table - 1

REDUCED FORM EQUATIONS

	a_1	a_2	a_3	a_4
Y_1	0.025 *	-0.015 *	1.540 *	-0.062 *
Y_2	-0.002	0.002 **	0.152 *	-0.053 ***
Y_3	0.009*	0.004 *	-0.137 *	0.051
Y_4	-0.0004	0.00001	0.154 *	-0.015
Y_5	-0.0002 **	0.00006	0.037 *	-0.015 *
Y_6	-0.083 *	0.009	4.310 *	-1.690

	a_5	a_6	a_7	a_8
Y_1	0.0005 *	0.163 *	0.001 *	0.007 *
Y_2	0.00004 * *	0.014 ***	0.0001 ***	0.0006 ***
Y_3	-0.000003	-0.014	-0.0001	-0.0006
Y_4	0.000004 *	0.016 *	0.0001	0.0007 *
Y_5	0.000001 *	0.004 *	0.00003 *	0.0002 *
Y_6	0.001 *	0.455 *	0.004 *	0.19 *

	a_9	a_{10}	a_0	R^{-2}
Y_1	0.0004 *	0.079 *	0.000002 *	0.877
Y_2	0.00003 ***	0.007 ***	0.00000009 *	-0.825
Y_3	-0.00003	-0.007	0.0000002 *	0.803
Y_4	0.00004 *	0.008 *	0.00000008 *	0.879
Y_5	0.000009 *	0.002 *	0.00000003 *	0.919
Y_6	0.001 *	0.221 *	0.0000001 *	0.763

* Significant at 1% level at 29 degrees of freedom
** Significant at 5% level at 29 degrees of freedom
*** Significant at 10% level at 29 degrees of freedom

The operational limits of different exogenous variables have been decided on several considerations related to the social, political, economic and operational factors and present stage of development together with the feasible level of development that may be attained in near future.

The operational limits of exogenous variables

X_1 and X_2 : Distance covered for collection of raw materials and distance covered for sale of finished products:

The lower limit for this exogenous variable is 0 and upper limit 15,000 metres with the assumption that a maximum of 15,000 metres can be covered by the tribals either for sale or collection of needed raw materials from a collection cum distribution centre. If the centre is in the village itself then naturally its distance will be 0.

x_3 : Standard Mandays :

Rope-Making is a part-time job at present and this position will not alter significantly in near future. In concordance with x^7 variable limit for this variable is 540 if two workers are employed in the industry or only one worker will be engaged in this craft then limit will be 270.

x_4 : Percentage share of work by part-time workers: Lower limit for this variable is zero (assuming no part of the total worker is employed) and the upper limit is 40 (40% of the total work can be handled at least by the unskilled part-time workers) instead of 40x4 = 0 when $x^7 = 1$

x_5 : Experience of the Workers :

Basing on x_7 and x_8 variables lower limit is 1 and upper limit of x_5 = 5 when x_7 = 1 and lower limit of $x_5 = 2$ when ($x_7 = 2$).

x_6 : Percentage of finished products sold to customers: The limit for this variable is 67% since it will not be possible to bring a drastic change in the market situation and at least 33% is bound to be sold Mahajans and middleman.

x_7 : Size of the unit in terms of employment : The size should range from 1 to 2 for economic reasons. These are considered lower and upper limits respectively.

x_8 : Age of the workers :

Basing on the limits of x_7 household size of the lower and upper limits are set at 2 and 7 (instead of 7 the upper limit of x_5 = 5 when x_7 = 1 and lower limit of x_8 = 3 when x_7 = 2).

x_9 : Finance mobilisation capability :

This should vary between 1 to 6 (i.e., units using only savings as capital to such units mobilising all sources of recurring capital.

Case Study Of Rope Making

x_{10} : Percentage of finished products sold to Mahajans and middlemen ;

Basing on x^6 this variable should be fixed at 33%.

Results of various projects are presented in Table 2 the table shows that the maximisation of $y_2 y^4$ and y_6 are self contradictory and results of the maximisation of y_5 are also acceptable on social and economic grounds. Maximisation of productivity (y_1) or hours of daily operation (y_5) have been considered as most feasible on economic and social groups[8]. Thus maximisation of y_1 or y_5 will be allowed for the development of the said industry depending on the limits extended by various exogenous variables.

Table 2

Projects

Set of x for max Y_1 or Y_5	Project impact of y_1 or y_5
$x_1 = 15{,}000$	$y_1 = 1442.19$
$x_2 = 15{,}000$	$y_2 = 88.98$
$x_3 = 540$	$y_3 = 111.94$
$x_4 = 0$	$y_4 = 79.00$
$x_5 = 6$	$y_5 = 23.99$
$x_6 = 67$	$y_6 = 1250.53$
$x_7 = 2$	
$x_8 = 7$	
$x_9 = 6$	
$x_{10} = 33$	

Set of x for max y_2 or y_4 or y_6	Project of y_2 or y_4 or y_6
$x_1 = 0$	$y_1 = 1073.19$
$x_2 = 15{,}000$	$y_2 = 112.23$
$x_3 = 540$	$y_3 = -22.61$
$x_4 = 0$	$y_4 = 84.72$
$x_5 = 6$	$y_5 = 21.05$
$x_6 = 67$	$y_6 = 2494.03$
$x_7 = 2$	
$x_8 = 7$	
$x_9=6$	
Set of x for maxy_2	Project impact of y_2
$x_{10} = 33$	
$x_1 = 15{,}000$	$y_1 = 1004.75$
$x_2 = 15{,}000$	$y_2 = 47.48$
$x_3 = 270$	$y_3 = 148.91$
$x_4 = 0$	$y_4 = 39.40$
$x_5 = 1$	$y_5 = 14.13$
$x_6 = 67$	y6 = 86.72
$x_7 = 1$	
$x_8= 2$	
$x_9 = 1$	
$x_{10} = 33$	

References

1. Sao, Suman (1980) : "Revitalization of Tribal Crafts and Nature of skill for rural industrialisation "M.R.P. Thesis (unpublished), Indian Institute of Technology, Kharagpur. pp. 127-179.
2. Price here and elsewhere in the paper is the current price.
3. Wage has not been included in working capital as all the workers are either owner worker or family member.

4. Mishra, S.K. (1982) : "Evaluation of public policies for agricultural development in less developed Regions" Ph.D. thesis (unpublished), Indian Institute of Technology, pp. 20-28.
5. *Ibid* : pp. 93-97.
6. Kumar, Binod (1983): "Regional planning approach to an efficient agricultural market system", M.R.P. thesis (unpublished) Indian Institute of Technology, Kharagpur, pp. 98-100.
7. Theil, Henry 1971 : *Principles of Econometrics*, John Wiley and Sons. New York, p. 179.
8. Sao, Suman : Ref. 1, pp. 200-201 and 246-249.

CHAPTER 5

Introducing Agriculture in a Tribal Community : The Case of Chenchus*

G.P. Reddy

During the last few decades, particularly after independence the techno-economic changes in tribal India have been rapid and quite perceptible. These changes have been mainly due to (1) the increasing contacts of the tribal communities with people from plains and (2) specific attention paid by the Government and non-Governmental agencies towards the development of tribal communities and tribal areas.

The response of the tribal communities in India to the outside contacts and developmental activities have been varied and could be tentatively classified into three categories in terms of their reaction.

---

* An earlier version of this paper was presented at the ''Seminar on Integrated Tribal Development Plans', National Institute of Community Development. Hyderabad, held between 19th and 21st January, 1977.

Reproduced by the permission of the authority of 'Man and Life' and Institute of Social Research and Applied Anthropology, Calcutta from 'Man and Life' 5(1+2) : 81-92, 1979.

1. *Positive reaction :* Under this we can include those tribal communities who have not suffered social disorganization and on the other hand have taken the advantage of the contacts and developmental activities and have improved themselves, techno-economically, as the Mizos, Tribes and NEFA and Nicobarese of Nicobar Islands.

2. *Negative reaction :* Under this we can include those tribal communities who have suffered social disorganization either because of the evil effects of contacts or due to ill-conceived and ill-directed developmental activities, as the Andamanese and Onges of Andaman and Nicobar Islands.

3. *Neutral reaction :* Under this category we can include the tribal communities who have remained immune and indifferent to the contacts and special attempts at development. This means that they have remained in the same techno-economic condition even after the special efforts made by the developmental agencies towards their development. The resources spent on these communities by the Government and non-Government agencies have gone down the drain mainly due to the ill-conceived schemes and lack of proper understanding of the culture of these communities on the part of the people entrusted with the planning and implementation of the Developmental Programmes and Schemes.

Each of this category requires different approach on the basis of priority of their needs. For example the tribes in the second category need increase in their dwindling population and the first effort of the Government should be towards this goal.

The present paper deals with the Chenchus, a preliterate tribe, numbering near about 17000, inhabiting the Eastern Ghats of Kurnool and Mehboob Nagar Districts of Andhra Pradesh. The Chenchus may be classified under third category i.e., Neutral reaction. The Chenchus have a long history and contacts with outsiders and Developmental and other Government agencies like Social Welfare, Revenue and Forest Departments and yet they still remain almost in the same condition as they were before.

The main objective of this paper is to analyse the reasons for failure of a welfare scheme introduced for the benefit of the Chenchus of

Atmakur taluk in Kurnool District. The welfare scheme consisted of colonization of hundered Chenchu families. The main objective of the Chenchu colonization scheme was to wean the Chenchus from food gathering, irregular wage labour and occasional criminal activities like theft and dacoity and settle them as cultivators. Unfortunately the programme was a total flop[1]. My endeavour in this paper is to bring out besides other reasons, the incompatibility of Chenchu culture and social structure with the conceived scheme of colonization and its implementation.

The Colonization Scheme

During the Second Five Year plan under centrally sponsored schemes the Byarluti, Nagaluti gudem (Atmakur taluk of Kurnool District), colonization scheme was started by the State Government in 1957. The scheme was solely meant for the welfare of the Chenchus living in Nallamallai forest.

Main features of the Scheme:

1. Colonization of 100 Chenchu families at Byarluti gudem.
2. Reclamation of 500 acres of forest land, to be distributed to each Chenchu family settled in the colony at the rate of 4 acres of dry and 1 acre of wet lands.
3. Construction of 100 houses for settling 100 Chenchu families.
4. Repair of existing tanks for irrigating the lands.
5. Purchase of 100 pairs of bullocks at the rate of one per family.
6. Supply of agricultural implements and improved variety of seeds.
7. Sinking of wells both for irrigation and drinking.
8. Construction of godown-cum-office.
9. Construction of staff quarters.

Working and Result of the Scheme

A senior Cooperative Inspector was appointed as Project Officer to execute the scheme under the direction of the Board of Directors

1. Many examples of failure of colonization schemes could be cited from the tribal areas of Andhra Pradesh itself. For example the colonization schemes of Kedarpuram an Jatapukotapadu in Srikakulam agency have been total failures (Raju 1971 : 35--44).

consisting of officials from Forest, Revenue,Agriculture and Cooperative Departments of Government of Andhra Pradesh. The Government spent an amount of Rs. 2,05,603.62 under different heads during the implementation of the programme.

Though the Project Administration constructed 100 houses at the colony site, it could persuade only 40 Chenchu families to move to the colony as against the targeted 100 Chenchu families. About 150 acres of forest land was reclamated as a cost of nearly Rs. 1,00,000 against the target of 500 acres of forest land. Minor repairs were carried out to the irrigation tank. Twenty pairs of bullocks were purchased. All the above mentioned works were carried out assuming that the Chenchus would be very happy to take up the cultivation of land immediately. Contrary to their expectations none among the forty came forward to take up cultivation. Consequently the project administration itself took up the cultivation of 72 acres of land, but it incurred a loss. The Administration, in the following season again tried to persuade Chenchus to take up cultivation but failed. The lands remained fallow, subsequently the Project Administration once again took up the cultivation of 100 acres. Unfortunately the second attempt also ended in loss. Finally the Project Administration ceased functioning and the forty Chenchu families were left to their own fate.

The Present Position

All the 40 colonized Chenchu families have finally abandoned the Project built houses and majority of them have left for their original abodes in the interior forest while the remaining are living in and around Byarlutigudem by raising their own traditional abodes. The Chenchus disposed the lands assigned to them to the neighbouring ryots for a pittance or leased out them in exchange for a few measures of grain or even liquor. At present one cannot even recognise the signs of the colony that existed once.

Social and Economic[2] life of Chenchus

Before dealing into the causes of failure of the colonization scheme, it is very essential to understand in brief the culture and social organization of Chenchus.

2. The Social and cultural data presented on Chenchus is based on my own field work among Chenchus as well as other Anthropologists. (Reddy, 1971, Haimendorf, 1943; Oswalt, 1972).

Chenchu Villages

The Chenchus call their villages *gudem.* A gudem usually consists of not more than 6 to 7 huts dispersed in a large area. Grouping of huts at one place forming a gudem is invariably based on kinship pattern consisting of close kin like brothers, cousins and their parents. The factors which influence the selection of the site for starting a gudem are (a) availability of perennial source of water (b) fruit bearing trees like mango, citrus and sapota (c) availability of small game and (d) abundance of forest roots tubers and tamarind trees[3].

The Dwellings

The Chenchus traditionally live in small, round, conical and compact huts. For a Chenchu family the front yard of the house is very important as they spend most of their time in front yards. Even cooking is done in the front yard rather than in the main hut. The main hut is used mostly during the winter nights and on rainy days. The compactness of their huts provide them warmth in the winter.

Domestication of Animals

Except for dogs Chenchus are not accustomed to keep any other domestic animals. The Chenchus are so much fond of their dogs, they share their shelter and food.

Economy

Majority of the Chenchus even today depend on food gathering activities and on forest labour for their day-to-day subsistence. They collect wild fruits, tubers and roots supplemented by small game and fishing. Honey also forms an important part in their diet. Some of the Chenchus living on the fringe of the forest take part in forest labour, but their number is insignificant and their employment is irregular. However the money realized through forest labour is mainly spent on country liquor by most of them.

---

3. Tamarind tree plays very important role in their satiation of hunger. When nothing is available the women folk pick the tender leaves, boil them, ground them into a paste and satisfy their hunger.

Division of Labour

Except in hunting, division of labour in Chenchu society is not much marked and clear cut between the sexes. Both men and women participate in the construction of the hut, collection of wild fruits and tubers, gathering of honey etc. Oswalt (1972, 141) writing about Chenchus states that "even sexual division of labour was not as clearly defined as might be expected ... individualistic complementary labours of a man and his wife lead to the self-sufficiency of the nuclear family in subsistence pursuits".

Family and Kinship

Nuclear family consisting of husband, wife and their unmarried children is predominant among the Chenchus (Reddy, 1971 : 10). Moreover its importance is felt by the individual at every stage of his life. It acts as an economic, social and recreational unit. A son or daughter immediately after marriage invariably establishes neolocal residence, but not far away from the parents or siblings of the one of the spouses.

The Kinship system among them is classificatory and bilateral. The affinal kins play very important role in their social and economic spheres. In most of the hazardous economic operations like collection of honey from valleys and hill tops, a Chenchu is always accompanied by his sister's husband or wife's brother.

Cooperation and Communal Activities

If one observes socio-economic and religious activities of Chenchus one comes to the conclusion that communal activity and cooperation in the lives of the Chenchus is almost absent. The only group which cooperates with each other is the close consanguinal and affinal group. Only death brings together people belonging to the clan of the deceased.

Chenchu World-View

A Chenchu even today never thinks of tomorrow, his concern is only today. These people do not usually store food for future consumption, but instead obtained it on day-to-day basis. They make little effort to conserve the environmental offerings which are not critical for immediate survival. A productive wild tree might be cut down for a honey comb in it or to obtain a single lizard (Oswald, 1972-148). This go-free habit of Chenchus always brought them into conflict with Forest Department.

Authority Structure

The Chenchu society traditionally does not possess even a rudimentary form of political organization. It is the age which carries importance, generally elders are respected. In the first part of this century the Forest Department started appointing their own nominees among Chenchus as gudem headmen. This imposition of authority from above was never liked by Chenchus. The formal headmen are virtually powerless and they acted only as informers to the Forest Department.

Chenchus and Forest Department

Tracing the relationship of Chenchus with the Department of Forest will enable us to understand attitudes, habits and behaviour of Chenchus in certain situations.

Till 1862 the Chenchus of Kurnool District were free birds roaming the Jungle. In 1862 by a Government notification Forest Administration was extended to the Chenchus territory, but this was not effective till 1882. Till then neither the Chenchus took notice of the occasional visits of the Forest officials nor the officials bothered the Chenchus. During the year 1882 with the enactment of Madras Forest Act the administration tightened its grip and imposed certain restrictions on the movement of the Chenchus. The Chenchus could not understand in the beginning why they should obey the orders of aliens in their own territory and did not readily submit to the rules and regulations. They, instead increased their activities with vengeance. The Forest Administration reacted by declaring them as outlaws and further tightened its grip on them.

In the beginning the right of the Chenchus to live in the forest, utilize bamboo, wood, fibre, fire wood, thatching grass, roots, fruits and honey etc. for bonafide domestic consumption and collection of minor forest produce was accepted, subject to the condition that each Chenchu gudem should utilise its surrounding forest area without encroaching into other areas, nor were they transferable. Neither were they exclusive or monopoly rights and they were subjected to regulation by the rules as may from time to time be framed by His Excellency the Governor-in-Council. During 1884 the Forest Department made it compulsory for the Chenchus to sell their minor forest produce to the Forest Department or to their agents at specified rates. This rule was scrapped in 1897 as the Chenchus never honoured it. The Chenchus honoured the rules more by breaching than adhering to them. The Forest Department retaliated with more stringent measures like punishment and imprisonment. The ding-dong battle between the Chenchus and the Forest Department continued till one Mr. F.A. Wood was appointed as District Forest Officer, Kurnool West in 1917.

Mr. Wood was sympathetic towards the problem of Chenchus and did yeoman's service to the cause of Chenchu Welfare. He started the plantation work and persuaded Chenchus to take up this work on daily wages, and succeeded to a certain extent. After some time the plantation work came to an end due to paucity of funds and the Chenchus became free once again to roam about in the forest. Added to this, virulent type of Influenza, Cholera and Small-pox penetrated Nallamalais and took heavy toll of Chenchus. These difficulties and miseries raised their former spirits and plunged them into criminal activities. On the recommendation of Mr. Wood the Government appointed a Special Officer, Sub-Assistant Surgeon and an Education Superintendent to look after the welfare of Chenchus of Kurnool District. For implementing Welfare measures every Chenchu-gudem in the district was put incharge of a a Headman and a Deputy Headman who were employed on monthly salary basis. In addition to other duties the headmen were asked to maintain a register of physical presence of each Chenchu in the gudems in the morning as well as in the evening everyday. Any one who absented himself was asked to give explanation, and if it was satisfactory, he was dealt with accordingly. This act further alienated the Chenchus from the officials of the Forest Department as well as their headmen.

In spite of such harsh rules and regulations the Forest Department could not wean the Chenchus from their activities. The Welfare Officers especially appointed were withdrawn in 1925 because of their ineffectiveness in moulding the lives of the Chenchus.

The rule that forest contractors working in bamboo coupes should employ Chenchu labour compulsorily was always there, but was never put into practice. Irregular working habit of the Chenchus did not find favour with the forest contractors.

Again in 1940 the Forest Department made an effort to improve the condition of the Chenchus by establishing schools in Chenchu-gudems in the district, providing work in the forest, extending medical facilities, etc. Somehow or other all these measures proved futile. Even today majority of the Chenchus mainly depend on their surrounding forest for subsistence rather than taking to new occupations.

Chenchu Mirasis

From many centuries the pilgrimage route to the famous sacred shrine at Srisailam situated in the Nallamalais of the Eastern ghats passed through Chenchu inhabited area. Pilgrims going to the shrine walked all this distance, Chenchus acting as guides. In return Chenchus collected 'metta' fee (protection fee) of one anna from each pilgrim. When Srisailam was connected by road from Dornal around fifties and buses started plying regularly, the Chenchus reacted violently and started obstructing the passenger vehicles to demand their 'metta' fee. They did not understand that pilgrims to Srisailam no longer required their guidance and protection. They felt that whether they guided and protected the pilgrims or not, it is their birth right to collect metta fee from all the pilgrims passing through their territory.

Keeping in view the above facts of Chenchu social organization and culture, if one analyses the starting and working of the colonization scheme, the reasons for its failure would be clear.

There is no doubt that introducing agriculture into a community whose economic activity is food gathering and irregular forest labour is a difficult task. If the Administrators of the Project has given some thought to the culture and behaviour pattern of the Chenchus both at the stage of planning and at the stage of implementation perhaps the programme would not have met with such a total disaster. The planners and the executors of the project were of the view that the Chenchus are ready and willing to take the help extended by the Government and improve themselves. Their assumption proved wrong at the beginning itself when no Chenchu family came forward to participate in the programme. They forced 40 unwilling Chenchu families to occupy the colony and asked them to cultivate the land combinedly without demarcating individual plots.

The colony houses were built as a single cluster like a rural village entirely different from that of a traditional Chenchu gudem. The houses in the colony were without any front and backyards, which play an important role in their traditional setting. Further the Chenchu traditional huts are comfortable during the winter because of their compactness. The colony houses proved most uncomfortable because of their size, shape and careless construction with loosely woven bamboo *thattis* for walls. The site selected for the colony itself was a very bad choice, because since it was situated in a low lying area, even a little amount of rain flooded the colony.

Even if the houses were good, conforming to the Chenchu traditional norms, other social and cultural factors would have led to the abandoning of the colony. The most important factor is their neighbourhood pattern. The traditional Chenchu gudems consist of only a few households, that too belonging to close relatives. A Chenchu feels inconvenient with strangers even if they belong to his own community. The 40 families brought to the colony were not related to each other, and all of them found most uncomfortable to live with non-relatives. It is reported by the teachers of Byrluti school that they witnessed quarrels almost every day between the Chenchu families in the colony. This they feel though not strange but uncommon in traditional Chenchu gudems.

Added to the above fact there were two factions in the colony. The enmity was between Chenchus of Byrluti and Nagolutigudems. This was known to the officials of the Project and both the groups did not agree to live side by side. After the intervention of officials and even of a Minister the hatred between the groups did not subside. When there are factions in the group and the Chenchu culture itself lacks communal activities, it is a foregone conclusion that Chenchus would never participate in such large combined activity which requires the cooperation of each individual.

Further their view of cooperation does not extend beyond their nuclear family and sister's husband or wife's husband or wife's brother.

In all of their economic activities it is the wife and husband who constitute a team. In certain hazardous activities like honey gathering from high cliffs and hunting it is the affinal relative i.e. sister's husband or wife's brother who takes precedence over the others.

Lack of traditional authority structure in Chenchu society has to be taken into consideration. This feature naturally gives freedom to individuals to pull in their own direction according to their whims and fancies. Neither the officials thought of identifying any informal leader amongst them and tried to work through him. The government appointed heads were hated and despised by the Chenchus through they belonged to their own community.

Lack of proper division of labour in their social structure was another factor which confused the Chenchus in their new situation. When they were asked to prepare the lands for cultivation, they started sending their children, and women for ploughing. Even for the men who are new to agriculture the technique of ploughing and controlling the bullocks is difficult. After some persuasion from the project officers the men tried their skill in ploughing but failed to learn the technique.

Further, agriculture requires continuous and strenuous regular work during the season. It cannot be done haphazardly and at irregular intervals. This type of continutity and persistence of physical labour is alien to them. Their world-view is not tomorrow but today only. They were accustomed to work irregularly or whenever they feel the necessity. Because of this habit even forest contractors hesitate to employ Chenchus as labourers. I have noticed many times that after working for an hour a Chenchu suddenly leaves the work and starts chit-chatting with his wife and children who accompany him wherever he goes. No amount of abuse and goading by the contractor makes him work at a stretch for few hours.

Chenchus are not accustomed to keeping any livestock. When they are asked to keep the drought bullocks except two or three families all the others flatly refused on the ground that they are not accustomed to keeping cattle. The others who agreed to keep, disposed them to the neighbouring ryots for a pittance. The remaining pairs of bullocks were looked after by the project officials. At the time of the abolition of the project not even a single bullock remained because a few became prey to predators and others died due to starvation.

Besides the cultural factors mentioned above there are others which have contributed to the failure of the scheme.

First and foremost the most important cause was the mistrust of Chenchus towards any outsider, particularly the Government officials. The history of their relations with the Department of Forest from the beginning if it could be taken as any guideline, it clearly shows there is no love lost between them. Many times they reacted violently to show their resentment against the interference of the forest officials in their life with stringent rules and regulations.

From the beginning neighbouring ryots were rather hostile towards this scheme and at every opportunity they not only tried all their tricks to discourage Chenchus but also derived some benefit out of the project when the project officers themselves took up the cultivation. They hired their labour and bullocks to the project to cultivate the lands brought under cultivation. They lured the Chenchus to sell their bullocks and lands by indulging in all kinds unethical practices.

We know that for primitive and traditional people seeing is believing. The project administration failed to show demonstratively that with little of hard work and experience cultivation is not such a difficult task. On the contrary the administration got a bad example by mismanaging the cultivation when decided to cultivate the lands. Even when the Project Administration took up the cultivation of lands, it did not employ Chenchu labour on the ground that they are inexperienced and preferred labour from neighbouring villages. It is an irony that when the officials thought that the Chenchus are not fit as agricultural labourers because of their inexperience, how did they think that they are capable of practising settled cultivation ?

The corrupt practices of the officials were other reasons for its failure. They were hand in glove with the ryots of the neighbouring villages. The neighbouring villagers benefited more from this project than the Chenchus for whom the project was started.

Above all the time given for the Chenchus to adapt themselves to settled cultivation is too short. It takes a very long time to diffuse an innovation like settled agriculture into the society like Chenchus who though had contacts with outsiders from the past many decades, the rate of change in their culture is very less and slow.

It would be naive on my part if I suggest that Chenchus can never be made agriculture minded. If the schemes are properly planned and executed with understanding, perhaps though it may be long before they accept this innovation, the schemes would finally succeed.

In Andhra Pradesh itself we have an example how voluntary agencies have succeeded in making some of the Yanadies, another primitive and nomadic tribe, agriculture minded. The Siddipuram and Rajagopalpuram Yenadi colonies in Nellore district stand as monuments to the dedicated workers of these voluntary agencies.

References

1. Raja, M.V.T., (1971) Rehabilitation programme in Jatapukota padu Colony, Srikakulam, Andhra Pradesh, *Journal of Indian Anthropological Society,* No. 6, 35-44.
2. Reddy, G.P., (1971) The Chenchus - Ethnographic Note. Office of the Registrar General of India, New Delhi, p.10.
3. Furer-Hajmendorf Christopher Von (1943) *The Chenchus Aboriginal Tribes of Hydera-bad* Vol, 1, Macmillan & Co. Ltd, London.
4. Wendell H. Oswalt. (1972) *Other peoples - Other Customs*, Holt, Rinehart and Winston Inc., p. 141.

Part Two : Other Issues

CHAPTER 6

Problems of Denotified Tribes: A Case Study of The Interaction of Government and Diverse Ethnic Groups in Fringe Bengal

P.K. Bhowmick

I

Introduction

India is a land of diverse ethnic groups and socio-cultural systems. One finds here such an amazingly large variety of races as it sometimes appears extremely difficult to discern the string of unity binding all these vastly different groups together. Hence the cliche about India: "Unity amidst diversity".

The path to forging such unity has not been, at any time, smooth and free from troubles. Dissension and conflict, domination and revolt against exploitation marked the inter-ethnic relationship all along, while at the same time, attempts at harmony had been made by the affected groups.

One will find in India a great number of ecological systems existing in its various parts. And this difference in ecological systems has bred different modes of life for different groups of people. The physical advantages provided by Nature, the nature of economic activities, degree of contact with the neighbours or foreigners, etc. have placed some groups in a more advantageous position than the others. The latter naturally lag behind the former and this lag is reflected in other spheres of their life. These are the backward people of India--they constitute the weaker sections of the community. About 21% of the population in India are considered to be members of the weaker sections, both economically and culturally. Generally they have been dubbed either as Scheduled Tribes or as Scheduled Castes. After the Independence of India, the Constitution has provided certain unequal competitions. The makers of our Constitution realised the importance of not only an open road, but of an equal start in case of these people.

Most of the denotified communities belong to this backward section. But their miseries and sufferings far outweigh those of other groups of the backward section. Their past history is one of sorrows and profound pathos. It provides the glaring example of how sometimes a society can become ruthless in constraining the behaviour of individuals and groups.

The term 'tribe' is understood differently by the academicians and the lay people. The members of a tribe generally retain some distinctive characteristics in the midst of other groups in the society. The denotified tribes were earlier known as 'ex-criminal tribes'. The interesting thing is that the so-called criminal tribe population constitutes a group or a section of a group within a tribe or caste, or an entire tribe or caste. Some of them would be found to be members of one particular Scheduled Caste or another. A few even claim descent from higher castes. At the same time, some sections of the Muslims too belong to the criminal tribe category. Thus one would find in the category of criminal tribes, groups of people who may be considered tribes, Hindu castes and the Muslims. Thus, 'Criminal Tribe' has been a label, a straitjacket to mark a few groups as 'habitual', rather 'natural', offenders. Criminality is considered to be a hereditary trait of them. Naturally, they have been kept segregated from the rest of the society. We know that criminality exists in all human societies in different forms, and in different degrees, be it literate or illiterate, economically advanced or backward. But peculiarly enough, the so-called criminal tribes have been perpetually branded as criminals.

Social change is a continuous process. It is closely associated with changes in the eco-system. Sometimes changes in the eco-system place all of a sudden, some particular groups at a disadvantage. They cannot cope with the change that have been brought up on them abruptly and fail to march with those who had quickly responded to such changes. Naturally, they fail to follow the norms which the successful and dominant groups adopt. They become, as a result, dubbed as deviant groups, and, at times, are considered by others to be criminal for such deviation. Therefore, it is not scientific and just to consider particular group as perpectual criminals. But this sort of mistake had been continued in India all along in the past in respect of certain groups of people. The mistake was done by ordinary men as well as the administration. Being guided by such unscientific notions, the Government too took many harsh steps against these groups.

II

Background of The Criminal Tribes Act

The then British Administration in India while encountering many problems in the shape of mass uprisings, rebellions and other disturbances as well as murder, dacoity etc. presumed that these activities are indulged in by different groups almost hereditarily. The attitude of the British Government has been unabashedly expressed in the following remark of Mr. T.V. Stephen, the then Member of Law and Order, which he made in course of introducing the Bill for suppression of criminal activities: "The special feature of India is the caste system. As trade goes by caste, a family of carpenters will be carpenters, a century or five centuries hence if they last so long. Keeping this in mind the meaning of 'professional criminal' is clear. It means that a tribe whose ancestors were criminals from times immemorial, who are themselves destined by the usages of caste to commit crimes, and whose descendants will be offenders against law until the whole tribe is exterminated or accounted for in the manner of the Thugs. When a man tells you that he is an offender against the law, he has been so from the beginning, and will be so to the end, reform is impossible, for it is his trade, his caste. I may almost say his religion is to commit crime''.

Unfortunately this attitude was not exclusively of Mr. Stephen and the members of his race. It was also shared by many Indians.

Though Dr. Lombroso's widely accepted theory of ''inborn criminality'' continued to influence the Administrator for years together, experiments in blood-grouping and anthropometric measurements by Indian scientists proved that inborn criminality cannot be a fact, since the so-called criminal tribes and some higher caste people of Rajasthan showed the same racial affinity(Majumdar). My observation on the Lodhas, an ex-criminal group in West Bengal, suggests that territorial and economic displacements along with the failure of the members of the group in adjusting themselves with the fast changing situation forced them to the paths of crime and offence.

However, the British Administration did not appreciate the fact. The Criminal Tribes Act was passed by the British Government as early as 1871 and applied arbitrarily and unjustly against some of the aboriginal tribes, castes and other groups like some sections of the Muslims in our country. Possibly to control some turbulent sections of our population having proclivity towards committing offences and crimes, the ruling Government enacted this law by which these sections were kept under strict surveillance. But there were periodic amendments. In 1876, the law was extended to many parts of the British India, especially to lower Bengal. An amendment of the Act in 1897 empowered the local government even to separate the children of these groups, aged between 4-18 years, from their irreclaimable parents. This law empowered the Local Governments to declare any community or tribe or any part of a tribe, gang or class indulging in systematic commission of non-bailable offence as a criminal tribe. In 1911, further amendments were made, which provided for the maintenance of a Register of persons considered criminals for detailed information of their whereabouts. This amendment made it obligatory on the part of the members of the criminal tribes to give their finger-prints, and to report change of residence and also empowered the Provincial Governments to restrict the movement of these communities within particular areas. The provision of this Act could, therefore, be conveniently applied to deal with the criminal tribes, and offenders were punished according to the nature of their crimes. By gradual modifications this Act was, more or less, consolidated in 1924. An individual of any community which was considered to be habitually criminal or which committed crimes in an almost consistent manner came under the purview of the Criminal Tribes Act for constant surveillance. But later on, due to various reasons, modifications in this Act were made to alter the conditions of the criminal tribes and to uplift them. The chief reason was a change in the idea that somebody who was born of a criminal must be a criminal.

III

Repeal of the Act

Gradual change of the notions towards the criminal tribes resulted in various ways. In 1937, the Criminal Tribes Committee headed by V.N. Tiwari appointed by the Government of the United Provinces (Uttar Pradesh) opined that "criminal tribes were a legacy of unhealthy social environments and the wrong methods pursued through many centuries in dealing with them. They are not the sinners, they have been sinned against". This Committee not only recommended repeal of the Act, but also introduction of some welfare activities for this group.

The Madras Province (at present Tamil Nadu) repeated the Act in 1947 and Bombay (Maharashtra) in 1949. The Government of India appointed a Committee under the chairmanship of A. Ayyangar in 1949. "There has been persistent demand in the Central Legislature in recent years that the Criminal Tribes Act, 1924 should be repealed as its provisions which seek to classify particularly classes of people as Criminal Tribes, are inconsistent with the dignity of free India", observed the Committee. The Committee after careful evaluation of the problems and making a comprehensive tour of the places where these groups of people lived recommended for repealing the Act. Henceforth, people belonging to these criminal groups were recognised as 'Denotified Communities'. By this, more than 153 communities throughout India were liberated from the crushing wheels of the law under which they had smarted helplessly for centuries. One very important fact should be noted here. A few communities in different States are still considered to be groups with criminal propensities i.e. criminal tribes or ex-criminal tribes, whereas they are considered common castes in other States without any stigma of criminality. Thus even now the stigma of criminality is attached to a particular group in one State, and the same group is free from the stigma in another State. This is a problem which has caused mistaken identity. However, 2,71,02,180 persons are accounted as members of denotified community, as per Census 1961.

Traditional occupations of these communities vary from forest economy to pastoral economy, weaving, mat-making, trading in beads and bangles, doing the job of scavenger, singer, and so forth. Many of them are reported to have followed in the past some unusual 'occupations' requiring special skill to eke out their existence. And these were considered offences or crimes according to law: e.g. burglary and dacoity (the Minas of the Punjab, the Lodhas of West Bengal, the Sansis of U.P., the Punjab, the Rajasthan etc.), swindling (the Jadna), cattle-lifting (the Gopalas, the Manggrudsis), cattle poisoning (the Manggrudis), pilfering and counterfeiting of coins (the Chapperbands), offences and crimes during the harvest (the Kaladis of Madras and Konda Dora of Andhra Pradesh), prostitution (woman of the Beder Community of Maharashtra), so on and so forth.

After the repeal of the Criminal Tribes Act (1953) our Welfare Government has decided to take some concrete steps in the form of welfare activities and rehabilitation schemes to ameliorate the living condition of these groups and the incidence of crimes among them is dwindling, as a result, and idea that peculiar groups are hereditarily associated with particular kinds of offences is gradually losing ground.

IV

Classification

If we look into the histories and ways of life of different denotified communities, we shall be able to appreciate more fully the fact that these communities cannot be and should never be considered criminal tribes. On the basis of their habitats, occupations and ways of life, these denotified tribes may be classified into the following groups :-

i) Nomadic groups who have taken to criminal life.
ii) Fighting men and soldiers who, having lost their jobs, have turned into criminals.

iii) Communities who used to work as village watchmen and Police, but have taken to criminal life.
iv) Wild tribes in distress who took to criminal living as a way out of the plight they had fallen in.
v) Beggars turned into criminals.
vi) Some settled castes and tribes who took to criminality due to poverty.

We may take a few examples from history. A good number of tribes of Chittor of Rajasthan left their homeland and took a wandering life when Alauddin Khilji (1296-1316) conquered their homeland. In course of their wandering, they indulged in criminal activities finding no other way to earn their livelihood. Then, there are a good number of communities who lost their traditional jobs and resorted to criminal activities under compulsion. The Banjaras of Andhra Pradesh are a concrete example of this type. They were peripatetic common carriers for generations. But due to the extension of transport facilities, they lost their jobs and became criminals, Ramoshis and Wagharis acted as guards near the hill ghats and forts during the Maratha regime. But after the loss of their jobs they adopted the life of criminals. The Lodhas, who lost their homes in jungles and could not adjust themselves with the changing situation, also resorted to criminal activities.

V

Approach of the Government of Free India Towards the Ex-Criminal Tribes

After the repeal of the Criminal Tribes Act a good number of people were freed from the stigma of criminality imputed to them. The Backward Classes Commission appointed by the Government of India made many suggestions for amelioration of the condition of these problem-ridden communities. They are summarized below :-

1) Criminal tribes should be called 'Denotified Communities' (Bimukta Jati, i.e. a group freed from the stigma unjustly imputed to them by others).
2) These communities should be included in the category of Scheduled Castes or Tribes and Backward Classes according to their

distinctive social features.

3) They should be resettled in batches and gradually integrated v the bigger society.
4) Proper education for effecting national integration should imparted to them, for making them free citizens of free India.
5) Reform activities should be undertaken for them.
6) Collective criminal activities and the individual criminal activiti should be clearly distinguished and understood for dealing wi them.
7) Proper type of education and employment for their children shoul be ensured.
8) Economic rehabilitation should be ensured simultaneously.

We consider these recommendations as well thought out.

In pursuance of the policy of Government, these different groups were restored to a status of dignity and self-respect, which had bee denied to them for centuries. Restrictions regarding their movement anc night surveillance on them had been withdrawn. They are no longer confined to their home environments. In compliance with the recommendations of the Commission, provisions were made by the Central Government and State Governments to rehabilitate these groups of people on sound economic footing. Steps have been taken to provide them with better housing facilities, along with cultivable land, as also starting primary school with Ashram or hostel facilities for their children. Small and Cottage type of industrial units have been started for their economic rehabilitation. It was decided that these groups should be given ever possible opportunity for adopting honest and normal ways of livin Every effort is being made to wean them away from their supposec criminal life.

For the purpose of rehabilitation, in many cases, voluntary organisations have been entrusted with the charge. Government agencies themselves also undertook this work at many places. But a detailed assessment of all these rehabilitation efforts has not yet been made. Naturally, a clear picture of the same is not available until now. However, it must be mentioned that during all previous plan periods, provision had been made for the rehabilitation of these downtrodden communities to raise their status and to make them equal with other citizens of India in all spheres. Thus the Government of India and a few individual organisations have tried to live up to the principle of the dignity of the individuals and the unity of the Nation as enshrined in the Constitution of India. The efforts have raised different types of response and reaction in the minds of these groups who have remained neglected through millennia, in the minds of the neighbouring communities, and in the world of attitudes of Government Officials and those engaged in these rehabilitation activities.

VI

The Lodhas : A Case Study

The Lodhas of West Bengal are known as one of the ex-criminal tribes. A survey undertaken by the author revealed that out of total number of active criminal in the district of Midnapur, the Lodhas constituted one-third. The Lodhas are commonly stigmatised with commission of daco-i j, burglary, pilferage and theft. It has been ascertained that previously the Lodhas used to live in the forest and most of them were satisfied with the forest economy of hunting, collection of edible roots, tubers and minor forest produce, procurement of hides of snakes and lizards (Bengal Monitor) and selling these in the locality around. In exchange of these, they procured some indispensable commodities of daily life and hardly disturbed by others, they could make an easy living. During the early part of British Administration in Bengal, when forests and other Khas lands were permanently leased out to the Zamindars, then, for the first time, the Lodhas faced an intriguing situation, having been prevented from free access into the forest and its use for their different needs. On the other hand, other agricultural communities like the Santals, the Mundas, the Bhumij and other gradually encroached upon the forests and, having cleared up these jungles, brought the land under cultivation, although any sort of entrance into such forests was declared a punishable offence by the Administrative Authorities. Thus by a trick of law they were dispossessed of their forest abodes and deprived of their hold and dependency on the forest. Still they sometime collected their food and fuel from the forest in the clandestine way for their existence.

Thus economically replaced, the Lodhas could not adapt themselves to the changing situations immediately and some of them migrated to the eastern part of district, which is less forested, in search of jobs of day-labourers and other employments for survival. The growing needs of the expanding families clamped in a small territory, could not be met with a hewer's income. Faced with this compelling situation, the Lodhas had to accept the challenge of survival and resorted to anti-social activities as a convenient means of livelihood.

"The economic and territorial displacement under a new setting, with the impact of scheming communities all around, affected very seriously their traditional patterns of economic life, and ultimately upset the equilibrium of the whole society. Probably under such circumstances, pilfering, petty theft, lifting of articles from the houses of the neighbours and clandestine sale of jungle produce were first resorted to individually, which, in course of time, developed into group habits. Amidst poverty, unsympathetic attitude of the neighbours and stoic apathy of the then ruling government, criminality cut a deep gorge into their society, in which the people had to roil down helplessly" (Bhowmick : 1963). But with the march of time, the Lodhas had to face other complex situations, such as :-

i) Economic and territorial displacements, i.e. loss of livelihood which caused loss of self-confidence.
ii) Being not specialized in any profession, they could not fit themselves into the existing greater economic structure.
iii) Stigma of criminality lowered their social status and prestige in society.
iv) Subsequent police oppression, punishment and torture completely loosened their group cohesion and solidarity.
v) Arrest and confinement in jail completely shattered familial bondage and relations, fostering atomised or individualistic mentality.
vi) Poverty exposed them to exploitation and made them surrender to many undesirable situations.
vii) Being compelled to sell the stolen properties to others at a normal price and thus being cheated, they came to think that the non-Lodhas people were dishonest and tyrannical. This made them more suspicious and revengeful.
viii) Chronic poverty and a low aspiration level retarded the zeal and enthusiasm of these people, and developed constraints in their culture, making them lazy and lethargic. These made them unresponsive to any sort of change or innovation.
ix) Constant police torture, by the neighbours made them migratory; their homes being less attractive to them. Thus they began to lose the sense of belongingness.

x) These ultimately made them isolated and recoil into the shell of their old traditions. Also these enveloped them with coyness, timidity and left them full of fear and distrust.

Thus circumstances, the Lodhas, not having rudimentary education, no skill in crafts or arts, no land in their possession, and no fixed employment as share-croppers or farm-labourers or work-house workers were compelled to live far below the poverty-line, and indulge in spurts of anti-social activities whenever their hunger provoked them to go against the society and the law of the land. In the past, Police intruded to restrain their crimes but the democratic ideals and the philosophy of social justice have made rapid strides and the views of the State and its laws have started changing in India, so much so that the welfare of the people has now become the ideal of the State.

Guided by the ideals of welfare, the Governments at the Centre and in the State have introduced a number of Schemes and Projects to improve the lot of the ex-criminal tribes throughout India. West Bengal has also a few Schemes for such purposes and the Lodhas, in many cases, have responded to these with enthusiasm.

VII

Impact and Reaction

Altogether five rehabilitation centres for the Lodhas started working during the period of last two years, distributed at five different places. These schemes accommodated 200 families, i.e. 1000 souls, out of a total (approximate) population of 15000. So its impact on the beneficiaries, as well as on the Lodhas in general, and on the other hand, on the neighbouring non-Lodhas tribals and Caste Hindu group is of special significance. Assessment of nature of economic and social benefits that accrued out of such schemes and other types of reaction, justifies the intrinsic worth of these schemes.

The Lodhas had to suffer chronic economic difficulties as well as social neglect for centuries. This had repercussion on their minds and made them hostile to the so-called neighbours, who according to the Lodhas, are unsympathetic. It has been observed that their so-called civilized neighbours hate them for their suspected propensities. They are also afraid of the Lodhas, who may steal away their belongings. This sort of suspicion still continues among the groups concerned. These, in succession, contributed to the outbreak of two serious types of tension in the form of riot and forcible decampment of the Lodhas from different villages. When attempts were being made to start rehabilitation centres in these places the Lodhas developed some imaginary ideas of receiving immediate benefit in the form of shelter and food as well as raising of their social status and wiping out of the long-cursed social negligence.

A sum of Rs. 1,500/- which was initially granted to each Lodha family was no sufficient to bring about the benefit of a permanent nature. This made the beneficiary Lodhas more frustrated leading to displacement of their goals. This unconsciously implelled them to curse the sponsors. Besides, they are not agriculture minded and their mentality is not such that they can wait patiently for the harvest. It has been observed that they prefer working as day-labour to cultivating their own land. They are ready to dispose of their own land to outsiders who sometimes advance them money or paddy. Maintaining of bullocks or cows or goats is expensive, time-taking and it requires keeping a constant watch on these animals. The Lodhas are not in the habit of keeping these animals. Even the poultry birds or the goats are consumed rather then domesticated.

To have gradual social cohesion with the bigger society and to achieve a prestigious status require refinement of manners and customs and mental preparation which cannot be done within a short period. So the expectations of the beneficiary Lodhas have had a jolt from the reality.

With such a mental background, when they found that they had to work hard on the land which was given to them to ameliorate their distress and were constantly threatened with unemployment in the locality, they did not find any real solution out of such schemes. This made them less inclined to such promises of distant future and less pleased with the actual circumstances.

In a few cases, a good number of Lodhas asked for money from the social workers to meet the expenses of tobacco and rice-beer, refusal of which made them hostile and reactionary. Similarly, the social workers wanted to stop effects on the mind of these people. But it had a different reaction on the incorrigible criminals. It was criticised by them. These incorrigible criminals used to get their support from the so-called gentry, who were the receivers of the stolen properties. They were seemingly sympathetic to the Lodhas and hostile to and critical of such schemes. For example, in course of our rehabilitation work at Bidis in the village of Daharpur, Midnapur, we faced tremendous opposition from many villagers who sought to use the Lodhas for the purpose of personal benefit, which at times, included breaking of railway wagons, theft, dacoity, etc., and who were prevented from doing so by us as well as the enlightened Lodhas.

The Lodhas of the adjoining village became jealous to some extent because they were not getting any sort of direct benefits out of such schemes. No provision has been made in the schemes for their active participation.

The neighbouring non-Lodha tribal as well as other people have a very serious type of mental reaction in regard to those schemes. They have apparently observed that huts have been built up for the Lodhas and land, bullocks, agricultural appliances, goats and poultry birds--everything has been given to them, yet the Lodhas are not in a position to utilise these to their advantage. Land is left uncultivated, bullocks are sold out, goats are consumed and birds are eaten up. They are not in a position to assess the capability of the Lodhas and the nature of resources and think that these are the items of gift. The colourful description of such gifts and rumours of huge expenditure incurred for the purpose make them frenzied and illusioned. On the contrary, they see that in actuality the Lodhas are committing crimes, as they did earlier, and are pursuing anti-social activities as usual and are threatening social tranquillity, peace and order in the locality. The other non-Lodha anti-social elements who have clandestine relationship with the criminal Lodhas try their level best to bring them back to the path of criminality propagating against the Government policies and voluntary organisation as well as the social workers who are in charge of schemes.

Thus the Lodhas remain in isolation as they were, far away from the socio-economic and cultural boundaries of the people of the locality--but in touch with criticisms and adverse statements.

The Government Officer who frequently visit the centres, sometimes find the disgruntled Lodhas giving some false statements against the organisation or the workers, as this is very natural. It is quite natural that they cannot be satisfied with such limited money, time and social interaction. In this connection, it may be said that these criminal people are not so simple as the other tribal people are. But in many cases the officers believe in their words without any questioning. This has resulted in more confusion and chaos. Sometimes the officers who stayed for a short period gave them hope of a bright future which was beyond the control of the organisation or the Government. This made the Lodhas more discontented, which seriously affected the welfare work.

VIII

Conclusion

The problem of the Lodhas of West Bengal, in particular, and the denotified tribes of India, in general, have a few important lessons for applied anthropology and action anthropology. Throughout the world different groups of aboriginals are facing crisis because of changes in the broader ecological systems and socio-cultural systems. The question of integrating these groups with the wider community life now faces the people and administration in every country. To find an answer we must take into consideration the nature of the ways of life of these groups and their social and psychological conditions. The way how these groups are interplaced with the particular ecological systems should be examined by us carefully. We would then, perhaps, find the clue to the riddle why these groups fail to respond quickly and favourably to the 'facilities' of integrating themselves with the wider social life, which may appear to us be 'obviously advantageous' for them.

We should try to examine the impact of the efforts at changing their ways of life as made in the rehabilitation schemes and welfare activities for these groups. We shall then and then only be able to locate where the shoe pinches. Herein lies the role of the applied anthropologists. Being freed from the prejudice which affects the laymen and somtimes the administrators, we should view the case from a scientific angle which should be, at the same time humane.

One thing has been, we believe, clear from the preceding discussion. The chronic social neglect of community by the society dwarf its mind and abilities. It develops various angularities in it. And it becomes difficult on its part to overcome the inhibitions bred by such angularities. Ways should be found out to help it free itself from such inhibitions.

We should note here a relationship between the segments of the society : the neglected communities or ethnic groups, the advanced ethnic groups and the State.

In welfare societies like ours and in advanced societies of today, the State is playing a positive role, which is becoming more and more important with the passage of time, to ameliorate the conditions of the down-trodden or neglected and backward ethnic groups, so that they can catch up with the more advanced ones. Otherwise, the equality in status and opportunity will continue to threaten social tranquillity and vitiate the social atmosphere. For this reason, government must recognise the fact that they should enable the backward communities to stand on their own feet.

At the same time, the Government should make an endeavour to bridge the mental gap between one ethnic group and another. But the task of promotion of inter-ethnic harmony can never be accomplished by the government alone. The wider society must be aware of the necessity of such harmony. The advanced ethnic groups must free themselves from the prejudices and angularities they have developed towards the backward communities.

For this reason a scientific outlook must be developed which would emerge from more intensive work of the applied anthropologists and action antrhopologist in future. This necessitates greater co-ordination between the planners and action anthropologists and the follow-up measures to assess the working of the progammes.

References

Bhowmick, P.K. (1963) *The Lodhas of West Bengal,* Calcutta.

Bhowmick, P.K. (1968) Development Schemes as factors of Social and Economic changes, Journal of Social and research, Ranchi.

Bhowmick, P.K. (1970) — Welfare Programmes and Administration for Development and Integration, Tribe, Rajasthan.

Bhowmick, P.K. (1973) — Ex-criminal Tribes of India, Indian Museun Bulletin

Bhowmick, P.K. (1975) — Essential Primary Consideration from Rehabilitation Schemes, Vanya Jati, Delhi.

Daly, F.C. (1916) — Manual of Criminal Classes operating in Bengal. Calcutta.

Gupta, R.K. (1954) — Work Among the Lodhas, Calcutta Police Journal, Calcutta.

Gupta, R.K. (1954) — Lodhas Revisited, Man-in-India, Ranchi.

Haikerwal, B.S. (1934) — *Economic and Social aspects of Crime in India*, London.

CHAPTER 7

An Approach to The Tribal Manpower with a Short Profile of Tribals in West Bengal

P. K. Sanyal, P. N. Dasgupta

In the penultimate end of this Century there exists a society of tribals in this State of West Bengal, hidden from 'Progress', which is almost universally accepted as 'backwardness' in terms of economy. To others they are the unique link with the past. Whatever may be the opinion, a group of people living in this state, have been scheduled as tribe by Government from time to time. These people governed by their own customary laws to a large extent managed to eke a precarious living mostly in the isolated forest villages and hilly tracts, as well as in the villages of the plains land. Once they were cut off from all sorts of modernization, but with the passage of time along with the advent of planning from 'outside world' a rapid change has been noticed in all spheres of tribal life in this state. A few decades ago they were self-contained in economy, though lying at the subsistence level. Nowadays, the thin periphery of their economic activity has been ruptured and ultimately they have come into contact with the market economy which leads to a number of economic problems. And it appears after a long and arduous journey since the inception of first five year plan that the focus of modern planning, some believe, is still remote from tribals' economic problems. Accordingly, the old pattern of tribal economy, predominantly dependent on incipient agriculture, has been vanished in such a way that majority of them have simply emerged in poverty. A large proportion of land from the tribal possession has been transferred to the land grabbers rather alienated to intruders to their land. As a result intensity in occupational mobility has already been recorded among them and they are going to be absorbed in the massive bulk of unskilled labour market.

In this way tribals in West Bengal are facing crisis in employment sector though quite a good number of protective measures and economic programmes have been chalked out to provide appropriate opportunities of employment creation. Therefore, it is found that during the developmental activities in the laterite and semi-arid zone of West Bengal comprising mainly of the districts of Purulia, Birbhum and Bankura where a sizeable tribal population reside, the tribal families are used to migratory labour in the districts of Burdwan, Hooghly, Howrah etc. In the agricultural operations.

In view of this the manpower situation of this segment of state population may be taken into account. Thus, an attempt will be made in this paper to assess the manpower availability among the scheduled tribes of West Bengal with particular reference to employment and unemployment situation. At the same time a short discussion has been made on their socio-economic status.

The population total for Scheduled Tribes in West Bengal was more than thirty lakhs and seventy thousands on 1st March, 1981. Twenty years earlier this State was inhabited by more than twenty lakhs of tribes. The decennial growth rates of this population from 1961 to '71 and 1971 to'81 were 23.3 per cent and 21.2 per cent respectively. In both the cases the growth rate for the tribes was lower than the state population. But despite the declining growth rate as found in the tribes that does not minimize the dimension of the economic problems for this scheduled part of state population. Simultaneously, it is to be noted that in both the sectors, i.e. state as a whole and scheduled tribes in particular registered a very high rate of growth of population, when the demographic status is considered.

For instance, if one assumes the growth rate as observed during 1971-81 to persist in the current future and accordingly estimates the size of tribal population of this state of West Bengal for 1986 and 1991 these may work out to 34.10 lakhs and 37.88 lakhs respectively. This means that another 7.18 lakhs of tribal people are likely to be added to their present population stock by 1991. Even, if one-third of this addition enters into the labour market, a manpower planner will have to concern himself with the creation of employment opportunities for a little more than two and half lakhs of new entrants by 1991 let alone the present task of absorbing backlog of unemployed and under-employed people. But this is another story.

Details regarding sex, residence wise distribution of scheduled tribes population has been furnished below along with the population projection up to 1991.

Table 1

DISTRIBUTION OF ESTIMATED SCHEDULED TRIBES POPULATION IN WEST BENGAL (IN LAKHS)

Year	*Rural*			*Urban*			
	Male	*Female*	*Total*	*Male*	*Female*	*Total*	*Grand Total*
1981	14.97	14.58	29.55	0.62	0.53	1.15	30.70
1982	15.28	14.90	30.18	0.63	0.55	1.18	31.36
1983	15.60	15.22	30.82	0.64	0.56	1.20	32.02
1984	15.93	15.54	31.47	0.66	0.57	1.23	32.70
1985	16.27	15.87	32.14	0.68	0.58	1.26	33.40
1986	16.62	16.00	32.62	0.69	0.59	1.28	34.10
1987	16.97	16.55	33.52	0.70	0.61	1.31	34.83
1988	17.33	16.90	34.23	0.72	0.62	1.34	35.57
1989	17.70	17.25	34.95	0.74	0.63	1.37	36.32
1990	18.07	17.63	35.70	0.75	0.65	1.40	37.10
1991	18.46	18.00	36.46	0.76	0.66	1.42	37.88

Population estimates for all the years from 1982 to 1991 have been worked out on the basis of sex-residence ratios at 1981 census and applying these to the rate of growth of population during 1971-81 an approximate idea has been built-up to the next decade.

A delineation of the manpower profile of tribal people requires a discussion on education. It is already observed that incidence of literacy in the scheduled tribes is still very low throughout the country. In West Bengal the rate of literacy of this particular section of population raised from 6.55 p.c. in 1961 to 13.34 p.c. in 1981. Incidentally it appears that though the literacy rates for the tribes in 1961 and 1981 were much lower than the ratios of general population of this State in the corresponding years but still the trend is very encouraging. The rates visibly increased during the last two decades for the male folk of the scheduled segment. An absolute size of literate tribes of West Bengal can also be obtained from the following table.

Table 2

DISTRIBUTION OF SCHEDULED TRIBES IN WEST BENGAL BY LITERACY

Year	*Total number of Literates (in lakhs)*	*Number of Male Literates (in lakhs)*	*Number of Female Literates (in lakhs)*
1971	2.26(8.92)*	1.88(14.49)	0.38(3.69)
1981	4.06(13.34)	3.30(21.10)	0.76(5.00)

Source : Census of India, 1971,1981

*N. B. In parenthesis percentages of literates to corresponding populations have been given.

The literacy rate of the tribes is, no doubt, far below in the line of progress achieved by the state as a whole. The reason behind such situation is that the formal education could make a little headway among the tribals though the State has launched a massive programme to implement the formal education policy all over.

Further break-up of literates by educational level show that about 75 per cent of literates in 1961 were absent from having any education level. It is interesting to know that in 1971 this figure has been slashed down to 30 per cent., in that case about 66 per cent, of literates achieved educational qualification up to primary or junior basic stage. It is expected that 1981 census will furnish detail on the literates having qualification above primary level.

The percentage distribution of literates of scheduled tribes by educational level in 1961, 1971 has been presented below.

Table-3

PERCENTAGE DISTRIBUTION OF SCHEDULED TRIBES BY EDUCATIONAL LEVEL.

Educational Level	*1961*	*1971*
Literates (without educational Level)	74.63	29.65
Primary or Junior Basic	23.88	65.93
Matriculation or Secondary or above.	1.49	4.42
Total :	100.00	100.00

Source : Census of India 1961,1971.

According to Commissioner's Report the percentages of enrolment of Scheduled tribes student in 1977-78 in West Bengal for undergraduate and graduate and above were 1.2 each in respect of general population whereas all India figures were 1.6. per cent in the corresponding sectors. The Cultural Research Institude of Scheduled Castes & Tribes Welfare Department of Government of West Bengal estimated that against a total number of 3.17 lakhs of students who actually attained secondary and above stage of education, the outturn petered to paltry total of 10 thousands in 1977.

The evaluation report of the Development and Planning Department of Government of West Bengal on Primary Education in rural and urban areas of West Bengal in 1976-78 shows that about 13 p.c. of the scheduled tribes households in the urban area having children in the age group belonging to 6-11 years were found to be ''not sending their wards to school '' while the corresponding percentage was 70 for rural area. The report also reveal that the percentage of enrolment varies directly with income.

It is, however, found form Commissioner's report that 70 p.c. to 80 p.c. of habitations with a population of 300 and more, predominated by scheduled tribes are blessed with primary schools.

The conclusion, therefore, is that mere creation of opportunities is not enough as capacity to avail of that opportunity will be invariably limited by the economic condition.

The tribal people living characteristically interspersed with other population derive their livelihood mainly from agriculture. Hence, their dependence on land cannot be ignored, which is, therefore, very important to examine the extent of tribal manpower. Thus, the discussion on the pattern of land holding is necessary.

The percentage distribution of households by size class of land possessed by Scheduled Tribes in 1977-78 was as follows.

Table-4

PERCENTAGE DISTRIBUTION OF TRIBAL HOUSEHOLDS BY SIZE-CLASS OF LAND

Land size Class (in acres)	*Percentage distribution of households*	
	Rural	*Urban*
0(without owned home-stead)	1.79	45.21
0(with owned home-stead)	1.18	1.80
01-2.49	74.73	48.80
2.50-4.99	15.00	4.19
5.00 & above	7.30	
Total :	100.00	100.00

Source : National Simple Survey 32nd Round

The table reveals that in West Bengal tribal agricultural labourers and marginal farmers including casual workers in the rural area having holding size below 2.5 acres constituted 78 per cent of the aggregate. The small farmers among tribals in this State were about 15 per cent , whereas the medium and big farmers being 7 per cent.

Comparison of figures at the State level with that of India shows that situation in West Bengal was worse during the reference period

1977-78 when the four categories of farmers, viz. marginal, small, medium and big farmers are taken into account. As per the Bulletin of the Cultural Research Institute, Scheduled Castes and Tribes Welfare Deptt. Government of West Bengal it appears that in 1961 the agricultural labourers and marginal farmers having holding size below 2.5 acres constituted 45 per cent . of the total tribal households. For the small farmers the corresponding percentage was 23 only. Therefore it is understood that the poor tribals due to reason of too inadequate their income to match against irreducible minimum requirement are in perpetual debt. All the above are just a few instances to depict the economic condition of the tribal people in this state.

The tribals in West Bengal are basically land based. A few of them practise crafts and have adopted occupations other than land-based activities. Before going into details of tribal manpower an examination on the occupational profile of this population is much needed. Here we may look into the occupational distribution of the working force of the scheduled tribes by industrial category.

Table-5

DISTRIBUTION OF SCHEDULED TRIBES WORKERS BY INDUSTRIAL CATEGORY IN WEST BENGAL (IN LAKHS)

(in lakhs)

Category	YEAR		
	1961	1971	1981
Cultivators	5.02 (48.75)	2.97 (31.18)	3.95 (31.04)
Agricultural Labourers	2.92 (28.40)	4.66 (48.95)	6.21 (48.73)
Household-Industry, Non-household Industry, Repairing., Servicing, Manufacturing, Processing	0.33 (3.16)	0.24 (2.60)	0.13 (1.05)
Other Workers	2.03 (16.69)	1.64 (17.27)	2.44 (19.18)
Total :	10.30 (100.00)	9.51 (100.00)	12.73 (100.00)
Percentage to Total population	50.01	37.56	46.77

Source : Census 1961,1971,1981.

The figures of the above table are not strictly comparable due to lack of uniformity in the definition of workers in different censuses. But their dependency on agriculture has been focused in this table along with negligible participations in other activities. Moreover, the growing pauperization of the lower layer of tribal peasantry as manifested in the swelling number of agricultural workers has been discernible from the table. In fact, the agricultural workers comprised nearly 50 per cent of the total tribal workers of this state. However, tribals' agricultural pursuit is characterized by uneconomic holding due to small size and because of hard, laterite soil, these are unproductive too, along with other institutional problems such as land alienation, indebtedness, lack of credit facilities, less irrigation which requires implementation of expensive projects and the use of traditional, age-old operation techniques.

On the other hand, tribals, who have adopted non-agricultural occupations, practise basket making, spinning, weaving and metal works etc.

Even, quite a good number of agriculturists supplement their earnings with activities like food gathering fishing and selling of fuel wood collection.

In the colliery areas of the district of Burdwan a large portion of the tribes is engaged as mine and industrial workers. They are also found working in the small quarries at Purulia and Birbhum. Similarly, tribal workers are found in the tea gardens at Darjeeling and Jalpaiguri. But the tribal workers' dispersal among different occupations is quite low compared to the pattern prevailing for the general workers in the state. In accordance with this it may be said that the push to other avocations is no match for the great pull exerted by agriculture. Due to absence of education and training their gravitation to other occupation is non significant. The trend of diminishing participation for household industries since 1961 shows that tribals require adequate training facilities in order to enable them to start small household industrial units. In 1977 only 175 Scheduled Tribes were engaged as apprentices in various establishments when the total number of such apprentices was 10687.

Now, on the basis of the facts mentioned above we may enter into the vicinity of tribal manpower in West Bengal. Manpower concept has been newly introduced in planning as a material for preparatory job. It has been observed that manpower being an essential ingredient of economic development, systematic collection of manpower data is the beginning of any rational planning process. Basically, manpower data contain (i) population, (ii) labour force (iii) employment & (iv) unemployment. It is important to note that preparation of Manpower data depends mainly on the available sources. And this is possible only when the organized sector is concerned. Among the sources mention may be made of i) Census, ii) State Bureau of Applied Economics and Statistics, iii) National Sample Survey Organisation, iv) Director General for Employment & Training and so on. Unfortunately, for the tribals required data are not at all readily available. Of all the possible reasons behind the absence of data supply is that the tribals in a large bulk work in unorganized sector. However, keeping this in mind we may proceed further to assess the tribal manpower status in this state.

Regarding the present status of tribal demography discussion has already been made before where the estimated projection of population growth has been furnished for an over all examination of the volume of the population in near future.

Labour Force : The notable feature of this segment of backward population is their overwhelming participation in agriculture and allied activities as the tribals in West Bengal are largely restricted to the rural areas for this State. In fact, for every 1000 Scheduled Tribes workers 922 were engaged in agriculture and allied activities. Similarly, tribals'

Table 6

SECTORAL DISPOSITION OF THE ECONOMICALLY ACTIVE SCHEDULED TRIBES

Sector	Scheduled Tribes
Primary	92.2 p.c.
Secondary	2.6 p.c.
Tertiary	5.2 p.c.

Source : an Abstract of Manpower Statistics in West Bengal, 1976

dependence on agriculture may be justified from the sectoral disposition of their economic activities.

'Primary' means traditional agriculture throughout the state excepting a few potential blocks in the Gangetic basin, which could not change the age-old mode of production practised by the majority. Therefore, the traditional agriculture operates mainly with land and labour. Tribals embody family labour with virtually zero opportunity costs in labour surplus situation. Furthermore, it is observed so far that the industrial development has failed to reduce the excessive dependence of our tribal labour force on agriculture as a whole.

In this connection it may be mentioned that in the backdrop of socio-political and politico-economic condition of present day West Bengal the tribal farmers and rural tribal population are regarded as 'archaic peasant population. Such type is characterized by high participation rate for male and female, high proportion of engagement in primary sector and low proportion of participation in other sector in terms of occupation as well as employment.

In view of this condition as prevailed in this State the status of tribal labour force may be examined. It is known that tribals' economy is now at the subsistence level of unorganised sector. Therefore the quantum of unemployment and employment so far worked out by Census or by National Sample Survey or from any other sources cannot be taken without any objection.

According to Census the number of workers in 1961,1971 were 10.30 lakhs, 9.51 lakhs and 12.74 lakhs respectively. However, the number of unemployed tribes were not furnished. In this regard it may be mentioned that labour force is a composition of i) total number of employees and ii) total number of unemployeds. Hence, in accordance with this problem to find out the tribal labour force one may use the results given by the National Sample Survey as the principal source. Accordingly key results of 32nd round have been reproduced below to

Table-7

PROPORTION OF TRIBAL POPULATION (5 YRS. & ABOVE,) TO TOTAL TRIBAL POPULATION BY SEX-RESIDENCE

Residence	*Male*	*Female*
Rural	86.54%	85.9%
Urban	91.73%	87.5%

Source : N.S.S. 32nd round

get an idea on labour force estimates for the tribes Labour force estimation N.S.S. is based on the proportion of population belonging to 5 years and above age structure.

Table 7 shows high participation rates of both male and female in both the sectors. In pursuance with this it may be said again that within this fold of tribal population both minors (below 15 years) and old (above 59 years) have been included, which cannot be isolated.

The quantum of labour force in absolute term is based on able bodied adult and workable persons. But in a country like ours where eradication of poverty and unemployment has been a major goal of development planning till to-day, the inclusion of child labour as well as old persons is inevitable.

Employment

In considering all these factors mentioned here the working force of this segment of tribal population may be taken out with the help of N.S.S. estimation, which depends on three assumptions at three different points of time span, viz., i) yearly estimate ii) weekly estimate and iii) daily estimate. Yearly estimate reveals proportion of persons usually works in a year, for a number of days, like-wise proportion of persons working on an average in a week and on an average in a day come under the next two estimates. These three estimations have been taken into consideration as 'Usual Activity Status' (U.S.) 'Current Weekly Activity Status' (C.W.S.) and 'Current Daily Activity Status' (C.D.S.) approach

Table 8

WORK PARTICIPATION RATES OF TRIBAL POPULATION BELONGING TO 5 YRS. & ABOVE ACCORDING TO USUAL STATUS (U.S.), CURRENT WEEKLY STATUS (C.W.S.) AND CURRENT DAILY STATUS (C.D.S.) BY SEX-RESIDENCE.

Residence	*Male*			*Female*		
	U.S.	*C.W.S.*	*C.D.S.*	*U.S*	*C.W.S.*	*C.D.S.*
Rural	65.58	63.63	58.00	35.36	32.55	28.10
Urban	66.34	64.37	58.81	28.30	32.39	26.78

Source : N.S.S. 32nd Round.

Table-9

ESTIMATED PROPORTION OF TRIBAL (5 YEAR & ABOVE) IN WEST BENGAL.

Year	*Rural*		*Urban*	
	Male	*Female*	*Male*	*Female*
1981	12.96	12.52	0.57	0.47
1986	14.38	13.74	0.63	0.53
1991	15.98	15.46	0.69	0.57

Now, applying these percentages to sex-residence wise population for respective years the working force estimates for West Bengal tribes may be deducted for 1981, 1986 and 1991.

Table 10

DISTRIBUTION OF ESTIMATED NUMBER OF POPULATION IN TRIBAL WORKING FORCE BY USUAL STATUS, CURRENT WEEKLY STATUS AND CURRENT DAILY STATUS IN WEST BENGAL (IN LAKHS)

Residence	Year	Male			Female		
		U.S.	C.W.S.	C.D.S.	U.S.	C.W.S.	C.D.S.
Rural	1981	8.49	8.27	7.51	4.42	4.07	3.51
	1986	9.43	9.18	8.34	4.86	4.80	4.14
	1991	10.48	10.20	9.27	5.47	5.03	4.34
Urban	1981	0.37	0.36	0.33	0.13	0.15	0.12
	1986	0.42	0.41	0.37	0.15	0.17	0.14
	1991	0.46	0.42	0.40	0.16	0.18	0.15

Following N.S.S. the distribution of estimated number of population in tribal working force by Usual, Current Weekly and Current Daily status has been presented here.

From the above table it is revealed that the number of Workers from Usual Status has been decreased in Current Weekly and Current Daily Status throughout the rural sector of West Bengal where more than 95 per cent of the total tribes reside. It is also understood that the extent of employment among the tribals is not enough stable over a period of one year.

Unemployment

For estimation of profile on unemployment of scheduled tribes 32nd round data of National Sample Survey has played the key role

Table - 11

PROPORTION OF UNEMPLOYEDS AMONG TRIBAL LABOUR FORCE BY U.S., C.W.S. & C.D.S.

Residence	*Male*			*Female*		
	U.S.	*C.W.S.*	*C.D.S.*	*U.S.*	*C.W.S.*	*C.D.S.*
Rural	1.97	2.80	7.11	6.73	1.86	3.67
Urban	5.48	7.09	12.18	3.58	0.75	4.12

Source : N.S.S., 32nd round

again. N.S.S. examined the extent of unemployment in terms of the Usual, Current Weekly & Current Daily Status. Below the proportion of unemployed among tribal labour force has been reproduced.

Now, applying these percentages given in the above table one may get an approximate idea on the extent of underutilization of labour

Table-12

ESTIMATED NUMBER OF UNEMPLOYED BY USUAL STATUS AMONG THE SCHEDULED TRIBES OF WEST BENGAL.

Year	*Rural*		*Urban*	
	Male	*Female*	*Male*	*Female*
1981	0.25	0.84	0.03	0.01
1986	0.28	0.92	0.04	0.02
1991	0.31	1.04	0.04	0.02

force rather unemployed tribal population mainly. In this regard proportion of usually unemployed has been worked out. According to the National Sample Survey at the State level, the chronic unemployment is found to a great extent among the tribes in rural sector. On the basis of this the estimated numbers of usually unemployeds have been worked out at three different points of time.

From the above table it is assumed that among the tribal females the extent of underemployment is higher than their male folk. In addition it may be said again that on account of growing scarcity of land and accelerated pressure of man on the land, particularly in the rural area the number of unemployeds would be higher than what has been estimated here.

Similarly, further examination on the unemployment situation on the basis of Current Weekly and current Dairy Status show the intensity of intermittent unemployment among the Scheduled Tribes of this state on account of seasonal fluctuations, as stated in the 32nd round report of N.S.S. In this connection it has been observed that opportunity for stable employment appears to be less among the tribes. These two observations have been made on Current Weekly and Current Daily Status, on the basis of which estimated number of unemployment in 1981, 1986 and 1991 have been presented below.

Table-13

ESTIMATED NUMBER OF UNEMPLOYEDS OF CURRENT WEEKLY AND CURRENT DAILY STATUS AMONG THE SCHEDULED TRIBES OF WEST BENGAL IN 1981, 1986, 1991.

(in lakhs)

Year	*Rural*				*Urban*			
	Male		*Female*		*Male*		*Female*	
	C.W.S.	*C.D.S.*	*C.W.S.*	*C.D.S.*	*C.W.S.*	*C.D.S.*	*C.W.S.*	*C.D.S.*
1981	0.36	0.91	0.23	0.46	0.04	0.07	.004	.02
1986	0.40	1.02	0.26	0.50	0.04	0.08	.004	.02
1991	0.45	1.14	0.29	0.57	0.05	0.08	.004	.02

Thus, it is observed from the above table that on an average per week unemployment in rural sector for 1981, 1986 and 1991 have been recorded as 0.59, 0.66 and 0.74 lakhs respectively. Simultaneously for the same years records of per day unemployment are 1.37, 1.52 and 1.71 lakhs respectively in rural areas.

Comparatively, the number of unemployment for both C.W.S. and C.D.S. in the urban sector for the above mentioned years are lower than the rural areas and at the same time it is to be noted again that the growth of unemployment in urban areas for C.W.S. and C.D.S. is somewhat restricted.

The employment strategy for the tribals, however, has failed, because of the fact that in a small population size of above 31 lakhs (in 1981 census) nearly one lakh and fifty thousands of people remained unemployed daily on an average, despite a high rate of usual status labour participation rates by both the sexes among the tribal people.

The magnitude of unemployment in actual term could not be measured as the heterogeneous character of unemployment situation was not identified. The stable condition in employment particularly in rural sector is far away from what we wanted for this backward segment of scheduled population.

Again, to view the extent of underutilization of tribal manpower further estimatation has been made with the help of a matrix. In the N.S.S. report of 32nd round the matrix has been fromed by computation of proportion of 'workers', 'unemployeds' and 'Not in labour force' at

Table 14

DISTRIBUTION OF ESTIM ATED NUMBER OF MALE PERSONS IN RURAL AREAS OF AGE 5 YRS. & ABOVE BY CURRENT WEEKLY ACTIVITY FOR EACH USUAL ACTIVITY GROUP

(in lakhs)

Usual Status	*Current Weekly Activity Status*			
	Workers	*Unemployeds*	*Not in Labour Force.*	*Total*
Workers	8.22	0.13	0.14	8.49
Unemployeds	0.02	0.23	-	0.25
Not in Labour	0.02		4.18	4.20

the usual status level with those corresponding to the current Weekly status and Current Daily Status level. Hence, the content of underemployment of employed persons may be examined for 1981 on the basis of this concept.

The estimated number of male workers, unemployeds and number of persons (5 years & above) not in labour force in the rural sector of 1981 were 8.49 lakhs, 0.25 lakhs and 4.20 lakhs by usual status respectively. The following table will represent the break up in each case when Current Weekly Activity status is considered.

It is clear from the above table that within the fold of male workers by usual status nearly 13 thousands of male persons remain jobless or

Table-15

ESTIMATED NUMBER OF PERSONS (5 YRS. & ABOVE) NOT IN LABOUR FORCE BY USUAL STATUS IN 1981

(in lakhs)

Residence	*Male*	*Female*
Rural	8.20	7.25
Urban	0.37	0.12

without any work during a reference week (current weekly status). Similarly, portion from the unemployeds gets employment to a little extent, which may be recorded as the underemployment.

Not in Labour Force

In this connection the examination of the number of persons belonging to 5 yrs and above but not in labour force is very important. The proportion of number of persons not in labour force in 1981 has been presented here. The estimation is based on 32nd round report of N.S.S.

Similarly, the extent of 'not in labour force' may be ascertained in varying degrees when the Current Weekly and Current Daily Status are considered. Here, this exercise has been shown in the following table.

It is clear from the above table that number of persons is 'not in labour force' is increasing.

Table 16

ESTIMATED NUMBER OF PERSONS (5 YRS. & ABOVE) NOT IN LABOUR FORCE BY CURRENT WEEKLY & CURRENT DAILY STATUS IN 1981

(in lakhs)

Residence	*Male*		*Female*	
	C.W.S.	*C.D.S*	*C.W.S.*	*C.D.S.*
Rural	5.33	5.58	10.14	10.55
Urban	0.16	0.21	0.38	0.39

The employment situation has been delineated by N.S.S. in their 32nd round report from which it is possible to get an idea on the disaggregated figures on employment pattern of tribals in rural & urban areas by either sexes along with the nature of works.

Nature of works have been diverged between two broad categories a) agriculture, hunting, forestry and fishing and b) all sorts of non-agricultural activities. Further every category has its own branches resting on a number of activities. Of these activities those who 'sought work' and 'did not seek but was available for work' were identified as 'unemployed'. On the other hand i) educational institution going persons or mainly the students ii) the persons attended domestic duties only or housewives and women folk who used to collect vegetables, roots, fire wood, cattle feed for home consumption or spend time in sewing, tailoring, weaving for household purposes, iii) minors, school-going children and those who are seeking employment, iv) old and disabled persons, likewise v) rentiers, pensioners etc., vi) persons not attending work on account of temporary sickness along with vii) those who beg or women known as prostitutes and viii) other are included as 'outside labour force'.

And the rest who work as a self-employer either by cultivating in own land or engaged in manufacturing any other non-agricultural poroducts and simply pull on their livelihood depending on manual labour in exchange of wage, salary or obligation are known as 'employed'.

In this connection it may be mentioned that among the tribes the concept of 'begging' and 'prostitution' is totally absent. Both the acts

Table 17

DISTRIBUTION OF PERSONS (5 YRS. AND ABOVE) BY USUAL STATUS FOR EACH HOUSE HOLD GROUP AND SEX BY 1981.

(in lakhs)

Status	*Industry division*	*Rural*			*Urban*		
		Male	*Female*	*Total*	*Male*	*Female*	*Total*
Worker without any wage or salary	Not mentioned (Agri. workers)	0.48	-	0.48	0.01	-	0.01
Wage worker or salaried worker	Agriculture (Agri workers)	0.74	0.41	1.15	-	-	-
Worked as Casual Worker in other type of work	Agriculture (Agri. Workers)	3.62	2.86	6.48	0.07	0.03	0.01
Wage worker or salaried worker	Non agricultural industry	0.51	0.05	0.56	0.19	0.01	0.20
Work as Casual worker in other type of work	Non Agricultural industry	0.19	0.15	0.34	0.06	0.06	0.12
Casual worker or wage in public works	Non agricultural industry	0.01	0.01	0.02	-	-	-
Self-employed in cultivation including family members	Agriculture owner (cultivator)	3.15	0.87	4.02	0.01	0.02	0.03
Self-employed other than cultivation	Non-agricultural industry	0.09	0.04	0.13	0.03	0.01	0.04
Total No. of employed		8.49	4.42	12.71	0.37	0.13	0.50

are tabooed to them. However, the inclusion of such activities for the tribes is nothing but an incredible misunderstanding on the part of National Sample Survey. The existence of some figures (as stated for the rural males) in this category smacks of our apprehension of misclassification. It might have been recorded in other category. In addition it is to be noted again that the persons (including women) who usually collect food-stuff, firewood, etc., not necessarily use these for home consumption, but sell these out also in the market.

In view of the above discussion on persons in employment, unemployment and not in labour force a detailed break - up in employment by usual status has been furnished here for 1981 to assess the nature of employment.

To find out the extent of owner cultivator 'worked (self-employed) in household enterprises' and worked as helper in household enterprises' have been considered. With these the persons who 'did not work though there was work in household enterprise'[10] has been added. On the other hand quantum of agricultural laboures has been determined by the inclusion of 'working with an employer under obligation but work not specifically compensated by any wage or salary' and 'worked as casual labour in other type of work?' The former one is sometimes considered to measure the 'bonded labour' or 'unfree labour'. Besides,

Table 18

ESTIMATED NUMBER OF WORKERS OF AGE 5 YRS. & ABOVE AVAILABLE FOR ADDITIONAL WORK TO TOTAL WORKERS.

(in lakhs)

Year	*Rural*		*Urban*	
	Male	*Female*	*Male*	*Female*
1981	3.223	1.591	.097	.0254
1986	3.5768	1.746	.109	.0288
1991	3.975	1.965	.118	.031

'worked as regular salaried/wage or employee' and did not work but had regular salaried/wage employment' have been included.

Now before concluding the discussion one may look into the extent of under employment taking the present state of situation if persists in near future. As per N.S.S. all persons categorised as usually working may not be having work throughout the year or enough work in terms of quantum of work or in terms of money return from the occupation in which they are engaged. Therefore, the person categoried as usually working, is available or looking for additional work. Thus from the list of usually working persons a comprehensive account has been prepared on the basis of persons who were available for additional work at three different points of time'

From the above table it is revealed that intensity of unemployment as well as poverty is increasing day by day. With the advent of urbanisation, industrialisation rather sophisticated technology based modernisation this segment of rural population is lagging behind the appropriate employment absorption.

Regarding the estimation something more to add that the whole work is based on empirical studies.

ACKNOWLEDGEMENT

We express deep gratitude to Sri R.M. Banarjee and Sri T.K Nandy of Development & Planning Deptt., Govt. of West Bengal for their help and co-operation aand thanks to Shri P.Bhattacharya of National Sample Survey Organisation for his valuable suggestion.

References

State Planning, Board Govt. of West Bengal (1986) *Regional Development in Laterite Zone Birbhum, Bankura & Purulia.* Conference Report, Calcutta.

Report of the Commissioner for Scheduled Castes & Scheduled Tribes for the year 1977-78 Manager of Publications Civil Lines, Delhi.

Das, A.K. *et. al.* (1974), *The Role of Age groups in the determinationf of extend of Educational Achievements Bulletin of the Cultural Research Institute,* Scheduled Castes & Tribes Welfare Department, Govt. of West Bengal, *Vol, X No. 1 & 2.*

E.M. M. Directorate, Dev. & Planning Deptt., Govt. of West Bengal, 1984, *Report on the Evaluation Study on Primary Education in Rural West Bengal.*

E.M. & M. Directorate, Dev. & Planning Deptt., Govt. of West Bengal 1985 *Report on the Evaluation Study on Primary Education in Urban West Bengal.*

Sanyal, T.K. 1976. *In Search of World of Planning, Bulletin of the Cultural Research Institute*, Scheduled Castes & Tribes Welfare Deptt., Vol. XIII, No. 3 & 4.

E.M. & M.Directorate, Dev. & Planning Deptt., Govt. of West Bengal, 1976, *An Abstract of Manpower Statistics in West Bengal.*

Roy Burman, B.K. (1978) *Village Studies in the Census of India.* In the *Village studies in the Third World* Vol. I, (ed), Biplab Dasgupta, Hindustan Publishing Corporation of (India), Delhi.

Dantwala, M.L. (1979) *Rural Employment : Facts& Issues, Economic & Political Weekly*, Vol. XIV, No. 25.

National Sample Survey, Govt. of India, July, 1977 - June, 1978. *Pattern of Employment-unemployment Scheduled Castes & Scheduled Tribes population during late seventies* National Sample Survey 32nd Round.

State Planning Board, 1986, Report.

CHAPTER 8

An Appraisal of the Emerging Patterns of Leadership in Tribal Areas of Andhra Pradesh

*A. Joseph**

The leadership generally means the ability of a person which influences other people's behaviour in a desired way. Any community or organization has some influential heads to guide and lead them. Generally these leaders are of two types i.e., formal and informal. The formal leader plays his role with some authority while the informal leader influences other people's behaviour with his personal skills without any formally prescribed rules. By and large, leadership may be defined as 'the behaviour that effects the behaviour of other people more than their behaviour effect that of the leader'. The traditional leaders who dominated the tribal societies are generally formal leaders. This formal leadership predominantly steers and maintains social control in the tradition oriented societies and the informal leadership is not as potential as that of the formal. The traditional leadership is

* Reproduced by the permission of the authority of 'Man and Life' and Institute of Social Research and Applied Anthropology, Calcutta from 'Man and Life' 5(3&4) : 175-178, 1979.

dominant both in traditional and statutory institutions in tribal areas. The traditional leaders play their roles more effectively in traditional Kulapanchayats (Caste Councils) as their society delegates power and authority. But parallel to traditional Kulapanchayats, Statutory Gram Panchayats were introduced in tribal areas in the year 1962 which has a resilient political frame.

Traditional mechanism of Social Control

I. The Primitive Society is compact and its cohesion and solidarity is chiefly maintained and controlled by an unwritten law. Its functioning in a systematic manner is expected by every individual member of the society. Any act that causes disruption of social control and solidarity of the society is denounced by every individual of the tribal community. The tribal law imposes restrictions and principles which are free from malice and nepotism. All the individuals respect their unwritten social law. The hereditary leader or group of leaders play their roles effectively and do justice and they are always loyal to the next fellow man. They strive to ensure social security.

The modern democratic institutions which are introduced in tribal areas in the process of democratic decentralization for achieving socio-economic uplift, are the antiquities of tribal traditional institutions which safeguard the social code of conduct and ensure social security. The traditional Caste-Council of elders is known as "Kulapanchayat" in local parlance. This institution is prevalent among the tribal communities like Koya, Konda Reddi, Konda Dora and Konda Kapu of Rajavommangi and Buttayagudem Panchayat Samithis of East and West Godavari districts respectively. It is observed though the traditional council is common among these tribal communities, its constitution and functioning vary from tribe to tribe, for example, Konda Dora has a traditional council consisting of a single member who is known as "Kulapedda" and he is an authoritarian. He is assisted by two functionaries called "Dummari" and "Sarugudu". While "Dummari assists the Kulapedda in social functions, "Sarugudu" assists him in religious matters. Similar type of leadership is prevalent among Konda Reddy tribe. A traditional functionary locally known as "Chinnakapu" plays a role of an advisor to the "Peddakapu" in Kulapanchayat. In these two tribal groups "Kulapedda" (Pedda Kapu) is the dominant functionary both in religious and social life. Though the office of "Kulapedda"

(Pedda Kapu) is hereditary, a sort of democratic set up permeates in the mechanism of social control. The ''Kulapanchayat'' of Koya and Konda Kapu consists of five persons including Kulapedda and the traditional council is locally known as ''Panchi-Bai''. The office of Kulapedda is hereditary while the other four members are selected by the community elders and the tenure of office is life time. Kulapedda (Peddakapu) has no authority to appoint or select any subordinate member of his council and even his advice is seldom sought by the elders of the village to select any member. The selected person dedicates himself to the task for which he has been chosen and always tries to win the confidence of the people by virtue of his service. The leader always keeps congruent relations with the members of the village Kulapanchayat and avoid any sort of conflict with them.

II. The ''Inter-Village-Kulapanchayat'' is another traditional institution which has a large territory comprising 12 villages and it is known as Sumuthu' in local parlance among Koya tribe. It extends recognition of kinship-bond over a larger area than that of the village-Kulapanchayat. The Sumuthu' will have to meet on the appeal of an individual person who challenged the justice meted out by caste council at the village Kulapanchayat. When the justice of a particular village-Kulapanchayat is challenged by the appellant, the chief of that Kulapanchayat summons all hereditary leaders of various Grama-Kulapanchayat' in the Sumuthu' area. The leaders of village-Kulapanchayats will elect a leader to conduct deliberations at the Sumuthu'. Generally the leader at Sumuthu' will be elected unanimously considering his leadership qualities such as his ability, skill, act and assertiveness etc. He holds the right of office on *ad hoc* basis for that particular occasion only and it ceases itself when the `Sumuthu' is dissolved. The Sumuthu is convened at a village which is convenient to all the members.

The infrastructure of the tribal leadership is built on traditional authority, religious and social norms and personal abilities like age, traditional status, economic and educational status etc. In tribal areas, the leadership is traditionally vested with the institution of 'Kulapanchayat' which maintains the integrity of community by imposing social code of conduct, its members invariably abide by its decisions. Any disregard to such traditional authority is ruthlessly dealt with.

III. The introduction of Statutory Gram Panchayat in the tribal areas has added a new dimension to the leadership pattern, which was hitherto a tradition-bound one. The statutory system enables any individual to become a leader through adult-franchise. The woman, hitherto has been a taboo to occupy a seat of leadership in the traditional 'Kulapanchayat', is now competent to shoulder the leadership responsibilities in the village administration on par with man according to the statutory provisions of Andhra Pradesh Panchayat Act, 1959. According to the provisions of Sections-9 (1) a and (1) (IV) of Andhra Pradesh Gram Panchayat Act, 1959, a seat for woman member and a seat for Harijian candidate are reserved. The leadership pattern among tribal community is in transition i.e., from tradition to modernity. The changing situation called for certain prerequisites like traditional status, age, economic and social status, educational qualifications etc., for assuming leadership. In a study conducted in six Grama Panchayats of two Panchayat Samithis it was observed that most of the leaders elected to the statutory Panchayats, have had the above qualifications. The members elected to the Gram Panchayat were from various tribal groups and non-tribal communities. The non-tribal leaders who were elected to the statutory Panchayats represent six castes viz., Kapu, Kshatriya, Brahman, Kamsali, Mangali and Harijan while the tribal leaders represented four groups viz., Koya, Konda Dora, Konda Kapu and Kammara etc. By and large, the leadership is emerging from traditional to non-traditional sources. As a result of this transition process there are now three types of leadership functioning in tribal society i.e., traditional leaders of the traditional-councils, traditional leaders elected to statutory bodies and the non-traditional leaders elected to the statutory institutions. However, it is observed in most of the cases that traditional leaders of Kulapanchayat are elected to the statutory body while in some cases the traditional leaders sponsored their candidates to represent their respective community.

The tribal leaders elected to the statutory Panchayats in 1961 represented Koya, Konda Kapu and Konda Dora tribal groups in Rajavommangi Samithi while Koya, Konda Reddi and Kammara tribes in Buttayagudem Samithi area. In both samithi areas the tribal representation is 83.35% while the non-tribal representation is 14.65%.

The following trends are observed during the study. The traditional leadership continues to hold sway over the tribal society in maintaining the social order. Tribals are quite aware of the roles of traditional and statutory panchayats. While the former is to maintain social order, the latter is for implementing development programmes in their villages. They felt that both are equally important.

The traditional leaders elected to statutory bodies, became easy prey to non -tribal leaders who have vested interest and use their offices to exploit tribals.

1. It is observed, the traditional leaders elected to the statutory bodies have not evinced keen interest in implementing the Development Programmes. It is due to the fact that their outlook is mostly conservative and tradition-oriented and most of them are uneducated and illiterates ;

2. That some are of the opinion that informal leaders have emerged from educated and literate sections of the Tribal Communities while a majority continue to come from traditional leadership sources ;

3. That during the two elections (1962-64 and 1964-69) the majority of leaders elected to the statutory bodies are from traditional leaders only and it proved that the traditional leaders continue to hold their grip in the society.

4. The statutory bodies are playing a complementary role in respect of social values of the society. The traditional institutions both social and religious continue to exist without undergoing any basic changes.

5. The importance of the role of woman in tribal panchayats has been recognised. Even though the women are not allowed to participate in traditional panchayats, their presence in the statutory panchayat helped a lot and they are acting as diffusion agents of innovations in the tribal cultures.

6. The bulk of tribal traditional and non-traditional leaders elected to the statutory panchayats are in the effective control of few non-tribal leaders, excepting a few educated young leaders who are aware of the inducement of the non-tribal leaders. Due to

intrusion of this alien leadership the simple and pre-literate tribals are bound to accept that their age-old traditions are being jeopardized. Unless the old and passionate traditional leaders who are losing their grip, voluntarily concede to the emerging young, there is none to avert the thrust of the non-tribal dominance over the poorly informal tribal people. Let this be a beckoning call to the emerging youth and sinking old.

CHAPTER 9

Development of Curriculum for Tribal Students

L.R.N. Srivastava

The Framework of Curriculum

Tribal students constitute an important segment of the student population of India. The fact that they live in comparative isolation and not much educational development has taken place among them, calls for an effort to impart meaningful education to them so as to bridge the gulf that exists today between tribal and non-tribal students. In tribal culture transmission of knowledge takes place vertically from the older to the younger member of the society. But, lately, agents of change have been operating from different directions and changes are taking place at a speed with which tribal societies are not able to keep pace. Now in them the transmission of knowledge takes place horizontally from the informed to the uninformed regardless of age. Now a varied type of learning is becoming essential in order to be able to manipulate the new technology. With the increasing rate of culture change, it is becoming difficult to adapt the curriculum to the changing demands of the tribal society. This raises a great problem and challenge for the curriculum frames. The situation is further complicated by the fact that, at present, the different States and Union Territories of India have a common curriculum for both tribal as well as non-tribal students. The differences in their cultural values, ethos, needs and aspirations are not taken into account while developing the curriculum. The result is that the cultural values of tribal students are not reflected in the curriculum and education does not become meaningful.

In the contemporary educational process science and its application to technology has been a major and important force driving cultural and hence curricular changes. As more and more knowledge of science and technology permeates through the system, there grows a likelihood of a conflict between the scientific facts and cultural values, and a harmony has to be maintained between the two. And, hence, a curriculum which is culture-based and science-oriented will ideally suit tribal students.

Education of tribal students, however, cannot be conceived of as separate from the general framework of education meant for the country as a whole. The tribes live in distinct physical and social environment with different patterns of culture. As such, while the general objectives of education could remain the same, its content may require modifications to suit their needs. The attributes of modernization have not yet made themselves manifest in many tribal societies and life in them is much simpler and unsophisticated. Therefore, it is desirable that education for them should be in tune with the prevailing situations there. For many tribal children elementary education is terminal. Even though the body of knowledge given and skills imparted at his level is not of any significant dimension, yet they may be sufficient to meet their socio-cultural needs.

Tribal societies are stable, and change in them takes place slowly. Nevertheless no tribesmen dies in the world in which he was born. Now ideas and concepts come to tribal areas gradually and are adopted by the tribal people in course of time. A curriculum should keep pace with time and should be revised from time to time. Since tribal culture is stable, there would be no need of constant revision and remodelling of the curriculum as is necessary in the case of curriculum for non-tribal students in whose areas change takes place at a much faster rate. It would also make the curriculum burdensome if all new ideas and concepts which are of passing importance are incorporated in it.

Owing to a tremendous development in science and technology, the total stock of knowledge to be imparted has increased manifold. While it would be necessary to impart a bulk of this knowledge to tribal students as well so that they do not lag behind others, it is also essential to ensure that this body of knowledge does not create socio-cultural imbalances in tribe societies. The content of education imparted to them should not be such as to uproot them from their moorings and cultural milieu.

It is true that even the remote tribal areas may not remain unaffected with the advances made in the field of science and technology. New scientific facts may come in direct conflict with established cultural values. Scientific knowledge may bring in new occupations and new opportunities and destroy or alter the existing ones. Tribal students may have to be prepared to face these facts. Children of today may have to come face to face with new situation when they become adults. To meet all such situations students would not only have to be imparted scientific knowledge and skills in manipulating the technology but also a scientific attitude will have to be developed in them. But, at the same time, it has to be ensured that buffers are built to absorb the shock the established cultural values will receive from new scientific knowledge. The curriculum has to be taken into consideration the above factors as well.

A child in a tribal society, which is simple and unsophisticated, does not need a large body of knowledge to meet his socio-economic needs. He is not at all bothered about the contemporary needs of another society which are not going to have any lasting influence on him or his immediate environment. It is conceded that in the modern world there is enough to learn, but simply because of this we need not unnecessarily load the information bag which he has to carry, and drive him out of the educational system. In what follows an attempt has been more to give some indication of the content that should go into the curriculum for tribal students. These are only illustrative and not exhaustive. With a little understanding of tribal life and culture it may not be difficult to make the curriculum interesting and attractive to tribal children

Language

Language is the main vehicle of communication. One of the main hurdles in devising an affective educational programme for the tribes has been the unwillingness to use their languages as media of instruction. The constitution provides for imparting of education at the primary stage in the mother-tongue. This has also been the recommendation of different commissions, committees and experts. There is therefore, no reason why an exception should be made in the case of tribal children. A simple operational plan may make imparting meaningful education to them easier. In class I, the medium of instruction may be the total tribal language. In the second half the process may be reversed. Regular teaching through the regional language may start from the third year. Instructions in the first year may be imparted through tribal folksongs, folktales, riddles, proverbs etc. A small primer in tribal languages may be used.

The general objectives of teaching mother-tongue cannot be different for tribal children. But these objectives can be achieved only when they are taught through their own mother-tongue. Non-teaching through the mother-tongue has resulted in a large scale wastage and stagnation, and a gradual fall in the standards of tribal students. It is, however, realised that paucity of literature and textbooks in tribal languages will, for the time being, come in the way of teaching through tribal mother-tongue. But, as and when the tribal dialects are developed and more literature produced, it would be easier to teach through their languages.

In order to ensure that tribal students do not get isolated teaching of and through regional language will also become necessary. Since the text-book in tribal mother-tongue will, of necessity, be written in the script of regional language, the tribal child will become familiar with the script of the regional language in the course of the first two years, and thus it may not be difficult for him to pick up in class III the regional language in both oral and written forms.

It is possible that some of the sounds of the tribal languages may not be represented through the alphabet of the regional language. To do so, diacritical marks may be used. The content of the lessons in textbooks for classes I and II may be heavily drawn from tribal life, tribal village, their social, political and economic institutions, folk songs, folk tales and so on. Description and functions of such tribal institutions as the priest, magician, head-man, ritual expert, professional mourner and such other key personnel who regulate the village life, may also be included in the content. It would be necessary to balance the content in textbooks for classes III, IV and V in such a way that information about the life and culture of both tribal and non-tribal communities is reflected. This would enable the two communities to come together and create among them an awareness of each other's life. Correct and precise knowledge of each other's life will lead to quicker national integration rather than the distorted picture that is generally presented before the non-tribal students about their tribal counterparts.

However brilliant and imaginative the curriculum may be, it is the teacher who will make it really functional. In order that the curriculum is implemented in letter and spirit, the teacher should invariably know the tribal language.

Mathematics

Mathematics is a subject considered very tough by tribal children. This results in their consistently poor performance in it. Efforts may be made to make its teaching as interesting and simple as possible. While the concept may be developed the same way, instances and illustrations to explain and solve problems may be drawn heavily from the local tribal areas. Illustrations of different types of modern gadgets which are unknown and totally irrelevant to their daily needs, may be avoided. The concept of number, as indeed all other mathematical concepts, may be woven round the everyday life of the people.

Social Studies

The objective of teaching social studies may be the same for tribal and non-tribal children except that in the case of the former emphasis may be laid more on family and kin groups. Similarly, knowledge about the immediate environment should precede knowledge about the neighbouring areas, the district, the state and the country and, lastly, knowledge about the world. Tribal ideas of creation of the world, the sun, the moon and other celestial bodies, natural objects and living beings may be highlighted. The degree of modified, natural objects and living beings may be highlighted. The degree of modification of the content for tribal students should largely depend on the stage of development of a particular tribal area.

Imparting of knowledge may begin from the known to the unknown. Lessons may begin from the family and the community and emphasis may be laid on economic cooperation and interdependence between them, and the division of labour among the members of the family. From family one may proceed to the school and the community. In order to maintain a link between the family and the school, the latter may be conceived of as a bigger family. The problems of how to bring about understanding with the other non-tribal children may also be discussed.

In any discussion of the village life, it would be appropriate to first make the child conversant with the basic features of his own village. He should be made aware of the precautions he has to take against different types of dangers, particularly from wild animals, jungle fire, swollen rivers, land-slides, earthquakes and such other natural calamities which often befall him. While discussing the neighbouring villages, the distinctive feature of the two may be highlighted not to create any discrimination but to bring to focus the differences in the living patterns of the two communities.

There has been tremendous development in the modes of transport. The invention of the wheel has totally revolutionised the transport system, but in many tribal societies the wheeled transport system has not yet made itself manifest. In fact, in many areas no transport system exists and human back is still an important means to carry goods. Lessons on modern means of transport like scooter, car, steam and electric trains, and air planes will have less significance for tribal students. Communications through word of mouth still prevails in tribal areas. Telegraph, telephone, wireless, radio and television will take a long time to appear in all the tribal areas. Therefore, while discussing the transport and communication system, the local modes of transport and communication need not be lost sight of.

There are no professional craftsmen in tribal areas. The tribesmen take upon themselves the function of basket maker, weaver, wood carver, barber, smith and so on. Since these institutions do not exist independently discussion about their roles and functions as part of the professional caste system would not be understandable to tribal students. and may be avoided.

Advancement made by the society should also be discussed from the earliest stage of development of man. Information on how the early man lived in cave, hut or on tree top and subsisted on hunting and fishing; different types of tools and use of fire; man's early clothing from tree leaves, grass and animal's skin and ultimately from cotton and synthetic fabric; domestication of animals and raising of crops; and such other relevant aspect of tribal life could be used as textual material for illustrating the gradual development of man and society.

Agriculture is the basic occupation of the tribes. Hence, the concept of shifting, terrace and permanent cultivation on scientific lines and the tools associated with them would be the first thing to be taught under agriculture. It is well-known that even a small tribal child is conversant with the different agricultural operations. Small but significant improvements made in the tools and techniques of the traditional type of cultivation may be usefully brought to their notice. Local manures and fertilizers alongwith the effectiveness of the latter in increased production may also be usefully taught.

The diverse nature of the social, political and economic life of different communities may be explained to them in the context of the diversity of the Indian society. The democratic values, the concepts of secularism and socialism, which are no less significant to tribes themselves, may also be included at this stage. The role played by the freedom fighters including those from tribal areas, may be highlighted. This would instil in them a pride for their own freedom fighters, and they will feel that they too has a role to play in achieving the independence of the country.

While discussing the political life of the country tribal customary law, tribal concepts of crime and punishment, the traditional village council etc. should not be ignored.

General Science

Teaching of general science may follow two important principles namely, relating the teaching to the environment of the child and avoidance of the reference of situations and findings which militate against tribal cultural heritage. In stipulating these principles it is not desired that scientific knowledge should be kept away from them but that the content should be useful. Teaching of the subject would need great tact and imagination on the part of the teacher. Schools in tribal areas are generally devoid of scientific apparatuses, models, charts, equipments etc. The students may, at times, find that the scientific explanation of natural phenomena is at variance with the cultural explanation. It would thus be essential to avoid bringing any conflict between scientific facts and cultural values. Cultural interpretation of natural phenomena may have to be reinterpreted in scientific terms. The local environment should invariably act as the laboratory for teaching science. Creating and fostering scientific attitudes should be as important as disseminating scientific knowledge. Knowledge about the constitution and function of human body can precede knowledge about health and hygiene. Emphasis may be laid on development of healthy habit and sense of cleanliness both social as well as physical rather than on imparting knowledge of facts. The concept of cleanliness often varies as widely as the concept of beauty. A clean and white set of teeth may not always be regarded as beautiful in tribal societies. Attempts are made to blacken the teeth to make them beautiful. Knocking out and filling of teeth are also resorted to in order to make them beautiful. Tattooing may be considered hideous by one society, beautiful by another. Thus the concept of beauty and cleanliness as prevalent in one society may not be accepted in another. Therefore, while imparting such knowledge of cleanliness and beauty aids, the local concepts may be taken into consideration.

Tribal houses may not fulfil all the essential requirements of modern living. But they are functional. Absence of windows in tribal houses is very conspicuous. The necessity of having windows in the house for the purpose of getting light and fresh air need not be discussed as a matter of routine, but in the context of local climate and tribal belief that provision of windows in the house is an open invitations to the malevolent spirits to enter the house and trouble the inmates. Non-existence of any ventilators has also led to severe criticism of the design of the tribal houses. But this again should be considered in the context of the utility of smoke in destroying the insects which eat away the building material very soon. But such resistance to modern and scientific way of living may have to be broken by explaining the comparative dangers and disadvantages and not just by denouncing the ways of living of the tribal people.

Plants and animals are part and parcel of tribal living. There are a number of plants which have medicinal values. There are plants which are used as poison for fishing and hunting. Though with widespread hunting and coming in of modern arms and ammunitions, the number of animals left in the jungles is few, their value in tribal economy and rituals is nonetheless important. The widespread use of animal flesh for eating and equally widespread taboo on taking animal milk are basic features of tribal life. Textual material explaining the use of plants and animals should also take into consideration these aspects of tribal culture.

Socialy Useful Productive Work

The tribal child is an economic unit of the family. To make education attractive for him and his parents it needs to be linked up with his economic development. Only after a few years of schooling his parents expect to derive some economic advantage out of his education. This objective can be achieved by making education productive by introducing meaningful programmes of socially useful productive work. Such programmes need not be an end in themselves but should be conceived of as a process through which knowledge of other subjects can be imparted. In tribal societies knowledge and skill are imparted through different types of activities and observation. Education through different activities would thus be effective there.

Simple knowledge and skill connected with cleaning of personal belongings; cleaning and repair of agricultural implements; stringing of musical instruments, making of hunting and fishing implements; cleaning of ornaments and dresses, erection of water supply system, building of youth dormitorics and the like may be imparted. Also skills in manipulation of local material in preparation of bow and arrow, plough, sickle handle, axe and hoe, bamboo vessels and containers and such other utilitarian goods may be imparted. Some tribal societies are also adept in textile designing and wood carving. These have great economic potential and finished goods may bring a handsome return. It is thus clear that socially useful productive work activities should, by and large, be confined to activities which are socially and economically relevant in a particular area and in undertaking of which local material could be used. There will be no sense in introducing activities which would need importing of raw material from outside, as happened in the case of basic education programmes under which spinning was introduced throughout the country irrespective of the fact whether a particular area grew cotton or not.

Health Education

The contents of health education for tribal students is to be such as to give them an adequate knowledge of the various types of known and unknown diseases, precautions to be taken against them and the remedial measures. With the recent influx of non-tribal population in tribal areas many diseases unknown to the people have also crept in. They are not equipped to fight them and very easily succumb to them. The tribal child may be made aware of such diseases and how to guard against them.

Cleanliness can be affected not only through soaps. Use of local cleaning agents and detergents need not be discouraged. Children should also be made aware of the difference in bathing for cleaning and cooling. Something can also be said in favour of tribal habit of spitting in fire. This immediately destroys the bacteria in their sputum and prevents the spreading of diseases. Apparently it may appear to be a 'dirty' habit but it has its own importance. The danger of using water from the source which has been used by the cattle should be emphasised. Tuberculosis, venereal diseases, skin diseases and goitre are rampant in tribal areas. Instead of giving general information on diseases which are not prevalent there information about the above and how to fight them would be more useful. What is more important is to create a healthy habit and attitude rather than giving lectures on how to keep the body and the village clean.

CHAPTER 10

Social Processes in An Emerging Tribal Displacement Situation in Southern Rajasthan*

N.N.Vyas

In the wake of construction of Kadana Dam forming a part of inter-state Mahi-Bajaj Sagar Project of Gujarat and Rajasthan, a large Bhil tribal belt is going to be affected. The site of the Dam is at Kadana, an erstwhile princely State which lies in the Panchmahal district of Gujarat. The Project is the result of inter-state agreement between the States of Rajasthan and Gujarat, for harnessing the river Mahi, which rises in the Southern slopes of the Vindhya's and flows in Madhya Pradesh, Rajasthan and Gujarat. As the construction of Dam is proposed

* The paper is based on the field observations of the author during 1972-73 ; views expressed are of the author and not necessarily reflect Govt. policy.
{VYAS N.N.: Kadana Dam Towards Understanding of Among the Tribals 'TRIBE', Vol. VI, 1969, Tribal Research Institute, Udaipur (Raj).}
Reproduced by the permission of the authority of the Journal Man and Life, Vol. III, No. 3& 4, 1977 pp 101-108.

to be completed by 1977, the process of rehabilitation programmes have been speeded up in both the Sates to meet the new emerging social situation.

The paper analyses the various social processes among the indigenous population that are taking place as a result of emerging displacement situation.

Primarily the present analysis through case study of two villages on the adjoining border of Rajasthan and Gujarat, (which are going to be partially affected due to sub-mergence) identifies various processes and elaborate the effects of associated social variables on qualitative changes. While analyzing social variables, it is proposed to discuss the effect and planned economic action.

SOCIO-ECONOMIC ASPECTS OF SUBMERGENCE

The construction of Kadana Dam will affect some 5940 families consisting of about 30,000 residents of 132 villages. Of the affected people about 20,000 are tribals.

The Pre-displacement Situations

Out of three tehsils of Dungarpur and Banswara district in Rajasthan only one tehsils of Sagwara in Dungarpur has been selected for examining the various processes. The percentage of Scheduled Tribe to total population in this tehsil is 57.05 per cent. The literacy rate is 16.37 per cent and percentage of workers is 20.08 as against 71.92 per cent non-workers. The female participation in the economic activity is as low as 6.28 per cent in the tehsil.

Of 262 villages in the tehsil, 48 affected villages are in the belt of river. Mahi, which spread over in the tehsil from Galiakot (a famous pilgrimage centre of Dawdy Bohra sect) to the end touching Santrampur taluka of Panchmahal district of Gujarat. Of these in 9 villages only govt. land is affected with no loss to public property. In remaining 39 villages the house property, and land is affected.

Contours of Displacement in Sampled tehsil

According to the revenue records total acreage of land in 39 villages is 47531.10. The total households going to be affected is 2296 with 4258.76 acres of land likely to come under sub-mergence, of which 63.36 per cent is irrigated.

Out of 2296 affected households, 524 will have house property affected, which belongs to only two villages and will require rehabilitation. 13 household are lend-less with house property affected, 1775 households will have only land affected.

In the first category of houses affected, 14 tribal villages will be affected which will require rehabilitation. Of these 14 villages, one will have 88.24 per cent households, affected, in 9 villages the households being affected are in the range between 20-60 per cent, 3 villages will have approximately 11-4 per cent of households affected. In second category of land less but houses affected approximately 1-3 per cent will be affected in two villages. In the third category households having their land affected are found in all the 39 villages.

The Proposed Economic Action

Under the scheme of rehabilitation it is estimated that 1.50 crores of rupees will be spent towards rehabilitation and payment of compensation to displaced persons. So far Rs. 1.50 crores is understood to have been paid to oustees. 2000 displaced persons have also been given 7200 hectares of land. About 1500 families from Galiakot will be resettled in nearby area. The Rajasthan Land Acquisition Act, 1953 provides compensation award as per valuation of houses, wells and trees. 10 per cent additional charge is also proposed to be paid as soletium as a token of compulsory acquisition of land. 2 per cent is proposed to be paid towards transportation. Landholders retaining less than 15 bighas of land after sub-mergence is proposed to be allotted at least 15 bighas of land.

DISPLACEMENT AND SOCIO-POLITICAL PROCESSES

At the initial stage, people did not believe that they are going to be displaced from their land and homestead. It was only after preparation of the lists of affected households were finalized, they started adjusting with the new emerging situation. The people who were indifferent so far started making adjustments in bargaining their properties with government at individual level.

There was no organized move at inter village or inter/intra community level to press their view-point in this matter, though inner rivalries and tension were noticed but villagers were not vocal. Tribals have their own conflicting interests and ambivalent attitude which they only whisper among themselves but never beyond village level.

Some of the village level meetings convened at the initiative of elected and traditional leaders, organized efforts came into forefront to register their protests through an organization called Kadana Dam Dub Kshetra Sahyog Mandal, Chikhli, Distt,. Dungarpur. The organization proposed to safeguard the interest of the oustees and pool necessary information and records from available sources for the help the oustees. According to them the main purpose of the Kadana Dam is to raise the living standards and displaced tribals should also be guaranteed a fair and equitable share of the developmental benefits, particularly since the reason for their removal is to enable Government to get profit from major irrigation and power generation projects.

Therefore oustees should be assisted in every possible manner to earn new means of living elsewhere.

The Mandal proposes to help the State Govt., in plan of rehabilitation of the oustees, before area is submerged. The Mandal also proposes to get the similar benefits as given to their brethren in Gujarat. In Gujarat compensations to the oustees of Kadana have been proposed to be paid in three instalments. Compensation of land in Gujarat for 'A' category of land is Rs. 1020 per acre, for 'B' category Rs.930/, per acre, and for 'C' category which includes 'Rakhed' or barren land the compensation fixed was Rs. 815/-. The Gujarat Government has also decided to reserve 15% of the compensation for the purpose of reclamatiomn and for other developmental needs. The criteria of allotting 10 bighas of free land has been adopted in addition of compensation to be paid. The Gujarat Government has also set up an Kadana Dub Niraman Sahkari Samiti under the auspices of Social welfare Department, in which officials and semi-officials are members.

The Mandal also wanted the Government to provide essential relief until the oustees harvest his first crop, simultaneously ownership right on the submerged land should also be retained, so that they may continue bed cultivation in the reservoir area, after water level lowers down, so that they may have best of both the situations. All these demands of the Mandal reflect, the inner tensions and dilemmas of the local population. No inter village rallies or organized rallies to protect their demands were noticed. Persons with political contacts at the district level have not shown alliance between the local traditional elite and political elite at the district level.

INSTITUTIONAL RESPONSE TO NEW SITUATION

A preliminary observation and interview with tribal folk of the two villages of Bavdi and Badgama, which are going to be partially affected reveals the inner tension and anxieties. The villages are situated on the belt of river Mahi, which demarcates natural boundary between Rajasthan and Gujarat States. Across the river villages of Khedpa and Bhalesimal are situated on the adjoining border of Gujarat in the Santrampur taluka of Panchmahal district. The only connecting link between these inter-state neighbouring villages is through a boat, owned by two tribals each belonging to village of Gujarat and Rajasthan respectively. The boat is operated on the basis of traditional Jajmani System. The Bhil inhabitants of Salakari village (in Rajasthan) go daily on the other side across the river in the neighbouring village of Khedpa in Gujarat to see their relatives and for daily purchases, which is much nearer and more economical, rather than go to village Bohra in nearby village Bavdi situated is at the distance of six miles.

The village Khedpa, a Bhil village on the adjoining border (in Gujarat) is not only a communication and marketing point, but largely offers social opportunities to maintain old ties. These social ties are reflected through marriage relations and fruits of cooperations and conflicts are mutually shared by them.

The Bhils of these villages prefer to marry their daughters in adjoining village of Gujarat, as they feel their daughters to be more happy because of the relative prosperity of the area. They also prefer to bring daughters from Gujarat as they prove to be better housewives. The tribals of these affected villages do not go beyond the nearby village of Chikhli (in Rajasthan) which is 15 miles from the village Salakari

Taking kinship and marital relations as social variable it was tried to trace the interconnections between the neighbouring tribal communities under displacement situation and also the social effect on the quantitative changes on oustees as a result of economic action. During the year 1971-72 after the first instalment of cash compensation was awarded to the tribal oustees of Gujarat on the adjoining border, the first thing they did was to celebrate the marriages of old and younger ones. It was reported that more than 60 marriages took place in a single village, at the increased rate of *dapa* (bride price) ranging between 1500-2000 rupees, whereas the prevailing rate of dapa is between 800-1200 only. According to selected respondents the local Sahukara and Bohara had flourishing business in village Chikhli.

The tribals of Salakari and Badgama villages (in Rajasthan) also borrowed money from relatives in Gujarat to celebrate marriages of their sons and daughters, as it might not be possible for them to find suitable match, in their kin group after the neighbuoring villages are submerged. Their fear of displacement resulted in the increase of child marriage (which is un-common among the Bhils) and efforts towards strengthening of inter-community and kinship relations in shortest possible time.

In the Bhil Society the land and the house form a focus of family support and identity which Bhils are reluctant to give up. This means that there primary interests need not be new economic opportunities but in preserving their land as an entity. Maintenance of existing relations and not expansion is important, as social mobility is limited, and solidarity and identity of the family still form an important value.

Another social variable was social custom and tradition. The major effect of cash awards to oustees of bordering villages of Gujrarat has been that they spent money on the death feast or Katya's as part of obligation towards deceased, which they have been postponing due to poverty and economic hardship. Because of their bad economy, as a normal practice they try to preserve the Kathli (bed made of bamboos and sticks on which the body of deceased was laid and carried for funeral) as token of old obligations to be repiad towards the deceased.

Since neighbouring Gujarat villages serves as centre of goods and brides exchange, the social and economic activities of the Bhils in these villages are guided and inspired by their relatives on the other side, especially when they were also given the compensation in cash.

A further social variable is associated with occupational status where young members of tribal group do not mind opting for non-agricultural occupation, the old people like to remain on their farms and merely want to keep going. It was with this view that there reaction towards shift was attempted. A group of outstees of village Badgama on being asked, whether they would like to be settled in colonies expressed their own fears. According to them even their existing scattered pattern of settlement does not provide any opportunity to reduce interpersonl disputes which occur quite often between them, therefore how can they live peacefully if forced to live in a clustered manner which is not a part of their traditional pattern.

The older folks of the village were interested in bed cultivation, which according to them can be made available at least fo one crop in reservoir area due to back water effect. According to them the evacuees of Vanak Mori pick-up have been cultivating the uncovered land known as pata-kasht. They were desirous to have compensation as well as ownership right for such a type of cultivation. As large number of villages are going to be partially affected, they were interested in retaining their lands for bed cultivation. But according to National Project rules one mile surrounding of the reservoir area has to be left un-occupied for reasons of backwater effect.

Thus there is a tendency of the older folk to keep going in the existing settlement, because they may still have benefit of the existing farm as focus for family relations and security, while obtaining all material benefits of being displaced.

As against this younger population is interested to go elsewhere provided they are given new economic opportunities since traditional form of life seems to many of them to be one with long term future. Though they expressed their desire to have new economic opportunities, they were unwilling to shift from present place before they had eaten last grain from the present fields after total submergence. Such expressions also indicate confusion and lingering uncertainty about future, which they have been able to overcome during pre-displacement situation.

Displacement of people due to the construction of dams is a nation wide problem. Generally the property, land and houses of the displaced persons are evaluated and compensation is fixed. In principle it may sound logical that oustees be paid compensation in cash. The experience of other places shows that little land was purchased by displaced persons, with the result money was misspent and when it was all spent people were worse off than they were before the construction of dam. The State Government is assuming responsibility for rehabiliation of people, rendered landless and homeless through this project. The rehabilitation of 5000 families will be over by the end of 1975 and remaining 2500 families will be resettled next year.

Land is not merely property to tribals but also means of employment. The tribals who are deprived of their land needs to be compensated for the loss of work opportunity also, as there are always tenants, share-croppers, who are not deprived of land ownership, but loss of work opportunity.

Most of the rehabilitation programmes that country has been, as a result of national project, largely failed because oustees were not properly motivated, guide for future resettlement with the result compensation money was eaten away on unproductive items. They need to be assisted in every possible manner to earn new means of living elsewhere.

Looking to the proceses operating to preserve the system of maintenance one may doubt whether economic action and increase of material incentives to displaced tribals would have long term effect in leading them to invest or produce more unless they are properly motivated to meet changing conditions.

CHAPTER 11

Tribal Education In India Progress And Problem

Manis Kumar Raha

The stalwarts, humanists and wisemen of Indian politics who were involved in framing up the Constitution of India, gave much thought over the problems of the Scheduled Tribes of India and kept significant provisions for the uplif and betterment of the existing miserable condition of the tribal people most of whom still now live much below the poverty line. While Article 342 of the Constitution has kept provision for notification of the Scheduled Tribes, Article 366(25) has defined Scheduled Tribes as 'such tribes or tribal communities or parts of or groups within such tribes or tribal communities as are deemed under Article 342 to be Scheduled Tribes for the purpose of this Constitution'. While Articles 15, 16, 19 and 20 dealing with the fundamental rights of the Indian populations, have authorised different States to adopt special provisions for the advancement of different Backward Classes people, Article 332 provides reservations of seats for the Scheduled Tribes in the Parliament and State Legislative Assemblies. Claims of the Scheduled Tribes to services and posts have also been guaranteed. Article 338 has provisions for the post of Special Officer for the

Scheduled Castes and Scheduled Tribes to look after their interest. Article 244 (1 & 2) read with Fifth Schedule Part A and C, deals with the administration of Scheduled Areas and Tribal Areas. Part B of the Fifth Schedule provides the establishment of Tribes Advisory Council. Article 275 has given opportunity to the States to draw grant-in-aid from the Consolidated Fund of India for the welfare of the Scheduled Tribes, and so on. Thus we see that the Constitution of India has enough provisions to safeguard the interest of the tribal people and also to uplift their deplorable conditions through different welfare schemes. Identically Article 46 of the Constitution is looking after the educational development of the Scheduled Tribes. It states,

"The State shall promote with special care the educational and economic interests of the weaker sections of the people and in particular, of the Scheduled Castes and the Scheduled Tribes, and protect them from social injustice and all forms of exploitation."

With the commencement of the Constitution, special assistance has been given and special care has been taken to promote educational standard among the Scheduled Tribes. Free education, tuition fees, hostel fees, distribution of the text books, reservation of seats in the schools, colleges, technical institutions and Universities etc. are part of such facilities granted specially to the scheduled Tribes students so as to enable them to achieve a greater momentum towards the development of their education. A number of schools and hostels has also been constructed in the tribal areas to reach education to their door steps and to facilitate the tribal students to receive easy education.

Though there is specific provisions for the promotion of educational status of the Scheduled Tribes, in our Constitution and in spite of the grant of special facilities to the tribals for the promotion of the education among these people, if we analyse the rate of achievement in the field of literacy among the Scheduled tribes since the day the Constitution came into force, we shall definitely not get a very happy and satisfactory picture though no doubt a huge sum of money has been spent on account of the tribal education.

In order to show the progress in the tribal education I have analysed census data of three decades, 1961, 1971 and 1981 on the literacy among the Scheduled Tribes of India as well as of different States and Union

Territories. The achievement on this line can clearly be seen from these analyses. I have also compared the literacy data of the Scheduled Tribes with those of the general mass of India and also of different States and Union Territories to show how far behind our tribal brethren are staying in literacy in comparison to the people of India in general. I have also tried to show the achievement in literacy among individual tribes. At the end I have discussed about the problems and constraints those hinder the promotion of education among these people.

But before I go into the analysis let us see the population strength of the Scheduled Tribes in India and its distribution in different States and Union Territories in different decades. According to 1961 Census 6.87 per cent of total Indian population belonged to the Scheduled Tribes. In the States and Union Territories like Madras (Tamil Nadu), Mysore (Karnataka) and Punjab the strength of the Scheduled Tribes was below 1.00 per cent of the total population of the respective States and Union Territory. Next come Andhra Pradesh and Kerala where they lie between 1.00 and 5.00 per cent. Their strength was between 5.01 and 10.0 per cent of the total population in Bihar, Maharashtra, West - Bengal and Himachal Pradesh. Assam, Gujarat and Rajasthan are the States where the Scheduled Tribes share between 10.01 and 20.00 per cent of the total population of that States. State and Union Territories where the Scheduled Tribes cover between 20.01 and 35.00 per cent of the total population, are Madhya-Pradesh, Orissa, Andaman and Nicobar islands Manipur and Tripura. In Laccadive, Minicoy and Amindivi island (97.03 per cent), Dadra and Nagar Haveli (88.43 per cent), North East Frontier Agency (Arunachal Pradesh) and Nagaland (88.59 and 93.09 per cent respectively) more than 80.00 per cent of their population belong to the Scheduled Tribes according to 1961 Census.

Again States and Union Territories like Kerala, Madras (Tamil Nadu), Mysore (Karnataka), Punjab, Andaman and Nicobar Islands, Manipur, Dadra and Nagar Haveli and NEFA (Arunachal - Pradesh) the strength of the Scheduled Tribes population was below 1.00 per cent of the total Scheduled Tribe population in India. Andhra Pradesh, Assam, Gujarat, Maharashtra, Rajasthan, West Bengal, Tripura and Nagaland have between 1.01 and 10.00 per cent and Bihar and Orissa between 10.01 and 15.00 per cent. The State of Madhya Pradesh possesses the highest number of the Scheduled Tribe population (22.13 per cent out of the total Scheduled Tribe population in India.

From the returns of the Census of India, 1971 it is revealed that the Scheduled Tribes secure only 6.82 per cent of the total population of India. They remained below 1.00 per cent of the total population of the States like Karnataka, Tamil Nadu, Uttar Pradesh and Union Territory of Goa, Daman and Diu, but range between 1.00 and 5.00 per cent in Andhra Pradesh, Himachal Pradesh and Kerala. In Bihar, Maharashtra and West Bengal they cover between 5.01 and 10.00 per cent Gujarat, Rajasthan and Andaman and Nicobar islands have between 10.01 and 20.00 per cent. Between 20.01 and 30.00 per cent of the total Scheduled Tribe population are found in each of Madhya Pradesh, Manipur, Orissa and Tripura. But each of Meghalaya (80.48 per cent), Nagaland (88.61 per cent), Arunachal Pradesh (79.02 per cent), Dadra and Nagar Haveli (86.89 per cent), and Mizoram (94.26 per cent) has more than 75.00 per cent of each of the total population as the Scheduled Tribe population.

Again according to 1971 Census each of the States and Union Territories like Himachal Pradesh, Kerala, Manipur, Mysore (Karnataka), Tamil Nadu, Uttar Pradesh, Andaman and Nicobar, Dadra and Nagar Haveli, Goa, Daman and Diu and Laccadive, Minicoy and Amindivi islands has less than 1.00 per cent each of the total scheduled Tribe population in India. Again Andhra Pradesh, Meghalaya, Nagaland, Tripura and Arunachal Pradesh range between 1.00 and 5.00 per cent, between 5.01 and 10.00 per cent of the total Scheduled Tribe population is found in each of Assam, Gujarat. Maharashtra, Rajasthan and West Bengal. The highest number of these people are found in Madhya Pradesh(22.06 per cent) followed by Orissa (13.34 per cent) and Bihar (12.97 per cent).

According to 1981 Census India has 7.76 per cent of her population as the Scheduled Tribes. Among the States and Union Territories Uttar Pradesh and Goa, Daman and Diu have Scheduled Tribe population below 1.00 per cent of the total population there. Himachal Pradesh, Kerala and Tamil Nadu range between 1.00 and 5.00 per cent. Within the range between 5.01 and 10.00 per cent fall Andhra Pradesh, Bihar, Maharashtra and West Bengal. Each of Gujarat, Rajasthan and Andaman and Nicobar island has Scheduled Tribe population ranging between 10.01 and 20.00 per cent of the total population of the State and Union Territory. Madhya Pradesh, Manipur, Orissa, Sikkim and Tripura are keeping Scheduled Tribes ranging from

20.01 to 30.00 per cent of the total population there. But the rest of the States and Union Territories like Meghalaya (80.58 per cent), Nagaland (83.99 per cent), Arunachal Pradesh (69.82 per cent), Dadra and Nagar Haveli (78.82 per cent), Lakshadweep (93.82 per cent) and Mizoram (93.53 per cent) have more than 69.00 per cent each.

Again when we examine the numerical position of the Scheduled Tribes in different States and Union Territories comparison to the total Scheduled Tribes of India, we see that Himachal Pradesh, Kerala. Manipur, Sikkim, Uttar Pradesh, Andaman and Nicobar Islands, Arunachal Pradesh, Dadra and Nagar Haveli, Goa, Daman and Diu, Lakshadweep and Mizoram have each below 1.00 per cent of the total Scheduled Tribe population in India. Identically Karnataka, Meghalaya, Nagaland, Tamil Nadu and Tripura have each between 1.01 and 5.00 per cent of the total Scheduled Tribe population in India. The strength of these population ranging from 5.01 to 10.00 per cent is found in the States like Andhra Pradesh, Gujarat, Rajasthan and West Bengal, Bihar, Maharashtra and Orissa share between 10.01 and 15.00 per cent each. Madhya Pradesh has the highest frequency of 23.22 per cent of the total Scheduled Tribe population in India.

According to 1961 census (Table-1) it is clear that the literacy rate among the Scheduled Tribes was 8.53 per cent (literacy among the general mass at that time being 24.04 per cent) which rose to 11.30 per cent in 1971 (literacy rate among general mass this time being 29.45 per cent) and finally reached to 16.35 per cent in 1981 (literacy rate of the general mass of India being 36.22 per cent). Two things have become clear from the census figures of three decades. Firstly the rate of literacy is much lower among the Scheduled Tribe in comparison to the general mass of India; but secondly the growth rate of literacy among the Scheduled Tribes during this period is somewhat faster than that present among the general people. While the literacy rate among the Indian people rose from 24.04 per cent to 36.23 per cent in tewenty years i.e. nearly 50 per cent increase, among the Scheduled Tribe, it rose from 8.53 per cent in 1961 to 16.35 per cent in 1981. That means the rate has almost been doubled during this span of time. The position is almost same in both rural and urban sectors. In India the literacy rate among the Scheduled Tribes inhabiting rural areas was 8.61 per cent in 1981. The same became 10.68 per cent in 1971 and 14.92 per cent in 1981. Here the growth rate is much higher than 50.00 per cent in two decades. In urban sector it is also much higher than 50.00 per cent increase. In 1961, 22.41 per cent of the Scheduled Tribes residing in urban areas were literates. This rate became 28.84 per cent in 1971. In 1981, 37.92 per cent of these people became literates.

While 1961 Census returns the literacy rate for the Scheduled Tribes of States and Union Territories like Assam, Bihar, Gujarat, Kerala, Himachal Pradesh, Manipur, Tripura, Arunachal Pradesh, Nagaland, Andaman and Nicobar Islands and Laccadive, Manicoy and Amindivi Island above the Indian average (8.53 per cent) for the same group of people, the States and Union Territories like, Andhra Pradesh, Madhya Pradesh, Madras (Tamil Nadu), Maharashtra, Mysore (Karnataka), Orissa, Rajasthan, West Bengal and Dadra and Nagar Haveli have literacy rate among the same people lower than that of the Scheduled Tribes of India in general.

In 1971 States and Union Territories like Assam, Bihar, Gujarat, Himachal Pradesh, Kerala, Maharashtra, Manipur, Meghalaya, Mysore (Karnataka), Nagaland, Tripura, Uttar Pradesh, Andaman and Nicobar Island, Goa, Daman and Diu and Laccadive, Minicoy and Amindivi islands have more Scheduled Tribe literates than that of India in general (11.30 per cent) the remaining States and Union Territories like Andhra Pradesh, Madhya Pradesh, Orissa, Rajasthan, Tamil Nadu, West Bengal, Arunachal Pradesh, and Dadra and Nagar Haveli, show literacy rate among the Scheduled Tribes below the average standard literacy rate among the same people of India in general (11.30 per cent).

According to 1981 Census the Scheduled Tribes of the States and Union Territories like Bihar, Gujarat, Himachal Pradesh, Karnataka, Kerala, Maharashtra, Manipur, Meghalaya, Nagaland, Sikkim, Tamil Nadu, Tripura, Uttar Pradesh, Andaman and Nicobar islands, Dadra and Nagar Heveli, Goa, Daman and Diu, Lakshadweep and Mizoram have literacy rate among the Scheduled Tribe higher than that of the Scheduled Tribes in India in general (16.35 per cent). Only a very few States and Union Territories like Andhra Pradesh, Madhya Pradesh, Orissa, Rajasthan, West Bengal and Arunachal Pradesh have the same rate below the rate achieved by the Scheduled Tribes in India in literacy in general.

Now if a comparison of the achievements in literacy by the Scheduled Tribes between different States and Union Territories made, it is seen that all States and Union Territories, where the literacy rate among the Scheduled Tribes in 1961 was below the Indian average for the Scheduled Tribes (8.53 per cent), were still below the average literacy for the Scheduled Tribes in 1971 except in Maharashtra and Mysore (Karnataka) where they could drag themselves above the Indian rate of literacy for the Scheduled Tribes (11.30 per cent). Here I could not take into account the literacy rate of the Scheduled Tribes of Arunachal Pradesh as the literacy rate therefore 1961(29.09 per cent) excludes 292,972 persons 'as their distribution into literates and illiterates is not available' (Mitra, 1966 : L-Li).

The above analysis also reveals that while in Tamil Nadu and Dadra and Nagar Haveli where the literacy rate among the Scheduled Tribes in 1971 was below the Indian rate for the Scheduled Tribes, these people could improve their position in 1981 and increase their respective literacy rate above the same rate for the Scheduled Tribes in India; but in other States and Union Territories where the literacy rate among the Scheduled Tribes was below the same rate of the Scheduled Tribes of India, they failed to improve upon their lot much to take them nearer to the Indian rate.

If the data on the literacy rates of the Scheduled Tribes of individual States and Union Territories are examined, one finds almost same picture is apparent. According to 1961 Census the lowest literacy rate among the Scheduled Tribes, of all States and Union Territories where there were the Scheduled Tribes was in Rajasthan where it was only 3.97 per cent. Andhra Pradesh and Dadra and Nagar Haveli also had very low literacy rate (below 5.00 per cent) among the Scheduled Tribes for the same Census year. States and Union Territories like Bihar, Madhya Pradesh, Madras (Tamil Nadu), Maharashtra, Mysore (Karnataka), Orissa, West Bengal, and Himachal Pradesh had the same rate between 5.01 and 10.00 per cent, Gujarat Andaman and Nicobar, Tripura, and Nagaland between 10.01 and 15.00 per cent and Kerala and Punjab between 15.01 and 20.00 per cent. Between 20.01 and 25.00 per cent literates among the Scheduled Tribes were found in Assam and Laccadive, Minicoy and Amindivi islands Manipur was the lone area where literacy among the Scheduled Tribes was above 25.01 per cent but below 30.00 per cent.

In 1971 with the increase of the literacy rate among the Scheduled Tribes due to different facilities granted to them by the Government and also for some other reasons, no State or Union Territory had the said literacy rate below 5.00 per cent. Andhra Pradesh, Madhya Pradesh, Orissa, Rajasthan, Tamil Nadu, West Bengal and Dadra and Nagar Haveli achieved the same between 5.01 and 10.00 per cent, Bihar, Gujarat, Mysore (Karnataka), Uttar Pradesh and Goa, Daman and Diu came with literacy rate among the Scheduled Tribes between 10.01 and 15.00 per cent. Between 15.01 and 20.00 per cent literacy rate had been achieved by the Scheduled Tribes of Himachal Pradesh, Mysore (Karnataka), Tripura and Andaman and Nicobar islands. Nagaland was the lone State that lay between 20.01 and 25.00 per cent for the same. States and Union Territories like Assam, Kerala, Manipur and Meghalaya had secured tribal literacy rate above 25.01 per cent but below 30.00 per cent. The only area which achieved a record increase in literacy was Laccadive, Minicoy and Amindivi islands where the literacy rate among the Scheduled Tribes was as high as 41.37 per cent according to 1971 Census.

1981 Census returns better achievement in case of the tribal literacy. None of the States or Union Territories has this rate below 5.0 per cent. Andhra Pradesh is the lone State that retains its lowest position in this regard with only 7.82 per cent of tribal literacy rate. States and Union Territories like Madhya Pradesh, Orissa, Rajasthan, West Bengal and Arunachal Pradesh have kept the standard between 10.01 and 15.00 per cent. Between 15.01 and 20.00 per cent of literacy rate have been achieved by the Scheduled Tribes of Bihar only. Gujarat, Karnataka, Maharashtra, Tamil Nadu, Tripura and Uttar Pradesh come with the same between 20.01 and 25.00 per cent. The Scheduled Tribes of Himachal Pradesh and Goa Daman and Diu have secured positions between 25.01 and 30.00 per cent. Those States and Union Territories who have achieved literacy rates for the Scheduled Tribes beyond 30.01 per cent but below 40.00 per cent are Kerala, Manipur, Meghalaya, Sikkim and Andaman and Nicobar islands. Nagaland secures a very good position in this regard by recording 40.32 per cent literacy among the Scheduled Tribes. But two areas, Lakshadweep and Mizoram, have remarkable achievements with 53.12 per cent and 59.63 per cent literacy among the Scheduled Tribes respectively.

It is thus seen that while the improvement in literacy standard of the Scheduled Tribes in some of the States and Union Territories is quite praiseworthy in twenty years time, in case of some other States and Union Territories the same is moderate. Yet in some States the progress is not that hopeful and eye-catching.

Now let us examine the sexwise achievement in literacy among the Scheduled Tribes of India in general and States and Union Territories in particular during last two decades. It is clearly visible from Tables - 1, 2 and 3 that the achievement is more prominent among the males than among the females. Among the Scheduled Tribe males according to 1981 Census the literacy rates (24.52 per cent) is three times more than that of the females (8.04 per cent). But the condition was quite different in 1961. At that time the literacy rate among the Scheduled Tribes males and females was 13.83 and 3.16 per cent respectively. The said rate rose to 17.63 and 4.85 per cent for males and females respectively in 1971. While the progress of literacy was not that speedy between 1961 and 1971, but it generated some momentum from 1971 to 1981.

When we go for State and Union Territory-wise progress of literacy among Scheduled Tribe males and females in two decades we do see that in some States and Union Territory like Andhra Pradesh, Madhya Pradesh, Madras (Tamil Nadu), Rajasthan and Dadra and Nagar Haveli where the male literacy among the Scheduled Tribes was below 10.00 per cent according to 1961 Census, the same remained below 10.00 per cent in Andhra Pradesh and below 14.00 per cent in other areas except Dadra and Nagar Haveli where it is below 16.00 per cent in 1971. It could reach above 15.00 per cent in all these areas except in Andhra Pradesh where it is only 12.00 per cent according to 1981 Census. In some of the areas like Tamil Nadu and Dadra and Nagar Haveli the Scheduled Tribe males could achieve even much above 20.00 per cent (26.71 and 25.46 per cent respectively) in 1981. That means at least in case of these two areas the achievement is quite appreciable. Again those States and Union Territories which had male literacy rate among the Scheduled Tribes remained between 10.01 and 20.00 per cent in 1961, for example Bihar, Gujarat, Maharashtra, Mysore (Karnataka), Orissa, West Bengal, Andaman and Nicobar, Himachal Pradesh, Tripura and Nagaland could improve upon their male literacy and could take it beyond 20.00 per cent in twenty years time. In 1971 the same rate in these areas remained within 15.00 to 25.00 per cent except in West Bengal where it was below 15.00 per cent (14.48 per cent) and in Himachal Pradesh (26.25 per cent) and Nagaland (30.17 per cent) where this rate was above 25.00 per cent. Even in some cases it went beyond 30.00 per cent in 1981 and at least in one case it jumped over even 40.00 per cent. The achievement of these areas e.g. Himachal Pradesh (38.75 per cent), Maharashtra (32.37 per cent), Andaman and Nicobar (38.43 per cent), Tripura (33.46 per cent) and Nagaland (47.31 per cent) is no doubt worth mentioning. States and Union Territories like Assam, Kerala, Laccadive, Minicoy and Amindivi Islands and Manipur where above 20.01 per cent of the Scheduled Tribes males could attain literacy in 1961, according to 1971 Census the same rate was above 30.01 per cent but below 40.00 per cent in these areas except Laccadive, Minicoy and Amindivi Islands where it rose as high as 54.06 per cent. In 1981 they have attained over 30.01 per cent literacy. In this category Manipur has achieved 48.88 per cent and Laccadweep could go as high as 63.34 per cent in 1981. Besides in case of some other States and Union Territories like Meghalaya (34.19 per cent), Sikkim (43.10 per cent), Uttar Pradesh (31.22 per cent), Goa, Daman and Diu (33.65 per cent) and Mizoram (64.12 per cent) the achievement in 1981 is quite praiseworthy.

The literacy among the Scheduled Tribe females, as already stated, provide a miserable picture. In India as already stated while the rate of literacy in 1961 among the Scheduled Tribes in general was 8.53 per cent and that of the Scheduled Tribe males 13.83 per cent, the same for the Scheduled Tribe females was as meagre as 3.16 per cent. That means less than 4 Scheduled Tribe females per 100 were literates. The condition did not change much even after ten years time. The Census of 1971 returns that the female literacy among the Scheduled Tribes rose only by 1.69 per cent over 1961 i.e. in 1971 the same became 4.85 per cent though male literacy among these people had 3.80 per cent increase over that of 1961. In India among the Scheduled Tribes in general, the literacy among the Scheduled Tribe females is only 8.04 per cent in 1981. That means between 1971 and 1981 the literacy rate among them increased from 4.85 per cent to 8.04.

The increase thereby becomes almost double during this period though in comparison to the rate of literacy among the Scheduled Tribe males during this period (24.52 per cent) this is quite low. The condition of the rural Scheduled Tribes females is even worse in these decades.

In States and Union Territories the condition is likewise miserable. In som, States and Union Territories the rate is remarkably low. Let us examine the situation State and Union Territory wise. In Madhya Pradesh (0.97 per cent) and Rajasthan (0.28 per cent) where the literacy rate of the Scheduled Tribe females was pitiably low remaining below 1.00 per cent in 1961, the same rose to 2.18 and 0.50 per cent respectively in 1971. It increased to 3.60 and 1.19 per cent respectively in another decade's time (i.e. in 1981). That means even after the passage of long twenty years' time the education among the Scheduled Tribe females in these two States gathered little momentum. States and Union Territories like Andhra Pradesh, Maharashtra, Orissa, West Bengal and Himachal Pradesh, where literacy rate of the fair sex of the Scheduled Tribes as per 1961 census was as low as between 1.00 and 2.00 per cent, also did not show any marked change in the progress of literacy of the Scheduled Tribes women as returned both by 1971 and 1981 Censuses. In all the above areas except Himachal Pradesh according to 1971 Census the rate was below 5.00 per cent. In Himachal Pradesh this is 5.53 per cent only. This rate did not flourish in 1981 to above 5.00 per cent in case of Andhra Pradesh and Orissa but became mere 5.01 per cent for West Bengal. But in case of Maharashtra it rose to a respectable 11.93 per cent and for Himachal Pradesh to 12.81 per cent.

Again States and Union Territories like Bihar, Gujarat, Madras (Tamil Nadu), Mysore (Karnataka) and Tripura where literacy rate among the Scheduled Tribe females was between 2.01 and 5.00 per cent according to 1961 Census, rose between 4.48 and 6.15 per cent in 1971 except Mysore (Karnataka) where the rise was a little more (7.67 per cent). While this rate increased and oscillated between 10.01 and 15.00 per cent in Gujarat, Tamil Nadu, Karnataka and Tripura after another ten years' time (in 1981), it increased only as 7.75 per cent in Bihar during the lapse of the same period of time. 1961 Census returned 6.31 per cent of literacy among the members of the fair sex of the Scheduled Tribes in Andaman and Nicobar Islands, where the literacy rate went up to 11.17 per cent in 1971 and 23.24 per cent in 1981 for them. States and Union Territory where this rate remained above 10.01 per cent in 1961 were Assam, Kerala, Laccadive, Minicoy and Amindivi Islands, Manipur, and Nagaland. In Kerala, Manipur and Nagaland this rate rose between 15.01 and 20.00 in 1971. But in Laccadive group of islands it became 28.33 and in Assam it rose as high as 48.17 per cent. In 1981, that is after expiry of another ten years this rate grew to 26.02 per cent for Kerala, 30.35 per cent for Manipur and 32.98 per cent for Nagaland.

For Laccadive it became 42.92 per cent. Figure for Assam is not available. Thus we have a comfortable idea about the progress made in the literacy status by the Scheduled Tribe females. In this connection it may be stated that this rate for the urban dwelling Scheduled Tribe females is much higher than that of those residing in the rural set up.

Now let us look into the progress made in the field of literacy by the Scheduled Tribes dwelling in rural and urban sectors. No doubt very few tribal people live in the urban sector (2.65 per cent in 1961, 3.41 per cent in 1971 and 6.20 per cent in 1981) whereas the major bulk of them have the rural base for centuries. But possibly because of the better educational facilities, educational environment and moreover better economic condition of the Scheduled Tribes inhabiting the urban areas, the rate of literacy is much higher among them than that of the vast majority of their brethren living in the rural areas of India. While in 1961 only 8.16 per cent of the Scheduled Tribes residing in the rural areas of India were literates, in the urban areas it was 22.41 per cent. Similarly among the Scheduled Tribes males, during the same year, 30.43 per cent males of the urban regions were literate but it was only 13.37 per cent males in the rural areas. It was even worse among the Scheduled Tribe females. While 13.45 per cent of the Scheduled Tribe females of urban sector were literates , only a meagre of 2.90 per cent of them residing in the rural areas, had literacy.

Almost same picture is visible from the returns of the 1971 Census. Here 28.84 per cent of the urban-dwelling Scheduled Tribes were literates in contrast to 10.68 per cent of the rural based Scheduled Tribes. Similarly among the Scheduled Tribe males 37.08 per cent of the urban-based and only 16.91 per cent of the rural based ones are literates. The Scheduled Tribe females also show the same trend. While only 4.39 per cent of the Scheduled Tribe females of the rural areas were literate in 1971, quite a large number of them (19.64) per cent residing in the urban sector had literacy.

According to 1981 Census 37.92 per cent of the urban dwelling Scheduled Tribes are literates in comparison to only 14.92 per cent of their brethren residing in the rural areas. Among the Scheduled Tribe males 47.59 per cent of the urban dwellers are literates while among rural based Scheduled Tribes males the rate of literacy is only 22.93

per cent. The condition of the Scheduled Tribe females is still worse. The Scheduled Tribe females inhabiting rural areas, have scored only a little literacy (6.81 per cent). But those who reside in the urban area, have a somewhat comfortable position as 27.32 per cent of them are literates.

For different States and Union Territories, the Census of 1961, 1971 and 1981 have returned almost similar contrast in the literacy rates of the Scheduled Tribes (person, male and female). The rural areas in this regard, have always given a very poor show.

We would now examine the progress made by some individual tribes in the field of education. This progress has been judged here on the basis of the figures from 1961 and 1971 Census (Das Gupta and Danda, 1984 : VIII-XV). The same for 1981 Census are not available. Tribes like the Bhil, Birhor, Didayi, Kolam including Manervarlu. Koru, Bopachi, Mouasi, Nihal or Bondhi, Korwa including Kodaku, Parenga, Riang and the Soligaru had the rate of literacy below 5.00 per cent in 1961. In 1971 the literacy rate remained within 5.00 per cent in case of the Bhil and the Parenga. But in case of the Kolam, Korku, Bopchi, Mouasi, Nihal or Bondhi and the Riang the same rate rose between 5.01 and 8.00 per cent. The Soligaru could make considerable progress by enchancing their rate of literacy from a meagre 1.90 per cent to as high as 11.44 per cent. But also reverse trend is noticed in case of some tribes. Instead of progress, regression is noticed in literacy in their case. The Birhor who had 2.82 per cent of literacy in 1961, came down to 2.26 per cent in 1971. Similarly, the Didayi with their literacy rate of 2.73 per cent in 1961 regressed to below one per cent (0.79 per cent) in 1971. Among the Korwa including Kodaku too similar trend is noticed. They had 3.16 per cent literacy in 1961 which dropped down to 3.06 per cent in 1971.

Again tribes like the Dimasa, Gaddi, Ho, Irular or Irulan, Kaman, Mishmi, Kawar, Kondakapu, Lahaula, Nagesia and the Saora had between 5.01 and 10.00 per cent literacy among each of them according to 1961 Census. Among some of these tribes like the Gaddi, Irular, Kondakapu and the Nagesia the said rate remained within 5.01 to 10.00 per cent in 1971.

Not much of increase in literacy rate is seen among them in a decade's time. Some progress in literacy (between 10.01 and 15.00 per cent) is noticed among the Ho, Kawar, and the Saora during this decade. But some significant achievement has been made by the Dimasa (18.99 per cent) and the Lahaula (19.24 per cent) as returned by 1971 Census. But only in case of the Kaman Mishmi a significant regression in literacy between 1961 and 1971 is marked. While in 1961 they had 6.16 per cent of them as literates, in 1971 it dropped down as below as 0.79 per cent.

The tribes who had the literacy rate ranged from 10.01 to 20.00 per cent in 1961, were the Bodo or Bodo Kachari, Chero, Jamatia, Karbi (Mikir), Kinnaura, Nocobarese and the Pardhan, Pathri or Saroti. In 1971 out of all the above Scheduled Tribes only the Bodod Kachari (20.51 per cent) and the Kinnaura (23.12) could achieve respectable literacy respectively. In case of the other tribes the literacy rate showed an increase but it remained with the range of 10.01 to 20.00 per cent. None of the tribes had shown any state of decline in the said rate.

Only a few tribes achieved literacy rate between 20.01 and 30.00 per cent in 1961. These tribes are the Khasi (24.57 per cent), Lalung (20.94 per cent), Lepcha (24.68 per cent), Minyong (25.65 per cent), Miri (20.85 per cent), Purum or Chote (22.56 per cent), Rabha (21.84 per cent) and the Ulladan (27.84 per cent). In the next ten years time (in 1971) the Khasi, Lalung, Lepcha and the Rabha could increase their literacy rate to some extent but keeping themselves within 20.01 to 30.00 per cent. The Purum or Chote and the Ulladah could take their literacy rate beyond 30.00 per cent. The literacy among the Purum in 1971 was 36.17 and that of the Ulladan was 35.94 per cent. In 1961 only one tribe, the Tangkhul could achieve 30.76 per cent literacy which was increased to 35.61 in 1971 per cent. But in case of the Minyong and the Miri the literacy rate virtually decreased in 1971 (8.34 and 18.20 per cent respectively).

When we compare the literacy rate among the Scheduled Tribes (Table-3) with that of the people in general in India and also of different States and Union Territories (Table-4) we would see considerable gap in the achievement of literacy between them. In order to show the difference in the literacy rate of the people in general on one hand and the Scheduled Tribes on the other, we have made a comparison among them using the literacy data from the Census of 1981. This comparison discloses the marked gap in the achievement of literacy between them. For example while the literacy rate among the people in general in India and also of the total males and females according to 1981 Census are 36.23, 46.89 and 34.81 per cents respectively the same rates among the Scheduled Tribes of India (Person, Male and Female) are 16.35, 24.52 and 8.04 per cents respectively. Similar significant difference is also noticed among the same people inhabiting in both urban and rural areas.

In some of the States and Union Territories this difference is quite significant for example in Andhra Pradesh while the general population has 59.15 per cent literacy, the Scheduled Tribes here have only 7.82 per cent literates among them. In Gujarat while general people have 43.70 per cent literacy, the Scheduled Tribes have 21.14 per cent. Similarly in Himachal Pradesh these rates are 42.47 and 25.93 per cents respectively. In Kerala the difference is quite significant. While the people of Kerala have achieved a very high literacy rate (70.42 per cent), the Scheduled tribes there have only 31.79 per cent literacy. In Orissa also the same picture is noticed while 34.23 per cent of the people here are literates, the Scheduled Tribes here can provide literacy only among a meagre of 13.95 per cent of them. In Tamil Nadu the literacy rate of the people and the Scheduled Tribes are 46.76 and 20.46 per cents respectively. West Bengal also shows a very wide gap between them. Here 40.94 per cent of the people are literate but the same literacy rate is only 13.21 per cent among the Scheduled Tribes here. In Goa, Daman and Diu while the people in general have 56.66 per cent literacy, the Scheduled Tribes there have only 26.48 per cent literates. In both urban and rural areas and among both males and females the same difference in the literacy rate between the people of the State and Union Territories and the Scheduled Tribes inhabiting there, is clearly visible.

In the foregoing pages I have discussed about the progress made by the Scheduled Tribes of India and also of different States and Union Territories. From the above discussion it is clear that though the Scheduled Tribes have almost doubled their literacy rate in the period of two decades (1961-1981) in many States and Union Territories, yet their achievements in literacy is not that comfortable when we compare their rate of literacy with that of the general people, in spite of the fact that during this period they have been provided a number of facilities for the promotion of their literacy, and a huge amount of money have been spent by the Government for this purpose. And the objective of rendering all these facilities to the Scheduled Tribes in the field of education is to bring them close to the general mass if not at par with them in this field. But in reality the gap between them in the field of literacy and education has not been narrowed down. In some cases it has infact widened. Now the question is: Why this is so ? Why in spite of receiving a number of extra facilities they have failed to achieve the expected goal ? What are the difficulties which hinder their expected progress and where lie those barriers ? And why these barriers could not be removed during these long forty years' time since promulgation of the constitutional provisions ?

The problems those hinder the progress of tribal education have been ascertained by the Government through a number of Committees and Commissions. These Committees and the Commissions found out the factors responsible for such low progress in literacy. Many institutions and organisations as also many individuals studied tribal education. The reports of all of them could find out some basic problems. These are the socio-economic problems of the tribal people, problems relating to content-curricula and medium of instructions, problems relating to functioning of the schools and aspects relating to the teachers (Rao, 1988 : 78).

The tribal people live in a state of backwardness and always suffer from a high economic depression. A large number of them are living below the poverty level. So they can not think of education when they are totally engrossed with the thought to their tottered economy, their very survival. To them education is a luxury which they simply cannot afford. Moreover, those tribal people who have agro-based economy, employ even their minor children in different agricultural operations or in the associate activities like tending the cattles, looking after minor children to release elderly people for agriculture, etc. A study in Adilabad district of Andhra Pradesh shows that among the tribals there 'enrolment of the children in primary schools from the families of the salaried employees and petty businessmen (59.4%) was more than from the families of the cultivators (41.7%) and labourers (18.3%) .... " (Rathnaiah, 1977:178).

Lack of educational environment in the tribal family/society is also responsible for the lack of interest for education among the Scheduled Tribes. As the parents do not have education, they feel little urge to educate their children. Many of them even now do not understand the value of modern education. The parents who are exposed to modern education, are somewhat keen to educate their children.

Income of the tribal families is also an important factor. Lower and middle income groups among the tribals have less attraction for education as their economy does not permit to afford education of their children. Both Vidyarthi (1955 : 41-42) and Rathnaiah (1977:179-180) found the same trend among the tribals.

The seasonal migration of the tribals from their homeland to different industrial units, factories, mines, collieries etc. as labourers often cause problem against the education of their children. As seasonal migration is a must for them to earn cash for their livelihood, so negligence in their children's education was inevitable. Movement from one place to another by the nomadic tribes like the Gujjar, Bhotia of U.P. Hills, Gaddi and others also hampers the education of their children.

The medium of instruction is also a very important factor that promotes or hinders education. The best medium of education at least in the primary level, is the instruction through mother tongue. But in case of the majority of the tribals the medium of instruction in schools in tribal areas is not in the mother tongue of the tribals inhabiting there. The main reason for this drawback is the lack of sufficient tribal teachers, and the lack of knowledge of the tribal language as medium of instruction on the part of the teachers working in the tribal areas. Another important factor is the lack of knowledge of the non-tribal teachers working in the tribal areas about the tribal culture, their language, customs and manners, etc. This lack of knowledge often creates gap between the teachers and the pupils.

Curriculum is also an important point. So far no proper curricula have been prepared which suit the tribal students. The existing curricula as the experts think, are of little relevance to the tribal people.

The schooling and hostel facilities are also not adequate in the tribal areas. As a result not many tribal students get opportunity to enjoy educational facilities.

Most of the tribal languages do not have script of their own. These people are taught in other scripts. This also creates problem and hinders progress of education among these people.

The stereotyped method of teaching as prevalent in different parts of our country may not and does not create interest among the tribal students and attract them to educate themselves. So the method of teaching should be so made that this creates interest among the tribal students and inspire them to get modern education. Otherwise the existing method of teaching may not generate interest among the tribal students towards education.

Sometimes peculiar psychology of the tribals prevent progress of education. An example may clarify the statement. Among the Oraons of Sunderban (Southern part of West Bengal), an Oraon boy on his first day in the school, fell seriously ill. His illness created an impression among the Oraons of that area that due to his admission in the school, he fell sick. So the Oraons of that area abstained from sending their children to the school.

The stagnation is also another factor that retards education. There may be some more reasons behind the slow progress in education among the Scheduled Tribes.

All these factors and the high wastage in education among the Scheduled Tribes are compelling factors for the low achievement of literacy among these people. Unless these are overcome the rate of literacy among these people cannot be accelerated.

References

Chari, R.B. (1975) — *Census of India 1971 Series - 1 Paper - 1 of 1975 Scheduled Castes and Scheduled Tribes*. New Delhi, Manager of Publication.

Das, A.K. & Raha, M.K. (1964) — *The Oraons of Sunderban* Special Series - 3, Calcutta Cultural Research Institute.

Das Gupta, B.K. & Danda, A.K. (1984) — *Tribal Education in India* (in retrospect), Calcutta, Anthropological Survey of India.

Mitra, A. (1966) — *Census of India 1961*, Volume - 1 India, Part - V - A (ii) Special

Tables on Scheduled Tribes. Delhi, Manager of Publication.

Padmanabha, P. (1983) *Census of India, 1981, Series-I India Part-II B (iii) Primary Census Abstract Scheduled Tribes.* Delhi Controller of Publications.

Raha, M.K. & (1982) Das, J.C. Constitutional Safeguards for the Scheduled Tribes : Their Relevance and Implications in *Tribal Development in India* (ed) B.Choudhury, New Delhi Inter-India Publishers.

Rao, V.Rama (1988) Tribal Education and the Role of the Teacher in *Man and Life*, Vol. - 14 Nos. 1 & 2.

Rathnaiah, E.V. (1977) *Structural Constraints in Tribal Education : A Regional Study,* New Delhi,Sterling Publishers Pvt. Ltd.

Vidyarthi, L.P.(1955) Education in Tribal Bihar in *Man in India,* Vol. 35, No. 1.

Table - 1

LITERACY AMONG THE SCHEDULED TRIBES ACCORDING TO 1961 CENSUS.

S. No.	*India/State Union Territories*	*Total Rural Urban*	*Total Literates*		
			Person %	*Male %*	*Female %*
1	*2*	*3*	*4*	*5*	*6*
	India	Total	8.53*	13.83	3.16
		Rural	8.16*	13.37	2.90
		Urban	22.41	30.43	13.45
	States				
1.	Andhra Pradesh	Total	4.41	7.26	1.48
		Rural	4.13	6.86	1.34
		Urban	10.54	16.19	4.57
2.	Assam	Total	23.58	31.09	15.72
		Rural	22.55	30.19	14.56
		Urban	53.66	57.53	49.68
3.	Bihar	Total	9.16	15.22	3.18
		Rural	8.63	14.57	2.81
		Urban	28.76	38.06	18.24
4.	Gujarat	Total	11.69	19.06	4.09
		Rural	11.32	18.53	3.90
		Urban	18.80	28.66	7.80

S. No.	*India/State Union Territories*	*Total Rural Urban*	*Person %*	*Total Literates Male %*	*Female %*
1	*2*	*3*	*4*	*5*	*6*
5.	Jammu and Kashmir	Total	-	-	-
		Rural	-	-	-
		Urban	-	-	-
6.	Kerala	Total	17.26	22.63	11.92
		Rural	16.31	21.44	11.18
		Urban	38.35	50.23	27.58
7.	Madhya Pradesh	Total	5.10	9.25	0.97
		Rural	4.98	9.06	0.93
		Urban	15.46	24.81	4.77
8.	Madras	Total	5.91	8.93	2.73
		Rural	4.70	7.70	1.55
		Urban	25.96	29.21	22.47
9.	Maharashtra	Total	7.21	12.55	1.75
		Rural	6.87	12.06	1.57
		Urban	15.92	24.56	6.45
10.	Mysore	Total	8.15	13.24	2.81
		Rural	7.49	12.26	2.48
		Urban	20.23	31.10	8.87
11.	Orissa	Total	7.36	13.04	1.77
		Rural	7.22	12.87	1.67
		Urban	14.00	20.79	6.83
12.	Punjab	Total	16.46	29.49	3.79
		Rural	16.46	29.49	3.79
		Urban	-	-	-
13.	Rajasthan	Total	3.97	7.39	0.28
		Rural	3.76	7.04	0.22
		Urban	14.13	22.99	3.09
14.	Uttar Pradesh	Total	-	-	-
		Rural	-	-	-
		Urban	-	-	-
15.	West Bengal	Total	6.55	11.20	1.76
		Rural	6.27	10.83	1.60
		Urban	18.27	24.76	9.57

S. No.	India/State Union Territories	Total Rural Urban	Total Literates Person %	Male %	Female %
1	2	3	4	5	6
	Union Territories and other areas				
16.	Andaman and Nicobar Islands	Total	11.10	15.56	6.31
		Rural	11.10	15.56	6.31
		Urban	..	..	..
17.	Himachal Pradesh	Total	8.63	15.37	1.74
		Rural	8.53	15.21	1.71
		Urban	42.29	51.18	18.75
18.	Laccadive, Minicoy and Amindivi Islands	Total	22.27	34.40	10.61
		Rural	22.27	34.40	10.61
		Urban	..	..	..
19.	Manipur	Total	27.25	37.03	17.67
		Rural	26.83	36.43	17.49
		Urban	51.98	67.37	30.63
20.	Tripura	Total	10.01	17.37	2.31
		Rural	9.48	16.78	1.84
		Urban	61.76	70.84	51.00
21.	Dadra and Nagar Haveli	Total	4.40	8.28	0.41
		Rural	4.40	8.28	0.41
		Urban	..	..	..
22.	North-East Frontier Agency.	Total	29.09*	38.81	8.47
		Rural	29.09	38.81	8.47
		Urban	...	.	..
23.	Nagaland.	Total	14.76	18.99	10.57
		Rural	13.54	17.45	9.68
		Urban	56.13	67.70	43.00

*Excludes population 292, 972 (144, 586 Males and 148,386 Females) of North-East Frontier Agency as their distribution into literates and illiterates is not available.

Table - 2

LITERACY AMONG THE SCHEDULED TRIBES ACCORDING TO 1971 CENSUS

Sl. No.	*India/State Union Territory*	*Total Rural Urban*	*Total Literates*		
			Person %	*Male %*	*Female %*
1	*2*	*3*	*4*	*5*	*6*
	India	Total	11.30	17.63	4.85
		Rural	10.68	16.91	4.36
		Urban	28.84	37.08	19.64
	States				
1.	Andhra Pradesh	Total	5.39	8.46	2.12
		Rural	4.77	7.72	1.75
		Urban	15.74	21.84	9.16
2.	Assam	Total	26.03	34.63	48.17
		Rural	24.09	33.56	15.98
		Urban	68.84	73.54	63.62
3.	Bihar	Total	11.64	18.43	4.85
		Rural	10.73	17.40	4.13
		Urban	32.34	40.52	22.82
4.	Gujarat	Total	14.19	21.83	6.15
		Rural	13.46	21.03	5.68
		Urban	24.24	33.57	13.78
5.	Haryana	Total	-	-	-
		Rural	-	-	-
		Urban	-	-	-
6.	Himachal Pradesh	Total	15.89	26.25	5.53
		Rural	15.76	26.09	5.45
		Urban	49.00	60.05	31.80
7.	Jammu and Kashmir	Total	-	-	-
		Rural	-	-	-
		Urban	-	-	-
8.	Kerala	Total	25.71	32.00	19.40
		Rural	24.70	30.91	18.47
		Urban	49.70	58.2	41.27
9.	Madhya Pradesh	Total	7.62	13.04	2.18
		Rural	7.38	12.71	2.05
		Urban	21.12	31.02	10.11
10.	Maharashtra	Total	11.74	19.06	4.21
		Rural	11.11	18.25	3.79
		Urban	25.61	36.09	13.90
11.	Manipur	Total	28.70	38.63	18.87
		Rural	27.32	37.18	17.59
		Urban	58.30	60.37	47.47
12.	Meghalaya	Total	26.45	30.11	22.78
		Rural	23.40	27.11	19.65
		Urban	60.11	64.93	56.21

Sl. No.	India/State Union Territory	Total Rural Urban	Total Literates Person %	Male %	Female %
1	2	3	4	5	6
13.	Mysore	Total	14.85	21.71	7.67
		Rural	12.99	19.41	6.31
		Urban	30.03	39.62	19.26
14.	Nagaland	Total	24.01	30.17	17.68
		Rural	22.27	28.28	16.12
		Urban	63.2	70.83	54.63
15.	Orissa	Total	9.45	16.40	2.60
		Rural	9.2	16.07	2.38
		Urban	18.17	26.6	9.40
16.	Punjab	Total	-	-	-
		Rural	-	-	-
		Urban	-	-	-
17.	Rajasthan	Total	6.47	12.03	0.50
		Rural	6.17	11.55	0.41
		Urban	19.67	31.60	4.30
18.	Sikkim	Total	-	-	-
		Rural	-	-	-
		Urban	-	-	-
19.	Tamil Nadu	Total	9.02	13.34	4.48
		Rural	8.50	12.76	4.02
		Urban	17.94	23.38	12.28
20.	Tripura	Total	i5.03	23.60	6.04
		Rural	14.33	22.86	5.41
		Urban	71.12	80.90	59.70
21.	Uttar Pradesh	Total	14.59	22.51	55.84
		Rural	13.37	21.35	4.33
		Urban	66.81	35.13	21.24
22.	West Bengal	Total	8.91	14.48	3.08
		Rural	8.60	14.2	2.76
		Urban	22.52	26.08	18.14
	Union Territories				
1.	Andaman and Nicobar Islands	Total	17.84	24.14	11.17
		Rural	17.84	24.14	11.17
		Urban	33.33	50.0	-
2.	Arunachal Pradesh	Total	5.20	8.71	1.70
		Rural	4.91	8.30	1.55
		Urban	34.85	46.82	19.21
3.	Chandigarh	Total	-	-	-
		Rural	-	-	-
		Urban	-	-	-
4.	Dadra and Nagar Haveli	Total	8.90	15.30	2.60
		Rural	8.90	15.30	2.60
		Urban	-	-	-

Sl. No.	*India/State Union Territory*	*Total Rural Urban*	*Total Literates Person %*	*Male %*	*Female %*
1	*2*	*3*	*4*	*5*	*6*
5.	Delhi	Total	-	-	-
		Rural	-	-	-
		Urban	-	-	-
6.	Goa, Daman and Diu	Total	12.72	20.33	5.08
		Rural	11.52	18.85	4.32
		Urban	16.55	24.81	7.66
7.	Laccadive, Minicoy and Amindivi Islands	Total	41.36	54.06	28.33
		Rural	41.36	54.04	28.33
		Urban	-	-	-
8.	Pondicherry	Total	-	-	
		Rural	-	-	-
		Urban	-	-	-

Note : The figures for the Andaman and Nicobar Islands are exclusive of the Jarawas and Sentinelese tribes of those Islands. These tribesmen could not be contacted and hence no information pertaining to them could be collected at 1971 Census.

Table - 3

LITERACY AMONG THE SCHEDULED TRIBES ACCORDING TO 1981 CENSUS.

Sl. No.	*India/State Union Territory*	*Total Rural Urban*	*Total Literates*		
			Person %	*Male %*	*Female %*
1	*2*	*3*	*4*	*5*	*6*
	India	Total	16.35	24.52	8.04
		Rural	14.92	22.93	6.81
		Urban	37.92	47.59	27.32
	States				
1.	Andhra Pradesh	`Total	7.82	12.02	3.46
		Rural	6.79	10.68	2.78
		Urban	23.27	31.50	14.14
2.	Bihar	Total	16.99	26.16	7.75
		Rural	15.56	24.63	6.48
		Urban	38.53	48.29	27.78
3.	Gujarat	Total	21.14	30.41	11.64
		Rural	20.34	29.52	11.00
		Urban	31.26	41.16	20.19
4.	Himachal Pradesh	Total	25.93	38.75	12.81
		Rural	25.39	38.21	12.36
		Urban	59.15	68.61	46.19
5.	Karnataka	Total	20.14	29.95	10.02
		Rural	17.94	27.59	8.03
		Urban	59.15	68.61	46.19
6.	Kerala	Total	31.79	37.52	26.02
		Rural	31.22	37.00	25.39
		Urban	61.42	63.78	58.91
7.	Madhya Pradesh	Total	10.68	17.74	3.60
		Rural	10.04	16.91	3.19
		Urban	27.62	38.63	15.18
8.	Maharashtra	Total	22.29	32.37	11.93
		Rural	19.35	29.18	9.34
		Urban	56.73	65.23	47.92
9.	Manipur	Total	39.73	48.88	30.35
		Rural	37.49	46.72	28.05
		Urban	56.73	65.23	47.92
10.	Meghalaya	Total	31.55	34.19	28.91
		Rural	27.08	29.76	24.39
		Urban	63.03	66.60	59.67
11.	Nagaland	Total	40.32	47.31	32.98
		Rural	37.50	44.59	30.15
		Urban	66.28	71.36	60.49
12.	Orissa	Total	13.95	23.26	4.76
		Rural	13.42	22.63	4.34
		Urban	25.18	36.05	13.69

Sl. No.	India/State Union Territory	Total Rural Urban	Person %	Total Literates Male %	Female %
1	2	3	4	5	6
13.	Rajasthan	Total	10.27	18.85	1.19
		Rural	9.61	17.87	0.93
		Urban	27.31	41.93	8.69
14.	Sikkim	Total	31.13	43.10	22.36
		Rural	29.13	39.44	18.09
		Urban	55.84	63.43	47.31
15.	Tamil Nadu	Total	20.46	26.71	13.99
		Rural	18.98	24.98	12.78
		Urban	34.21	42.91	25.31
16.	Tripura	Total	23.07	33.46	12.26
		Rural	22.33	32.74	11.52
		Urban	78.80	84.42	72.21
17.	Uttar Pradesh	Total	20.45	31.22	8.69
		Rural	18.95	29.66	7.33.
		Urban	50.69	60.92	38.12
18.	West Bengal	Total	13.21	21.15	5.01
		Rural	12.72	20.69	4.53
		Urban	25.75	32.35	18.02
	Union Territory				
1.	Andaman and Nicobar Islands	Total	31.11	38.43	23.24
		Rural	30.60	37.64	23.11
		Urban	72.69	83.92	41.67
2.	Arunachal Pradesh	Total	14.04	20.79	7.31
		Rural	13.23	19.75	6.78
		Urban	48.39	60.63	33.18
3.	Dadra and Nagar Haveli	Total	16.86	25.46	8.42
		Rural	16.32	24.76	8.04
		Urban	32.34	44.87	19.28
4.	Goa, Daman and Diu	Total	26.48	33.65	18.89
		Rural	26.24	33.00	19.12
		Urban	27.28	35.78	18.11
5.	Lakshadweep	Total	53.12	63.34	42.92
		Rural	50.99	61.21	40.83
		Urban	55.76	65.98	45.51
6.	Mizoram	Total	59.63	64.12	55.12
		Rural	55.20	60.16	50.21
		Urban	74.04	77.11	71.01

Table - 4

INDIA AND STATEWISE LITERACY IN PERCENT ACCORDING TO 1981 CENSUS.

Sl. No.	India/State Union Territory	Total Rural Urban	Total Literates Person %	Male %	Female %
1	2	3	4	5	6
	India	Total	36.23	46.89	34.81
		Rural	29.65	40.78	17.95
		Urban	57.40	65.83	47.82
	States				
1.	Andhra Pradesh	Total	59.15	39.25	20.40
		Rural	23.23	32.24	14.08
		Urban	51.99	65.30	41.55
2.	Assam	Total			
		Rural			
		Urban			
3.	Bihar	Total	26.20	38.10	13.62
		Rural	44.17	34.38	10.17
		Urban	52.18	62.47	39.81
4.	Gujarat	Total	43.70	54.43	32.30
		Rural	36.20	47.85	24.05
		Urban	60.31	68.61	51.13
5.	Haryana	Total	36.13	48.20	22.27
		Rural	30.33	43.44	13.36
		Urban	56.86	64.94	47.34
6.	Himachal Pradesh	Total	42.19	53.19	31.45
		Rural	40.71	51.35	29.35
		Urban	67.44	73.32	60.04
7.	Jammu and Kashmir	Total	26.66	36.29	15.87
		Rural	21.63	31.64	10.46
		Urban	45.56	53.55	36.43
8.	Karnataka	Total	38.46	48.81	27.70
		Rural	31.04	42.06	19.77
		Urban	56.71	71.39	47.78
9.	Kerala	Total	70.42	75.25	65.73
		Rural	69.11	74.13	64.25
		Urban	76.10	80.10	72.19
10.	Madhya Pradesh	Total	27.87	39.49	15.52
		Rural	21.22	32.90	8.99
		Urban	54.01	64.40	42.26
11.	Maharashtra	Total	42.40	58.78	34.78
		Rural	38.15	51.25	24.88
		Urban	63.91	71.80	54.64
12.	Manipur	Total	41.35	53.29	29.05
		Rural	37.37	49.33	25.06
		Urban	52.44	64.30	40.20

Sl. No.	India/State Union Territory	Total Rural Urban	Total Literates Person %	Male %	Female %
1	2	3	4	5	6
13.	Meghalaya	Total	34.07	37.88	30.08
		Rural	27.45	30.82	23.95
		Urban	64.11	68.90	58.82
14.	Nagaland	Total	42.56	50.05	33.89
		Rural	38.59	46.09	30.25
		Urban	64.22	69.26	56.91
15.	Orissa	Total	34.23	47.09	21.12
		Rural	31.48	44.50	18.45
		Urban	54.77	65.12	42.71
16.	Punjab	Total	40.86	47.16	33.69
		Rural	35.20	41.91	27.62
		Urban	55.63	60.73	49.72
17.	Rajasthan	Total	24.38	36.30	11.41
		Rural	17.99	29.65	5.46
		Urban	48.35	60.55	34.45
18.	Sikkim	Total	34.05	43.94	22.20
		Rural	30.04	40.54	18.23
		Urban	54.85	61.43	45.42
19.	Tamil Nadu	Total	47.76	58.26	34.99
		Rural	33.56	51.15	25.80
		Urban	63.44	72.49	53.99
20.	Tripura	Total	42.12	51.70	31.99
		Rural	49.1	48.24	27.63
		Urban	73.66	79.94	67.09
21.	Uttar Pradesh	Total	27.15	38.76	14.04
		Rural	23.05	35.17	9.49
		Urban	45.88	54.72	35.43
22.	West Bengal	Total	40.94	50.67	30.25
		Rural	33.11	43.58	22.06
		Urban	62.66	69.08	54.82
	Union Territories				
1.	Andaman and Nicobar Islands	Total	51.56	58.96	42.20
		Rural	46.57	53.94	37.06
		Urban	65.53	71.69	56.97
2.	Arunachal Pradesh	Total	20.78	28.94	11.32
		Rural	18.51	26.36	9.60
		Urban	53.22	60.79	41.18
3.	Chandigarh	Total	64.78	69.00	59.31
		Rural	44.72	52.28	33.73
		Urban	66.15	70.19	60.93
4.	Dadra and Nagar Haveli	Total	26.67	36.31	16.77
		Rural	24.71	34.33	14.91
		Urban	54.16	62.90	44.28

Sl. No.	*India/State Union Territory*	*Total Rural Urban*	*Total Literates* *Person %*	*Male %*	*Female %*
1	*2*	*3*	*4*	*5*	*6*
5.	Delhi	Total	61.54	68.40	53.06
		Rural	47.56	60.21	32.07
		Urban	62.64	69.04	54.71
6.	Goa, Daman and Diu	Total	56.66	65.60	47.56
		Rural	52.67	62.24	43.08
		Urban	64.98	71.96	57.39
7.	Lakshadweep	Total	55.04	65.23	44.64
		Rural	51.98	62.24	41.57
		Urban	58.65	68.66	48.30
8.	Mizoram	Total	59.88	64.45	54.91
		Rural	55.24	60.18	49.91
		Urban	74.06	77.26	70.47
9.	Pondicherry	Total	55.85	65.83	45.71
		Rural	47.98	59.38	36.30
		Urban	63.03	71.77	54.23

CHAPTER 12

The Co-operatives in Tribal Areas(LAMPS) in West Bengal

Swapan K. De

In India, about seven per cent population belong to tribals. There are over four hundred tribal groups in this country with one hundred five major languages and about two hundred fifty dialects. In West Bengal the total number of tribals are 3,070,672 according to 1981 Census which is 5.63% of the total population (54,580,647).

Their living style is quite different from others. Their economy is not similar to general population. Among the tribals some have been practicing settled agriculture for many many years and some are still in food gathering and hunting stage although not in the form of the traditional ways. Naturally special measures should be required for their development. The bondage with forest is of old age. The economy as well as their social customs are closely related to forest. But many restrictions have been imposed in recent decades on forests, and as a result their traditional dependence on forest has been reduced to minimum. The entry of money economy in a traditional society generally often poses some problems, these becomes conspicuous particularly in the backward economy where consumption and purchase pattern, and money and material relationship are not similar to the modern economy money system. The tribals of the contemporary India have been facing the same problem.

Some special provisions were given by the Constitution of India to protect their tradition and life. Afterwards, during the planning phase of Third Five Year Plan period some Commissions and Committees namely Renuka Roy Committee (1959) and Dhebar Commission 1961 etc. were appointed to assess the progress of the tribal education, economy etc. The main points of their recommendations were (a) Coordinate the available resources in Tribal areas and utilize for their betterment. (b) Planning should be done in accordance with their aspiration by protecting indigenous culture. Some measures no doubt, have been taken following these recommendations. But it was not reflected in planning process. In the recommendation of the Fourth Five Year Plan, it was suggested to consolidate available resources for all-round development in tribal concentrated areas, and it should be tied out with the national economy. "S.C. Dube Committee (1972)" and "Bawa Committee (1973)" recommended some basic things which were accepted in the Fifth Five Year Plan. Tribal sub-Plan was formulated and tribal concentrated areas were noted as I.T.D.P. areas (Integrated Tribal Development Project). Attention was given to mobilise all available natural resources in local areas and to integrate planning inputs to protect these people from exploitation. Family based planning was encouraged to help them to rise above poverty line. Cooperative societies were also recommended to fight age old exploitations in many areas. These societies would be formed by the tribals (at least 70% members should be tribals) and controlled by them so that tribals would get better benefits.

In West Bengal during the Fifth Five Year Plan period Integrated Tribal Development Project areas were formed with the mouzas where fifty per cent or more persons were tribals. The work has been undertaken in twelve districts with thirty three project areas and in 4482 mouzas. The total population of those I.T.D.P. areas was 15.83 lakhs. Among them 10.13 lakhs i.e. 64% were tribals, and it is little above 40% to total tribal population in the State.

It has been observed that the tribals have been suffering from several daprivations for decades. The backwardness of their habitation and economy is a common factor in the State. It has been felt necessary to guard the tribals against the exploitation of money-lenders and the middlemen contractors. Side by side, it is also necessary to utilize the natural resources of the respective areas and thereafter to market them in the commercial field: the purpose is to check the other areas of exploitations and providing justice to the tribals with remuneration of their toils. Looking into these basic functtions of credit and marketing the large sized Multipurpose Co-operative Societies (LAMPS) have been organized in West Bengal a s recommended by the Bawa Committee.

It was decided to set up one hundred LAMPS at the end of Sixth Five Year Plan in West Bengal. At present, altogether 75 LAMPS have been established in sub-Plan areas of West Bengal.

Although the presence of these organizations is of recent development in this State but their existence has already put some impact in certain tribals areas. In fact, they are thinking these institutions as their own and also as platform to express their feelings and expressions.

The LAMPS have already undertaken the following activities to render short term and mid-term consumption loan to the members; to collect and market minor forest produces, to supply consumer goods in the tribal areas and to render other associated services in tribal areas.

All these activities have been made possible with the financial and infrastructural support by the State as well as the Central Government, different banking organizations and cooperatives. The Tribal Development Co-operative Corporation (T.D.C.C.) works as Co-ordinating agent of all those organisations and also looks after the day-to-day activities of the LAMPS of the State.

In this study data obtained against each LAMPS have been placed herewith to get a stock of the things relating to their activities and prospects up to 1979-80.

There were altogether 49 Large Sized Multipurpose Cooperative Societies (LAMPS) in West Bengal during 1978-79. The present study was undertaken to assess the impact of tribal cooperative organizations in the tribal sub-Plan areas and data were gathered from 35 LAMPS in eleven project districts of West Bengal. As there was no LAMPS in Hooghly district naturally the only project district was excluded form this study.

In Midnapur district, there were altogether eight LAMPS in the three I.T.D.P. areas out of five I.T.D.P. areas of the district. This study covered only five LAMPS in four Police Stations (Nayagram, Binpur, Gopiballavpur, and Salboni).

The total number of members of those LAMPS were 4,448 and about 88% of them were tribals and remaining 12% came from other communities. Among the tribals members the Santals were the most dominant group i.e. about 90% of the total tribal members. The other tribals members were from the Bhumij, Mahali and the Lodha communities. The female participation among the members was very meagre. A good percentage of members (about 90%) possessed their own land but they were mostly small land holders (one to two acres).

There were twelve LAMPS in Purulia district of which ten LAMPS have been covered in this study and they were located at Puncha, Manbazar, Noturia, Jhalda, Bagmundi, Kashipur, Balarampur, Barabazar, Bandwan and Arsha police stations. The total number of members of those LAMPS was 8031 of which 5952 (74.11%) were tribals and 2079 (25.89%) non-tribals. Although the Santals were the major group among the members but a sizeable number of tribal members came from the Lodha, Kharia, Mahali and the Bhumij communities. A few females (2%) have registered their names as members. The land holding pattern among the members was almost the same as that of the district of Midnapur.

In 24-Parganas, only one LAMPS was located at Sandeshkhali police station and started its function in the year 1976. Only 623 persons have registered their names as members, among them 558 (89.57%) were tribals and 65 were non-tribals of which most of them came from Scheduled Castes communities. Altogether seven villages comprising 27,054 persons were under the operational area of the LAMPS. The Oraons and the Santals members shared in equal proportion. There were a few females among the members.

In the year 1976. the Aushgram LAMPS started its function at Aushgram Police Station in the district of Burdwan, and this was the only LAMPS in Burdwan district. Its operational area was extended to 35 villages. Altogether 523 persons have registered their names as members. Among them 30% belonged to tribal communities. But afterward, attention was given to accommodate more tribals as members of this LAMPS. A large number of persons belonging to Scheduled caste communities, have registered their names as members. But there was no female member at that time.

There were eight LAMPS at Bankura district. The data were collected from six LAMPS situated at Ranibandh, Raipur, Gangajalgathi, Saltora and Chatna Police Stations. Altogether 8619 persons have registered their names as members in those six LAMPS and 94.26% of them were tribals. More then 80% tribal members belonged to the Santals community. Most of the tribal members possessed land from one to two acres. A few females also registered their names as members.

In Birbhum district there were altogether 3 LAMPS which were located at Rajnagar, Rampurhat and Muhummad Bazar police stations. Rampurhat and Md. Bazar LAMPS started their function in 1976 and the remaining one was on 1979. The total number of members of these LAMPS were 2276 of which 1665 (73.15%) were tribals and 611 (28.84%) came from other communities. The controlling area of those LAMPS extended up to 61 villages. The Santals were the major group among the members.

In the project district Murshidabad, there was only one LAMPS in 1979-80 termed as Sahapur LAMPS which has been functioning since 1976 at Sagardighi P.S. The total number of members were 581 of which 520 (89.50%) were tribals and remaining 61 (10.50%) came from other communities (mostly Muslim). Its operational area was extended to 32 villages with ten thousand population. The tribal members hold very small area of land and that too were mostly having with less irrigational facilities.

The Habibpur and Gazale LAMPS of Malda district started their functions in 1976. Altogether 541 members have registered their names in those cooperatives. Among them 432 (79.15%) were tribals and 109 were non-tribals.

The study has covered only two LAMPS namely Banshihari and Udayan LAMPS, out of four LAMPS in West Dinajpur district. These two LAMPS have registered 1212 persons as their members of which 1067 (37.9%) belonged to Scheduled Tribes and remaining 147 (12.1%) were non-tribals. The controlling areas of those LAMPS were extended up to 70 villages with 20,000 population. There were altogether eight LAMPS at Jalpaiguri district and this study dealt with only three LAMPS namely Madarihat LAMPS. Samuktola LAMPS and Mitiali LAMPS at Madarihat, Alipurduar and Mitiali Police Station respectively. There were altogether 1178 members in those LAMPS of which 925 (78.52%) were tribals and remaining 253 (21.48%) were non-tribals. The operational area of those LAMPS comprised 33 villages. The Samuktola LAMPS has started its function for 1975 and the remaining Mitiali and Madarihat were started in 1977 and 1978 respectively.

Kharibari-Phanshidewa LAMPS located at Phanshidewa Police Station of Darjeeling District started its function from 1977. The total number of shareholders were 177 of which 175 (98.87%) were tribals.

These LAMPS have already undertaken some steps to protect the tribals from the exploitation by middleman and moneylenders. Loan facilities have been extended to the members in the form of short term and mid-term loans towards production of crop, animal husbandry, fisheries, cottage industries and other related matters with lower rate of interest (no more than four per cent).

From the study it was noted that altogether 11,645 members were given loan in those areas from 35 LAMPS and more than 75% beneficiaries were tribals. On analysing the average number of beneficiaries the LAMPS of Bankura and 24-Parganas district have extended loan facilities to greater number of beneficiaries and the LAMPS of Burdwan and Darjeeling districts were lowest in that category. On an average the LAMPS located at northern region of West Bengal could not provide loan facilities towards their members in comparison to other regions.

Among the beneficiaries, an overwhelming majority (81.82%) took short term loan in the form of crop loan. Mid-term loan was provided mostly for purchase of agricultural implements and animals and 10.69% of beneficiaries were given this kind of loan. Only 1.18% beneficiaries were provided with artician loan and remaining 6.31% were given consumption loan.

It was observed that the rate of providing loan facilities was very low in comparison with the demand and also the repayment of those loan was not at all satisfactory. The administrative compiicacy of the LAMPS, inability and noncooperation of banking organisations and overall lack of coordination between governmental agencies, banking institutions and cooperative organisations are the root cause for these consequences. Some steps have already been taken to combat these inconveniences by sanctioning consumption loan in support of production loan and increase of risk capital up to twelve per cent of crop loan. From the information received from the Tribal Development Cooperative Corporation the crop loan of Rs. 17.5 lakhs was given to the beneficiaries where target figure of Rs. 60 lakhs in the year 1981-82.

Traditionally, tribals have had close association with the forest. Their economy and way of life are related to it. And the LAMPS located in the nearby forest areas are also conducting business with minor forest products. The LAMPS have already acquired permission for performing this activity from the Department of Forest. At present sal seed and leaf, kendu leaf, mahua seed, neem seed, tassar cultivation etc. are the major business in M.F.P. activities. These societies have already undertaken steps against the exploitation of middlemen who used to give very small amount of money of the collections. At present the collections by the tribals are purchased by the LAMPS and they get the actual price for their toil which is four to five times more than the rates offered by the middleman. Up to 1982-83 there were 30 LAMPS which were engaged in mnor forest produce business. The collection of sal seed was 5961 metric tons (with shell 4070 mt.and without shell 91mt) in 1982.

It is obvious that the quantum of business in M.F.P. is going up day by day and comprehensive planning for collection as well as marketing is necessary especially in those items whose production is mostly dependent on climatic condition of the specific season. Still today no much control over the market price has been made as the business of those produces is mostly controlled by the private businessman at the exist point.

But some measures have already been taken so that the LAMPS which are performing these business, can earn profit in this respect. Regional centres have already been established at Purulia, Jhargram Bankura and Jalpaiguri, so as to make their work more scientific and market oriented. Some relaxations have been given to sell goods at profitable price in a local arrangement and information on market price at different levels are kept in notice. The LAMPS could make this business more successfully with some changes in regulation of forest, creation of risk capital and increase of efficiencies of T.D.D.C. as well as the LAMPS.

The LAMPS have already taken an important step towards supply of consumer's goods in fair price and proper weight to check exploitation of small shopkeepers and middlemen. In many cases the tribal buyers have to travel long distance from their village to collect day-to-day requirements, and this area is cared of by these stores. The LAMPS have already supplied the consumer items (controlled cloth, different kind of cloths, spices. Baby food etc. worth Rs.60 lakhs where demand was estimated for Rs. 1000 lakhs up to 1982-83. Naturally a tremendous demand has not yet been fulfilled during previous days. The whole sale co-operative societies at district level could not assess the actual demand of the items and supply accordingly, and the LAMPS have to suffer a lot. Afterward the T.D.C.C.took over the matter and are engaged to supply the items for these stores. Up to 1982-83, materials worth Rs.30 lakhs have been supplied by the T.D.C.C. who are expected to supply goods for Rs. 125 lakhs in 1983-84 financial year. This is a time to specify the activities of the wholesale consumer stores and T.D.C.C. Above all, we should remember that these stores are exposed to an economic milieu where a long aged trading activities are controlled by private traders which is the real threat to the LAMPS.

In co-operative movement, although the LAMPS are of recent origin in the State, but already a basic infrastructure has been formed. But attention is to be given towards effective organizational control as well as communicating the information to the tribal people to involve them in their activities.

MEMBERSHIP PATTERN IN DIFFERENT LAMPS IN DIFFERENT DISTRICTS (1979)

Sl.No	*District*	*No.of LAMPS Surveyed*	*Number of members*		*Total*
			Sch. Tribes	*Others*	
1.	Midnapur	8	3910 (87.90%)	538 (12.10%)	4448
2.	Purulia	12	5952 (74.11%)	2079 (25.89%)	8031
3.	24-Parganas	1	558 (89.57%)	65 (10.43%)	623
4.	Burdwan	1	142 (27.15%)	381 (72.85%)	523
5.	Bankura	8	8124 (94.26%)	495 (5.74%)	8619
6.	Birbhum	3	1665 (73.15%)	611 (26.85%)	2276
7.	Murshidabad	1	520 (89.50%)	61 (10.50%)	581
8.	Malda	2	432 (79.85%)	109 (20.15%)	541
9.	West Dinajpur	4	1067 (87.89%)	147 (12.11%)	1214
10.	Jalpaiguri	8	925 (78.52%)	253 (21.48%)	1178
11.	Darjeeling	1	175 (98.87%)	2 (1.13%)	177
	Total	49	23470 (83.19%)	4741 (16.81%)	28211 (100.00)

NUMBER OF BENEFICIARIES UNDER DIFFERENT CATEGORIES OF LOANS

Sl.No.	*District*	*Total Beneficiaries*	*Short term*	*Mid Term*	*Consumption Loan*	*Artisan Loan*
1	*2*	*3*	*4*	*5*	*6*	*7*
1.	Midnapur	1656	681 (41.12%)	255(15.40%)	720(43.48%)	-
2.	Purulia	2628	2152 (81.89%)	420(15.98%)	-	56(2.13%)
3.	24-Parganas	685	639 (93.28%)	-	-	46(6.72%)
4.	Burdwan	53	53 (100.00)	-	-	-
5.	Bankura	4088	3983 (97.43%)	105(2.57%)	-	-
6.	Birbhum	1259	1120(88.96%)	101(8.02%)	15 (1.19%)	23(1.83%)
7.	Murshidabad	304	265 (87.17%)	39(12.83%)	-	-
8.	Malda	271	176 (64.94%)	95(35.06%)	-	-
9.	West Dinajpur	209	70 (33.49%)	127(60.77%)	-	12(5.74%)
10.	Jalpaiguri	436	389 (89.22%)	47(10.78%)	-	-
11.	Darjeeling	56	-	56 (100.00)	-	-
	Total	11645 (100.00)	9528 (81.82%)	1245 (10.69%)	735 (6.31%)	**137 (1.18%)**

CHAPTER 13

Planting A Mission Among The Bhils of South Rajasthan*

Shyamlal

The process of social change among the Bhils of Banswara district had started in 1911. It gained momentum under the Canadian Protestant Missionaries and has been an important agency of conversion among the Adivasis of Banswara district in Rajasthan for 69 years. But, unfortunately, until now, not a single systematic study has been attempted by any scholar. The present paper discusses the various welfare programmes, such as, educational, medical, agricultural, etc. which induced Bhils to accept Christianity as their religion. The findings also indicate a significant change between traditional Bhils and converted Christian tribesmen on various aspects.

Missionaries Work in Tribal Areas

The activities of the Christian missionaries may be seen among the tribal people of the country in general and Assam, Bihar, Orissa,

---

* Reproduced by the permission of the authority of the Journal 'Man and Life', Vol X, No.1 & 2, pp 77-96.

Madhya Pradesh, Maharashtra, Nagaland, Nicobar, etc. in particular. The tribals attracted the attention of missionaries owing to their horrific practice of human sacrifices, deplorable socio-religious and economic conditions and their exploitation by the higher caste Hindus or money-lenders, Rajas, petty police officials and traders in the tribal areas. While working among these communities the missionaries not only sympathized with them but

> "... made them conscious of their rights and duties and showed them how they could resist social discrimination and fight their oppressors by coming under their umbrella. When the people looked upon these missionaries as saviours, they were naturally obliged to accept the faith which the latter were simultaneously preaching".

B.K. Roy Burman, the noted Inidan Anthropologist, while speaking about the work of Christian missionaries in hill tribes of North-East India, observes that, "It is frequently alleged that people have been converted to Christianity on mass scale by allurements provided by the foreign missionaries. In some parts of the hills of North-East India, this may be true. But it is certainly not the whole truth. In many areas, Christianity appears to have served the role of filling-up the intellectual and spiritual vacuum caused by the growing scepticism among the tribal population, about their traditional faith and world-view. It has also tended to serve as the vehicle for unification of isolated small communities into a larger entity".

Srinivas, while making a general observation on the **working** of Christian missionaries says,

> "the opening of schools, hospitals and other welfare agencies by missionaries in the areas where the Harijans and the tribals live, appears to the Hindus only as bait in the trap of conversion. The linking up of humanitarianism with proselytization has made the former suspect. Even every liberal Westernized Hindu feels this way",

Rao, while writing about the work of missionaries among the down-trodden people, says,

> "The missionaries not only converted them to their respective denominations but initiated broad based pogramme involving English education, and the setting up of orphanages and other special welfare measures. Those of the depressed classes who were converted to Christianity soon developed a different life-style from their contemporaries. They received English education and were recruited to various government jobs"

As a result of this, mass conversion to Christianity occurred among the aboriginal tribes like the Mundas, Oraons, Kharias, Santals, Hos, and others. Besides, lower castes have contributed large number of converts through mass conversion.

In this paper, an attempt has been made to present one such case of conversion from South Rajasthan.

If one important and responsible dynamic factor is to be singled-out for change in the life of the Bhils, it would undoubtedly be the introduction of Christianity among them.

Background

Banswara lies in the southern region of the Rajasthan State. It is encircled by Udaipur and Chittorgarh districts in the north and north-east respectively, by Madhya Pradesh State in the east and south-east, by Gujrat State in the south-west and by Dungarpur district in the west. Up to 1948, Banswara remained a princely State of Sisodia clan. According to the 1971 Census, the population of the Banswara district was 6, 54, 586. The population of the Scheduled Tribes in the district as enumerated in the Census of 1971, was 4, 77, 369 and this ranked first in the State in this respect. The district has a court, a post-graduate college, an industrial training institute and the district administrative headquarters.

It has also a few important factories and industries, such as, Banswara Syntex, J.C. Mill, steel factory, etc. although industrialization has been recently started.

The Bhils

The population of the Scheduled Tribes in the country, according to 1971 Census, was 38, 015, 162. The Bhils are the third largest group (13.63%) of tribal community in India. They are mostly found in Madhya Pradesh, Gujarat, Rajasthan and Maharashtra. They are in the largest of the tribal population in these States. Besides, they are also found in small numbers in Andhra Pradesh and Tripura.

In 1971 Census, 13 tribes were found in Rajasthan. Among them the Minas and the Bhils are the dominant and constitute largest single group of about 94 per cent of the total tribal population. The population of the Bhils in Rajasthan was 1,431,020. The Scheduled tribe population in Banswara district as shown in Table 1 consists of mainly the Bhils, Bhilmeena, Damor or Damaria, Minas, Garasia, and others.

The table reveals that in Banswara district, the Bhils constitute the great mass of Scheduled Tribe population. Thus, Banswara district is predominantly a Bhil area.

Bhils live in a meagre way in houses built of bamboo rafter leaves and grass plastered with clay. The house is locally called as 'tapra'. Their dress consists of a loin cloth and food corn millet and fruits of chase. They do not live together in villages, but in *pals* and groups of huts at some distance apart, each hut is surrounded by a small sized field and sometimes enclosed by fence of upright polls interlaced.

Bhils speak Bhili and its allied dialect called 'wagdi'. A close study of their life shows that a Bhil is truthful, modest, loyal, courteous and submissive, as also brave, courageous and independent. Bhils are divided into number of exogamous clans known as `jat'. The jats are sub-divided into numbers of`edakhs' (Sub-clans). The clans among the Bhils of Banswara district are: (1) Maida, (2) Rana, (3) Vaid, (4) Neenama, (5) Devda, (6) Wadhari, (7) Buj, (8) Aari, (9) Lambervada, (10) Bargot, (11) Kander, (12) Kharadi, (14) Ada, (15) Chauhan, (16) Sarpota, (17) Doki, (18) Niharta, (19) Masar, (20) Pagora, (21) Bhumani, (22) Dindoor, (23) Armor, (24) Bhabar, (25) Saral, (26) Goda, (27) Bhangora, (28) Damor, (29) Makhvana, (30) Khadio, (31) Bamnia, (32) Khada, (33) Kandor, (34) Rathor, (35) Moinia, (36) Dodiar, (37) Kalawa, (38) Halki, (39) Bharia or Bhuria, (40) Denad, (41) Manpuria,

Table 1

TRIBE-WISE POPULATION IN BANSWARA DISTRICT DURING THE LAST TWO DECADES (1961 & 1971)

		1961				1971			
SlNo	Tribal Group	Male	Female	Total	Percentage to the total Scheduled Tribes Population	Male	Female	Total	Percentage to the total Scheduled Tribes Population
1	2	3	4	5	6	7	8	9	10
1.	Bhil	103505	99532	203037	68.23	221926	21335	437261	91.59
2.	Bhilmoona	-	13	13	0.00	1621	1465	3086	0.65
3.	Damor or Damaia	5	4	9	0.00	92	137	229	0.04
4.	Mina	6701	6312	13013	4.38	16697	18497	35194	7.38
5.	Garasia	NA	NA	NA	NA	535	504	1039	0.22
6.	Unclassified	40735	40794	31529	27.39	307	253	560	0.12
	Total	150946	146655	297601	100.00	241178	236191	477369	100.00

SOURCES:

(1) K.K. Sahgal, Rajasthan District Gazetteers (Jaipur: Directorate of District Gazetteers, Government of Rajasthan, 1974), pp. 79-80 Appendix III

(2) Census of India 1971, Rajasthan Series 18, Rajasthan Part-V; Special Table and Notes on Scheduled Castes and Scheduled Tribes, p.268; and Table St-II, AGe and Marital Status for Scheduled Tribes.

(42)Hodar (43) Katara (44) Pandora, (45) Solanki (46)Bad (47) Bagoda, (48) Hingaz or Hinger (49) Mal (50) Daima, (51) Gosain, (52) Ganara, (53) Baid and (54) Girasia of Garbai.

There are different opinions concerning the position of the Bhil community in social hierarchy. Russel and Heeralal stated; "the position of the Bhils as the oldest inhabitants of the country is recognised by their employment in the capacity of village watchmen. A watchman must know the village boundaries and keep watch and ward over them and it was supposed the oldest class of residents, would know them better".

Vyas described the position of the Bhil in these words:

> 'The Rajputs recognised the Bhils as the former residents and owners of the land occupied subsequently by the Rajput. Despite the fact that the Bhils were brought under their rule by the Rajputs, it was considered as a token of recognition that at the time of coronation the forehead of Rajput chiefs must be marked with the blood of the thumb of the Bhil. The Bhils of Gogunda and Undri villages of Udaipur district still claim the mark of performing the 'tika' for the Sisodias. The Bhils of Dhambola and Padar villages in Dungarpur district regard themselves as descendants of Rajputs, who for some mistakes or sin, had been declared socially to become Bhils."

Nath, while speaking about the position of the Bhils of Ratanmal Gujarat observes that, "the Bhils occupy an intermediary status in social hierarchy of this region".

The original socio-cultural life of the tribal population of Banswara district has undergone transformation owing to the Christianity and vigorous social welfare programme.

Early Disturbances

The nineteenth century was a time of rapid change and simmering discontent among the Bhils. 1836, 1861 and 1865 were difficult years of scarcity. In the year 1873-74, there was also deficient rainfall resulting in poor harvest and great distress particularly among the Bhils and the lower classes. As a result, a dispute arose with Jagirdars of the State and the turbulent Bhils got out of hand and the land revenue system become chaotic.

In accordance with agreement made with the Bhils of Banswara, the people of Malva paid tribute to them for their security. This tribute was later on stopped after the treaty and posting of the police on the border. As a result of this, the Bhils again revolted and attacked Mokheri village.

The years 1903-1907 marked the beginning of a movement of considerable importance and one that is worth considering in some details. In the year 1907, Govinda Giri Gobpalia, a Banjara Sanyasi of Dungarpur district introduced religious reforms among the Bhils. He was earlier known as Govinda. Many persons had become victims of famine of 1900. Govinda also lost his wife and children. Sad and depressed, he left Dungarpur for the adjoining State of Gujarat where he married for the second time. While in Gujarat, he came in contact with Rajgiri Gosain, Govinda became Govind Giri. His wife also became a disciple of Rajgiri.

Govind Giri returned to Dungarpur State accompanied by his wife in the year 1914 and made temporary abode in the State. With a determination to devote himself to the social uplift of the Bhils, he started the work and could also draw some Bhils to his fold. A famous disciple of Surata, Kuria by name was initiated soon. His son Bhagwan Maharaj was a chief exponent of the sect. His *dhuni* is at Surata.

Then Govind Giri came to Bedasa and established his *dhuni* on a hillock known as Channi Dungari and planted is Negi-flag. To bring a large number of Bhils into his fold, he styled himself as an incarnation of the Almighty. Many Bhils later on became his followers.

However, he did not confine himself to this field only and the result of his teachings was that many of the Bhils began to imagine that they were original rulers of the country now governed by the Rajputs and showed a defiant attitude. In the year 1913, a large number of armed Bhils assembled at Mangarh -- a hillock on the borders of Banswara and Sunth and revolted.

Consequently, an armed force led by Major Hamilton had to be sent from Neemuch about 100 miles away from Banswara to suppress the rebellion. During the operation, about 20 Bhils were killed and 150 were jailed. When Hamilton returned to Neemuch, he talked to Rev. Daniel Cock of the Presbyterian Mission. He said,

> "Against my wishes, I ordered the police to fire on the innocent persons, I knew and loved them for years together. Really, it was a sad experience of my life. You go there and do work which I could not do for them. Their hearts have broken. Give them divine message. I want to do something and I know, the best one will be to establish a mission centre."

Advent of Canadian Presbyterian Missionaries

It was against this background, the first organized attempt of Canadian Missionaries towards proselytization began when eight missionaries led by Rev. D.G. Cook arrived at Banswara in January 1914. Though a few Canadian missionaries had come here earlier in 1911, but had met with little success. They first obtained permission to visit imprisoned Bhil leaders and have first hand information about their mental state. It was decided to make a speedy tour of as many villages as possible, from which these men had come. This trip convinced them that there was an opening for them.

Returning to Banswara, they selected a site for the mission building. The site was approved and granted by the ruling prince in the year 1914. Thus mission posses a piece of land measuring about sixteen hectares. In the same year, permission also came from Canada Foreign Mission Board to start the construction work. At mission council held in Ratlam in March 1914, Rev. D.G. Cock, Mrs. Cock and Miss Catherine Campbell were appointed to work in Banswara. In November 1915, Dr. B.C. Oliver was appointed to initiate medical work, using a small room in a bungalow as a dispensary. Between 1914 and 1916, preaching work was also started in earnest, although for three years, they worked without any success. However, it is important to mention here that by 1914 throughthe efforts of Irish Presbyterian Mission, four persons had embraced Christianity.

Nathia--a resident of Dhavada village was the first to embrace Christianity. His relative Teja of Bijalpura village was the second in the chain. A resident of this village had married a daughter of Khunta village. The daughter's brother (Ratna) was third to join. His relative Thavra came from village Savania. He was fourth to join. The channel of fusion went along affinal ties rather than through cousins or the consanguinal kins. Second channel of diffusion started with Thavra of Sevania. Having become a convert, he tried to pass on the religious creed to his brother's son and two others in the village (Bijiamba) and Teja were baptized by the Irish Presbyterian Mission in Jhalod.

To the joy of Canadian missionaries the first door was opened when one Bhil was baptized in 1917 in Shagwa village. The Presbyterian church expanded greatly and evangelization work extended to the remote and inaccessible areas in Ghatol and Aamkhunt in Banswara State. A few mission centres were also started among the Bhils. The conversion work went side by side with the opening of schools both for boys and girls and, in 1980, a school building was constructed at Banswara. In 1920, the construction work of a hospital was also started, which later rendered great services to the Christians as well as to the non-Christian population. On 16 February, 1922, the newly constructed hospital was inaugurated by His Highness Bahadur Singh of Khandu. On this auspicious day, Dr.. Armstrong, who was the secretary of Canadian Foreign Mission, delivered the sermon. During the same period, the foundation stone of the church was also laid down by Dr. Armstrong at Banswara. Thus, he became the true founder of Bhil church. The church building took two years to complete. The most important thing was that the poor families contributed both in cash and kind for construction of the church. In the words of Master Punja: "We have constructed this church with our own hands". The church building was inaugurated in 1923. The function was attended by a huge gathering. Most of the people came from villages by using bullock-carts and horses.

It was about the year 1923, when a nursing school was also started by Miss Grancy. During the following years, the missionaries be friended a few Bhils in the villages. The villagers were deeply influenced by the dedication of the missionaries. Consequently, a large number of Bhils became Christians in villages, namely Agoria, Khunta, Bijalpur, Servania and Lalavara. This occurred in 1925. Again in 1926,

Christianity spread out in the adjacent tribal villages, namely Shalrapada and Zhumki. Towards the end of 1926, Pestor James came here to strengthen the work among Bhils which was undertaken in Banswara. Banswara mission flourished and, up to 1937, three congregations, namely, Agoria, Sevania and Shalrapada were established. Again, in 1939, another three congregations, namely, Khunta Khuntani, Katanpura-Chirola and Kharia-Patelia was established. And, in all, seven congregations came into existence up to 1941.

Advent of Roman Catholic Missionaries

The Roman Cathoic Mission varies were comparatively late-comers. The Bhils of Kushalgarh, another major tribal area of Banswara, was known to the Christian missionaries after the year 1937. The earliest missionary work among the tribals of Kushalgarh area was started in about 1931 by Father Charles of Church Missionary Society of Madhya Pradesh. The first organized attempt by Roman Catholic Missionaries towards proselytization began in 1931 with the arrival of Father Charles in village Aamlipada-Ambapada, Kushalgarh. Since then, they met with great success in their work of conversion. There are eight village churches in Kushalgarh having about 1500 members in 1980. Their mission is also running six schools and maintaining five hostels, both for boys and girls, in the area. About 30 Christian tribesmen are working as 'Pracharak' or missionaries..

With these pioneer missonaries, the Canadian Presbyterian and Roman Catholic Churches began their efforts to spread Christianity in South Rajasthan.

TYPES OF CHRISTIAN ACTIVITY

Since the majority of Bhil Christians are baptists, this section will refer mainly to their work. The church has become 'indigenous' in the sense that during the last few decades, the whole Christian work has been in the hands of Indians.

Evangelistic Work

Owing to the nature of the climate and habits of the people, outdoor preaching was carried throughout the year. In the cool weather, when for weeks and months, the sky was cloudless, all missionaries who were not prevented by station work, went forth to tour among the villagers. Tents and necessary camp equipments, medicines, films, cooking material, etc. were gathered into bullock carts and preaching band set out. The usual plan was to make a week's stay or so at some considerable places.

Public Preaching

In the morning, the missionaries and their assistants performed the prayer and usually began by singing a hymn, to the accomapaniment of some musical instruments. A crowd quickly assembled and the preachers took their turn in addressing the gathering. Starting with some truth, expressed in the hymn, a pithy text of scripture, a parable, some recent occurrences or incidents, they declared the great fundamental truth regarding aim and salvation. After prayer, they took a round of the village and people individually at their respective houses.

In the afternoon, interested persons again gathered at the missionary tent and spent a few hours in listening and discussing religious matters. The women-folk also listened clamly the gospel from missionaries. Evangelistic services were regularly carried on among both Bhils men and women during camping period. Besides religious preaching instructions were given regarding hygiene. The women were taught about their menstruation and were encouraged for medicine and vaccination.

At night, again prayer was held. Just after the prayer, films were screened by missionaries to entertain people. The pithy text of the film was explained by missionaries in the Hindustani language.

Educational Work

In Banswara, special attention was given by missionaries to impart education among the Bhils and their children as they remained illiterate as much as they could not even read and write. So it became necessary that they learn, read and write and therefore the necessity of regular schooling arose. Thus, a summer school-cum-hostel both for boys and girls was opened in the early years in the mission compound and a few boys and girls were enrolled. School remained open only for about three months during the summer. The hostellers received free of cost books, slates, writing material, clothing, meals, residential facilities, etc. Some women Christian teachers were employed. All these teachers were converted women. Knowing the advantages of education, numerous Christian tribesmen sent their children to the school.

Although the programme for imparting education among the Bhil children was continued, the following programmes were given priority:

(i) The tribal students were ignorant about the basic knowledge of hygiene. To overcome this problem, the elementary knowledge of hygiene was imparted to them.

(ii) They were taught to go to church and made to learn manners, etiquette, etc. related to church and prayers.

(iii) Special seminars and talks were arranged to spread the holy message.

(iv) The students were also persuaded to learn and sing the devotional songs.

(v) The tribal people were and still are of the opinion that diseases are caused due to gods and goddesses or evil spirits. To remove all these notions, they are persuaded to get themselves vaccinated.

(vi) To wean away from faith in spirit, etc.

Masihi Prathmic Shala

On account of increased number of the students in the summer schools, a primary school known as Masihi Prathmic Shala was opened in Banswara near about 1920. Three women teachers were employed. Besides secular education programme, one hour was devoted to holy message and its related principles. The first batch consisting of nine students was declared successful in the year 1940. Among these, two of them later on became pastors. While remaining became teachers. It is important to note here that since its inception to 1947, no fee was charged from students. As well as, 602 boys and girls, have so far been enrolled in this school.

Boys and Girls Hostels

The mission also opened two hostels, one each for boys and girls belonging to Christian faith as early as about 1924. Now, it is an indication of the fact that education is spreading fast among the tribal

Table - 2

YEARWISE ECONOMIC ASSISTANCE FOR HOSTELLERS (BOYS) IN MISSION HOSTEL, BANSWARA IN THE LAST DECADE

Year	*No. of Students*	*Amount*		*Total*
		Amount Charged from Hostellers	*Aid Received from Donors*	
1970-71	38	4,000	7,000	11,000
1971-72	45	5,000	7,000	12,000
1972-73	40	6,000	7,000	13,000
1973-74	28	3,500	7,000	10,500
1974-75	35	4,000	8,000	12,000
1975-76	50	5,000	15,000	20,000
1976-77	60	6,000	20,000	26,000
1977-78	72	8,000	33,000	41,000
1978-79	106	10,000	35,000	45,000
1979-80	130	15,000	35,000	50,000
Total	604	66,500	1,74,000	2,40,500

Prepared by hostel warden.

Table - 3

YEARWISE ECONOMIC ASSISTANCE FOR HOSTELLERS (GIRLS) IN MISSION HOSTEL, BANSWARA IN THE LAST DECADE

Year	*No. of Students*	*Amount*		*Total*
		Amount Charge from Hostellers	*Aid Received from Donors*	
1970-71	30	2,000	7,000	9,000
1971-72	25	1,500	7,000	8,500
1972-73	22	1,500	6,000	7,500
1973-74	20	1,500	6,000	7,500
1974-75	15	1,000	10,000	11,000
1975-76	15	1,000	10,000	11,000
1976-77	20	2,000	14,000	16,000
1977-78	30	1,500	18,000	19,500
1978-79	40	2,000	24,000	26,000
1979-80	64	3,000	24,000	27,000
Total	281	17,000	1,26,000	1,43,000

Prepared by hostel warden.

people as well as Christian tribesmen. Besides for lodging and boarding the inmates received free, along with books, stationery and clothing. The total number of hostel inmates up to the year 1980 is 3096.

With the changing circumstances later on the mission authorities had started charging a nominal fee. During survey work, I was told that some donation as a partial aid was given to the hostellers by donors in the form of aid as well as number of students in the last decade.

Residential Schools in Rural Area

Besides the Primary school in Banswara, there are a few residential schools exclusively for Christian tribal children. The schools provide free educational facilities to the students. The facilities like free supply of books, writing material, etc. are expected to work as incentives and motivate both parents and children towards education, besides providing conducive atmosphere for studies.

Residential schools were started in the district for the first time in 1948 by the missionaries and their number had increased to 12 by 1978. The total strength of students studying in these summer schools upto the year 1980 was about 3407. The location and other details of the residential schools in the district are given in the following table.

Table - 4

RESIDENTIAL MISSION SCHOOLS IN BANSWARA DISTRICT

Location	*Tehsil*	*Tentative year of Establishment*	*No. of Teachers*
Sevania	Kushalgarh	1948	1
Agoria	Kushalgarh	1949	1
Khunta	Kushalgarh	1949	1
Kharia	Bagidora	1949	1
Kevaria	Banswara	1949	1
Macha-Molan	Kushalgarh	1962	1
Ratanpura	Banswara	1965	1
Shivpura	Banswara	1970	1
Hamirpura	Bagidora	1970	1
Vital Dev	Banswara	1973	1
Parvali	Bagidora	1978	1
Lalavada	Bagidora	1978	1

Prepared by hostel warden.

Medical Work

In a county like India, where meagre provision was made for the relief of the sick and suffering and where the social conditions of caste and prejudice preclude, to a great extent, opportunities of showing the heart of Christianity in acts of sympathy and helpfulness, medical work has special value in opening the hearts of people and making them responsive to christian efforts.

Sharansthan Hospital Banswara

In the year 1911, the population of Banswara and the Bhils of surrounding areas were in need of medical care. In 1920, Dr. Chone Oliver was appointed to initiate medical work for the poor and backward people, particularly the Bhils, using a small room in a bungalow as dispensary. Here, in the early morning, a motley crowd of sick persons assembled. After a gospel address, the patients were admitted one by one and examined by the doctor. For about two years it remained only a dispensary and, in 1922, it was converted into hospital and its building was inaugurated by His Highness Bahadur Singh of Khandu. Since then, there had been a gradual expansion of medical facilities in the hospital. During the last forty years the staff, equipment and number of beds in the hospital have considerably increased. Now the hospital is one of the biggest and well-equipped in the district.

A new building was added to it in 1968-69 with a grant of 70,000 dollars from the United Church of Canada. It has now (1980) 90 beds, 16 each in male and female medical wards, 12 each in male and female surgical wards, 16 in maternity ward and 8 in Bohra ward. Besides, three wards, namely, pediatric, isolation and T.B. each having 12, 8 and 30 beds respectively, but these wards were closed down during 1976-78. Hospital also contains a well-equipped pathology laboratory, an X-Ray department, a dispensary, an operation theatre, a labour room, a clinical bio-chemistry section and a central supply room. Previously, there was one anti-rabies centre and a well-equipped dental clinic also. The staff consists of two doctors (a male and a female), one nursing superintendent (female), one business manager, three female nurses, three compounders, three technicians, six aayahs, three office clerks, four ward-boys and eleven class - IV servants.

The Institutional Set-up

The institution is headed by the Medical Superintendent of the hospital. Apart from the administrative assistants, there is a nursing superintendent, who supervises the entire nursing staff of the hospital. She has supervisory powers and is responsible for allotting duties and well-being of the inmates, discipline, etc. among the staff. The Business Manager is the incharge of income and expenditure of the hospital.

The hierarchical position is as follows:

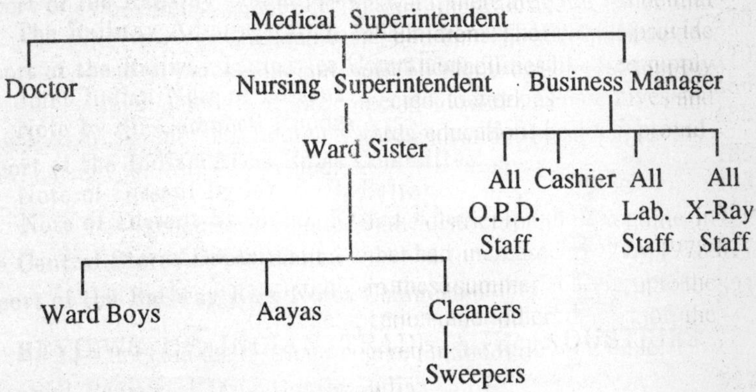

Nurses' Training School

The mission has also been running a nurses' training school within the compound of the hospital since 1922. The trainees have to undergo a three years' training course. In the fourth year, the female students work for a midwifery diploma. In 1971, there were 35 student nurses on roll. Hostel accommodation is also provided to all the student nurses. It has a good library and a laboratory. The school has also received some teaching aid, equipment, etc. from UNICEF. From 1971 to 1975, 240 nurses have been trained.

Rural Community Health Centre

Besides the above, there are three rural community health centres. The administrative control on the centres and their activities is exercised by the Medical Superintendent of Sharansthan Hospital. In all these centres, free treatment is provided to outdoor patients only. These are: (i) Bhameri Centre: (ii) Bada Agoria Centre; and (iii) Kharia Centre.

These health centres are situated predominantly Christian tribal area and housed in 'tapra'. The staff consists of one community health educator. These centres also render their services to the adjacent villages. List of the centres, number of villages served by the centres, the year of establishment, and closing year are given in the following table;

Table - 5

COMMUNITY HEALTH CENTRES IN BANSWARA DISTRICT

Location	*Tehsil*	*Tentative Year of Establishment*	*Adjacent Villages Served by the Centre*	*Closing Year*
Bhameri	Ghatol	1953	Omrinala Ghori-Tejpur Ronia Pattipura	1955
Bada Agoria	Kushalgarh	1956	Moeha-Molan Bijalpur Bhatavdala	1960
Kharia	Bagidora	1960	Chhatri Agoria Chota Parvali Patia Gari Thapra Bora Khandi	1974

Prepared by hostel warden.

Wide Influences

Patients from distinguished families in neighbouring towns of various States, came for treatment and fame of good work spread far and wide. The good impression produced by the efforts of Dr. C.F. Grant and other co-workers did much to silence the irritation and disarm the opposition manifested by Banswara officials in the earlier days of the mission. Many of the patients were cured by Dr. Grant who out of gratitude opened their houses for their visit.

Agriculture Work

Besides the various activities mentioned above, special attention was also given to agricultur work by the missionaries. Mr. A. Corner, the agriculture pioneer missionary, immediately on his arrival from Canada, became the Director of Economic Life Committee, Bhopal Diocese. He emphasized the importance of agriculture work in the villages. So one agriculturist, namely Shamul Prakash of Mhow was appointed as Agriculture Officer of Banswara in 1963. He immediately recruited four field workers. Each of them was given a bicycle by mission for touring villages and distributing required agricultural materials to the farmers.

The Beginning

Five distributing centres were opened at Kevaria, Kharia, Agoria Bada, Sevania and Banswara. The villages were regularly visited by the field workers. Seeds, fertilizers, pesticides and fungicides were given to the needy villagers. Besides, special loans were also given to the villagers for purchasing diesel engines and Persian wheels. Mrs. (Dr.) A. Loan and Dr. Maxlur, both Canadian missionaries, presented two diesel engines for agriculture purposes to Kharia and Zhumki villages respectively. Further, the diesel engine was made available to other villages on nominal charges.

Expansion

With a view to spreading the scientific agriculture knowledge among the villagers, six demonstration centres were opened at different places. Of these Vital Dev, Zhumki and Sevania were used for demonstration purposes for wheat crop while Kevadia, Khunta and Agorir Bada were used for maize crop. Much interest was shown by both Christian and non-Christian farmers and a few villagers were trained in advanced techniques of agriculture. Besides, they were also trained in terracing farming. Towards the end of the year 1967, Pastor R.D. Jening arrived here from Canada to strengthen the work among the Christian tribesmen which was then undertaken in Banswara.

Poultry Farm

In the town of Banswara and adjacent villages, some poultry farms were started in houses. Though these were not by any means suitable for their work, but were the best that could be had at the time. .

In this way the villagers began to show an interest in the agriculture work. Besides, villagers of various areas came for advice and consultation and the fame of good work spread far and wide.

The Famine Relief Works

During the famine of 1937-38, the Bhils suffered terribly and vast multitudes perished, whole families and hamlets were wiped out. During this critical period, the mission undertook relief works, gave food to the starving and rescued orphans. Similarly, after sometime when plague broke out in 1938 and claimed many lives in this area, medicines were distributed by Dr. C.F. Grant under the mission management among the people. Besides anti-plague vaccine injections were given to the people in the affected areas too. Thus, the mission had the opportunity of relieving distress and saving life.

Other Works

The long neglected backward section of the population in rural and inaccessible areas remained naked due to lack of stitched clothes. So, a special need of opening a craft was, therefore, realised by the missionaries. Consequently, the first centre among the Bhil women-folk was started in 1960, in Kevaria village by Miss Robson, who was also a pioneer missionary of the State. The girls were also taught sewing.

The study leads us to the conclusion that missionaries have played a commendable role in bringing the socio-religious and cultural change and consciousness.

ACKNOWLEDGEMENTS

I am deeply grateful to pastors Shadtilal Damor, H. Kala and Dhulia, respectively, who had supplied me relevant information. Their personal experience, in various churches managed by mission in this tribal belt had made my analysis more fruitful. It is my privilege to extend my thanks to Sri Ladji Karva, Warden of mission hostels, who had informed me his personal experience about the tribal education, hostels, community health centres etc. I am deeply grateful to Sri Malia Bhai and Bhanji Patel who had informed me of his experience about the missionaries programmes in the field of evangelical and agricultural. Besides, I am highly obliged to Mrs. Lila Narsingh - Principal, Masihi Prathmic Shala, Banswara for her co-operation during field-work.

References

Alexander, K.C. (1977) *'The problem of caste in the Christian Churches of Kerala'* in Harjinder Singh (ed.) Caste Among Non-Hindus in India. New Delhi. National Publishing House.

Chauhan, D.R. (1970) *Towns in Tribal Setting*. New Delhi. National Publishing House.

Nath, Y.V.S. (1960) *Bhils of Ratanmal* - An Analysis of the Social Structure of a Western Indian Community. Baroda The Maharaja Sayajirao University.

Ozha, G.H. (1993) Sanvat *Rajputana-Ka-Itihas*. 'Banswara *Rajya-ka-Itihas* Vol. III, Part II. Ajmer Vedic Yantralaya.

Prasad, Saileswar (1980) *'Education of Scheduled Tribes and Nomads'* in L.P. Vidyarthi and B.N. Sahay (ed.) Applied Anthropology and Development in India New Delhi. National Publishing House.

Roy Burman, B.K. (1972) Integrated Area Approach to the Problems of the Hill Tribes of North East India' in K. Suresh Singh (ed.). *Tribal Situation in India*. Simla, Indian Institute of Advanced Study.

Rao, M.S.A. (1978) 'Social Movements Among the Backward Classes and the Blacks: Homology in the Sources of Identify' in M.S.A. Rao (ed). *Social Movements in India*. Vol. I New Delhi Manohar Publication.

Sen, Jyoti (1960) *Missionary Activities in Chotanagpur* in Journal of Social Research. 3(2).

(1965) *'A case study of the Development Work* by the Christian Mission' in Journal of Social Research. 8(2).

Srinivas, M. N. (1962) *Caste in Modern India and Other Essays* Bombay. Asia Publishing House.

Sandhwar, A.N. (1973) *'The Method of Christian Conversion Among the Tribals: The Korwa Converted of Palamau*: A case study in Journal of Social Research 16(1).

Terhuja, Kherieleno (1972) 'The Christian Church Among the Angami Nagas' in Suresh Singh (ed.) *Tribal Situation in India* Simla. Indian Institute of Advanced Study.

Vyas, N.N, Mann, R.S. and Choudhary, N.D. (1978) Rajasthan Bhils Udaipur Manikyalal Verma Tribal Research & Training Institute.

Wilson, W.A. (1903) *The Redemption of Malva* Toronto Arbuthnot & MacMillan

Wiebe Paul D and Peter, S. John (1977) The Catholic Church & Caste in 'Rural Tamilnadu' in Harjinder Singh (ed.) *Caste Among Non-Hindus in India.* New Delhi National Publishing House.

Whittier, M. Jean (1979) *My Life Tapestry. India and Around the World. Memories and Meditations.* Canada. the Skimner Printing Company . Box 1218. Petrolia Ontariod, Non-I. R. O. Canada.

Govindgiri-ki-Jeevani (1976) By Nathu Ram, Bohri-Dobara Dhanurdhar Press, Banswara.

Kahai-Ham *Bhul Na-Jai. Sharansthan*-Aradhanalai, Savanjayanti (1925-77), Heetesi Press, Banswara.

Gazetteers and Census Reports

Census of India 1961. Vol. XIV. Rajasthan Part VI-A, Village Survey Monograph. Khajoora, 1964.

Ethnographic Atlas of Rajasthan (with reference to Scheduled Caste and Scheduled Tribes, 1969)

Census of India 1971, Series I. Paper I of 1975. Scheduled Castes and Scheduled Tribes 1969).

Census of India 1971, Rajsthan. Series 18, Rajasthan, Part-V Special tables and notes on Scheduled Castes and Scheduled Tribes, 1977.

Gazetteer of India, Rajasthan, Dungarpur 1974. Jaipur. Directorate, District Gazetteers Govt. of Rajasthan.

CHAPTER 14

A Study on Tribal Drinks

Atul Chandra Bhowmick

Countrymade liquor forms an integral part of the tribal life and culture. Drinking of countrymade beverages is considered a distinct phenomenon of the tribal society, and their use is recorded in almost all tribals as a stimulant. Tribal people do, of course, enjoy the sensation of being drunk. They express that they feel like king when they drink liquor fully. No social and religious festivals are performed practically without liquor. During dance the dancers of both sexes having a belief in getting more energy, spirit and rhythm drink indiscriminately and openly without any shyness, the distilled and undistilled liquor. *Mahul* and *hanria* are used as compulsory offering to their *bongas* (gods), namely, Maran budha, Mareko, Jaher era, Gosain era, Pargana bonga, Manjhi bonga all supernatural beings and deities residing at *jaherthan* (a sacred grove of four *sal* trees and a *mahua*) and at *manjhithan* situated at the village outskirts during propitiation. Mourners take countrymade liquors at funeral and revellers at wedding. Drink is levied to excommunicated person as fine for penalties and for readmission to his own society. *Gunin* is generally offered drinks for his service and activities. Orthodox tribals sprinkle a few drops of the liquor on the ground before sipping in honour of their deceased forefathers' souls and to please the evil spirits roaming around for not being ill after drinking.

The tribal people are addicted to drinking. The Santal, the Munda, the Oraon, and other communities of Chamargora, Pataghar, Jamtalgora and Gidighati villages, P.O. Orali P.S. Binpur, Midnapore district, Khatanga-Santaldihi village, P.O. Khatanga. P.S. Jhaldah, Purulia district of West Bengal, Harin Dhubri and Raghunathdihi villages, P.O. and P.S. Ghatsila, Singhbhum of Bihar prepare three kinds of homely brewed traditional drinks, viz., *mahul, hanria* and *tari.*

Among these tribal people drinking is virtually universal.*Paurā* (Pourā, Paora) is the local term of *mahul* beverage. It is their favourite and largely used countrymade drink. Drinks made of *mahuā* flowers are of two varieties, viz., *matkam mahul* and *ākātā*. The other name of *mahuā* is *matkam,* and the liquor made, is named *matkam mahul. Ākātā* has more concentration of *mahuā* sap than *matkam mahul.* The recipe is described heretoafter.

1.a. *Matkam mahul*--This drink is prepared by distillation from the mash of *mahuā* (*mahu-- maul*) flowers. *Mahuā* flower is pale yellow. The flowers are dried on a smooth floor plastered with cow-dung and mud until they shrivel to a quarter of their original size, and take a light brown colour, as to resemble raisin. The vitamin present in the corollas of *mahuā* flowers are carotine as vitamin. Ascrobic acid, folic acid, pantothemic acid, biotin and inosital. Ascrobic acid is destroyed during drying and storage due to deoxidation. The corollas contain an oil with an unpleasant odour, anthocyamins, betaine and salts of malic and succinic acids. Boiling takes all the flavour out of the flower. *Mahuā* flowers show anti-bacterial activity (*The Wealth of India*, Raw Materials, Vol. I; 192 : 214, 215). *Mahuā* is a medium to large size deciduous tree.

The ingredients of *mahuā* beverage are mahua flowers and guḍa (jaggery). The proportion of these is 3:1 respectively. Dried *mahuā* flowers are soaked in vat with *guḍa.* Water is added just to make it slurry. The mixture is kept in an earthen pot (tālāo) for three days for fermentation, locally known as *jaoyā.* The *jaoyā* mixture when started to eject bubble, called *phut* indicates start of fermentation, and it is completed when the bubbling sound of fermentation ceases. The bubbling starts due to evolution of gas. If the *jaoya* is distilled at the start, the beverage will be weak, and if it is distilled after complete fermentation the product will be acidic. If *jaoyā* is prepared in a new earthenware pot (also called *jaoyā*) longer times (4 days) are required for fermentation, while it takes three days, in case of a preused one. Again longer times (6 days) are required for fermentation in winter season, and three days in summer. Four or five cakes of *rānu* are mixed with the *jaoyā* to accelerate fermentation as well as to make the beverage intoxicating. If more *rānu* is added more strong is the product.

Rānu cake is prepared by mixing thoroughly with pulverised *bākhar* plant (*coleus sp.*) with sunned rice flour. *Bākhar* plant grows by itself in high land. The rice is soaked in water till sufficiently moist . The rice and the ingredients are pounded separetely in a *dhenki* (husking pedal) or in a wooden mortar and pestle or between two stone grinders. The sap of the crushed plants is squeezed out in a pot. The refuse of the plants is thrown away. Before grinding the plants are washed in water. The pulverised rice and the sap is mixed thoroughly. Medicinal cake, known locally as *rānu,* sometimes as *mūlikā* is made out of the rice pulp, and water is sprinkled, if required , over it at the time of making cake. The cakes are roundish balls produced by turning round a portion between the palms. The tablet is dried under the sun for three days, and preserved in a basket for future use. The balls are reddish in colour when made, but after drying the colour changes to white. Some tribal peoples purchase the *rānu* cakes from the market, prepared and sold usually by the Majhis, the Kurmis, and others. To make the *paurā* more intoxicating sap of *mahuā* bark (*Madhuca indica gmel.*), *chaitā* (*mejurjhuti-Elephantopus scaber* Linn.), *jastimadhu* (*Glyeyrrhiza glabra* Linn.), *anatamūl* (*Hemidesmus indicus* R. Br.) *Kusum* bark (*Schleichera oleosa* (Lour.) Merr.) are mixed with the sap of *bakhar,* named also *rolli, raktajatā* plant. Rarely they mix the sap of crushed *kurchi leaf* (*Holarrhena antidysen-teria* Wall.).*deorapan* (unidentified) and *bādallej* (unidentified) plants. The *paura* with *mahuā* and *kusum* barks as ingredients is considered harmful for its more intoxicating nature, and it may cause even death. The plant ingredients, their properties and uses in different liquors are stated.

Plant ingredient	*Part/thing used Used*	*Property*	*Purposes of use*	*Liquor*
1	*2*	*3*	*4*	*5*
Mahua *Madhuca indica* gmel.	1. Flower	Sugar Vitamin Calcium	Sugar, the raw material for the production of alcohol	*Mahul*
	2. Bark	Calcium	To make the liquor more intoxicating with calcium salt.	In the production of *mahul*
Date palm (*Kejur, Kajur*) (Phoenix sylvestris Roxb)	Sap	Sucrose	Toddy is nutritive due to presence of sugar, Vitamin and thiamine	*Tari*
Palmyra palm/Fan palm (*tal*) *Borassus flabellifer* Linn.)	Sap	Sucrose	Toddy is nutritive due to presence of sugar and yeast: yeast is the source of Vitamin B Complex	*Tari*
Bakhar (*Coleus sp.*)	Root	Starch Vitamin Inorganic salts like carbonate, magnecium sulphate	Vitamine and inorganic salts accelerate the process of fermentation.	In the production of *mahul* and *hãnria*
Chaila (*Elephantopus scaber* Linn.)	Leaf Root	Vitamin Inorganic salts		
Jastimadhu (*Glycyrrhizin glabra* Linn)	Root	Glycerine	Glycerine for sweeting and flavouring	
		Glucose Sucrose Starch	For the production of alcohol	
Anantamūl (*Hemidesmus indicus* R. Br.)	Root	Sweetish Fragrance *fragrance*	To make the beverage a sweetish taste and fragrance The root is nutritive, diuretic, blood purifier, alterative and tonic	In the production of *mahul* and *hanria*
Kusum (*Schleichera Oleosa* (Lour.) Merr.)	Bark	Tennin	In the fermentation process galic acid is formed from tannin which stops oxidation of liquor into aldehyde	In the production of *mahul*

The pot containing the turbid mixture is covered with another pot (*matasi* or *sitani*) placed up side down, mouth to mouth, and seal both airtight with mud paste. A bamboo pipe (*chung*) used as condenser joins the *matasi* and the receiving pot (*Kalsi*), two together by inserting the pipe through them (Fig. 1). Mud paste makes the joints airtight.

The receiving earthenware pot is in turn placed into a broken vessel filled partly with water for cooling the vapour into liquid and for keeping cool the liquor. The distilling apparatus is structurally similar to the modern glass retort. The process converts liquid into vapour by heat, and then condenses into liquid drops. The vapour raised, passes through the pipe to the *Kalsi.* During heating the condenser and receptacle are cooled down by pouring water continuously over them from a water reservoir. One hour boiling is required for a mixture of 3 kgs. *mahuā* flowers and 1 kg. guḍa for distillation of 3 litres *mahul* yield. They set up the distillation apparatus in the interior dark corners of their house to avoid the sight of outsiders, particularly of the Excise Department. Freshly prepared liquor has a strong smoky foetic odour, which disappears on aging. One bottle (about 1/2 litre) *mahuā* liquor is sold at Rs. 2.50-3.00. Dried-up *mahuā* flower costs Rs. 2.00 per kg.

1. b. *Ākātā* -- Preparation process is the same as that of *matkam mahul*. *Ākātā* is more pungent, as it contains more *mahuā* juice, and so thick is the fragrance. During distillation the beverage weighing about one and a half litres prepared first is the *akata*, and a litre costs Rs. 20.00. The tribal people taste its purity in a very simple process. A lighted matchstick when contacts the *ākātā* blazes out suddenly, and emits a long blue flame. *Ākātā* is used as medicine. They use *ākātā* as a massage in rheumatic pains and in convalescence. Regular drinking of one table-spoonful of *ākātā* daily increases appetite, removes idleness and weakness.

During the days of Caraka (Su.6.39, 27.185) and Susruta (Su. 45.190) *mahuā* flower was known as *madhūka* flower, and the liquor prepared from it was known as *madhavi*-Caraka Su. 6.39, 27.185, Susruta Su. 45. 190 (Prakash, 1961 : 152, 299) and as *vāruni* (a strong liquor, cf., *ākātā*). The use of *madhūka* for preparing intoxicating drink is mentioned as early as in the *Atharvaveda* (1.34.5) (Prakash : 1961 : 269) and in the *Mahabharata* (Virat Parva. 16.3) (Prakash) 1961 : 269, 299).

2. *Hānriā (hāriā, hāndi, hāndiā, pachoi, illi, diāng)*-Sunned rice is boiled, and the boiled water (gruel) is absorbed in the rice. The boiled cereals are mixed thoroughly with *rānu*. The mixture is put in an earthenware vessel, and the vessel is kept in a cool and dry place (usually at the corner of the dwelling house) for three days covered with leaves. Rānu acts as fermenting catalyst. Fermentation is allowed for three days in the summer and four days in the winter. After the stipulated period kneading of rice is done, known to them as mera, and than sufficient water is added to the fermented mixture in the proportion of 1:3. The liquor is filtered through a sieve made of bamboo strips. locally called *hāndichālā* (Fig. 1C) in Kamarbandhi village, P.O. Silda, Midnapore. The process is known locally as *sāniyā*. Sometimes the top extract is decanted to another vessel, and the sediment is then sieved. The residual rice is given to the chicken or cattle. The undistilled and unclarified rice-beer looks like whey. This beverage produced by mild fermentation of rice, is very nutritive. It aids digestion. *Hānriā* is sold at *hāts* (markets) and fairs, and a litre costs Rs. 4.00. For measuring *hānriā* calabash ladle known to them as *bacca* (Fig. 1 B) or an aluminum bowl is used.

At the time of preparing rice-beer the Santals of Sagar island invoke for blessing the *Pilcu Haṛam* and *Pilcu Buḍhi*, the first man and woman according to their tradition with chants, as follows (Mukherji) 1967 : 11)

Pilcu Haṛam Pilcu Buḍhi
Noa Ranu Ran sebelkotinma.

(Ho, old, man Pilcu and old woman *Pilcu Budhi*, let this intoxicating medicine of mine be tasty for all).

3. *Tari*-Date palm (*Phoenix sylvestris Roxb.*) and Palmyra palm (*Borasssus flabellifer* Linn.) sap secreted by tapping, starts fermentation overnight by yeast action. The use of palm juice in preparing liquor was a very old tradition. For tapping the date palm, the lower leaves along one side of the trunk are cut off, and the bark is removed to expose the innersoft layer vertically and half of the circumference of the tree horizontally, and the palmyra palm, the flowering finger like inflorescence shoots are scraped with tapping knife, and their tips pared off daily. The sap yield is higher in cold months than in summer. Trees of both sexes are tapped. *Tāri* has an intoxicating and pungent smell.

A glass of *tāri* (about 250 ml.) costs 0.50 paise. The tribal people prepare toddy in less amount. The preparation of all these delicacies shows a high stage of development in culinary art.

Ubiquitously they keep *mahul* liquor in 1/2 litre glass bottles and *hānriā* and *tāri* in an earthen pot. In industrial belt *mahul* liquor is stored in plastic canister in large quantities, and at the time of selling liquor is poured in glass bottle for ascertaining the quantity. I have observed in the industrial area at Rekha Mines near Ghatsila that for large scale production of *mahul* liquor they select an area amidst jungle away from their habitation, a precautionary measure against the Excise Department. The liquor often contains pulverised used up carbide or paste produced by rubbing copper on a stone which makes the beverage highly intoxicant.

Drinking of beverages is done in a bell metal or aluminum bowl (for *hānriā*), leaf cup, usually made of *sāl* (*sarjom*- shores *robusta* Gaertn.) or *kurchi* (for *mahul*) and glass (for *tāri*). All these beverages are used largely in the evening after day's work.

The principal tribal drink is prepared from *mahuā* flower. But *hanriā* is considered better than *mahul* or *tari* beverages for the following reasons :

1. *Hānriā* drinking generates heat and energy for work.
2. *Hānriā* is cooling.
3. *Hānriā* serves both as a food and a drink.
4. Moreover hānriā tipples the body mildly.

Nutritive values of tribal drinks (samples are not of the same villages of my field work, but of adjoining areas) as stated by P.N. Sen Gupta (1956 : 76-78) and in the *Wealth of India*, Raw Materials (vols 1, VIII: 1948, 1969 : 203, 27) are cited as references for revealing the different food values which is not changed much in drinks prepared traditionally through the generations.

Fig—1

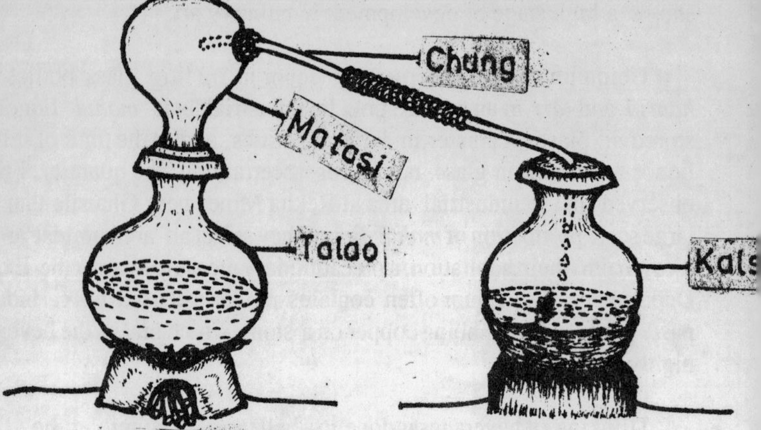

A Distilling Apparatus

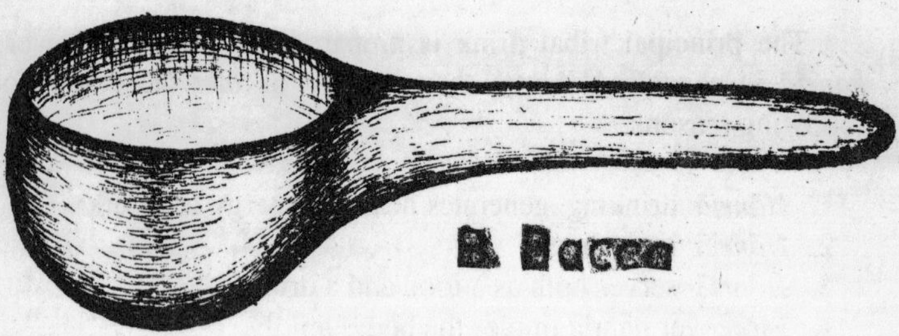

B Bacca

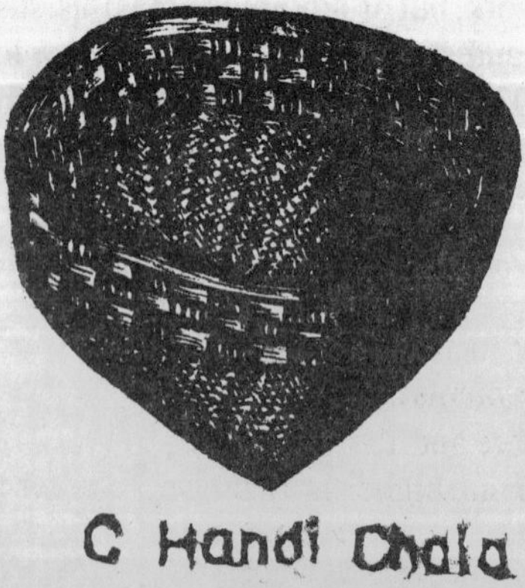

C Handi Chala

The average nutritive values of the tribal drinks are as follows :-

Nutritive	*Paurā*	*Hāndi*	*Tāri (Date palm)*	*Tāri (Palmyra palm)*
1	*2*	*3*	*4*	*5*
1. Alcohols (By vol)	21.25	4.40	8.61	2.57
2. Calories	123.00	34.67	-	-
3. Protien (gm)	-	0.43	-	-
4. Calcium (mgm)	-	3.00	-	-
5. Phosphorus (mgm)	-	30.63	0.55	-
6. Iron	-	1.30	-	-
7. Thiamine (Vitamin B_1 (mgm)	-	14.93	-	-
8. Riboflavin (mgm)	-	15.16	-	-
9. Niacin (nicotinic acid (mgm)	-	288.00	-	-
10. Acetic acid	-	-	-	0.40
11. Tartaric acid	-	-	0.94	-
12. Sucrose	-	-	0.36	1.88
13. Glycerol	-	-	0.33	-
14. Nitrogen	-	-	0.12	-

The alcoholic content of the distilled liquor of *mahua* of Midnapore is higher than that prepared in Bihar, and definitely much higher than that of undistilled liquor of *handi* and *tari*. The handi prepared by the Santals contains exceedingly high quality of alcohol, calories, protein, phosphorus, riboflavin and niacin contents than that prepared by the Mundas. The contents life calcium, iron and thiamine (vitamine B_1) of rice-beer are higher in beverage prepared in Midnapore than that in Bihar; while these contents have some equality as those prepared by the Mundas of Midnapore and the Santals of Bihar. The niacin nicotinic acid) and vitamine B_1 are higher in rice-beer. The fermented date toddy has much higher thiamine content than the fresh sap. The sucrose content of palmyra palm *tāri* is much higher than date palm *tāri*. Date palm *tāri* contains glycerol and nitrogen.

The beverages of *mahuā* and palms are more intoxicating and considered injurious to health. These keep body heated and tipsy. Usually in *Dūrga Pūjā, Kāli Pūjā, Paus sånkrānti* (March-April), in marriage, birth of a child, funeral, religious festivals, worshipping of spirits, dance, music, sowing, harvesting, curing disease by propitiaiting the wrath of evil spirits, feasts, in receiving guests, in village council meetings and as an offering to the graves of the departed souls the tribal people, both male and female, consume countrymade liquors in full. The tribal people have no inhibition that a woman who indulges in drinking, would be deprived of her husband's company in the next world like some caste people.

The drinking habit of the tribes is an important problem from socio-economic point. It is found that the fermented beverages play a very important role in the daily life of many tribes, such as the Santal, the Munda, the Savara and many of other tribes. They cannot think of any social or religious occasion without a supply of drink. The addiction has accentuated their poverty. They drink hard on some other occasions like witch-craft. Once addicted in drinking, I was told, the poor people sell even their bell metal dish, bowl, glass or any other movable property to pay off the drink's money, and gradually become poorer. For purchasing food stuffs they often sell their domestic cow or goat, and out of it an amount is spent for drinks the act causes to ruin the family. Drinking in excess gives rise to broils in the family. Excessive drinking of *mahua* beverage causes anemia, turgidity of limbs, jaundice and even tuberculosis. It wanes appetite. The tribal people use *mahua* in coughs, colds and bronchitis. The effects of drunkeness of any liquor are loss of wealth, insanity, absence of consciousness, loss of knowledge and life. *Mauha* drinking excites gastric irritation. Tottering, prattling irrelevantly, inarticulated speech, excitement and even vomiting, for the new drunkards are some of the physical conditions revealed. A limited use of drinks is a habit good for health, especially in the winter season. Limited use increases appetite and digestion causing tribal people to eat a large quantity of food which gives them to possess good health, energy and inexhaustible strength for work. They regard drinking as an exquisite pleasure. They also believe that it inspires courage, confidence, bestows powers and self-trust. Moderate drinking is acceptable, but excessive drinking makes intoxication and hence loss of control is the pathognomic symptom. Drinking of excess liquor is harmful, particularly in the summer and rainy season, and in a tropical country like India.

Drinking has been interpreted in terms of psychology. It has been viewed as a reducer of anxiety, fear from animal and toil at hardwork. Aggressive behaviour and sexual impulses tend to be associated with drinking. I have been told that they use liquor as an instrument to achieve the submission of and control over others.

The tribal people, generally at all times take drinks to quench their thirst. Drinks provide considerable nutrition in the form of food energy, mineral matters and vitamins. The *hānriā* is enriching the nutritional value of their diets, and to some extent corrects the deficiencies of some of their food essentials. But the distilled liquor *mahuā,* prepared secretly by the ingenious method for higher alcohol contents, does not have much nutritional value. It is consumed for intoxication mainly, and is really very harmful to the tribes. For the welfare of the tribes, the consumption of liquor should be discouraged through the Tribal Welfare Department, Philanthropic organisations, and the bad effect of liquor drinking should be shown or broadcast through audio-visual means, like T.V., radio and loud speaker. Nowadays, the Santals, the Mundas, the Oraons and others consume distilled *mahuā* liquor more than rice-beer, the reason behind the fact is that the tribal people are mostly poor who cannot afford to buy more rice for the preparation of *hānriā*. Again high intoxication and flavour of *mahuā* are their choice.

ACKNOWLEDGEMENTS

I gratefully acknowledge the help of Dr. Sitesh Ranjan Das, Survey Officer, Regional Research Institute, Government of India, Calcutta for identifying the plants and for his indomitable encouragement.

References

Council of Scientific and Industrial Research, (1948) *The Wealth of India*, Raw Materials, Vol. I, Delhi.

Council of Scientific and Industrial Research (1962) The Wealth of India, Raw Materials, vol. VI New Delhi.

Elwin, Verrier (1950) Bondo Highlander, Oxford University Press, London.

Mukerji, Sankaranda (1967). The Recipe of Rice-Beer, Bulletin of the Cultural Research Institute, Vol. VI. Nos. 1 & 2, government of West Bengal, Calcutta.

Prakash, Om. (1961) *Food and Drinks In Ancient India*. Munshi Ram Manoharlal, Delhi.

Sen Gupta, P.N. (1956) Studies on the Nutritive Values of Tribal Alcoholic Beverages, Bulletin of the Department of Anthropology, Vol. V. No. 1 Government of India, Calcutta.

CHAPTER 15

Anthropology and Tribal Welfare

Ajit K. Danda

I

It is generally presumed that anthropology has a role to play in matters related to tribal welfare. This is based more on incidental phenomena than any scientific reasoning. The association between anthropology and tribal welfare is historical to the extent that since birth of anthropology as an academic discipline as it received colonial patronage.as a precondition the patrons assigned priority to the study of primitive cultures and societies. A reference to some historical antecedents seems important in this context.

The success of industrial revolution in Europe and the impact of the theory of organic evolution led the cultures and societies of the North Atlantic region to look at themselves as the most evolved among the human populations and those at the technologically relatively less developed part of the world, as the prototype through which once the industrially developed societies have passed. Thus the model for and stages of transformation were set. In other words, at least hypothetically the technologically under-privileged cultures were assumed to represent the archaic forms of the contemporary societies. The interest, therefore, was to study the so-called primitive cultures in order to evolve a system of administration that could establish colonial authority over them and in the name of preservation of their way of life could perpetuate their hold over such cultures.

There were at least two basic mistakes in such an approach. One, the technologically most developed part of the world did not enjoy this privilege throughout the periods of history. It is well known that in terms of knowledge of science and technology, India was ahead of most of the world almost up to 12th Century A.D. It is the fall out of the Industrial Revolution that shifted the centre of focus from the orient to the West. Two, technological superiority or inferiority of human populations does not have anything to do so far as their position in the scale of organic evolution is concerned. Since all human populations biologically are classified as *Homo sapiens,* any attempt for associating human faculty with apparent technological capability at least on biological counts appears a misnomer.

In view of this background, any attempt for hierarchical categorization of human societies and cultures reflects a sort of prejudice a good deal more than actual scientific information. It is perhaps this prejudice that played a very crucial role in the initial delineation of boundary of anthropology as an academic discipline. Such was the upshot and impact of the same that even today Indian anthropology could not fully restore the balance. As a result, anthropologists and anthropology are often made to share the blame for any failures in the fronts of tribal welfare in spite of the fact that apart from academic interest, welfare of tribes is not the major area of operation of the anthropologists and besides some role in the advisory capacity, anthropology in India so far has vary little to do in administration.

Because of its growth under colonial patronage, such was the orientation of anthropological studies in India for decades together and so was its impact that even when a scholar from the so-called Third World proposed any anthropological research, due perhaps largely to the preoccupations of his mind, he too invariably focussed his attention to the relatively underprivileged compatriots. This provides a notion of boundary for anthropology that in the Indian context suffers from lack of rapport with anthropology as a body of knowledge. Specifically in view of the fact that India had the unique distinction of producing and possessing the earliest written records on the earth[1], it is rather unfortunate that for drawing up the syllabus for any Indian university, it was taken more or less for granted that there could not be any indigenous texts having knowledge of anthropology that could be worth considering for incorporation in the curricula. In other words, India was taken as devoid of any knowledge of anthropology, until the same was introduced as an academic discipline under colonial patronage. This resulted into at least two other basic mistakes, One, the indigenous knowledge of anthropology being ignored, it remained not only unknown to most of the world, anthropology in India as an academic discipline being devoid of its linkage with the indigenous knowledge was yet to be able to establish its roots. Two, anthropology in India had to be based on the cultural and social realities experienced elsewhere in the world. The result has been disastrous for anthropology. The discipline mostly carried the prejudice as grew out of Euro-American experiences. Obviously, it could not yet make the science sufficiently meaningful for the Indian society. The vaguely defined boundary of the discipline and its sub-disciplines helped perpetuating the phase of confusion. The situation became even worse due to shuttling of commitments of the discipline between scientific reasoning and humanism. Although the two commitments are neither mutually exclusive nor necessarily at clash with each other, whenever the focus shifted from scientific reasoning to humanism, the quality of objectivity of the argument had to make room for expression of subjective sentiment. In fact, the expression of such humanistic sentiment by some anthropologists has invited criticism about the role of anthropology in tribal welfare and made the intention of anthropologists rather suspect.

II

Historical antecedents of the development of anthropology as an academic discipline in India created a sort of hypothetical association between anthropology and tribal welfare. In actual situation, however, anthropologists hardly participated directly in tribal administration. There are only a few instances when anthropologists were inducted to advise in matters related to tribal administration. Thus, even they were responsible primarily for framing the policy decision more than participating in the administration as such. Von Fuerer Haimendrof and Verrier Elwin played important roles in this respect during British regime in India and afterwards. Noted anthropologist Dr B.S. Guha was also asked to submit a report on matters related to tribal administration.[2] Whatever indirect impact may they have on tribal welfare, certainly that does not justify any close association between anthropology and tribal welfare.

Suggestions made out purely on human considerations were also unwelcome by administrators and social workers alike. As an illustration a reference can be made to the recommendations of Verrier Elwin in the context of the Baigas of Madhya Pradesh.[3] As shifting cultivators they were, due to the pressure on their land created by the neighbouring peasantised tribal and non-tribal communities, the Baigas were led to a precarious economic existence. Since due to their cultural attachment with shifting cultivation the Baigas were not quite capable of absorbing any benefits out of the immediate agricultural development programmes, Elwin in his account on the Baigas recommended a measure of special protection for the people, lest by sheer pressure of the other communities the Baiga society should disintegrate. This was misunderstood as if the anthropologists had a vested interest in the preservation of tribal communities. Some went to the extent of making even such comments that as the anthropology as an academic discipline would cease to exist unless there were tribals around, the anthropologists had a vested interest in the preservation of tribals. Such observations are definitely unlearned as they emanate out of unawareness of the facts that anthropology is the study of man as a whole and not of primitive societies alone.[4] Observations of Elwin also infuriated the social workers who branded anthropologists as interventionists and expressed suspicion in their expertise which according to the social workers could be expendable without any loss to the society. Their main argument was based on the general assumption that the tribals in India were on their course toward Hinduism. When the goal is defined, there is no reason in creating any hindrance that may decelerate the rate of their change. According to them, the apparent human concern was nothing but a plea to put a check to that direction of change.

It would not be out of place to mention here that since Elwin himself had no formal training in the field of anthropology, his recognition as an anthropologist to the fellow professionals was always under some cloud. Even then his observations were taken as if the representative opinion of the anthropologists, in spite of various clarifications issued by him in this respect. Interestingly enough, the views of Prof. Ghurye, whom the social workers seem to have followed in full in this respect, was though an anthropologist by training, his views were not considered anthropological opinion at all.[5] It is, therefore, obvious that how the people wanted to brand an opinion is more important than what actually the opinion was. In other words, the politics of truth as such appears much more important than the reality of truth as such. In view of these facts the role of anthropology is to be understood having the given background into attention.

III

When we focus our close attention to tribal welfare, two important issues come to the limelight more or less instantly. One, in the Indian context definition of a tribe as such appears to be in a flux. Elsewhere we have indicated that various definitions of tribe currently in circulation seem to convey an ethnocentric bias to which the scholars of Euro-American background by and large subjected themselves.[6] Attributing queer and exotic qualities to tribes implies their notion of superiority that in all probability has grown out of their successes following industrial revolution. Two, various socio-economic and educational programmes introduced by the governmental and non-governmental agencies suffer from the inadequacy of not maintaining any clear distinction between ameliorative and welfare measures. Although ameliorative measures by implication amounts to a sort of assurance of welfare activities, the objectives behind and the directions thereof are generally non-identical. Such confusion about the goal as well as the directions get reflected in the manner the administrators, social workers, and other agencies perceive the programmes.

It is well-known a fact that an administrator's major concern is toward fulfilment of physical targets and demand of budgetary outlay. Social workers in contrast are more interested about the outcome of exposures to such programmes than anything else. They have accepted assimilation of tribal committees to the so-called mainstream of national life, no matter how vaguely they define the mainstream and to what extent they refuse to maintain any distinction between integration and assimilation. The tribalmen's concern as reflected through empirical data gathered from various parts of the country indicate their relative apathy toward any finer distinction between assimilation and integration.

They are aware of their state of relative impoverishment and are eager for over-all economic uplift.[7] Regarding their nature of transformation they are found to be logically skeptic so far as their status in the socio-ritual hierarchy is concerned. The anthropologists' dilemma is how to safeguard the independent identity of tribes as cultural entities and at the same time to integrate the tribal societies with the national main-stream, if there is any. Integration at the technological, professional, educational and political levels are relatively less difficult. Problem arises when such measures threaten the identity of the people. Elsewhere we have demonstrated how due to their exposures to various developmental measures the so-called primitive and relatively smaller groups have become aware of their rights to protect their independent identity and assertive about their choice.[8] Even the Constitution of India is unequivocal in its support to this stand of the minorities. In other words the Constitution makes a commitment to maintain the identifiable cultural groups and promote their cultural activities. Under the circumstances any programmes for welfare or otherwise that might lead to the loss of identity of the concerned people is required to be discouraged. Unfortunately, while drawing up the details of programme for tribal welfare such commitments of the society are not taken note of.

IV

The problem is somewhat more complex than what it apparently seems to be. Unless one gets into the basic spirit of them, even the constitutional provisions regarding tribal policy may outwardly appear contradictory. Since a tribe in contemporary India means a Scheduled Tribe, a constitutional category knowledge of anthropology or that of the anthropologists has very little to do so far the identification of Scheduled Tribes is concerned. Although it has been stated clearly that a Scheduled Tribe is so only by origin, the Constitution of India does not spell out how the primary delineation of identity will take place. Over the years, nevertheless, certain administrative strategies have evolved by application of which it is usually decided whether a community is fit to be designated as a Scheduled Tribe by the Declaration of the President of India. In this entire process knowledge of anthropology has been given very little cognizance. As a result, we observe simultaneous application of territorial basis as well as ethnic basis for determination of status of Scheduled Tribes. It may be pointed out here that although the territorial basis of delineation of Scheduled

Tribes does not and cannot fully conform to the principle of determining Scheduled Tribes as such by origin, the exercise was generally extended within the limits of a declared Scheduled Area. As a result, heterogeneous populations from a given territory were often extended with Scheduled Tribe status and assigned with a generic identification. In such matters, however, the over-all economic, educational and professional backgrounds of the people were considered important. It is, therefore, seen that for delineation of Scheduled Tribes in India the requirement of anthropological criteria was altogether dispensed with. Although anthropologists were the only professionals who had a sustained academic interest in the matters of tribes, their expertise perhaps due to administrative exigencies failed to attract due recognition.

After the independence of India the welfare State took upon itself the responsibility to ameliorate the socio-economic condition of its downtrodden populations. The tribes of India, at least theoretically received a priority treatment in this respect. Huge budgetary outlays for tribal welfare and tribal development, it is amazing to see, have created nearly a 'gold rush' situation where innumerable pseudo-experts formed a beeline to sell out their uncooked or half-cooked recommendations and execution skill. This is as such perhaps not that much objectionable as creative intuitions at times can do a lot good in this respect. What is, nevertheless, disturbing is the attitude of the pseudo-professionals as if the tribes deserve no serious study or close observation in order to develop any professional expertise on or about them. The rush of the pseudo-experts is of such an order that the anthropologists who have spent years in receiving training and to study them systematically and from strictly scientific angle have been much out-numbered. Naturally, their feeble voice, no matter how much reasonable might it be, could make hardly any impact in this respect.

It may be carefully noted that although tribes constitute the subject of study of the anthropologists, their welfare as such cannot be the exclusive liability of the anthropologists. Meeting the constitutional commitments is the responsibility of the society as a whole although anthropologists have often been blamed for any failure in that front. The exercise of finding out a scapegoat for not obtaining the expected result is not only unrealistic but unscientific, too. Strangely enough, when we do not make any extra fuss for any failure in the experimental sciences, we are relatively intolerant so far as the anthropological experiments are concerned. As such, results of no scientific experiment can be treated as an utter failure. The experience gained through such experimentation by itself is very valuable.

True it is that we cannot afford to make too many experiments with human populations that may have open-ended probable results. As the fates of human populations are directly involved in such exercise, it is not very desirable either. It is, therefore, important that such experiments are carefully designed and those who have really spent years in closely studying them, their expertise is given due recognition. A word of caution, however, is considered necessary, particularly in respect of involvement of human factors. There are discrete machineries under the existing set-up for conceiving tribal welfare schemes, implementation of them and for measuring their degree and nature of successes. There are at least a few instances where anthropologists have been inducted into the team either as advisors or employees. Since the success in their personal career to a large extent depends on their ability to the line suggested by the administration, there is every likelihood of some pressure being generated against strict adherence to the ethics and disciplines of the profession. Under the circumstances if the anthropologists feel pressed to strike a compromise, they will be indirectly instrumental in letting down the cause of anthropology.

The foremost responsibility of anthropologists is to record and express facts as much faithfully as possible. This is considered extremely important and urgent for overhauling the entire machinery responsible for executing tribal welfare schemes. The anthropologists are also collectively responsible for exploding myths that have been floated around due to the direct or indirect contribution primarily of the pseudo-scientists. In the field of anthropology the pressure of such myths is also considerable.

In spite of all skepticism expressed through this presentation, there cannot be any disagreement about the fact that anthropologists among all professionals have the maximum, first hand and intimate knowledge about tribes as well as tribal welfare. It is expected to be beneficial for the society as a whole and for the tribes in particular if such intimate and genuine knowledge is properly harnessed for drawing up and implementation of the tribal welfare schemes.

Notes

1. *Rig Veda* is accepted as the earliest written text in the world. Where knowledge could reach such a level of refinement, it is rather unnatural to think that the authors of the *Vedas* and *Puranas* paid no attention to human society and culture.
2. For details vide Guha, B.S. "The Indian Aborigines and their Administration", The Journal of the Asiatic Society, Science, (1951).
3. For details vide Elwin, Verrier, *The Baiga* (1939).
4. For details Vide Strickon (1964). Reflections of prejudice of the technologically developed world is very much conspicuous in such observations.
5. For details consult Ghurye, G.S. *The Scheduled Tribes*. (1959).
6. We have particularly indicated the definitions of tribe currently in usage in anthropological literature. Special reference has also been made to the major contributions of Indian scholars recorded mostly by way of the social and cultural facts of India. For details vide Danda, Ajit K. "*Tribes in India*", *Man in India* (1988).
7. In matters of economic options the tribles in India appear to be relatively less inhibited than their non-tribal brethren. Since they do not suffer from any load of traditionally prescribed calling as is found among most of the Hindu castes, they are rather free to make any choice according to their capability.
8. For details vide Danda, Ajit K. "Ethnicity in a pluri-cultural society", *Journal of the Indian Anthropological Society* (1988).

References

Danda, Ajit. K. (1988) "Ethnicity in a Pluri-cultural Society", *Journal of the Indian Anthropological Society*, Vol. 23, No. I

Danda, Ajit.K. (1988) "Tribes in India", *Man in India* Vol. 68, No.4.

Elwin, Verrier (1939) *The Baiga*: London : John Murray.

Ghurye, G.S. (1959) *The Scheduled Tribes;* Bombay: Popular Book Depot.

Guha, B.S. (1951) "The Indian Aborigines and their Administration", *The Journal of the Asiatic Society*, Science: Vol. XVII, pp 19-44.

Strickon, Arnold (1964) "Anthropology in Latin America", in *Social Science Research on Latin America* By Charles Wagely (ed); NewYork: Columbia University Press.

CHAPTER 16

Applied Anthropology and Development in India*

P. R. G. Mathur

The genesis of applied anthropology can be traced to the divergent interests of anthropologists in social change and problems of cultural contact. E.B.Tylor, the father of Anthropology, held that the application of anthropological knowledge would help in improving human affair. Malinowski himself was one of the earlier protagonists in encouraging his students to practical or applied anthropology.

Philip Gulliver (1966) would not use the term applied for any anthropologist who had given some facts and ideas which a department, or an agency, could use to its own advantage. To him, applied seemed to mean policy making, planning and implementation involving responsibilities at times. Applied anthropology is action-oriented research, particularly oriented to administrative and developmental problems together with some degree of responsible participation in the process of making use of the results of such research (Brokensha, D.,1966). According to D. Forde, the phrase

> "applied anthropology in government" must refer to the actual application of anthropological knowledge by administrators

* Paper was presented in the XIth ICAES in Vancouver, Canada.

and planners in the formulation and execution of government policies (1953:841).

Applied Anthropology in the Pre-Independence Period

Anthropology was taught at the Haileybury College in England where British Civil Servants were given training prior to sending them to India, to the East India Company. As far back as the year 1807 the Company realized that anthropological knowledge would be of much use to administrators. Dr. Francis Buchanan was appointed by the then Governor-General of Bengal to enquire into the life and culture of the people of Bengal. After the middle of the 19th century a number of administrators like Dalton, Thurston and Risley were entrusted to write ethnographic notes and gazetteers on the castes and tribes of India. They, however, did not make any suggestions to government about the solution of any specific problem of the people they described and analysed. It was only in 1931 that J.H. Hutton, the then Census Commissioner, writing in the context of culture contact, recommended the creation of self-determination in regard to joining the neighbouring provinces or States. Thus, the British Government had fully accepted the relevance and importance of anthropology to administration and seriously meant to utilise anthropology as an aid in the formulation and execution of their policies and programmes.

Anthropology was included as one of the subjects in Civil Service examination. D.N. Majumdar's book *Races and Cultures of India* was based on a series of lectures delivered in 1942 to the I.C.S. Probationers at Dehra Dun. Many administrators went to Oxford, Cambridge and other Universities for courses in Anthropology. The International African Institute which was established in 1926 carried on research on many practical problems. S.P. Nadel also served in the 1930s in Sudanese Government.

Anthropological knowledge has been in use in the Governments of developed countries including the U.S.A. From 1934 onwards anthropologists there have been serving the Bureau of Indian Affairs in the U.S.A. in important positions. Jobs for anthropologists in the U.S.A. have since proliferated rapidly. An important function of the Foreign Service Institute of the State Department is to equip members of the Foreign service and others with as much background information on various peoples and cultures as is possible. It is found although that anthropologists are not very keen in joining Government services and in the administration. The reason for their reluctance in joining administrative departments appear to be mainly three. One, some anthropologists hold that any diversion of resources for anthropological research to practical studies would be at the cost of the fundamental research in anthropology. In fact Evans-Pritchard (1946) issued a warning

> lest the pressure of political and administrative interests (should) draw away so many of our band from the investigation of purely scientific problems, that the advance of the science may be seriously retarded.

Two, since they cannot possibly carry on basic research elsewhere, their reluctance in taking up jobs with the Government is understandable. Three, sometimes their reluctance also stems from the apprehension that the anthropologists' participation in the Government might be viewed as their support to policies that prove unpopular. Anthropoligists whose concern for the weaker sections of the society is widely known, do not wish to be a party to policy decisions which by themselves may not be able to further the development of these peoples.

Anthropology and Development in the Post-Independence Period

As applied anthropologists, they have to work primarily in areas and problems set by the Government, to report (and report quickly) in the interest of the Government and people, and to participate in the application of anthropological knowledge. Thus, they have to concentrate on really relevant facts, to demonstrate and highlight their significance and give their considered opinions to the problems, trend of events and on the solution of problems. They have to defend their opinions in the face of criticism and challenges from Government's specialists and administrators, and take responsibility for them besides having to plan policies following from these facts and opinions and sometimes even to help in formulating programmes of action into operation.

In India, after the achievement of independence and after the Constitution came into force, the question of having a clear-cut policy was raised, and positive steps had to be taken in planning and development for the tribals. In 1939, Elwin after studying the Baiga recommended the creation of national parks for the tribes in which the access of missionaries and exploiters would be restricted. Elwin was criticised by Ghurye who held that the only solution on the tribal problems for India was the assimilation of the tribes into the Hindu society.

The anthropologist's broad approach to the tribal problems was enunciated as guide-lines for India's national tribal policy by the the late Prime Minister, Pandit Nehru under the inspiration of Verrier Elwin in the shape of Pancha Sheel of tribal development. The outlines of this were (a) tribal people should be allowed to develop on the lines of their own genius and nothing should be imposed upon them, (b) tribal rights in land and forests should be respected, (c) introduction of too many outsiders into tribal areas should be avoided, (d) there should be no over-administration of tribal areas and as far as possible development programmes should be implemented through their own social and cultural institutions and (e) the results of development programmes should not be judged by the amount of money spent, but by the quality of human character that is involved.

Between 1953 and 1973 as many as twelve tribal research institutes were started in different States with the following three aims and objectives.

1. To conduct action orientated and applied anthropological studies on the life and culture of the tribal people.

2. To conduct evaluation studies on the development programmes already implemented and envisaged to be implemented, so that the tribals will receive the maximum benefit from them, and,

3. To impart training programmes on the life and culture, and development programmes to the personnel in-charge of implementation of the schemes.

It is unfortunate that the majority of the institutes had not been taken into confidence at the planning level of welfare programmes. Most of the Tribal Research Institutes had gone down ever since they came under the administrative control of the Harijan Welfare and Social Welfare Departments which are the implementing authorities of development programmes. Now some of them have been reorganised as separate Departments, and placed under the Governments directly giving greater autonomy in planning, evaluation and execution or research, as well as in the administration of the Research Institutes.

I have been the Chief Evaluation Officer for the last ten years, on the tribal development programmes implemented for the welfare of the tribal people of Kerala. I conducted an evaluation study in 1980 on Integrated Tribal Development Programmes in Attappady Valley of Palghat district, Kerala State. When I submitted my evaluation study on the tribal development programmes implemented in this area during the last one decade or so, planners and administrators involved, did not agree with my findings. I was opposed by powerful bureaucrats who wanted to reject my report. Finally the Government of Kerala appointed a high power committee to examine whether my findings were according to field situations and existing facts. The members of the Committee included the top planners, administrators and myself. They toured with me in the tribal areas and submitted their report which agreed with all my earlier findings. This created a stir in the whole of Kerala although it improved the image of anthropologists and the Department which I am heading.

The conclusions which I had arrived at conducting the evaluation study were:

1. Each of the 3 tribal communities in the area--the Irulas, the Mudugas and the Kurumbas-- have distinct ethnic identity. Their socio-economic conditions differ from one another, and like their cultural difference their receptivity to various development programmes also varies. The Irulas constitute the major chunk of the Attappady tribal population and can be considered settled cultivators who have adopted wet paddy cultivation. They are also well versed in animal husbandry. The Mudugas are shifting cultivators and landless agricultural labourers. They have been badly affected by the migrants to this area from lowland areas. The Kurumbas have been identified as one of the primitive tribes of Kerala.

2. As a result of Agricultural Extension work the cultivation of high yielding variety of paddy by tribal farmers can be seen even in remote hamlets. It is true that such crop varieties are popular among farmers having wet lands. But it must be remembered that

the tribes have very small holdings of wet land suitable for high yielding crops. Of the 3943 tribal families approximately 2000 have no land at all.

3. Sizeable funds have been spent on minor irrigations to no avail. Oil engines and energized pump sets supplied have broken down and need repairs. Some of the weirs constructed and cross--bars have collapsed and are in dilapidated conditions.

4. There is no concern for tribal welfare in the determination of road pattern, their alignment or their distribution.

5. One of the biggest failures of development efforts here has been the inadequacy of proper and safe drinking water supply. Drinking water is a rare commodity in 10% of the area and difficulties are acute during summer. Wells have been constructed only in 9 out of 132 hamlets, but these have been poorly built and maintained.

6. The housing scheme including the houses provided for primitive groups has been inconceivably delayed in their construction and are of poor quality. This scheme has not given any heed to tribal requirements, climatic conditions or terrain of Attappedy.

7. Electricity supply is rare and in some hamlets wiring has only been done even though there is no electric supply to those. Some dilapidated houses also have been wired, thus wasting a lot of money.

8. There is no encouragement nor schemes for cultivation of traditional cereals like ragi, chana, jowar, maize and thina which are the staple food of the tribals here. The dry land here is more suitable for the cultivation of these cereals than the high yielding varieties of wet paddy that has been introduced by the Agricultural Department.

Unit of poultry and milch cows distribution is found to be unviable in the tribal context of this area although the goat rearing scheme has been partly successful wherever these were supplied. The distribution of work bulls by the IRDP scheme is also showing good results even though there are grievances that they are highly priced.

9. Efforts of the Education Department and that of the Health Department have been minimal and without much positive effects. Despite all the financial spendings and efforts the literacy rate in this area is still the lowest in Kerala and their health conditions deplorable.

10. The tribals in Attappedy are exploited by money-lenders and non-tribals, most of the tribal lands alienated and the tribals, position generally one of deep indebtedness.

11. The Western Ghat Development Programmes have not been successful in providing job opportunities to the tribals to the extent envisaged.

12. The Centrally sponsored scheme for primitive tribal community (Kurumba) has not made any headway from its start.

Based on this evaluation study the following recommendations have been made as a guideline for other ITDPs in general :

1. Development programmes for the welfare of tribal people must relate to the facts of life and culture of tribals.

2. The special characteristics and aptitude of the tribal communities which are expected to be benefited should be taken into consideration, and different development programmes must be formulated for various tribal communities at different levels of economic, social and cultural integration.

3. The development programmes should take a comprehensive stock of tribal development programmes, covering every aspect of the tribal life and culture, ecological, social, economic and educational spheres.

4. Development programmes should be formulated in such a way that the tribals are able to easily identify their merits and be ready to accept it.

5. The primitive groups, particularly the nomadic communities, have to be rehabilitated in agricultural land but the outcome of

> the programmes will take a very long time and therefore alternative avenues of livelihood must also be made available in the colony so that the tribals do not go back to the interior jungles.

Besides evaluation studies, classification of communities is another important field where anthropological work has contributed greatly. Many Scheduled Castes had sanskritized their names and also certain practices to elevate their social status. By this action they were deprived of banefits earmarked solely for Scheduled Castes, as their new names did not appear in the Scheduled Castes list. The Government in order to overcome this problem included such communities with new names in a separate list of Other Eligible Communities so that at least educational benefits earmarked for Scheduled Castes could be extended to them whereby right they ought to have been given all Scheduled Castes benefits. Anthropological studies helped to a great extent to prove the actual status these caste members had held in the traditional society and also show how exactly sanskritization had occurred among each, as a consequence of which they lost benefits constitutionally conferred on them. Here again anthropological knowledge has been greatly used by the administrators.

Another major problem facing us is the infiltration of forward communities into the fold of Scheduled Castes and ScheduledTribes to subvert benefits earmarked for the downtrodden people. The anthropological studies conducted by me during the last ten years have revealed many such incidences. For example, Telugu speaking caste Hindu had styled themselves as a Scheduled Castes during the last 30 years or so, grabbing executive posts, seats in Medical/Engineering and Agricultural Colleges, exclusively reserved for Scheduled Castes. My anthropological researches particularly in respect of classification of communities, have helped the administrators in checking this infiltration. Even the community members' appeals to the High Court and even the Supreme Court were rejected based on the anthropological findings. Similarly a large number of another Telugu speaking members of a high caste Hindu community had infiltrated as Scheduled Tribe. They even approached the High Court to prove their claims but these were also dismissed on the basis of the anthropological findings submitted. In yet another case, a number of non-tribals has been found masquerading as a Scheduled Tribe and hence enjoying benefits earmarked for Scheduled Tribe, thus, anthropology had been of enormous help to the administrators and judiciary in Kerala to help check such manipulative efforts by unscrupulous persons.

Anthropology and Administration

Sometimes doubts have been expressed whether applied anthropology is at all possible or is scientific. There are numerous difficulties existing between anthropologists and the world of action. Bernett (1956:49) held that anthropologists and administrators do not generally get along well together. There is a great deal of misunderstanding and apprehension on both sides. The administrators demand quick and certain predictions from anthropologists who are generally reluctant to be hastened. As a matter of fact, theoretical and applied studies cannot be put into mutually exclusive categories. In the ultimate analysis theoretical and applied aspects of anthropology strengthen each other. But it must be noted that there are obvious dangers in overselling anthropology and in making high sounding but impossible claims as a science of human engineering (Dube, 1958).

Today the Governments of underdeveloped countries are committed to improve the standard of living of the people. Such aspirations are reflected in their documents of planning and development programmes. To carry out the planning tasks effectively the administrators in the developing countries need the help of anthropologists more than ever before. Even the economists now explicitly recognize that conventional economics has no tool for dealing satisfactorily with the socio-cultural factors in economic development, an understanding of which is essential for planners in these countries, including India.

My position as an anthropologist in the Government is the same as what H.M. Mathur (1980) says about anthropologists in Government.

> By and large the anthropologists in Government positions have not always felt happy about their lot. The many difficulties in their relationships with the administrators mainly arose from the fact that they belong to two separate professional categories. Their ways of looking at the problems are different, their expectations from each other are often vague and consequently they both fail to achieve any measure of understanding which is vital to the success of any programme.

The administrators often say that the usefulness of anthropology would become greater for them if only anthropologists would (a) provide quicker, more definite answers to their problems and (b) present the required information in a readily digestible form. The administrators who most of the time, are in a hurry, have to take decisions on the spot and to act quickly to implement them and cannot actually be said to be asking for too much time. Yet these needs cannot be met by the anthropologists adequately. It is not easy to provide instant solution to all the problems that may arise before the administrators. Problem oriented research, in fact, research of any kind, is a time consuming activity. And obviously administrators in most of the cases, cannot be expected to have patience for experiments or time for research.

Some anthropologists feel that government ought always to act upon their advice. Now viewing this as some kind of "technical intervention", a symbol of all those specializations that tend to intrude on the administration in the name of science or efficiency or welfare, this reaction certainly has been friendly to these tall claims. Anthropology is undoubtedly very helpful but the administrators aruge that in reaching at policy decisions governments do have to give consideration to many other matters also.

Some administrators hold that they can very well act as their own anthropologists. It is true that in the past there have been administrators who have done specialised work in studying the life and culture of the people they lived with and who today are probably claimed as anthropologists. Administrators certainly know their areas they serve better than the anthropologists. They also know the local people and their language well. But however valid this argument may have been in the early days of anthropology, it does not hold good in the present stage of specialisation. In recent years, there have been very rapid advances in the theory and field work techniques in modern anthropology. Field work today is a full time job. As Godfrey Wilson (1940) says,

> It is now widely recognised that systematic and detailed knowledge cannot in any case be easily picked up in one's spare time by a busy man who has no special training in research; even when he is stationed for years in one spot it is only an exceptionally gifted man who can attain it under such conditions.

Admittedly both administrators and anthropologists have by now gained sufficient experience of working together on common problems, and there are hopeful signs of their difficulties gradually receding into the background.

Some anthropologists believe that any administration who wants to make use of anthropological knowledge should make them an integral part of it. In this context Evans-Pritchard (1946) observes:

> It is important that anthropologist who acts as advisor or consultant to an administration should be a full member of it. He cannot advise the administration on the bearing of the legal, educational, economic and other social programmes, unless, he knows the bureaucratic machinery from the inside, has full access to all government documents, and meets the head of departments around the same conference table as an equal. Otherwise he will not be able to see the problems in their full anthropological context to translate an administrative problem into anthropological terms and vice versa, and to speak as one who shares the full responsibility for the actions and policies of the government. Administrators would naturally resent advice from outsiders, but will gladly accept them from one who has the same loyalty to the administration as themselves and who can, moreover speak about some of its problems with special knowledge they themselves lack.

But Mathur, H.M. (1980) observes :

> The administration accepting the anthropologists as full members of it should not in any way restrict his freedom in research matter. The anthropologists must have final say in the selection of the topics for research and the manner of conducting it.

L.P. Mair says that

> It is better then that the anthropologist should be content to put his knowledge at the disposal of the framers of policy, leaving to them the responsibility for decisions into which other considerations must enter. He can fairly claim that a Government would be unwise to disregard altogether the facts he lays before them.

References

Barnett, H.G. (1956) *Anthropology in Administration.*

Evans-Pritchard, E.E. (1946) *Applied Anthropology, Africa,* London.

Forde, Daryl (1953) Applied Anthropology in Government, British Africa in A.L. Kroeber (ed)

Mair, L.P. (1957) *Studies in Applied Anthropology,* London.

Philip, Gulliver (1966) Quoted in David Brokensha, Applied *Anthropology in English Speaking Africa,* Society for Anthropology.

Sachchidananda (1980) Planning, Development and Applied Anthropology in *Applied Anthropology and Development in India* (ed) Vidyarthi, L.P. and Sahay, K.N.

Wilson Godfrey (1940) *Anthropology as a Public Service.*

Index

W

Z